OF MOONS AND MONOLITHS

Collected Essays

OF MOONS AND MONOLITHS

Collected Essays

Richard Behrens

NINE MUSES BOOKS

Nine Muses Books

New England, USA

NineMusesBooks.com

ISBN-13: 978-0-9912784-3-5

Cover art and book design: Stefani Koorey, peartree-press.com *for Richard (1964-2017)*

"Everything in life is just for a while."
—Philip K. Dick, *A Scanner Darkly*

Also by Richard Behrens

Lizzie Borden: Girl Detective
(2010, Pear Tree Press)

The Minuscule Monk
(2015, Nine Muses Books)

*The Audible Amnesiac and
Other Lizzie Borden, Girl Detective Stories*
(2018, Nine Muses Books)

Garden Bay Stories
(2018, Nine Muses Books)

Of Moons and Monoliths
(2018, Nine Muses Books)

Acknowledgments

Sincere gratitude to all those who contributed to Richard Behrens' GoFundMe page to make the posthumous publishing of his writing possible and fulfilling his wish to publish his collected essays into one volume, *Of Moons and Monoliths*. A heartfelt thank you to Susan Behrens, who masterfully edited Richard's works. We also gratefully acknowledge Catherine Behrens for her expert copy editing, Robert Brett Sherry for his beautiful introduction, James Taddeo for his fine prologue, and David Lavoie for his assistance in gathering Richard's essays. Thanks also to Marc Reed for his update on *Almost Gone* and for his support of Richard's book projects. Special thanks to Stefani Koorey for her creative cover design and skillful book design.

ACKNOWLEDGMENTS

TABLE OF CONTENTS

III. REVIEWS

IV. HISTORICAL WOMEN AND TRUE CRIME

PROLOGUE

From what Richard told me, because I honestly don't remember the event, we first met in Keene, New Hampshire, in 1993 when I was all of three-and-a-half. It was a family reunion at his parents' house. The specifics of how we are related are complicated, and Richard is technically my second step cousin once removed. As such, he knew my family but hadn't got the chance to meet me yet. On that day he found me playing with my newest Lego set. My first words to him were, "Not all Germans were Nazis." Obviously, that clearly left an impression on him.

The next time I saw him twelve years had passed. At Thanksgiving we met again in earnest. I had heard stories of the legendary "Cousin Richard" from my Uncle Frank and Aunt Kate, but I was excited to finally meet him. And so we met and discussed the things one normally does when one first meets: obscure Pink Floyd albums and the racist revisionist history in *Gone with the Wind*.

A year and half later we began what became a weekly series of phone conversations. I was battling depression and reached out to Richard, who responded kindly and compassionately. When we discussed whatever issue was weighing on me, we often escaped into esoteric conversations of Jungian psychology, consciousness in particle physics, the military industrial complex, even the history of the anarchist movement. At first, I did far more listening than talking. I was amazed that one person could contain so much knowledge about such an eclectic array of ideas. Everything from Nietzsche to *Star Trek* and back again. His words became like a balm for my deep gashes of depression, not because he provided me with some magical remedy, but because his vast knowledge and love for learning reminded me of the things in this world that are worthy of loving and learning. Our weekly chats became almost an experience from another Universe. Richard had me enthralled in his wisdom and wit, and it felt like some great privilege to be able to speak with him. My college studies provided more fodder for discussion, whether it was white privilege in America, prose poetry, or experimental quantum mechanics.

I think what I will remember most about Richard is his tremendous book collection. I say this not only because I helped him move and catalogue his vast collection, but because of his relationship to books. For Richard, a bookstore was an exhilaration surpassing any amusement park. A well-stocked public library was as essential to him as clean air and food. Richard is probably the only person who not only read every single book he bought, but extracted the essence of each text and assimilated it into his own mind. He devoured books voraciously, and he was kind enough to share with all.

But he was more than a repository of ideas. Richard created new ideas on his own, and many far more original than the leading pundits are oft to spout. The ideas contained in this book are far from the simplistic rhetoric that passes for public discourse. Richard was an intellectual and indeed a truly unique thinker who synthesized his knowledge into an incredible understanding of the human psyche and humanity's role in the greater whole of the universe.

James Taddeo
Yonkers, New York
July 2018

INTRODUCTION

There never will be words enough to express the great love for literature, passion for the dramatic arts, and fondness of pen to paper held by my friend, colleague, and editor, the author of this collection of scholarly works, Richard D. Behrens. Even though recently embarking on a new path to somewhere hopefully far more adventurous than that of our mundane existence, Richard continues to share with us his astute understanding of the mysterious, intriguing, comical, and veiled nature of humankind through his prolific words of power. His stories stoke a fire within which illuminate so many new ideas and unexplored emotions.

Having been so fortunate to work under this masterful mind, this less adept writer is inspired by Richard's creative force to achieve greater heights in my own works. A part of him lives in each of my tales. This same experience is shared by many who knew this exceptional writer. Therefore, it is with such delight that his voice once again resonates through this collection of essays entitled *Of Moons and Monoliths*. Richard continues to share his wisdom while riding the lunar rhythm of time, with its immortal and eternal enlightenment, breaking through the obvious into a realm of unimaginable potential. His will to express shines brightly, unlimited by time or space, radiating his special kind of joy.

Thank you, dear friend, for allowing us to further delve into your world of endless possibilities!

Robert Brett Sherry, D.C.
Providence, RI
July 2018

Editor's Note

Richard Behrens was a prolific writer of both fiction and non-fiction and his work has been published in numerous journals since the start of his writing career in the late 1980s. What has been gathered for this book of collected essays, are those that best represent a cross-section of his favorite topics and interests, but by no means encompasses all, or even most, of his writings. In most cases, the essays included in this book had been selected by Richard personally when he first conceived of and titled it *Of Moons and Monoliths*. Every effort was made to try and locate the original publication source of each essay, but in some cases, largely due to publications being out of print or no longer having an on-line presence, the original source could not be located at the time of this book's printing. Each essay has been thoroughly edited, and therefore does not appear exactly as it did in its first publication.

MYSTICISM

MOONS AND MAGIC

"Any technology sufficiently advanced is indistinguishable from magic."

—Arthur C. Clarke

One afternoon, I had the pleasure of being present for a two-year-old boy's first glimpse of a commercial airplane cutting a line across the sky. Initially, Maxwell seemed frightened, ready to bolt behind his father's legs, but then a strange smile broke out on his face and he pointed up in the air, barely knowing what he was looking at, not even having a word for it. His father knelt by his side and said, "Airplane!" as if it were the most marvelous thing in the world. The father, a fiber optics engineer, stood back up to adult height and said to me, "Isn't it funny? Max doesn't know anything about aviation infrastructure!"

Those were wonderfully true words. In order to understand what an airplane is, there is so much we have to either learn, take for granted, or just have programmed into our subconscious. Not only do we have to understand that there is man-made machinery that can travel across the sky (ancient chariots and flying saucers not withstanding), but we also have to realize that this machine is serviced by an entire industrial manufacturing infrastructure. The more we learn about the politics and economics of the airlines industry, the less marvelous or full of wonder the sight of an airplane in the sky is to us.

Maxwell was experiencing a numinous moment so full of magic that all he could do was marvel at it all. But to an adult mind with an adult brain, knowing about airplanes, the inventors who built them, the pilots who fly them, and the industry that manufactures and profits from them, it is just another loud machine on its flight pattern. Perhaps the two-year-old was experiencing something spiritual, religious even.

His experience of seeing the machine for the first time, before a word was applied to it, before an adult gave him the clue that it was safe and ordinary, was no doubt akin to the emotions and spiritual currents that coursed through our primate ancestors as they huddled in their caves watching lightning storms slash across the sky, or feeling the rumble of earthquakes, or watching strange beasts stampede across the flat lands, or encountering an angry cave bear in the lonely crags of the mountains, or just having the experience of giving birth or dying of old age. So many unanswered questions, so many moments of magic and wonder. So many Gods and spirits lurking just behind the hard veil of matter.

The magical content of Max's first encounter with an airplane is hard for an adult to reproduce at will, because we have rationalized and studied and measured and quantified so much that we now live in an age which, although not necessarily void of things to marvel at, is layered in so many concepts and labels and measurements over those things that we have literally lost our ability to wonder at them. We are so used to the experience of watching television and following a story played out by actors, that we cannot even imagine what would happen if a desert nomad who has never encountered anything electronic or digital, or industrial for that matter, would see the same television program and be convinced that weird spirits are talking to him through a metal box. Australian Aborigines who had grown up in Paleolithic conditions, when confronted by a Hollywood movie projected onto a large screen, have expressed puzzlement and confusion, and sometimes grasped at supernatural straws to explain what was happening to them.

It seems that our minds are shaped in early childhood to demystify and to render mundane in our consciousness the truly strange and unexplained phenomena that rage all about us. When we pick up a remote control for a television and change the channel, manipulating the audio-visual device from a distance, we take for granted the infrared waves that are accomplishing the task, just as Max's father took for granted the phenomenon of a machine weighing several hundred tons being able to fly gracefully across the sky. We take comfort in the fact that science has explained those infrared waves or the physics of aeronautics. Scientists aren't confused by it, so why should we be? But anyone who takes the time to look deeply into science, particularly Einstein's Relativity, or Quantum Physics, would see that infrared waves are just as elusive and mysterious as the voices of the thunder gods on their mountains were to primitive man. We generally ignore this and use the remote control in a mundane way to do our bidding, enact our will upon the television. All around us, we can see evidence of man's so-called domination over the forces of nature turned into mundane technology that few of us question, but all of us use to get our business done.

But a Cro Magnon, transported in time from the past into a modern-day city, would see a lot of strange looking human beings gesturing with their hands and waving around small devices that make light, images and energy dance about them. He would see cyclopean structures populating the sky. He would hear the voices of humans who are miles away appearing in the thin air from small hard shells. He would be confronted by sophisticated lingual systems, be it speech or mathematics, that would enable humans to interact with the forces of nature in a way that completely outdistances his own attempts to please the thunder and the hurricanes through the use of religious rituals in a dark cave. Where once he witnessed a group of huddled cavemen trying to appease the spiritual forces for the plentiful growth of food or good fortune on the hunt, he would now witness our modern shamans, or mathematicians and physicists and computer engineers, utilizing magical systems like calculus, computer science, biochemistry and mechanical engineering, all powerful languages and procedures to harness the powers that were once the exclusive domain of the Gods.

Likewise, what would happen to us if we were magically teleported a few hundred years into the future? How would our "modern" minds react to the technology and the common everyday machinery of 2206? Science fiction has always been around to speculate about what this technology will be like, but most sci-fi that has been written so far was created before the recent advent of the information age, and its prejudices and predictions are based upon the model of Newtonian Mechanics that has dominated most of science since the late 1600s. Few people who take science for granted realize that Newtonian Mechanics, the every day "common sense" physics that we see at work around us when we drop things on the ground, drive our cars, build bridges, or design airplanes, is only one model amongst many. When we get to the realm of the extremely large (like traveling at the speed of light between star systems), Newtonian Mechanics must concede to Relativity physics, since "common sense" mechanics cannot explain the broad range of phenomena that will occur. Likewise, when we enter the realm of the extremely small (i.e., the murky world of sub-atomic particles), Newtonian Mechanics is equally inadequate as a model of explanation and prediction. Quantum Physics, which, for over 100 years now, has been perplexing, confusing and challenging some of our most treasured ideas about reality and consciousness, would be the model to use on such a small scale of measurement.

The body of literature that we know as science fiction is a literature of the Newtonian age. Perhaps other forms of literature will emerge to give voice to our interplay with other ways of perceiving and processing phenomenon beyond the world of classical science. Indeed, if we stretch our definition of science fiction (with apologies to Hugo Gernsback, who invented the genre), we can see that the evolution of human consciousness has been a theme in much modern and post-modern art and literature.

Friedrich Nietzsche kicked off the 20th century with his controversial philosophical novel *Thus Spoke Zarathustra*, which used as a metaphor for his complex ideas on metaphysics and religion, a stormy prophet known as Zarathustra who proclaims the advent of the Ubermensch. Translated as either Overman or Superman, the Ubermensch stands in relation to the human being, as the human being does to our ancestral apes. This Ubermensch will emerge from the rubble of our bankrupt philosophical and metaphysical systems and will transcend the equally bankrupt Christianity that has failed to produce anything but a "slave race" of weak spirits. To Nietzsche, the Ubermensch is the transcendence of the Western mind trapped in its moralities and Christian weaknesses. The Ubermensch is "beyond good and evil" and strives for a "re-evaluation of all morals." It is not hard to see why Nietzsche was much beloved by Adolph Hitler, although it is doubtful that Nietzsche would have seen the Nazi party's use of his ideas as anything more than a complete misunderstanding of his work.

Regardless, the composer Richard Strauss wrote a famous passage of music represented the rising of the human consciousness from the ape beast to the human being to the splendor and glory of the Ubermensch. The music, which also represented a Sun rising over the mountain where Zarathustra has exiled himself, feels like the rising on three steps towards a solar altar, the last step of which brings the listener to the transcendence of being human. This passage turned out to be one of the most recognizable pieces of music in western culture, and not just because it was used by Elvis Presley to accompany his advent onto performance stages.

In the mid-to-late 1960s, science fiction novelist Arthur C. Clarke and film director Stanley Kubrick created *2001: A Space Odyssey*, a novel/movie combination that sparked a cultural phenomenon. Its powerful use of the opening bars of Strauss' "Thus Spoke Zarathustra" over an image of the Sun, the Moon and the Earth lining up in splendid and transcendent symmetry, is the key to the entire movie and its own three-fold structure. Like Nietzsche's evolution path, *2001* starts with the primate apes that were the human race, the Dawn of Man, reasonless beasts struggling for survival in the dirt of a primal Africa and shows the exact moment when our ancestors discovered technology and took the first step towards the domination of nature. This is the step of the Earth.

The second step is the Moon. The narrative jumps millions of years forward to the advent of man to the lunar surface where a celestial mystery is revealed to a human race that has technologically progressed to the point where it can reach the Moon. The third step is one that takes humans beyond technology and reason into the dark abyss amongst the stars, and climaxes in a psychedelic and mystical journey that is unlike anything else that was ever committed to Hollywood celluloid.

Oddly enough, neither Clarke nor Kubrick was interested in expansion of consciousness, or mind-altering drugs, or were even particularly religious or spiritual (Kubrick distinctly declared himself an atheist), but both of them had a profound understanding of what it is like for a primitive consciousness to be confronted by the numinous. Their intention was to create a powerful vision of the role that technology has played in the evolution of human consciousness and the inevitable transcendence to the next step.

Arthur C. Clarke's statement that "any technology sufficiently advanced is indistinguishable from magic" is a both a rebuttal of magic and a positive understanding of it. There is little need to think of magic and science as being mutually exclusive opposites. Indeed, models of consciousness do exist that can reconcile them. But if our consciousness is that of a primitive ape, or a child, the experience of higher phenomena that are beyond the range of our consciousness' ability to process, would appear to us as angels and demons, as supernatural, Gods and Goddesses, dream spirits. In short, if a savage human, stripped of all the conditioning and education of the modern world, was to experience virtual reality decks, or computer games, or a trip on an airplane at 27,000 feet, such an individual would believe that they had been whisked away into a supernatural realm, and wouldn't be able to process the experience the way that we would. To him, he may return to his jungle home claiming that he spoke with angels and demons, rode on chariots of flames, and saw phantoms of strange creatures who didn't exist.

2001: A Space Odyssey was based on a short story by Arthur C. Clarke called "The Sentinel." This simple tale concerning a survey team that uncovered a buried alien artifact on the Moon is the germ from which the expanded story was developed. Part of Clarke's brilliance as a science fiction writer is his understanding of the vast amounts of time and space that exist in the universe, and how the human race and all of our history are but mere fleeting moments in a vast continuum. The alien technology in his stories, whether they are the monolith of "The Sentinel"/"*2001*" or the space probes of "Rendezvous with Rama," are silent, relatively inert, and incredibly patient. They move with the glacial slowness of stones and can wait tens of thousands of years just to achieve one objective. The monolith of "The Sentinel" has been placed on the Moon millions of years ago in anticipation that the growing life forms on the planet Earth may one day become intelligent enough to reach it and trigger off its interstellar radio pulse. This is the trigger signaling the aliens behind the monolith that mankind is ready. But ready for what?

"The Sentinel" doesn't answer that question, but leaves the reader filled with a sense of wonder of what would happen next. But "next" may be thousands of years from now. Whoever is at the other end of that radio pulse may take thousands of years to get back to Earth. Perhaps they have seeded the galaxy with tens of thousands if not millions of these monoliths, providing stepping stones for all potential species of the galaxy to contact the race of beings that is billions of years ahead of them.

This is the conceit that seized Stanley Kubrick's imagination, and he knew that the story that they would develop from "The Sentinel" needed temporal elbow room, indeed a few million years. It seemed obvious that the story of Mankind's evolution from human to super being would be more dramatic and have more authoritative voice to it if the range of evolution was stretched backwards to include the steps that we already have taken. This is why Clarke and Kubrick added on the "Dawn of Man" sequence, one of the most remarkable and powerful sequences ever displayed on film.

What is so powerful about this 20-minute vignette about our primate ancestors is that we are looking at something remarkable: the small tribe of apes that is destined to become the human race facing possible extinction because of hunger and thirst. They are living under appalling conditions, fighting a daily struggle for meager sources of food. We see the apes eating from plants and berry-producing vines that are themselves shriveling from the drought. They are clustered around a water hole, fighting off a rival tribe of apes for the small amount of water left due to the horrific drought. They have not yet taken any of the evolutionary leaps that would lead them to becoming Men, but they are suffering horribly, and a sensitive viewer would find their unhappiness, their feral existence, unbearably sad in light of the fact that they are struggling to become "us."

Kubrick brings in his own thematic touches with the two tribes fighting over the water hole, clearly pre-echoing the American-Soviet conflict hinted at later in the film. They are not yet meat eaters, they are weak and stupid, they exhaust their energies jumping up and down trying to scare the other tribe, but they have no defenses outside of making a lot of noise. It is clear that the first tribe to discover some form of weapon that would break the stalemate would survive the drought, and the other tribe would perish. This again pre-echoed the nuclear weapons balance of power that threatened to destroy the human race in the later part of the 20th century. To understand the opening sequence of *2001*, one must see this parallel and how the depiction of destructive tribal rivalries is played out in many Kubrick movies, including *Dr. Strangelove* with the Cold War itself, *A Clockwork Orange* with futuristic street gangs, *Full Metal Jacket* with a platoon of Marines in Vietnam, and his other films that portray warfare and the herd mentality that creates it.

Once Kubrick has established the basic crisis that the apes are encountering, the possibility of their tribal extinction due to their inability to adopt to their environment, he shows how they take the first step towards becoming human. They wake up in the morning to find a single black monolith, about 7 feet high, standing in the middle of their sleeping circle. The soundtrack, which has been void of music until this point, now plays a haunting Ligeti piece that sounds like the quivering of angelic beings undergoing some form of ecstasy. It's strange music, alien, beyond our comprehension. Something different is happening, something that a modern mind cannot comprehend any more than the apes.

The ape who first sees the monolith, Moon Watcher as Clarke calls him in the novel, reacts at first with fear and rage. He growls and bares his teeth at the thing, makes meager attempts to use the same tactics of scaring off his enemies that he tried with the rival apes at the water hole. But clearly this is something several orders of magnitude higher than a rival ape. It stands against the sky, dark and silent, presenting a passive and ineffable face. It is simply there for the Apes. Its motives, methods and subjective experience are forever incomprehensible. The mind of the apes is not yet advanced enough to even detect that it is confronting intelligence. Moon Watcher even dares getting close enough to try to bite the rock.

Eventually, the apes touch the stone. At first, they seem to be touching it in order to determine if it is hostile or friendly, but as their fingers play along its surface, they settle down, and some of them stroke it slowly and press their palms against it. Their ape consciousness is too feral and survival-based to feel anything resembling our current emotions, but the monolith seems to have a calming effect on them. Kubrick includes a shot of several apes crouched around the stone, touching it, starting to feel awe, perhaps even starting to think.

In the novel, Clarke has the mechanisms within the monolith explicitly start teaching the apes, showing them how to hunt, how to use weapons, how to fight—he even calls the chapter "Academy"; but Kubrick keeps it cryptic, simply portraying the apes doing something to the stone that resembles religious worship. In this shot of the film, we are watching the very first adoration of a God by humans.

Moonwatcher is aptly named, since the base instinct at the core of mankind is to reach for the stars, and the Moon of course is the first step in that journey. The ape doesn't know what the Moon is any more than he understands the monolith.

Clarke's novel reveals to us that the monolith is one of many that have been scattered about the globe. Further, the monoliths seem to be scattered through the galaxy and the experiment on Earth is just part of a larger attempt to stimulate intelligent life forms throughout the universe. A monolith has been buried on the Moon, three million years before it is discovered by a group of American astronauts. When the black slab is exposed to sunlight, it is activated, and sets off a piercing radio signal that blasts across the solar system, directing itself at Japetus, one of the moons of Saturn. The mysterious structure was a trigger, a signal to some other switching station of alien technology in orbit around Jupiter, that the human race is ready. Without hesitation, the entire American space program is reconstituted to provide a spaceship that would take a team of scientists to the far moons of Saturn, prepared for contact with alien intelligence.

Originally, Kubrick had planned to show aliens descend from the skies and interact with the man-apes, teaching them skills and stimulating their intelligence. After doing some screen tests, he decided that it was best to go with an abstraction, to hint at and imply that alien intelligence is at work, but to leave the harsh image of a jet-black slab to stand alone as a receptacle of any meaning you chose to hurl into it, be it religious, scientific or philosophical. One of the most revealing statements that Clarke makes about the Monolith in the novel, one that reinforces Kubrick's insistence that it is an abstract on which we can impose our own interpretations, is that "it was only the outward manifestation of forces too subtle to be consciously perceived. It was merely a toy to distract the senses, while the real processing was carried out at far deeper levels of the mind" (page 217).

Clarke's use of the term "magic" when describing how advanced technology may seem to primitive minds may explain another cultural phenomenon that has dominated the 20th century. The last 100 years has seen an impressive growth in occult sciences, of which the Rosicrucian Order of the Golden Dawn and Aleister Crowley have been the most prominent voices, that has attempted to stimulate higher consciousness through a complex set of systems including yoga, meditation, Kabala and ceremonial magic. Crowley, who studied the magical arts throughout his entire controversial career, has defined magic as "causing change to occur in conformity with Will," a statement that puts a large emphasis on an intense focus on individual consciousness and an exploration of the different layers of consciousness. Often mistaken for a Satanist by his detractors, Crowley has said that he did not need to invent anything supernatural to explain spiritual phenomena. His system of magic had the slogan, "The aim of religious, the method of science." He rigorously believed that the spiritual phenomena that occurred while using magic and yoga to alter consciousness, could be scientifically modeled and studied. He encouraged, through the use of what he called "scientific illuminism," people to take magical practice as a form of experimentation. When certain things are performed, certain results occur. And this is true of magical phenomena just as much as it is of scientific phenomena. As a matter of fact, this way of thinking is what led to the birth of science out of the magical arts in the first place.

Therefore, the higher layers of consciousness, when descending into the rational and conscious mind, can reveal themselves as an awesome array of entities, spirits, demons, angels, gods and goddesses. Rather than believe in their empirical existence, one is encouraged to see them as gateways to a higher understanding of various parts of our minds, parts that we often ignore and rarely experience except in dreams and during drug trips. Perhaps, like *2001*'s Monolith, the deities and spiritual beings of our collective mythologies, religions and dreams are merely "outward manifestation[s] of forces too subtle to be consciously perceived" and that the "real processing" is going on deeper in the mind that we can even imagine.

Upon its release in 1967, *2001: A Space Odyssey* was immediately embraced by a pop culture already awash in psychedelic and cosmic imagery, a cultural phenomenon that was labeled by the press "the Age of Aquarius." This was the generation that was following the Beatles into Pepperland and the Rolling Stones into pacts with the Devil. *2001* become one of those heady experiences that one can only fully appreciate while stoned out of one's mind, but like the Monolith that patiently waits millions of years to reveal its purpose, it is possible that the ultimate meaning and message of the film and novel will only become more apparent as we enter into what Ray Kurzweil has called an "age of spiritual machines," a period of human existence where technology will be used to propel us to higher levels of consciousness, indeed to the point where computer consciousness will be the vehicle through which we will travel, where man and machine will merge and cast behind them the frail limitations that have haunted our relatively small consciousness and mortal bodies.

To revisit our hypothetical trip into the year 2206, we may find in the future that some of the more mystical and far-out notions of quantum physics, may not only be accepted by the average lay-person, but our very consciousness may be transformed and changed by it, in much the same way that the emergence of Newtonian science during the 1600s and 1700s made vast changes in the way we think and how we relate to the world. Our "modern" Newtonian minds may peep into the future and see a range of phenomena that is just as baffling, strange, terrifying, and counter to our "common sense" as the Cro Magnon would experience if he were transported to 2006.

Imagine if you will, waking up in the year 2206 and being so disoriented by what you see around you, that you find it difficult to know how to filter out the important elements. Weird creatures move about you, and you cannot determine whether they are humans or androids or projected holograms. They interact with you, attempting to communicate, but the process of communication is much faster and far less verbal than what you are used to. The room itself shifts and changes, like the Holodeck from *Star Trek*, and ordinary objects like chairs, tables, and doorways seem to change instantaneously as quickly as television channels being flipped by someone with a remote control.

Once you have pin-pointed who are the "humans" and what general environment you are in (it seems to be someone's house), you cannot determine with any certainty whether a person you see before you is an entity unto himself, or if he is only a distributed part of a whole that is dispersed throughout a series of people. In short, you cannot perceive whether his consciousness is local or non-local. Everyone seems to be telepathic. They are communicating with each other via a medium that is beyond your comprehension, just as our theoretical Cro Magnon would not be able to comprehend radio or television waves.

The people around you are also insubstantial as ghosts. They flicker in and out, seemingly becoming invisible, teleporting themselves from one room to another. Or even more bizarre, seemingly teleporting in and out of each other. They seem like aliens, strange creatures that cannot possibly be your descendants. There is little of your own world that you recognize. Images, information, communication and the physical environment keep moving at a colossal speed. You cannot comprehend the quantum computers that are working beneath the scene, processing information at billions and trillions times the speed of the most powerful computers of 2006. What would ordinarily take a fleet of mainframe computers a thousand years in our time would take less than a billionth of a second for a quantum computer to process since it possesses billions of times the processing power of a single human brain of today. Since you have not been born into a quantum age of computing and have never experienced the mind-bogglingly fast speeds of its processing, you cannot follow the rapidity of what is happening about you. You cannot even imagine where the processors are located. In the walls? In the strangely shaped objects that keep morphing and moving about you? In the minds and bodies of the humans that are in the room with you? Perhaps the chips and nanobots are everywhere and they have become an integral part of what it means to be human.

Suddenly, you realize that you cannot possibly function in this world. The Cro Magnon teleported to 2006 may have a chance of learning simple ways of being, wearing modern clothes, walking up and down staircases, perhaps learning primitive aspects of our languages, but the physical structures of his brain and the shape and textures of his inner consciousness have been shaped by a very different environment, so he can never truly be like us. In your case, in 2206, you do not share the same physical biology, far less the same brain structure. You do not know if there is even any organic metabolism going on, or has the carbon-based human body been replaced by a complex series of quantum systems that control reality on the subatomic level using computers that are only a few atoms in size, nanocomputers and quantum processors that manipulated and build and rebuild the structures around you. In short, by 2206, the human being has shed its physical body and has become a series of shifting physical forms and information patterns that constitute a non-local self.

As Arthur C. Clarke writes in *2001: A Space Odyssey*, "The first explorers of Earth had long since come to the limits of flesh and blood; as soon as their machines were better than their bodies, it was time to move. First their brains, and then their thoughts alone, they transferred into shining new homes of metal...In these they roamed among the stars. They no longer built spaceships. They were spaceships" (page 185).

The fact that it all happened through the evolution of science doesn't for one nanosecond take away the surreal spiritual power of watching consciousness without a stable physical body control the forces of nature.

To you, that would be supernatural. That would be magic.

First published in *The Journal of Advancing Technology*, Summer, Volume 4, 2006.

THE MAGUS OF OZ

"The appetite of our age for occultism demands to be satisfied, and while with the mediocrity of people will result in mere sensationalism, it will lead in many to higher and nobler and bolder thought; and who can tell what mysteries these braver and abler intellects may unravel in future ages?"

—L. Frank Baum, *Aberdeen Saturday Pioneer*, 22 February 1890

It is popularly believed that Aleister Crowley spent the last years of his life a sordid junkie in a ratty boarding house. On the contrary, despite an impoverished financial situation and the savagery of a world war raging about him, Crowley lived in pleasant lodgings in a seashore guesthouse called Netherwood in Hastings where he was quite prolific, writing and publishing books, overseeing the creation of Lady Frieda Harris' inspired Tarot paintings, maintaining correspondence with occultists all over the world, and managing the affairs of the Ordo Templi Orientis. He was in his twilight, physically ailing and still addicted to heroin, and had been discredited in the English press; but by the time he moved into Netherwood he had attained the rank of the Grand Old Magus of Magick and had followers on every continent. Not bad for a seventy-year-old who had long since exhausted his family fortune and had been publicly crucified as the "Wickedest Man in the World."

Crowley's decision to live in Hastings had more to do with his severe asthma and the London Blitz than any financial desperation. His colleagues had been concerned about his health and feared the bombings would do him in. Netherwood seemed the perfect atmosphere for him since the couple that ran the place, the Symonds, encouraged their tenants' Bohemian tendencies, arranging for concerts and lecture series, hosting a range of interesting talent, including the guitarist Julian Bream and the noted philosopher Jacob Bronowski.

He had arrived in early January 1943, in an ambulance that also carried his rather large book collection and his paintings. He was a gaunt and aging figure wearing knickerbockers and silver-buckled shoes, greeting everyone with that peculiar phrase: "Do What Thou Wilt Shall be the Whole of the Law." Although his behavior may have been considered a bit dotty, his landlords found him a charming eccentric who was not out of place in a Bohemian guesthouse. Perhaps the Great Beast could even lecture on mysticism, or explain his curious system of philosophy called Thelema, which had caused such a fuss over the years.

From his small room at Netherwood, Crowley corresponded with Jack Parsons in California about the L. Ron Hubbard affair and the *Book of Babalon*; scribed the *Caliphate Letters* to Grady McMurtry, establishing the succession of the OHO; and met with such luminaries as Kenneth Grant, Gerald Gardner, John Symonds, Louis Wilkinson, Dion Fortune and James Joyce biographer Richard Ellman. He continued to write, despite his ill health, preparing the proofs for *Liber Aleph* and organizing his literary estate.

His landlady, Kathleen Symonds, found the Great Beast quite amusing, particularly his penchant for tossing the I Ching sticks for every day decisions, including whether or not to go to the dentist. He loved wandering in the garden, admiring the rabbits, and had no qualms whatsoever about Kathleen watching him self-inject heroin. He engaged the hotel's guests in erudite conversations and made quite a splash at a local chess club where no one seemed to be able to beat him. His pungent pipe smoke preceded him into every room and he would often be seen wandering the grounds, lifting his palms to the Sun in adoration. As far as Kathleen Symonds could remember, he was never actually seen practicing what he called "magick" and had nothing demonic about him, except for his curiously sculpted eyebrows.

All manifested beings must pass, and the incarnation known as Aleister Crowley died peacefully in his bedroom at Netherwood in 1947, leaving behind a rich legacy of literary, spiritual and historical importance. Despite a funeral in England, his ashes were buried at the foot of a suburban tree in New Jersey and nothing remained of his physical being except the recordings, books, poems, photographs, memories and that strange philosophy called Thelema with its occasional and scattered followers around the world.

Over the years, quaint anecdotes and urban legends about Crowley were propagated through various biographies, including the famous claim that his last words were "I am perplexed!" The staff at Netherwood had their own fond memories to relate to future generations about the Victorian eccentric who had been their guest for several years. One of these stories stands out, suggesting a hint of a magical moment that could have occurred if Mrs. Symonds had only been familiar with her guest's penchant for fairy tales.

A local cinema was screening *The Wizard of Oz* and Crowley expressed some interest in seeing it. His landlady dismissed the movie as something for children that would hold no interest for him and encouraged him to ignore it. One can only wonder what the Great Beast would have made out of the film had he insisted on attending. He processed the world in his own peculiar and arcane way, through a mind that had been trained for more than half a century in mystic languages and the Hermetic Qabalistic tradition that had been passed down to him through the order of the Golden Dawn. In *Book Four*, he had interpreted the nursery rhymes of Mother Goose through the lens of this symbol system. Old Mother Hubbard had been transformed into Binah the Great Mother, and Humpty Dumpty had turned into the Akashic egg of Hindu mythology. Once having read the Mother Goose chapter of *Book Four*, it is not difficult to imagine how Crowley might have interpreted the tale of Dorothy Gale and her adventures in the Land of Oz.

At the time that Crowley asked his landlady about *The Wizard of Oz*, it had been in release for more than five years. Produced by Metro-Goldwyn-Mayer in Hollywood, it was based on the first in a popular series of children's novels by L. Frank Baum, a Chicago journalist who had made his reputation with a ground-breaking book on window dressing before achieving immortality through children's literature. Baum had joined the Theosophical Society in 1892 and studied the mysticism that influenced his refashioning of children's literature. The Oz books abound with magical rites, mythical characters, spiritual archetypes and occult references, including a division of the land of Oz into four quarters, each represented by a different elemental color. His intention was to take the classic structure of European folk tales, as represented by the works of the Brothers Grimm, and remove the disturbing elements, purifying it for a more innocent audience. As a result he invented remarkable tales of fantasy, deeply rooted in the American experience. The world-wide acceptance of the books and the colossal success of the

Hollywood film in 1939 suggest that Baum had tapped into a universal imagination, much the same way that George Lucas did with his *Star Wars* franchise and J.K. Rowling with her *Harry Potter* novels many decades later.

Fueled by literary success and a popular stage production of the story, Baum went on to pen twelve more Oz books before his death in 1918. By the time MGM filmed the musical with Judy Garland, the book was already four decades old. When Crowley wrote *Liber Oz*, his declaration of the Thelemic rights of man, in 1941, he was aware of Baum's use of the word Oz, but refused to change the name of his book just because Hollywood had co-opted it. The word appeared as early as *The Book of Lies* in the context of the Hebrew letters Ayin and Zain, which add up to the number 77. The reference is to the Devil card on the Tarot and, more specifically, to the Phallus as a generative power of magic. One can only imagine what Crowley made out of Baum's use of the word.

The plot of *The Wizard of Oz* needs no repeating, since the story and its characters are so well known, so beloved, and so archetypal to our conception of a children's fantasy tale that the world of advertising sees the characters from the Hollywood film as the most recognizable secular images in our culture. Hollywood had filmed the story for the screen several times before 1939, including an animated feature and a 1910 silent version co-starring Oliver Hardy. The story had also been adapted for the stage in 1902 and had enjoyed a very long and successful run both as a traveling show and on Broadway. It had been transformed into a musical revue, with the songs included in the show changing as often as the cast. Several actors, including the vaudeville team of Stone and Montgomery, were already extremely well known for playing characters such as the Scarecrow, the Tin Woodsman and the Cowardly Lion; by the time Ray Bolger, Jack Healy and Bert Lahr put on their make-up, all but the smallest children in the audience already had a conception of who these characters were, what they were supposed to look like, and how they were supposed to behave.

It is unrecorded how much of the story Crowley knew, whether he had seen any of the previous film versions or had attended any of the stage performances, which were quite popular in the 1910s when he was living in America. It is quite possible that in all the years of ushering in the Aeon of Horus, promulgating the Law of Thelema, editing occult journals, running various hermetic brotherhoods and secret societies, not to mention his Abbey in Cefalu, and attaining the grade of Magus, he had little time for trivial entertainments, his familiarity with Mother Goose rhymes notwithstanding. It is quite possible that if he had set foot inside the Hastings cinema to see *The Wizard of Oz*, he would have experienced the pure joy of learning the story for the very first time.

Aleister Crowley spent several decades training his mind to think in terms of magical correspondences, to interpret all phenomena as a microcosmic reflection of higher realities, often connected through a complex system of correspondences and interdependencies. No small task, but well worth the effort for an aspiring magus for whom even the simplest Hollywood film contained magical formulae and archetypes. *The Wizard of Oz* is a magically pregnant film, ripe for interpretation, in that its plot elements and fantastical imagery had already been shaped by a Theosophist.

> *"To know thyself" is considered quite an accomplishment, which it has taken us, who are your elders, months to perfect. But now"* [the Scarecrow] *added, turning to the others, "let us get aboard and start upon our journey."*
>
> —*The Land of Oz*, L. Frank Baum

Aleister was nearly thirty years old when he saw his first motion picture but had always recognized their full magical potential. He didn't get to the cinema very often but appreciated the media. Mankind had already harnessed the primal fire to warm his caves, hollowed out tree trunks to navigate and master the oceans, captured the winds to drive great ships to conquer continents, and exploited the earth for its minerals to build the machinery of empire. Somewhere in the midst of all that he had somehow conquered light itself. Events long since past were encoded into strips of celluloid and brought back to animated life upon the screen through light projection. The phonograph had done a similar service to sound, invented by the man who amusedly was known as the Wizard of Menlo Park, but this new medium captured both light *and* sound. Watching a movie was like seeing a dream. They call it the Silver Screen, and that is an appropriate name for this Treasure House of Images. In the Yesodic sphere, images dominate, and the motion pictures had redefined the way that we look at images.

Imagine: The film is being screened at a matinée, so just before noon, Crowley puts on his tweeds and lights his deep-bowled pipe with his favorite tobacco. The landlady's husband has been charged with the task of taking Aleister to that silly child nonsense since Mrs. Symonds has important tasks to take care of, such as scheduling a series of lectures for the intellectual improvement of her tenants. The two men stroll into town and buy tickets at the box office. Mr. Symonds spends several minutes convincing Aleister that he must extinguish his pipe if they are to go inside the cinema, and the old magus does so reluctantly.

The Wizard of Oz begins with the MGM lion roaring in the midst of his solar circle over some symbol that looks suspiciously like the Winged Disk. Aleister has seen this before and has always been amused by its evocation of force and fire. He even does some quick Gematria of the film studio's name: Mem-Gimel-Mem. Two hanged men flanking a high priestess riding a camel into the Abyss. Art for Art's Sake. Leo the Lion. What a splendid emblem! Solar phallic and full of strength! The film is already sealed with a potent talisman.

The opening credits are projected over a sepia-toned painting of clouds. Aleister does not recognize any of the names in the credits since the Great Beast has not been prone to take in any Andy Hardy movies over the years. Then a message from the filmmakers. For forty years, Time has been powerless to put the story's kindly philosophy out of fashion. Aleister ruminates upon the veracity of that statement. After all, the Aeon of Horus is just about forty years old, he thinks to himself. Perhaps this *Wizard of Oz* will be the first film to embrace the Law of Thelema. We shall see.

Now a drab Kansas landscape, with a little girl running along a dirt road. She is wearing a checkered gingham dress and at her heels snaps a little terrier. She calls him Toto but Aleister immediately decides that its real name is Totem. He must be much wiser than Dorothy herself for he bit the evil Miss Gulch in self-defense. What a name! Gulch! Aleister thinks of deep ravines under black skies. The black wraith who gobbles up light and life, is now after the dog. It is up to Dorothy to save Totem from that wicked old witch. What better way to open a movie, Aleister chuckles to himself, than to have Babalon the Dark and Mighty coming forth with her voracious appetite for annihilating existence.

Dorothy lives on a farm with her aunt and uncle. Many who have taken up the hero's journey, like Moses, are orphans. Even that ridiculous American comic strip hero, the one with the solar sigil on his chest who can leap over tall buildings with a single bound, even he was orphaned, raised on a farm by foster parents. The Aunt and Uncle are old enough to be Dorothy's grandparents. Can they be the Great Mother and Father? It is now certain that Dorothy will not just remain a little girl on a farm. Something inside her will evolve over the course of this picture. The three farmhands, Zeke, Huck and Hickory, will somehow be the agents of her evolution. One is brutish, herding the swine; another is romantic and dreaming of a statue in his honor; and the third is absent-minded and dull-witted, bashing his own hand with a hammer. They are each in their turn trying to teach her something.

Dorothy wants to go over the rainbow, to a place far away, where nothing can hurt her. She sings a lovely song in a surprisingly mature voice about troubles melting like lemon drops over the chimney tops. Such surrealistic imagery in such a sentimental song. The place she is longing for, which she sings about to Totem, is far, far away, beyond the Moon, beyond the rain. In a single instance, Aleister realizes, she is describing the Supernals beyond the Veil of Paroketh, the clouds covering the gray Kansas sky, blocking the rays of the Sun and the Technicolor. Aha! Aleister sighs. She is in Malkuth looking up, and the great light of Divinity is appearing to her as visions of candy and rainbows.

Mr. Symonds has dozed a bit but straightens up and grunts to his friend, "I hope you're not bored, it does get better, you know." "I'm sure it does," Aleister says with a smile.

Now Miss Gulch comes to the farm to take Totem and stuffs him into a picnic basket, an act as elegant and terrifying as the kidnapping of Hansel and Gretel. She is hatchet-faced, Victorian, full of heartless principles, like the Plymouth brethren of Aleister's youth. The dog escapes and returns to Dorothy. Running off across the farmlands, they disappear into the vastness of the American landscape. They stumble across the circus wagon of a charlatan magus, an old wizard with his crystal ball and turban. Aleister expects the old man to take Dorothy to his Abbey to perform her daily solar adorations, cast circles, keep a magical diary. The old magus is running his mystery school out of a broken-down circus wagon, probably cheaper rent than a farmhouse in Sicily.

He is a fake, obviously, but he has a heart and works magic upon Dorothy, convincing her that home is where she belongs and sends her back to her loving aunt, who misses her very much. Professor Marvel, who boasts of his acquaintance with the Crowned Heads of Europe, has performed a kindly act of white magic.

Then, the tornado comes across the land, ravaging, eating up houses, tossing cows high into the clouds. It is Miss Gulch returned in her more devastating form, another agent of annihilation. Dorothy is locked out of the storm shelter, cut off from her family and farmhands. Aleister remembers a painful incident from his childhood, before his awakening, when he carried that barbarous name of Alexander. His father, a member of the Plymouth Brethren, had been obsessed with the coming of the Kingdom and filled his son's imagination with that day when the righteous would ascend and leave behind the profane to a dying earth. Such feelings of exclusivity vanished like smoke one day when Alexander came home to an empty house. After wandering the silent rooms, he went into a panic, thinking that his mother and father had ascended into the Kingdom and left him behind. He now sits mesmerized, staring at the movie screen, remembering the feeling of helplessness, one he swore he would never feel again. He has found his emotional way into the character of Dorothy and felt the samsara of her existence: the absence of her parents, the approaching storm before which she stands mortal and defenseless, the advent of a terrible Abyss from which she will be annihilated and cease to exist.

A glass window blown from its frame knocks Dorothy unconscious and she falls onto her bed just as the winds cast her entire farmhouse high into the air. Then there is a mesmerizing sequence of special effects that Aleister does not expect, a crossing of the Abyss. The images of earthly life on a Kansas farm speed past the window, all caught into the melee: a barn; a cow; farmhands in a boat trying to steer their solar chariot; Miss Gulch on a bicycle in her element, the wilderness of winds. She transforms into a hag on a broomstick, a dark nightmare, an eldritch wraith cackling with her loathsomeness, the spirit of the twister revealing her true face.

Then a bump and it is all over. The house is down on the ground, the air quiet. Dorothy picks up Totem and heads for the door. Aleister is on the edge of his seat, breathless, grasping for the pipe in his mouth that cannot be lit, knowing that beyond the farmhouse door will be some glorious city of pyramids, cyclopean architecture, watch towers from which the Lords of the Elements observe the corners of the universe.

The door opens onto some of the richest colors and tonal textures that Aleister has even seen on a motion picture screen. Here indeed is the Technicolor House of Images, Yesod in its most visceral form. Munchkinland: the astral plane, the undeveloped self-cradled at the

THE MAGUS OF OZ 21

base of the spinal column, populated by small men, women and children in bright felt clothing, carrying sunflowers and lollipops. There are soldiers, politicians, even a mayor and a coroner. What a glorious microcosm of human society. And they celebrate their day of independence, for Dorothy has dropped her house on their former tyrant, the Wicked Witch of the East.

Dorothy is celebrated as a Good Witch for having liberated the Munchkins from their tyranny. There are two other witches present. Glinda of the North floats in as a bubble and then transforms into a radiant queen with magic wand and flittering voice, her soft feet not hurting the little flowers. The Witch of the West is green and evil and appears in an explosion of purple smoke and flame. Her sister is dead under the house, her feet covered in Ruby Slippers. Aleister frowns. What about the Witch of the South? Is she a pillar of flame, the pure essence of Fire? Did not the filmmakers diligently research a copy of 777 to bring magical symmetry to their mythology? Not to worry, for the Masonic temple has no candle in the South. There is a mystery concealed.

The two witches are now fighting over Dorothy and the Ruby Slippers. They are charmed and cannot succumb to the demands of the Wicked Witch, who disappears in a violent explosion. The Munchkins have been celebrating their liberty from the tyranny of the Wicked Witch of the East, but now there is a new danger. Dorothy wants none of this and wishes to go home, typical of an aspirant who has only risen to the grade of Neophyte. As soon as the path becomes too perilous, they do everything possible to abandon it and return to the familiar territory of Malkuth.

The path begins with the first steps: Follow the Yellow Brick Road. In the town square, the Road begins in a spiral like a Kundalini snake unraveling upwards towards the higher chakras. Aleister knows that road only too well. He knows that as soon as Dorothy passes beyond the Watchtowers at the borders of Munchkinland, traveling due north out of Malkuth along the 32nd path, she will have only begun her journey towards the completion of the Great Work. Perhaps she too will travel to Ceylon and study Buddhist meditation, wander the wastes of the Gobi desert and invoke the spirits of the Aethrys, turn invisible in Mexico, receive the Logos in Cairo, edit a journal of occult studies in Detroit, initiate neophytes into the Great White Brotherhood in London. But no matter what path her solar orbit will take, she will certainly go through ordeals, receive initiations, master the elements, and ascend through the celestial spheres and converse with the Angel. Her soul will merge with the body of Nuit and consume her like a hungry lover ready to annihilate her being. In order to conquer death, one must first die. Ding, dong the Wicked Witch is dead!

But wait, Aleister, this is a Hollywood movie. Enlightenment will not be so violent. Just sit back while Mr. Symonds snores and pay attention. The best is yet to come.

A Scarecrow hangs from a pole in a corn field. He is stationed at a crossroad with his arms pointing in conflicting directions and cannot tell Dorothy which way to go. Like Dante at the beginning of the Divine Comedy, she is lost in the woods. She releases the Scarecrow, who dances like rubber across the yellow road, complaining that he doesn't have any brains. Aleister may be the only member of the audience that knows the Scarecrow for what he is: the first Tarot card of the Major Arcana. The Fool has brought with him the Element of Air and the first holy letter Aleph. Aleister, who has recently meditated upon his own manuscript *Liber Aleph*, *The Book of Wisdom and Folly*, knows the Fool is really Parsifal who sees the Holy Grail but does not recognize it because he has not yet attained Wisdom. He is also Pan, Dionysus, the Green Man of Spring, the embodiment of Zero who is at once nothing and everything, the sum of all potentials and possibilities.

No brains indeed! All straw, he claims, tapping his head, but he has enough brains to know what he doesn't know: why ocean meets the shore, what a symphony is; he knows that Abraham Lincoln did a lot of thinking. That he can even formulate the questions tells much and promises much. Dorothy invites him along on the journey to the Emerald City so the Wizard can give him a brain, and as such Dorothy has consecrated her first elemental weapon, bound him to her like a Goetic spirit, and they set off along the Yellow Brick Road with Totem dancing behind.

The next element she encounters is Water and the holy letter of Mem in the form of a Tin Man, all hollow like the wretched of T.S. Elliot's poem. Also similar to the Hanged Man of the Tarot card that bears his element, he is frozen in a place of punishment. Once thawed out and oiled, he sings more sweetly than the hillbilly straw man, yearning for love. His face is oval and cherubic and tender. He even knows his Shakespeare, quoting Romeo and Juliet, an odd state of affairs when a metal-man from an astral world knows the works of the Bard. Lastly, he is all silver, reflecting his lunar nature. Once consecrated by Dorothy with the contents of his oil can, she binds him to her and the three of them, plus Totem, take off down the road.

If Dorothy has successfully fought Air and Water, there is only Fire left to master. Lions and tigers and beasts, oh my! The king of the jungle bounds out of the woods, growling and snapping. Of course, the solar monarch, the great beast, which Dorothy must tame like the woman on the Strength card harnessing the powers of the Lion. This is the letter Tet, the fire in the heart of the sperm cell, the energy of lust that drives the universe. But this Beast does not yet have his courage. He whimpers and cries like the Slave that he is, not realizing that he really is a King with his will enslaved to fear. He even calls himself a sissy and a dandy and resorts to lisping to show his feminine nature. He does indeed need a session with the Wizard, as badly as the neurotic needs to have a talk with Doctor Freud.

As Dorothy dances down the road with the bound spirits of Air, Water and Fire, the Elemental Quartet is now complete. They are off to the Emerald City to formally receive recognition of their elemental powers; but between them and the Wizard is the dark Abyss. The Wicked Witch is in her evil tower, surrounded by the winged monkeys, the yelping servitors who mindlessly do her bidding. She has one last weapon to hurl against them in her bid to keep them from reaching the Wizard: the Poppy Field.

The Abyss is where the adept, so road weary from his mystic journey, sojourns in forgetfulness. He is tempted to lie back and let all his labor go to waste, forgetting himself at the crucial point when even his Angel has abandoned him. As the Quartet crosses the field of poppies, the opiates in the air go to work and they start falling asleep, lured away from the Great Work. Aleister has spent many a day enraptured by the effects of opium and knows very well the need to lie down and go on the nod. But the Good Witch of the North reappears just in time, casting her wand over the crippled scene and countering the deadly narcotic with the healing veil of snow. Dorothy and the others awaken and take off, bounding for the Emerald City. As the voices sing on the soundtrack, they are indeed out of the night and into the light. They have passed through the Night of Pan, the stage of ego death, and can now approach the Great Oz.

"All magic is unnatural [said the scarecrow, wisely] and for that reason is to be feared and avoided. But I see before us the gates of the Emerald City, so I imagine we have now overcome all the magical obstacles that seemed to oppose us."

—*The Land of Oz*, L. Frank Baum

They knock upon the front gate because the bell is out of order (Aleister can't help but laugh that the glorious city of the Logos would have a mechanical failure), but instead of a skull-capped Doctor Dee answering their call, the door is opened by a Herald with a comical face, green clothing and great bulging buttons that are just ripe for busting. He is the type of buffoon one would expect when approaching the Great Wizard. He behaves very cruelly towards them, denying them entry, even claiming that the Great Oz won't see them. But wait, isn't that the same actor who played Professor Marvel? The Wizard is indeed very wise; he hides his true face under the mask of comedy.

The Emerald City is a giant stage set that suggests the main square of an indoor city, complete with street traffic, horses, and good citizens. The Horse of a Different Color is pulling the open carriage of a Cockney cabbie, suggesting that they have arrived in London, not one devastated by the Blitz, but awash into its own stability. The good people of Oz have a convenient straw-stuffing station for the Scarecrow, as well as a metal-buffing machine for the Tin Man. The Sissy Lion gets a perm and a bow in his hair, and Dorothy is treated to a manicure. After one has crossed and achieved the Knowledge and Conversation of one's Holy Guardian Angel, one is entitled to a bit of chakra cleansing.

They are charged up for their encounter with the Great Oz and treat the Lion to a riotous crowning ceremony, with a flower pot substituting for a crown and a throw rug for a royal cape. The Lion even sings a song about courage that proclaims the Law of the Strong. "What makes a King out of a Slave?" the Lion asks regally. Aleister nods and mutters to himself: Fear is failure, and the forerunner of failure; and courage is the beginning of virtue. "Yes, my dear Cowardly Lion," he concludes, "courage does indeed make a King out of a Slave. It also makes the flag on the masthead wave, just as you said, but that is a matter which cannot be revealed in clear language until you have advanced to a certain degree."

The Wicked Witch appears over the skies like a dive-bombing Messerschmitt, terrifying the populace. Her broomstick belches forth

fire and smoke, forming the letters that demand that Dorothy surrender. The citizens of Oz are confused, scared, their complacency cast
aside. Aleister knows what they are experiencing, for it has not been
so very long since the citizens of London huddled in their shelters
while the Germans dropped fire upon their houses, demanding their
own surrender.

Fueled with a renewed sense of urgency, the Quartet are let into
the Sanctum Sanctorum of Oz the Great and Terrible, who appears as
a disembodied head floating above a billowing storm of fire and smoke.
Here is Jehovah inside the Temple dwelling in all his terror over the Ark
of the Covenant. This is the pillar of flame that went before the tribes of
Israel conquering their enemies. The Quartet can barely stand in their
terror and the Lion sounds a retreat and jumps through a window. They
have been given their quest, to bring back the broomstick of the Wicked
Witch of the West. The Wizard knows that this is a suicide mission,
and ultimately the broomstick must be worthless junk to him, but he
knows that the Elemental Trio will benefit from the quest in ways they
cannot yet comprehend.

The Witch's castle is a bit of real estate that you would expect in the
neighborhood of the Abyss, bleak and blasted, craggy and mountainous,
not conducive to human survival. The witch can fly in and out on her
broomstick, but the Elemental Trio must scramble over rock and weeds
and in the process get assaulted by the army of flying monkeys. Dorothy
is then trapped within the Witch's castle and must be rescued.

Mr. Symonds has awakened along with Dorothy in the poppy field
and nudges Aleister with his elbow to announce, "I like this bit."

The castle tower resembles an outpost in Russia with Siberian
guards wielding large sabers marching to the barbarous evocation of
"Oh-Ee-Oh! Ee-Oooh-Oh!" a bit of sonority that belongs most properly in *Liber Samekh*. The Elemental Trio outwit the guards, storm the
castle, and rescue Dorothy, but the Witch tosses fire on the Scarecrow.
Dorothy drenches his arm with water from a nearby bucket and inad-
vertently splashes the Witch. Then the Witch melts, bemoaning her
fate, and cursing a universe in which such a trivial thing as Dorothy can
outwit her wickedness. "What a world! What a world!" she rasps as she
melts, and Aleister thinks to himself, "Yes, indeed, what a world!"

Armed with the broomstick, they return to the Wizard. "Pay no
attention to the man behind the curtain!" comes the voice of the charlatan through the smoke and fire. Totem has pulled back the curtain

of a small control room, unveiling the Professor from the fairgrounds, who has used his knowledge of technology to perform what appears to a limited intelligence as magic. The man is a fake, but a genuine fake. He has great wisdom to bestow, even if he does not command the supernatural. But he seems like a man of science whose true message would be mocked, so he presents the harmful fiction of the giant floating head of smoke and fire to maintain his authority. Like the Magus, he must lie in order to propagate the Truth, and now he bestows the Truth on the Elemental Quartet. The Scarecrow doesn't get a brain, but he gives him a diploma. The Tin Man doesn't get a heart, but he gets a testimonial. The Lion gets a medal for bravery. These weapons are mere formalities, for the true reward of Ra-Hoor-Khuit is inside of them.

Dorothy is despondent, and begs the Wizard to take her home, back to the land of E. Pluribus Unum. They climb into the Wizard's balloon but due to a faulty launch (he does not know exactly what he is doing), he takes off without her. Dorothy is once more plunged into despair. She has ascended along the path of serpent, along the road of brick, crossed the Abyss, conquered Babalon the Great and arrived at the Palace of the Magus. But now she is stranded and cannot go home.

The Lady Nuit arrives from the Ain Soph in the form of Glinda and reminds Dorothy of her Ruby Slippers. She clicks the heels together (three times, of course) and speaks the magic formula that returns her to Malkuth, or the Kansas farmhouse where she lies in bed after the twister. Familiar faces emerge from the mists of dream: the three farmhands, the aunt and uncle, Totem, and even Professor Marvel. They had all been there in her dream, and so many marvelous things had happened, but all Dorothy wanted to do was to come home, and she did. And there's no place like it.

The music swells, the lights come on, the projector grinds to a halt, and Mr. Symonds nudges the stunned Aleister with his hat. "Bit of a kid's play, isn't it?" he asks. "Most decidedly," Aleister says, getting to his feet and donning his overcoat.

All the way home Mr. Symonds does all the talking, mostly about the plans for the spring lectures and how his wife wants to repaint the front hallways. Aleister says very little, seems to be absorbed in thought. As they approach Netherwood, he pulls back a bit, telling his landlord that he needs to be alone. The landlord stops on the front porch, turns to see his curious tenant standing in the road, lifting his palms to the setting Sun, muttering something or other about a boat crossing the sky.

That man is quite unique, Mr. Symonds muses. Seems to have started some sort of religious nonsense. But quite creative. Wrote a bit of poetry in his youth. Reminds me a bit of the old Wizard in that movie.

The spring turns to winter, and another year passes. Aleister stays more and more in his room and tends to his strange affairs, receiving visitors and writing manuscripts. He keeps a box under his bed with some funds in it, and insists, despite his ill health, on smoking those odorous pipes. Then one day, he lies in bed, staring at the ceiling, knowing that his moment has come. It is time to cast off this incarnation and be absorbed into the infinite.

He calls them all to his bedside, every one of them: the Buddhist Monk from Ceylon, the Hierophant from Paris, the Hollywood film actress from Cefalu, the Scarlet Woman from Cairo, the young poet from the desert, the soldier from California, the editors and publishers, the Plymouth Brethren congregation and ministers, the Secret Chiefs, the Hierophants and Grand Masters, the mountain climber from the Himalayas, the publishers and editors, all his various lovers and whores, his dead children, his neophytes and acolytes, the elementals he had summoned in pyramid chambers and the demons he had raised in the wastelands, the preterhuman intelligences that gave him his most sublime poetry, the wanderers and mystics he had been in previous incarnations, his gods and goddesses, even those. They all stand around his bed and watch him as he dies.

He calls out to them, "I had a dream, and you all were in it. You, Allan, you were there. And you McGregor. And even you, my dearest Rose, without you there would have been no Equinox of the Gods. And my most beautiful Nanturk, even you were there in the end. I love you all for you have made this orbit so very enjoyable. I did my Will and I hope you continue to do yours in this or any other incarnation. Perhaps I'll see you all again in Eternity."

They all take their leave, one by one, disappearing into the Nothing, going back to the continuity of existence from which they once had emerged. Aleister finds himself standing in his old Victorian jacket, young again, a full head of hair, wild-eyed and full of energy. A light is shining brightly in the distance and he sees a sandwich shop next to a railroad station.

"I am so very thirsty," he admits to himself. "Before I take my leave, I'll stop for some ale and a bite to eat. There's an old man and an old woman there who I would very much like to meet once more before the

Lady Nuit comes to absorb me back into her body. Perhaps I will join them at home for tea and it will be like old times.

"Oh Great Mother and Great Father, there's no place like Home!"

First published in *Behutet: Modern Thelemic Magick & Culture*, Issue 55, Spring 2013.

THE BAVARIAN ILLUMINATI

1. THE ILLUMINATI IN EUROPE

The Bavarian Illuminati was officially active as a secret society between 1776 and 1785, the only documented years of its existence. Modeled after the Freemasons, the society promoted the doctrines of the Enlightenment, the philosophies of such thinkers as Voltaire and Diderot, and a social order freed from the shackles of church and state. The nature and purpose of the Illuminati could only be understood in the context of the revolutionary years during which it was politically active. The society was organized in the very year in which the American colonies declared their independence from the English crown, and such rebellious activity was frequently occurring throughout Europe at that time. But there was no less likely a place for such a society to arise than the Electorate of Bavaria, which had remained, even after the dissolution of the Society of Jesus in 1773, a Jesuit stronghold.

While the American rebels had the luxury of a vast ocean between them and the King that they rebelled against, the liberal free-thinkers of Bavaria had to maneuver within a heavily theocratic society that allowed its citizens little room for organized defiance. The Jesuits dominated the social, political and spiritual life of the country. A Jesuit was often the counselor and confessor of many high-ranking aristocrats and politicians and their rigid scholasticism ruled the universities. It was only at the University of Ingolstadt that liberalism created an academic beachhead through the activity of a very unusual young man, Adam Weishaupt (1748-1830), who at the age of twenty-seven had become the dean of the faculty of religious law, the first non-Jesuit to do so.

Deeply influenced by the philosophy of the Enlightenment, Weishaupt voiced his own radical views in a very indiscreet manner. This prompted the Jesuits to take action against him, questioning his appointment, disputing his salary, and attempting to limit his free speech. Weishaupt, who had experimented with Freemasonry but found that fraternity lacking the teeth he needed to fight the system, responded by founding the Order of the Illuminati. Its initial mission statement was to guide young men to perfect themselves both spiritually and philosophically so they could manifest in their lives and in the society about them the ideals of the Enlightenment and the cult of Reason. These young men were to be trained, educated and eventually placed into positions of authority within Bavaria where they could help the country shake off the shackles of the civil and ecclesiastical authorities.

At first, Weishaupt called his society the Perfectibilists. The name may have been clunky but it emphasized the belief that an individual could evolve into a paragon of an enlightened man who had transcended blind faith with the faculty of reason. While this was not an uncommon philosophy at the time, it was highly dangerous from the perspective of monarchs, church leaders and the dominant social order of Europe. To them, Weishaupt's society was an army of revolutionaries corrupting the youth and calling for an overthrow of thrones and altars. The Illuminati were initially only five students and it is very doubtful they could have triggered such a significant revolution on their own, but the dramatic revolt in the American colonies in July of 1776 made even a small gaggle of Bavarian students spouting youthful ideals more of a serious threat.

It is no coincidence that the Order was officially founded on May 1, 1776, just as the American colonies had found their sure path towards armed revolt against their monarch. The liberal views of the Enlightenment had spread like wildfire through the nations of Europe, and the trouble in the colonies was a harbinger of revolt back home on the continent. From this perspective, a society like the Illuminati could have manifested anywhere and anytime. Yet what distinguished this radical group in Bavaria, as we shall see, was the effectiveness with which the Bavarian government came to suppress them, and the rampant propaganda and paranoia that resulted from their destruction. The Bavarian Illuminati became, in the years following its dissolution, a world-wide symbol of the dangers of secret societies and a source of irrational political paranoia.

The first incarnation of the Order as conceived by Weishaupt consisted of three simple grades: Novice, Minerval, and Illuminated Minerval. At the level of Novice, a young man was mentored by a representative of a higher grade through a series of studies and examinations that intellectually grounded him in the vast literature of the Enlightenment. The Novitiate was expected to improve his moral character, to perfect his intellectual and philosophical views, and to help recruit others into the ranks of the Order. He was also expected to file details about his private life, including the contents of his library and the names of all his relations. An Illuminati Novitiate was expected to be completely loyal to the Order, making it his entire life, and to sacrifice all for the sake of the movement. All the time he was kept ignorant of the identity of others within the Order. It wasn't until promotion to Minerval that the young man experienced fellowship with his comrades. It was also in this second grade that he was assigned Novitiates of his own to guide. An Illuminated Minerval was expected to be an initiate of such perfected moral character that he was ready to go forth into Bavarian society, infiltrate its aristocratic and political ranks, and change society from within.

The whole structure was held together by a complicated system of instructions and initiation ceremonies, much of which reflected the prevailing liberal philosophies and Freemasonic ideals of its day. Weishaupt desired serious resistance to the standing social order and demanded much of his followers. He ordered strict control over his Novitiates, promoting violations of their personal privacy and a paranoid atmosphere of surveillance. The Illuminati believed in a free society, but they were also raising an army of rationalists who must be committed and disciplined. Seeing the Illuminati as university students fired by youthful idealism and the ferment of the times about them, one can only wonder what they would have accomplished if they had not been suppressed. Liberty, equality and fraternity were lofty words but in history they often had to be created and maintained through violence. The Illuminati ideal was to morally perfect individuals within society and to allow the changes to propagate. There was no evidence of Illuminati plans for physical violence or political assassination.

The Bavarian Illuminati were not the only organization at that time that strove for these ideals, so it is a bit difficult to see why they were singled out by the governments of the world to epitomize the evil force behind the scenes of history ready to destroy church and state to obtain absolute power. After four years, Weishaupt had recruited hardly more than sixty members and his Order was threatened with extinction due to financial troubles alone. It was time for Weishaupt to take his sketchy Masonic off-shoot and bring it to the next step.

Baron Adolph Franz Friedrich Ludwig von Knigge (1752-1796) was an aristocrat, diplomat, author and poet who had devoted much of his attention to the Freemasons and the Rosicrucians. His interest in the Illuminati helped to forge a bridge between the Masonic Lodges within Germany and the new Bavarian Order, and he was instrumental in restructuring the initiatory path and working out the higher grades. The new system looked something like this:

First Class
    Minerval
    Illuminatus Major
Second Class
    Apprentice
    Fellow
    Master
    Illuminatus Major
    Illuminatus Dirigens
Third Class
    Priest and Prince
    Magus and King

Clearly, this was a more mature and sophisticated system that bridged the initiatory gap between the Illuminati and the Masons. At the rank of Illuminatus Dirigens, however, a member swore an oath to unbind himself from all other secret societies and to dedicate himself solely to the administration and well-being of the lower grades of the Illuminati. Only members in the ranks of the Third Class were relieved of administrative duties and dedicated to the work of freeing society from the shackles of church and state. The Areopagites of the Order, all members of the Third Class, had distributed control over territorial provinces, twelve in number, and answered to the Supreme Magus and King, Adam Weishaupt.

The alignment with Masonry paid off in a huge way and after the establishment of the provinces and their administrative bodies, the ranks of the Order began to swell. Within three years, membership had grown to several thousand located in many parts of Germany, Austria and Switzerland. With the recruitment of several important aristocrats, most particularly Duke Ferdinand of Brunswick and Prince Carl of Hesse, as well as the poet Goethe (author of *Faust*), the Order not only flourished but began to challenge the authority of some of the more prominent Masonic bodies. The Illuminati took the general congress of Freemasons at Wilhelmsbad by storm and triumphed over many of its rivals, including the Order of Strict Observance, a more conservative branch of the Masons that had unsuccessfully attempted to eliminate occult teachings within their fraternity. The Order of the Illuminati had grown exponentially beyond a small band of students, and it was only a matter of time before the government acknowledged and responded to the new threat.

A lower ranking member of the Illuminati believed to be disillusioned with Wieshaupt wrote a disparaging letter to the duchess dowager of Bavaria, which included samples of secret initiation ceremonies, warning her that the Illuminati were challenging the authority of both church and state. He accused the leadership of the Order of being agents working for Austria against the Bavarian throne. Shortly after, the Monarch of Bavaria launched edicts restricting the activities of secret societies and explicitly denouncing the Illuminati. A large number of members subsequently defected, providing the government with many informers who were willing to turn evidence against the Order. Under such pressure and judicial inquiries, the Order quickly collapsed and Weishaupt had to flee to another country rather than risk arrest and interrogation. A police raid on the home of a high-ranking member yielded a large cache of intimate documents, including membership rosters and several hundred letters between the Third Class and their Magus. The evidence was devastating, especially a document that proved that Weishaupt, after the death of his first wife, had impregnated his sister-in-law and had performed an abortion to avoid a scandal. This revelation of Weishaupt's personal morals sealed the perception that the Order of the Illuminati was spreading an atheist philosophy and a corrupting disdain for existing authority. The crown of Bavaria had all the evidence it needed to suppress the Order, crushing it completely.

After the destruction of the Bavarian Illuminati, the Rosicrucians, who were still influential throughout Germany, began to fan the flames of paranoia, persuading other Dukes and Kings that the virulent strain of Weishaupt's philosophy was a serious threat to their security. The upper grades of the Illuminati, they claimed, were still operating in secret and capable of organizing revolts against church and state. With the outbreak of the French Revolution in 1789, many believed that the Illuminati were directly involved in the terror and violence that emerged from that uprising, including the murder of the French king. The conspiracy theorists of their day came up with all sorts of connections, largely imagined, between the remnants of the Illuminati and the French Masonic Lodges.

The fantasies and fictions of these conspiracy theories reached their fullest form in two books, both published in 1797: *Proofs of a Conspiracy Against All the Religions and Governments of Europe, Carried on in the Secret Meetings of the Free Masons, Illuminati, and Reading Societies* by John Robinson, and *Mémoires pour servir à l'histoire du Jacobinisme* by the Abbe Barruel. Both books meticulously mapped out the evidence for connections between the Illuminati and the French Revolution, mostly offered without any empirical or historical proof. The hidden agenda, according to both authors, was to subvert and destroy the governments of Europe and to put an end to all religion. The lodges and secret societies of both Europe and the Americas were the vehicles for anti-Christian philosophies. As paranoid and inaccurate as these two books may have been, they were to influence and dominate political paranoia for the next two centuries.

2. RELIGIOUS LIBERTY AND AMERICA

The Plymouth Colony, founded with the arrival of the Mayflower in 1621, was populated by a separatist Protestant sect from Scrooby, England, that had spent ten years in Holland before booking passage to the New World. Although they shared the North American continent with Spanish, French, Dutch and Swedish colonies and were eventually overshadowed by the much larger Massachusetts Bay Colony, the Pilgrims at Plymouth emerged over time as the archetypal symbol of our national origin. It is their harvest feast that we recreate on Thanksgiving and when we generally think of the seventeenth century New Englander, images from the *Scarlet Letter* or the Salem Witch Trials come to mind, but ultimately, we think of Governor Bradford, Miles Standish, Massasoit the Sachem, Squanto of the Wampanoag and the whole cast of characters from the Plymouth story. Our projection of American origins onto the Plymouth Colony is so ingrained that we teach our children a sanitized version of a very complex and violent story, claiming that the Pilgrims were early advocates of religious liberty, that they risked the dangers of the Atlantic crossing and the hardships of survival in the New England wilderness to escape the religious tyranny of their native land. A reasoned revision of the Pilgrim legend would show that the original New Englanders did not come to the new world seeking religious tolerance, but instead to found a society in which their religion could reign without interference.

After the founding of New England, it took over a hundred and fifty years and a political revolution for a separation of church and state to pass into national law. During the century-and-a-half before the ratification of the U.S. Constitution, there was a prolonged struggle over the standing order that every community in the New England colonies was required to tax its citizens to support the state church. The Congregational model of church governance that had sustained the colonies from the beginning stubbornly held its domination over New England society despite the growth of Quaker, Baptist and Methodist churches. The Great Awakening of the early 18th century saw a proliferation in the number of Christian denominations, which posed a number of challenges to the Puritans. Many of these new churches soon demanded to be exempt from the taxation that funded the state religion.

At the commencement of the American Revolution, the idea of taxing people to support churches that they did not even attend became more overtly ironic. If the Sons of Liberty were willing to lay down their lives to avoid paying taxes on tea, a substance they could easily avoid by choosing not to drink it, why were they so reluctant to help a Quaker become exempt from taxation to support a Congregational church? The American Revolution forced a massive psychological shift in the way that people viewed the concept of liberty, which necessarily included the liberty to worship according to individual conscience. With the ratification of the Constitution, a separation between church and state became state law, and the Puritan monopoly on governance had at last been loosened. After the Revolution, New England may have remained a Congregational culture, but religious liberty for members of other denominations had been greatly advanced.

Many of the governing bodies of New England lost a good deal of power under the new rulings. The General Court of Connecticut, for example, in the years before the Revolution, had a virtual monopoly on the governance of the church. It controlled every aspect of religious life in its colony, including the chartering of congregations, the calling of new ministers, the fixing of their salaries, and rulings in disputes within the church. Having surrendered such latitude of power, the

American Puritans were not going to go so gently into the night of Enlightenment philosophy.

The publication of Thomas Paine's *The Age of Reason* in 1794 was a barometer of how sensitive the New England clergy were to the whole cult of reason. Paine's determination was to provoke a revolution in religion, much the same way that his earlier work *Common Sense* had provoked a political revolution. Along with other books such as Ethan Allen's *Reason: The Only Oracle of Man*, *The Age of Reason* challenged institutionalized religion and questioned a literal interpretation of the Bible in favor of a natural religion. Sermon after sermon was published decrying the threat to religion that Paine's philosophy posed. The public dialogue that poured forth from writers and clergymen was deeply symptomatic of how the political upheavals of the 1790s, including the French Revolution and its bloody aftermath, had reshaped political and religious life within America.

At first, the newly-founded nation of the United States responded positively to the revolution in France. It had been born out of the same philosophical roots and had overthrown a monarchy in favor of a free society. The French had helped the colonies win their independence by supplying weapons and financial aid, and by going to war against Britain. However, the French revolt soon deteriorated into a reign of terror, mass murder, and regicide with the beheading of Louis XVI in 1793. Many Americans were aghast at the lengths which the revolutionaries, the Jacobins in particular, were willing to go for political power. An estimated 40,000 people lost their lives under the reign of terror, an atrocity that did not go unnoticed by New England clergy, who associated the violence with the anti-religious fervor that had come to dominate France.

Many French churchmen were arrested and murdered, their lands confiscated, and many were made to swear an oath to the existing regime. With the adoration of the Goddess Reason in Notre Dame Cathedral in 1793, the agenda of the revolutionary forces was clear: the Christian religion was to be abolished completely. In America, the churches turned towards the United States government to aid them in their support of the threat to religion and were met with a curious indifference. After the clergy had been asked to support the nation's political revolution even with their lives, the government did little to defend the churches during the anti-religious crusades.

Further, a sharp political division had formed between the political parties known as the Federalists and their strongest opponents, the anti-Federalists (or Republicans as they were sometimes called). The debate was over the necessity for a strong centralized government vs. a loose confederacy of states, an on-going conflict that grew from the ratification debates over the U.S. Constitution. But the schism was along international alliances as well. As the horrors of the French revolution became undeniable, and as war tensions grew between England and France, the American Federalists tended to side with England while the Republican opposition saw the ideals of the French as relevant. A controversial trade treaty with England negotiated by John Jay in 1794 further incensed and divided the American public. Secret societies known as Democratic Clubs began to appear before Congress in which dissenters voiced their anti-Federalist politics. After these clubs were publicly denounced by George Washington, there was a growing fear of revolutionary groups organized with the aim of overthrowing both church and state. A terrorist threat in 1798 to burn the city of Philadelphia led to mass evacuations and further denunciations by the government and also fanned the fires of political paranoia.

3. The Illuminati Scare of 1798-99

By 1798, the New England clergy and their churches were deeply affected by the political divisions that were polarizing the country. The churches tended to side with the Federalists, especially empathetic to their fear of Democratic clubs and any secret society that was promoting a rationalist view against the presiding social order. The clergy began making their pulpits a platform from which to preach political rhetoric that was often in favor of the Federalists. Their loathing for the ideals of the French revolution and the measures taken against the Catholic Church in France led to an explosion of sermons, pamphlets and declarations decrying the atheist and anarchic menace that was ravaging Europe in both real and imagined forms.

The publication of the XYZ Dispatches, letters from American diplomats in France who had been asked to bribe French officials to ensure that country's cooperation in the war with England, stirred anti-French sentiments even deeper and almost drove the United States into an all-out military conflict with their former ally. France was perceived as a breeding ground for atheism, violence, anarchy, and, in the eyes of the New England clergy, the international Illuminati conspiracy.

The great outbreak of New England Illuminati paranoia started in Charlestown, Massachusetts, in the form of a lecture given by Reverend Jedediah Morse. Morse was an influential geographer who was known as the father of American geography because of his pioneering textbook on the subject, the first that was tailored to the newly founded nation. He was educated and erudite, having earned a degree in divinity from Yale University. The intellectual accomplishments that ran in his family were eventually passed down to his son, Samuel Morse, who invented the telegraphic shorthand known as Morse code. Yet despite his intelligence and intellectual rigor, the Reverend was responsible for an outbreak of political paranoia, blind accusation and hate mongering that has since become a periodic staple of the American rhetorical landscape.

On May 9th, 1798, Morse gave a sermon that, on the surface, didn't differ much from hundreds of other sermons being published at the time, anti-French rants which warned congregations of the dangers of French irreligion. He was graphic and precise: the French meant to destroy both church and state and were determined to plant the seeds of their revolution in America. However, Reverend Morse added a twist which was to turn into a veritable storm. Morse had read *Proofs of a Conspiracy* by John Robinson and was convinced that the Illuminati had not only catapulted France into revolution but had infiltrated the United States and were determined to overthrow the newborn nation. Not only did they want to plant their agents in all offices of the land, Morse pronounced, they also wanted to control the newspapers, libraries, booksellers and post offices, destroy Christianity and spread their blasphemies and obscenities into every area of life. Robinson's book had convinced Reverend Morse that the Illuminati had firmly rooted itself in America, but had failed to compromise the Freemasons since, after all, the illustrious George Washington was a Freemason. However, the Illuminati had perverted the purity of the Freemasonic order and had exploited schisms within it.

Inspired by Morse's outrage, other reverends followed suit and by the summer of 1778, debates filled newspapers, especially the *Massachusetts Mercury*, over the notion that the Illuminati had infiltrated America and were planning its overthrow. Adding fuel to the fire was none other than the President of Yale College, who addressed his entire student body on the Fourth of July, emphasizing the threats and dangers to the nation. His unusual take on the matter was that God had planted the

Illuminati on earth to destroy the anti-Christian empire of Europe and to cleanse the world of Popery. By ridding France of Catholicism, the Illuminati were actually doing the Will of God. But of course, God would not tolerate such a revolution to happen in the United States.

Some voices of reason tried to raise skepticism about Robinson's book, questioning the book's sources and proofs, but men like Reverend Morse, who fired off letter after letter on the matter, claimed that Robinson was a scholar of great integrity and his theories had been accepted by erudite men of both clergy and state. That alone assured its truthfulness. Anti-Illuminati paranoia was further fanned by the arrival of Abbe Barruel's *Memoirs of Jacobinism* as it was finally translated into English and brought across the Atlantic for publication. The roots of the conspiracy were laid bare at last, as well as its central role in the French revolution. Such a nefarious organization could compromise any religious group or political party no matter how seemingly pious or patriotic. Paranoid thoughts started to circulate about the Quakers. Apparently, by believing in brotherly love, universal equality, pacifism, and by conducting meetings dedicated to "private business," the Quakers looked as if they had been infiltrated. Eventually, Thomas Jefferson, with his strong penchant for anything French and his belief in that country's eventual redemption as a political ally, was accused of being the head Illuminatus in the United States.

The reaction of the American government to the Illuminati scare was a fascinating study in the deep divisions that existed in the young nation. George Washington, after hearing of Morse's crusade against the alleged conspiracy, commented, "It is not my intention to doubt that the doctrine of the Illuminati and the principles of Jacobinism had not spread in the United States. On the contrary, no one is more satisfied of this fact than I am." Thomas Jefferson, on the other hand, called the Reverend by the nickname of "Illuminate Morse" and claimed that the Abbe Barruel's writing was the "ravings of a Bedlamite." Jefferson praised Weishaupt and confessed that he shared the man's belief in the perfectibility of mankind. The belief in evolution of the human race to the point where self-governance obviated the need for a political government was, according to Jefferson, the same vision held by William Godwin, the political philosopher that had influenced the principles behind the founding of America, and was therefore admirable. According to Jefferson, this desire to free themselves from the tyranny of both church and state and to live as perfected men in a free

society was the philosophy so threatening to ignorant men like Morse
and Robinson and which they considered to be blasphemy.

As the war of words and paranoia spread through the newspaper
columns of Massachusetts and Connecticut, the voices of reason began
to creep in. Critics of Morse claimed that the Charlestown Reverend
had his own political agenda, to promote Federalism and to defend the
powers of the church which, in the wake of the American Revolution,
was becoming less relevant to public life. His stance was pure bigotry
and political propaganda. So zealous was the Reverend that he would
fabricate his own evidence and deceive his readers with documents pur-
porting to be membership rolls from crucial American-based lodges of
the Illuminati. Eventually, the accusations of Morse and others like Dr.
Dwight of Yale University (where Morse had gotten his divinity degree)
were silenced by public mockery. A letter from a German scholar was
eventually published in the New England newspapers that scoffed at the
whole notion of a world-wide Illuminati conspiracy and fundamentally
debunked Robinson and his silly book. Morse was eventually shamed
into silence.

The Illuminati scare diminished, but the Masonic movement had
suffered some collateral damage from the entire affair. Their reputation had been tarnished by their circumstantial connections with the
Illuminati in its real or imagined form, and in 1828, there emerged on
the political scene a third political party whose platform was unabash-
edly anti-Masonic. The third was followed by another party called
The Know-Nothings or the Nativist Movement which was virulently
anti-Catholic, so much so that as the Washington Monument was being
constructed a group of Nativists stole a building stone that had been
donated by the Pope. The war for religious liberty, or each religion's
own personal perception of what religious liberty should be, raged on
decades after the signing of the Constitution.

In recent decades, much has been made of the Illuminati, elevating
them in popular mythology to the status of the sinister force behind the
New World Order, giving them credit for everything from the inner
workings of the world banking system to the outcome of presidential
elections and assassinations. Modern day incarnations of Reverend
Jedidiah Morse have appeared in the guise of popular conspiracy theorists like David Icke, Alex Jones and others who spread paranoia about
both Freemasonry and the Illuminati, often confusing and confound-
ing the distinctions between the two and creating pseudo-histories in

which the normal rules for empirical proof don't exist. Popular novels like *The Illuminatus! Trilogy* by Robert Anton Wilson and Robert Shea jokingly played with the more paranoid theories to create an entertaining piece of science-fiction, but only tossed more gasoline onto the fire by becoming cult classics. Hollywood movies such as *National Treasure* and *Angels & Demons* have exploited the myths about both organizations for entertainment purposes as well but are virtually worthless as sources of information about the secret societies. It seems as if an entertainment-saturated audience wants so badly to believe in a conspiracy to rule the earth that they completely ignore any history or hard facts of what we do know about the Masons, the Illuminati and any other secret society that has ever tried to improve the world by producing philosophical and spiritual initiates.

Perhaps the Illuminati will never go away, as long as human beings continue creating fantastical mythologies out of their own cultural, religious and political anxieties. It could very well be that relegating the entire notion of a world-wide Masonic conspiracy to Hollywood entertainment is the perfect cover for the real organization that feels the best secrecy lies in putting all their secrets in plain view and thereby rendering them invisible. Either way, the history of the Bavarian Illuminati was a small battle in a long war between the monarchical powers of Europe and the secret organizations that opposed them. There was nothing different about Adam Weisphaut's Order that could explain the special treatment it received, except that it had the unfortunate, or fortunate (depending on how you look at it) timing to start up operations at the birth of both the American and the French Revolutions. Weishaupt himself would not be displeased to hear that so many people are still terrified of his band of students, although he would be extremely glad to hear that after two hundred years of the American political experiment many of his values and political ideals have become part and parcel of our everyday life. In that sense, the Bavarian Illuminati did transform the world.

First published in *Behutet: Modern Thelemic Magick & Culture*, Issue 50, Autumn 2011.

FOLK TALES: A
MYSTICAL APPROACH

In *Book Four* of his magnum opus *Magick, Liber ABA,* Aleister Crowley devotes separate chapters to explanations of the traditional weapons of magic—the Wand, the Cup, the Sword, and the Pentacle. Yet in the very middle of the explanation, he unexpectedly inserts an "interlude" in which he takes up a challenge from co-author Soror V to demonstrate that "everything contained the truth." This insight, similar to that of William Blake's image of "eternity in a grain of sand," is applied by Crowley to a series of standard nursery rhymes with an interpretative technique that is Qabalistic in nature and loaded with the mystical insights of a master magician.

In a single chapter wedged between the Yod/Heh and the Vav/Heh of the magical weapons, Crowley walks us through the meaning of Little Bo Peep, Little Jack Horner, Old Mother Hubbard, Humpty Dumpty and a few other well-known rhymes. With mystical deftness, he improvises a few interpretations that crack open not only the names of the characters but the nature of their adventures. Old Mother Hubbard becomes the crone aspect of Binah; Humpty Dumpty is revealed as the Egg of Spirit falling into the Abyss; the Mouse who runs up the clock is the snake of Kundalini; and Taffy the Welshman becomes Taphtatharath, the Spirit of Mercury. One can sense Crowley having fun and laughing aloud as Soror V hurls at him one Mother Goose rhyme after another, challenging him to prove that everything is inside of everything, that the truth is in the lie, the whole is in each part, and eternity is indeed in a grain of sand.

Crowley confesses that anyone who believes his interpretations are as much a fool as anyone who believes that the original authors of the nursery rhymes had any mystical intentions as they composed them. In this paradox lies a profound mystery, one that I believe lies at the heart of—well, of course—everything, but I'll limit it for now to writing and magic.

At the heart of Magick is the Holy Qabalah, which is built upon the Hebrew alphabet. The letters are sacred beings in themselves, and even their physical shape as they are drawn on the page has earned mystical significance. Although the letters of the Hebrew alphabet historically evolved from earlier Semitic alphabets and did not spring fully formed from the primal utterance of the Logos (at least not literally), they are powerful audio-visual metaphors for the energies that did emit from that primal utterance. The devotional reverence paid to them as holy beings and their powerful application in mystical formula and ritual can only be explained by the notion that historically evolved symbols such as the Hebrew letters tap into some archetypal pattern that pervades the universe. The Tree of Life is a glyph that maps out this pattern, and all of ceremonial Magick is based upon it. This is the interpretive tool that Crowley used to crack open Humpty Dumpty, Little Bo Peep, and the others.

Crowley's was far from the first to attempt such an exegesis. For centuries, scholars have searched for deep structure within the narratives of fairy tales, myths, and nursery rhymes. In 1812, the Brothers Grimm published a collection of what they called household tales, which included many of the stories that have since become staples in the world of children's stories: "Cinderella," "Snow White," "Sleeping Beauty," "Rapunzel," "Rumpelstiltskin," the "Frog Prince," and "Hansel and Gretel," to name a few.

Before the Grimm Brothers collected tales, they were scholars of philology, the science of how language changes over time. It was not a large step from the evolving nature of language to the evolving nature of stories in popular folklore. These stories emerged spontaneously from the consciousness of the European mind and were filtered through the Germanic culture in which the Grimms lived. Their sources ranged from peasants to genteel aristocrats. Often, they would collect as many variants of the story as possible and then extract the common elements to form an essential and original kernel—the tale presented in their published collections. The fact that they learned their analytical technique from philology, the study of language, and applied it to the simplistic folk tales of common people is ripe with Qabalistic suggestiveness.

Another collector of folklore and culture was Harry Smith, an

American anthropologist and filmmaker who, in 1952, put together a vast compendium of music for Folkways Records, which he called *The American Anthology of Folk Music*. Over the course of twelve carefully sequenced vinyl sides, Smith presented folk ballads, socials, blues, spirituals, and expressive songs that ranged from tales of the old country to church and dance music of the Depression era. Most of the recordings were taken from Smith's impressively large collection of 78rpm records and presented with an accompanying booklet filled with Smith's own distillations of each track's significance. Considering that Smith himself was a ceremonial magician, and one who put great personal significance on the Holy Qabalah and the language of Magick, it is not surprising that the track notes in the booklet are as suggestive, foolish, profound, and full of "lies" as Crowley's notes on Mother Goose.

Yet Crowley's interlude was an amusing side note known only to readers of *Book Four*, while the respective collections by the Brothers Grimm and Harry Smith literally changed the world. The household tales, later to be known as fairy tales, of Wilhelm and Jacob Grimm instilled fundamental narrative structures into the minds of everyone who grew up in western culture. The tales took on new dimensions as Walt Disney stamped his own brand name on them. For example, "Snow White" became *Walt Disney's Snow White* and the envisioning of the characters by Disney's artists has become inseparable in people's minds from the stories themselves.

As for Harry Smith's anthology of folk music, it led directly to the revival of the folk, blues, and rock music that reshaped western culture, giving birth to entire artistic genres. Folk legends such as Bob Dylan and Dave Von Ronk have confessed to the enormous role that the anthology played in their artistic development. To this day, Nick Cave and Natalie Merchant are lovingly crafting new and vibrant versions of the folk songs first bootlegged by Harry Smith more than 66 years ago. One could argue that without Harry Smith's diligent research and remarkable liner notes, jazz and big band music would not have been toppled from their thrones as the reigning giants of popular music, and there would have been no folk/rock revolution, no *Rolling Stone* magazine, no Woodstock, and no Grateful Dead dancing bears. Can you sense an alternative history novel emerging here?

While the myths collected by the Brothers Grimm and the songs collated by Harry Smith were originally spontaneously generated from common people without any commercial or financial motivation, when they were repackaged for mass consumption, the resulting products acted as magical talismans to reshape human consciousness. This was no small feat, and one has to wonder what kind of punch the original materials were packing in order to raise such transformative energy when popularly anthologized. One can argue that Walt Disney's cartoons were brilliant works of art and that a song such as "Blowing in the Wind" by Bob Dylan speaks eternal truths, but the art and the truths needed to come from somewhere first before winning Academy Awards and Grammys or appearing on the Ed Sullivan Show.

When the masses react viscerally to *Star Wars* or *The Wizard of Oz* or *The Lord of the Rings*, they are responding to a magical vocabulary that, much like the languages studied by the Grimm Brothers and the narrative structures in the folk ballads collected by Smith, changes over time, taking on the flavor and seasonings of the specific culture in which they land—whether it be Germany in the late 1700s or the mountains of Appalachia in the early 1930s. Walt Disney painted eternal pictures through the Hollywood film system and Bob Dylan crooned truths from a Greenwich Village coffee house, but both were channeling folk consciousness.

So here I take up the challenge that Soror V proposed to Crowley back in 1919 and will dip into both the Brothers Grimm book of children's tales as well as Harry Smith's 78rpm record collection. Like Crowley, I am trying to crack some juicy Qabalistic nuts and I claim that anyone who takes me seriously is as much a fool as anyone who thinks that I am joking.

One story that we all learned from the Brothers Grimm is that of "The Frog King." We remember the plot as a princess kisses a frog and transforms him into a prince. In the original Grimm story, however, the princess, who is instrumental in breaking the spell cast over the prince by an evil witch, does not actually kiss the frog but throws him against a wall in an act of disgust-induced violence.

Perhaps it would be best to start at the beginning and summarize the tale as the Brothers Grimm recounted it.

A king's daughter, escaping the heat of the summer in a deep dark forest, sits beside a spring under a linden tree. She is playing with a golden ball, tossing it about, but accidentally drops it into the spring where it disappears under the water. Her cries of despair are heard by a frog that emerges from the water and tells her to stop her sniveling.

After rejecting offers of material wealth in exchange for retrieving her ball, the frog says that he'll fetch the ball for her but first she must promise to love him forever, invite him to sit beside her at the king's table, and into her bed. She immediately agrees, but as soon as the frog retrieves the ball for her, she snatches it and runs away, never intending to give the frog his promised reward.

The next day at a feast set before the king, the princess is eating from her golden plate when the frog comes splashing into the court and stands before the table. The king, hearing of the princess' dilemma, orders his daughter to keep her promise since a promise should never be broken. Reluctantly, the princess brings the frog with her to her bedchamber, where she attempts to kill it by hurtling it against a wall. Instead of dying, the frog immediately transforms into a beautiful prince and the princess falls instantly in love.

An odd coda to the story involves the appearance at the court of Faithful Heinrich, a servant of the prince, who had been so consumed with sorrow over his master's transformation into a frog that he had to place three wooden hoops about his torso to prevent his chest from bursting with sadness. After the re-appearance of the prince, Heinrich is elated and the prince and princess, driving in his coach, are alarmed when they hear cracking noises that they believe to be the coach coming apart. The couple soon trace the sound to the breaking of the hoops around Heinrich. Faithful Heinrich, as well as the prince himself (and presumably the princess), have all been healed.

While there are as many interpretations of this tale as there are folklorists who have written about it, there is no mistaking that some sort of psychic and/or psychological transformation has occurred that has deep archetypal meaning in the mystical universe. A creature of the lower order, a swamp beast that is ugly and awkward, becomes, through some sort of unintentional act of violence, a human being; and not just any human being, but a handsome prince worthy of marrying a king's daughter. Any child hearing this tale, especially a young girl, takes away ethical and moral lessons from the narrative: don't judge a book by its cover, for even the most loathsome can return true love; a frog may be a prince, or, as students of *The Book of the Law* may well know, yonder beggar may be a king.

In the Grimm's version, the princess is described as being so lovely that the sun is filled with wonder when it shines upon her face. This brings to mind the Shekinah, which is a Hebrew word for "dwelling" or "setting." In the Hebrew Bible, the Holy Ineffable "dwells" within a Tabernacle (mishkan) and fills it with a cloud of light. As the sun shines down upon the princess, filling her with light, so does the prince fill her with light. The Prince, a character who embodies the energies of Tiphareth, the central Sephiroth in the Tree of Life, corresponds to both the Sun and the Holy Guardian Angel.

The golden ball, which the princess has reduced to a mere toy to play with when she grows bored, is the Sun with its radiance obscured. The glory of the Sun has been hidden by a witch (one can only think of the dark aspect of Binah when there are evil witches about) and can only appear as an ugly creature of the lower order, one whose intentions seem very selfish at first: he wants the princess to love him and to share her bed. But when he is transformed into a prince, all his darkness, ugliness, and selfishness fade away and he shines as the radiant light of the heavens yearning to form a union with the physical universe, represented by the princess.

Kissing the frog seems like a nice romantic alternative to killing the frog by smashing it against a wall, but the act of violence brings out another mystical truth in the magical formula behind the tale. The princess is disgusted by the frog and rejects him, even tries to kill him. In many real-life mystical experiences, the aspirant is likely to find the most radiant spiritual experience in something that had previously been a triviality or an unpleasant aspect of life. The most mundane things, be it is a person, a teaching, or a symbol can be transformed into something profoundly meaningful, even to the point where the aspirant can no longer imagine living life without it. One example could be the symbol of the pentagram, which many associate with black magic and evil intentions. Yet the mind is capable of being reshaped to receive the energies of the pentagram, deconstructing and casting aside all previous associations with it, filling it with fresh spiritual insight, and then reaping the benefit of its surface simplicity and spiritual meaning.

In mystical literature, there are innumerable references to the relationship between the aspirant and the higher energies that are received. Crowley's *Liber LXV* includes a dialogue between the Holy Guardian Angel and the Magician. Previous to the attainment of Knowledge and Conversation of the Angel, the Magician thinks that the HGA is eluding him, concealing himself on purpose in order to torment, but "Thou wast long seeking Me; thou didst run forward so fast that I was unable to come up with thee. O thou darling fool! what bitterness thou didst crown thy days withal" (*Liber LXV*, 1:25).

The tossing of the frog against the wall in an attempt to kill it also reminds us of the story of Jesus Christ being crucified, although there are many interpretations of that mythos as well. It does make sense, however, that if the frog is a concealed prince who represents Tiphareth and the energies represented by Jesus Christ, a dead and resurrected solar deity, then the transit from being a frog to a prince would involve some form of crucifixion. In this respect, the princess has acted in the same way towards the frog as the Roman administrators and the rabble of Jerusalem responded to the rabbi Jesus. Their first instinct was to kill him, to make him suffer, and to get rid of him so he wouldn't love them unconditionally anymore.

How many of us have done this very thing—hurting the ones we love, pushing away those who really care about us, choosing to concentrate our energies on those who are bad for us because they pander to our baser instincts? Indeed, while the Beloved is waiting for us to recognize our own relationship to ourselves, we are truly crowning our days with bitterness. We need some sort of seismic event to make us realize that we must die to our lower selves in order to attain union with our higher self. The formula of death and resurrection can be applied to so many things and at so many levels that the flinging of the frog against the wall is much more powerful an image than the kiss we all remember from the Walt Disney movie.

To nail down this point, we must look at an obscure text by Aleister Crowley, written in New Hampshire, USA, and which describes a ritual that both illuminates and confuses the points that I have made about the Frog King tale. It is called *Liber LXX—The Cross of a Frog*. In it, Crowley describes a ritual that makes a mockery of the death of Christ by sacrificing a pond frog that has been consecrated as Christ himself. It is short and nasty and really seems like Crowley getting in one more blasphemy at the Christianity of his childhood. Crowley describes the rite as "the ceremonies proper to obtaining a familiar spirit of a Mercurial nature as described in the Apocalypse of St. John the Divine from a frog or toad." He describes the strange consecration in which the officer of the rite represents a snake, a creature that naturally feeds on frogs. He details the capturing of the frog, placing it overnight in a chest, giving it gifts of frankincense and myrrh, then baptizing it in the name of Jesus of Nazareth, worshipping it, asking it to perform miracles, then arresting it and condemning it to crucifixion. In its sentencing, the frog is accused of plaguing the officer in his youth, depriving him of all pleasures, and the frog is held responsible for the spiritual slavery that the officer had to endure. Finally, it is declared that "the Slave-God is in the power of the Lord of Freedom" and that the spirit of the frog shall be absorbed into the officer, who is revealed to be the Great Beast himself, so he can declare the Law of Thelema to all mankind, "the truth that I utter, the falsehood whereof shall deceive men."

This last bit is very reminiscent of a passage from *Liber B vel Magi*, in which Crowley, speaking as the Logos of the Aeon, declares, "In the beginning doth the Magus speak Truth and send forth Illusion and Falsehood to enslave the soul. Yet therein is the Mystery of Redemption" (*Liber B vel Magi*, 1).

This verse is a key to *The Cross of a Frog*. Crowley could not have heard a frog croaking in the New Hampshire night and decide to write a nasty bit of blasphemy just for the sake of it. While there is clear hostility against Jesus Christ in the rite, Crowley also recognized that the older spiritual energies that reigned in the previous Aeon must be subsumed into the new laws, and that the Magus must speak falsehood in order to liberate mankind. There's no doubt that *The Cross of a Frog* is meant to be tongue-in-cheek. But while the utterances of a Magus (Crowley), limited by both human language and the structures of consciousness of the people who hear his words, are spoken tongue-in-cheek, they are heard with the most severe solemnity. In fact, Crowley's whole approach to Mother Goose rhymes is that they are deep mystical truths being concealed in foolish doggerel. The Word is inherently false because it can only be a referent to a system of energies that are beyond words. Hence, the tale of the crucifixion of a frog in New Hampshire is as much a fairy tale as The Frog Prince tale itself.

In Harry Smith's anthology, the song "King Kong Kitchie Kitchie Ki-Me-O," otherwise known to modern school children as "Froggy Went a Courtin'," is a mystery wrapped inside a simple folk tune. The song may have had its origins in London during the 1580s (its earliest known appearance being in the register of the London Company of Stationers). To title it as "a Most Strange Wedding of the Frogge and the Mouse" makes it sound like a piece of Chuck Jones animation for Looney Tunes, but Harry Smith's description of "zoologic miscegeny achieved in Frog-Mouse nuptials, Relatives approve," brings us back into the realm of mystical interpretation.

The story is simple: Froggy goes to visit Miss Mousie to ask her to marry him. He finds her surrounded by four suitors, whom he proceeds to murder, after which he takes Miss Mousie as his bride and they live in a hollow tree along with an owl, a bat, and a bumble bee. Some say this was a satirical complaint against the Queen of England (perhaps Mary Stuart) and an unpopular suitor, but the actual origin and its purpose cannot explain its popularity. That can only be explained by a magical formula within the action of the song.

The Frog and the Mouse are lunar creatures, but the winning suitor of any romantic tussle is always the solar prince. Froggy is indeed Miss Mousie's Prince Charming, who exercises his prowess to win her love. The murder of the suitors, while horrible on the surface and certainly politically incorrect by today's standards, is a form of banishing. The magician (the frog prince) dispels the evil energies around the physical object of desire (the princess) before absorbing her into his being and experiencing rapturous union. One cannot obtain the true love, be it a romantic relationship or a personal encounter with one's higher self (Holy Guardian Angel), without performing a high banishing that makes the demons go away. While Miss Mousie's suitors deserve no punishment (they were simply hanging around Miss Mousie on the day when Froggy came 'a courtin'), folk lore and mythic narrative need not apologize. The suitors must be banished in order for the Prince and the Princess to come together in union and reign together from their throne (the hollow tree). One can even argue that the four suitors suggest that the four elements must be conquered before the magician masters his spirit.

It is doubtful whether Chubby Parker and His Old Time Banjo, who recorded the song in 1928, was thinking of the solar energies of Tiphareth when he learned the chords. However, the narrative is built upon the myth of the transformation within oneself that brings the sun and the moon together into an alchemical marriage. The popularity of the song, with all its variants—the endurance of its lifespan and the way in which children take to its interior world—speaks volumes about its magical potency and why it helped make Harry Smith's *Anthology* a talismanic agent of change within the world.

The frog's mythic role as the earthly disguise for the hidden solar prince is inescapable in our culture. The frog is a natural symbol of transformation because it starts out as a tadpole, an aquatic creature, and eventually becomes a lung-breathing land amphibian. Frogs are also a symbol of fertility as the flooding of rivers often coincides with the multiplication of frogs. In popular culture, the frog has played a powerful role. Where would *Wind in the Willows* be without Mr. Toad, or *The Muppet Show* without Kermit the Frog? In fact, Kermit's bizarre relationship to the ever-needy Miss Piggy reminds one of "King Kong Kitchie Kitchie Ki-Me-O" and the courtship between Froggy and Miss Mousie.

As for Faithful Heinrich, the servant of the Frog Prince who walked about in wooden hoops to keep his chest from bursting from sorrow over his lost prince, one can only think of the Ape of Thoth, or as Bob Dylan fashioned him, "the ragged clown behind."

In tying the folk song and the tale together with an obscure ritual by Aleister Crowley known as *The Cross of a Frog*, I have attempted to elevate the reader's mind to such a point that you could never again visit a frog pond without some Qabalistic pattern seizing your imagination.

While this may seem like a lofty aim, I'd like you to consider the impossibility of creating any story, whether in word or song, without tapping into these archetypal patterns. Crowley's claim that "everything contained the Truth" implies that any bubblegum rock song or trashy mass market paperback contains the eternal wisdom of the universe, just as any tragedy by Shakespeare or psalm from the Bible. The only difference between low-brow and high-brow entertainment is the level of intelligence attributed to the creator, the subtly of the use of language, the respect for the audience's maturity, and the intention for publication (to make money, to stroke the ego of the author, to convey a sense of wonder at the beauty of the universe, to disturb people). Beyond these, the reason why the story or song exists is because it is the nature of humans to express the universe, and when we do so, these patterns ultimately emerge. There is no point in debating whether the writer or lyricist actually meant it that way; it just happens.

Another example is the well-known tale from the Brothers Grimm, "Hansel and Gretel," and a recorded performance from 1927 by Nelstone's Hawaiians called "Fatal Flower Garden," preserved on Harry Smith's *Anthology of American Folk Music*.

"Hansel and Gretel" strikes a disturbed chord in our imaginations. It is a tale full of cruelty towards children, attempted murder, and cannibalism. The story may have originated in the early 1300s during a great famine that plagued all of Europe, when massive crop failure caused the death of millions. The scarcity of crops led to the hording of food by aristocrats and many families resorted to infanticide and cannibalism to survive. During this period, there was already a series of folk tales that chronicled the adventures of small children who could outwit monsters and survive on their own despite the failure of adults to protect them—a theme that has descended into our popular culture through film series like *The Lord of the Rings* (if Hobbits can be considered children) and *Harry Potter*.

Hansel and Gretel are the children of a simple woodcutter and his wife (stepmother in later versions) who are suffering the effects of the Great Famine. The parents have little food to spare and discuss if they should abandon their son and daughter in the woods so they would have more food for themselves. In some versions, the mother suggests the infanticide while the woodcutter-father is horrified. He only goes along with the plan under great pressure. The mother's logic is very rational: the entire family will perish if they do not kill the children. They don't know that their son Hansel has overheard their entire debate and has comforted his sister Gretel by telling her that he will drop stones on the ground as they are led into the woods so there will be a trail to find their way back. Indeed, after being abandoned by their parents in the woods, Hansel leads his sister back to safety. The parents make a second attempt to abandon the children in the woods, and this time Hansel leaves a trail of breadcrumbs to lead them back to safety. However, the children are not so lucky this time: the birds of the forest eat up all the breadcrumbs and Hansel and Gretel are truly lost and abandoned.

The children are led by a white bird to a house made entirely of candy, with walls of bread and windows of glazed sugar. As they greedily start to eat the house, a voice asks from within: "Nibbling, nibbling like a mouse/Who's nibbling at my house?" to which the children reply, "The wind, the wind doth blow/from Heaven to Earth below." What follows is truly a nightmare. An old witch comes hobbling out of the house and captures the children as they devour her roof and windows. She has built the house out of candy in order to lure children to eat them. She tosses Hansel into a barn and gives Gretel the charge of fattening him up with food every day. The sister is fed so meagerly, she begins to starve.

Eventually, the witch prepares for her cannibal feast by lighting up the fire of an oven. She orders Gretel to climb inside to see if it is hot enough to roast Hansel, but Gretel tricks the witch into entering the oven herself. After dispatching their tormentor, the two children race back into the forest with some of the witch's precious pearls and gems but find that they cannot cross a river that has no bridge or stepping stones. Spying a passing duck, they ask him to help them cross where there is "no path nor bridge." The duck accommodates them and the children are able to make their way back to their parents' cottage. There they find their mother dead and their despondent father happy to see his lost children. These three live happily ever after.

There is a sense of triumph in this tale. Two tormented children prevail over those who tried to kill them, a witch is dispatched, and a family is reunited. However, there are some troubling caveats. Most of the story revolves around parents trying to kill their own children, the witch is a cannibal maniac, a young girl murders an adult (albeit in self-defense) by thrusting her into an oven, and the mother (significantly changed to status of stepmother in later versions) dies before being reunited with the two children that she had plotted to murder. One can argue that the tale grew out of the terrible ordeal of the Great Famine, and thus that the dark tone of Germanic folk tales prevails, but one can also suggest that there is something of deeper mystical significance going on here.

In all living creatures there is the perpetual anxiety of being devoured. If we temporarily set aside our sense of domination over the animal kingdom, we might remember how terrifying it must be to have lived when our only defense against certain beasts was to climb trees and to throw stones, well before the invention of spears or firearms. Deep within the psyche is a primal terror of being ripped apart while still alive, a terror that extends to the taboos on cannibalism and our demonization of anyone who practices it. This anxiety is also manifest in other Brothers Grimm tales like "Little Red Riding Hood," where an old woman and her granddaughter are eaten whole by a big, bad wolf.

We are also terrified of being devoured in other ways: in losing our minds to the various mental illnesses that destroy our reason and consciousness and through incurable diseases that often seem unstoppable, that eat us alive from the inside. All these anxieties have been expressed in many forms, from the monster Grendel in the great epic *Beowulf* to the serial killer Hannibal Lecter in *The Silence of the Lambs*. Interestingly enough, Dr. Lecter is a psychotherapist who exploits his genius to rip apart people's psyches before feasting on their physical bodies.

Beyond the fear of being eaten alive or the fear of losing one's mind to madness, being threatened with death by an evil adult strikes a dark chord in the minds of children. To make Hansel and Gretel's dilemma even more disturbing, they have been abandoned by their parents (and what can be more terrifying to small children than to have the protection of their parents completely withdrawn) and they are lost in a forest, a situation that often symbolizes a completely despondent spiritual state. This three-fold problem of parents trying to kill them, being lost in a forest, and enslaved by a cannibal witch seems very hopeless. I contend, however, that "Hansel and Gretel" is more than just an adventure story with horror elements—it also contains a magical formula that students of the Holy Qabalah would find all too familiar.

Aleister Crowley gives the first clue in his small essay on the Mother Goose rhyme of "Old Mother Hubbard": "Who is this ancient and venerable mother of whom it is spoken? Verily she is none other than Binah..." (*Book Four*, Page 89).

Here Crowley refers to the Sephirah of Binah, a symbol for the Great Mother who stands in equilibrium with Chokmah the Great Father. These two Supernals are positioned in perfect balance above the Abyss, that chasm that exists between the phenomenal world that can be apprehended by ordinary consciousness and the divine world. The Great Work is a journey up the Sephiroth starting at Malkuth which is rooted in the density of matter towards an ever more refined and deepening understanding of the relationships between all things. Ultimately, the journey culminates in the Ultimate Source at Kether.

Binah and Chokmah can be seen as analogous to Yin and Yang, the archetypal male and female principles that inform all reality. In this analogy, Kether is the Tao, the union of Yin and Yang into a primal oneness. Crossing the Abyss is, in Crowley's magical system, an experience that takes one's consciousness into that realm. Taking the Oath of the Abyss is a high magical achievement, one that Crowley laid claim to, but it is not without its price.

To cross the Abyss, one must become a child. Like the astronaut at the end of *2001: A Space Odyssey*, who is seen after his own transit through a Star Gate as a huge embryo floating in space, the magician leaves behind everything he has and everything he is, stripping away the trappings of ego and mundane consciousness (for they can serve no purpose in his new realm). He must leave all behind, or else he is in danger of having to confront Choronzon, the Lord of Da'ath, a dark Sephirah that sits within the Abyss, like a Black Hole devouring light. This monster is poised at the very threshold of human consciousness into divine consciousness and threatens the madness that will ensue if one enters into a divine realm with the trappings of Ego still intact.

The Holy Guardian Angel, who has been the crowning achievement of a vision of Tiphareth, the solar Sephirah, forged with the Magician's being, abandons him at the portal of the Abyss. Even the Angel shall desert Thee, it is said, and one must face the Abyss alone. Perhaps this is the reason why Gandalf dies in the Mines of Moria in *The Lord of the Rings*, leaving Frodo and Sam alone in their quest, or Obi-Wan Kenobi in Star Wars, who surrenders himself to the light saber of Darth Vadar so Luke Skywalker can awaken the Force within himself. Each hero has to cross his own Abyss, abandoning not just everything he has and is, but consciousness as he knows it.

The Abyss transcends human reason and intellect. Before entering the Star Gate in *2001: A Space Odyssey*, Dave Bowman must destroy HAL 9000, a computer that is the pinnacle of science and reason, the organizing principle of the spaceship and an extension of human consciousness into outer space. He reduces HAL's mind to that of a child. Recall how the computer started to sing "Daisy," which is remembered from its first lesson, hence once more becoming a child. By destroying the computer, Bowman enters into his own Abyss, alone and unaided by anything human to guide him. According to Crowley's mystical experiences of the Abyss as recorded in *The Vision and the Voice*, the surrender must be total:

> *Beware, therefore, O thou who art appointed to understand the secret of the Outermost Abyss, for in every Abyss thou must assume the mask and form of the Angel thereof. Hadst thou a name, thou wert irrevocably lost. Search, therefore, if there be yet one drop of blood that is not gathered into the cup of Babylon the Beautiful, for in that little pile of dust, if there could be one drop of blood, it should be utterly corrupt; it should breed scorpions and vipers, and the cat of slime*
>
> *—Liber 418, The Vision and the Voice, The Cry of the 11th Aethyr, IKH*

But what has this to do with "Hansel and Gretel"? My analysis of a folk tale may have spiraled into the esoteric realm of high mysticism. However, the purpose of folk tales is to bring these visions down into the ordinary range of human consciousness where Binah the Great Mother can appear as an old woman giving her poor dog a bone, and

Choronzon the Dark Lord of the Abyss can appear as a cannibal witch ready to devour young children.

It is significant that Hansel and Gretel are abandoned in the woods by their own parents, the only source of protection they have ever known. They try to maintain a connection with the lower worlds by leaving behind stones and breadcrumbs, but all is in vain. They end up a prisoner of the witch and being fattened for a cannibal feast. Besides Choronzon threatening to eat the babes in the Abyss, the witch can also represent Binah (or Babalon) who waits, as Crowley indicated borrowing some imagery from Dr. Dee's Enochian visions, in the City of the Pyramids to welcome the magical aspirant to the other side of the Abyss.

Does this mean that Hansel and Gretel are magicians aspiring to the grade of Magister Templi, attributed in the system of the A.A. to the Sephirah of Binah? Qabalistic journeys are not always carried out by wealthy poets on a trust fund who sport a rather large technical vocabulary of Hebrew, Latin, and Greek. Sometimes they are ordinary people hurled into extraordinary circumstances. Not everyone is seeking attainment and a grade in a secret society. The fear of abandonment and dissolution of self is shared by children, adults, and magicians alike.

So, is the "crossing of the Abyss" an opportunity to touch something divine on the other side of mundane consciousness and to transform into a Magus? Or is it a dangerous ordeal where all is stripped from you, all certainty is gone, and you are faced with imminent extinction? Can it also be a period of dramatic transformation, where you have gone through difficulties that change you forever and strengthen you by making you more yourself than you have ever been? Perhaps it is all these things.

Either way, the Ego always intervenes. Those who are suddenly faced with death often get highly motivated to embrace the inevitable, and to see the dissolution of being as a "good" thing, one that is part of life, that is only a transit from a state of being to a state of non-being. To grasp at the things of this world at the moment of death ensures suffering, like the sugar and bread that make up the walls and windows of the witch's cottage, objects of desire that put Hansel and Gretel into the vulnerable state that leads to their capture.

If the witch can be interpreted as Binah the Great Mother, she is also a vast ocean into which all rivers dissolve, returning to their source. An individual raindrop can have a fierce sense of identity, but when it falls into the sea it becomes one with a vastness that obliterates its sense of self. The atoms that made up its being, however, are still in circulation. They are still part of reality and can be drawn back into the atmosphere to become other raindrops not yet born. In this sense, the ocean is seemingly oblivious to the cares and needs of the tiny raindrop, but it embraces the drop into its bosom, giving it back a primal unity. If the rain drop insisted upon maintaining its "ego," then the act of merging back with the ocean would be a terrible death and the ocean could be viewed as a cannibal devouring its own.

So, what is the significance of Hansel and Gretel escaping the witch, even defeating her, and returning to their parents' cottage? Is this some form of triumph over death? Notice that the mother is dead upon their return, which raises the curious question of whether the mother had any correspondence with the witch. Was their triumph over the witch also a defeat of the mother who opted to kill them rather than attempt to feed them? From a Qabalistic point of view, the children have passed through Binah, having conquered its energies, and have now moved on to Chokmah, the Great Father, in their continual journey towards Kether, the Primal Unity.

There's another more pedestrian explanation for their return. In *Book Four*, Crowley discusses a similarity in the stories of Mohammed, Christ, and Buddha. In each case, there is a disappearance, a gap in the men's lives in which they go to some remote place for quite some time and come back to preach a new Law. In short, Crowley tells us, "a nobody goes away, and comes back a somebody" (*Book Four*, page 8). Whether it was a divine vision in a cave, or an encounter with a God in a wilderness, or an overcoming of the temptations of mental delusion to achieve spiritual awakening, a human being goes somewhere else and comes back with an actualized consciousness.

Hansel and Gretel do not return to their parents without difficulty, for they come to a wide river, another variation on the Abyss theme, across which they can see no path. They must rely on a water creature, a duck, to carry them across one at a time. As simple as this may sound, it is a form of attainment in itself. They return to their father having conquered the devouring mother, freeing themselves from time and space, two babes in the Abyss that have conquered the Dark Lord of Da'ath and arrived safely at the Supernals.

Did the author of "Hansel and Gretel" have any of this in mind? Crowley would suggest that anyone who believes that is as much a fool as he who thinks that the author did not have any of it in mind. Such is the paradox of storytelling. "For the curse of His grade is He must speak the Truth, that the Falsehood thereof may enslave the souls of men." (*Liber B*, v. 14)

Yet, there are stories in which the children do get killed and devoured by the witch. In Harry Smith's seminal *Anthology of American Folk Music*, there is a song entitled "Fatal Flower Garden" that narrates such an outcome. The song was recorded by Nelstone's Hawaiians (the Alabama duo of Hubert Nelson and James Touchstone) in 1929 at the height of the Hawaiian guitar craze in American music. This style of playing, which included holding the guitar on the lap while running a slide over the strings, was being widely used by many musicians and was later to become a standard part of country western music. When one hears Hawaiian guitar, one thinks of dancing Hula girls and a tropical paradise setting. It is soothing and relaxing, offering some serenity. But "Fatal Flower Garden" packs a punch, since it is derived from an Eastern European fear of the old Gypsy Woman, the outsider who will steal and kill your children if they are not careful.

> *It rained, it poured, it rained so hard,*
> *It rained so hard all day,*
> *That all the boys in our school*
> *Came out to toss and play.*
>
> *They tossed a ball again so high,*
> *Then again, so low;*
> *They tossed it into a flower garden*
> *Where no-one was allowed to go.*
>
> *Up stepped a gypsy lady,*
> *All dressed in yellow and green;*
> *"Come in, come in, my pretty little boy,*
> *And get your ball again."*
>
> *"I can't come in, I shan't come in*
> *Without my playmates all;*
> *I'll go to my father and tell him about it,*
> *That'll cause tears to fall."*

She first showed him an apple seed,
Then again gold rings,
Then she showed him a diamond,
That enticed him in.

She took him by his lily-white hand,
She led him through the hall;
She put him in an upper room,
Where no-one could hear him call.

"Oh, take these finger rings off my finger,
Smoke them with your breath;
If any of my friends should call for me,
Tell them that I'm at rest."

"Bury the bible at my head,
A testament at my feet;
If my dear mother should call for me,
Tell her that I'm asleep."

"Bury the bible at my feet,
A testament at my head;
If my dear father should call for me,
Tell him that I am dead."

The torrential showers that open the song can be likened to the great sea of Binah. The ball that is being tossed about by the boys we have met before—the golden ball that represents the self that gets lost. The attempt to recover the ball often leads to a struck bargain as in "The Frog Prince" when the Princess' golden ball is offered back to her by the Frog who makes her promise to marry him. In that tale, the Frog had very good intentions and when his final form was revealed, the Princess was very happy. In "Fatal Flower Garden," however, the ball is recovered by the old Gypsy woman who has nothing but ill will towards the small boy who had dared to enter the fatal flower garden.

There is no hint as to why the old woman would want to hurt the child, but it is clear that she is going to kill him. She entices him in with apple seeds, some rings, and a diamond, just as the cannibal hag of "Hansel and Gretel" seduces the young children with a candy house. The little boy realizes that she is going to kill him and gives instructions on what to tell his parents when they come calling. His mother, he insists, should be told that he is asleep, but his father can be told the truth.

"Fatal Flower Garden" is based on an earlier song called "Sir Hugh, or the Jew's Daughter," (itself based on an alleged English incident in 1255), in which a Jewish woman dressed in green abducts a small boy while he plays ball, takes him to an upper room of her house, and then cuts off his head with a penknife. It was not uncommon in that age for Jews or Romani people (Gypsies) to be accused of child abduction and murder, which often resulted in violent action against those marginalized communities. Perhaps it is for this reason that Leopold Bloom, the Jew of Dublin, sings the song with Stephen Dedalus, the Poet, in Chapter 17 of James Joyce's *Ulysses*, a novel that deals extensively with the role of the outsider/Jew in society.

Joyce describes Stephen's reaction to hearing the "Ballad of Sir Hugh" in the following manner:

> One of all, the least of all, is the victim predestined. Once by inadvertence, twice by design he challenges his destiny. It comes when he is abandoned and challenges him reluctant and, as an apparition of hope and youth holds him unresisting. It leads him to a strange habitation, to a secret infidel apartment, and there, implacable, immolates him, consenting" (*Ulysses*, James Joyce).

Admittedly, this is a very grim ballad, and perhaps it would not even be worth mentioning in a mystical analysis of folk songs, but I had a very peculiar thought about the child-murdering gypsy woman in "Fatal Flower Garden." How do we reconcile the sinister and bestial creature that can murder a little boy with the Great Mother of Binah? Is she the dark side of the three-fold goddess, Hecate ill-dignified, the all-devouring monster of time that takes all lives without discrimination? Isn't the Great Mother supposed to be warm and nurturing and responsible for all that is beautiful in nature?

There's a clue in the three items that the gypsy woman tempts the child with. First, she offers him apple seeds, which are very earth-bound, potent containers of life that you plant in the ground to initiate growth. The earth is Malkuth at the base of the Middle Pillar of the Qabalistic Tree of Life. Then she offers him a golden ring, which is a solar symbol, positioning us at Tiphareth, the center of the Tree and the organizing principle of being human. Finally, she offers him a diamond, an age-old symbol of the higher chakras that correspond to Kether at the top of the Tree, the opening of the inner perceptions that pierces through the veils of matter and reveals the reality behind the curtain. As evil as the gypsy woman's ulterior motives are, she tempts him up the ladder of consciousness from base matter to spiritual awakening, from the earth, up towards the Sun, and beyond to the sphere of the fixed stars, represented by the diamond. Yet between the golden ring and the diamond lies the Great Abyss.

If crossing the Abyss involves a surrendering of Ego and an abandonment of all that we perceive ourselves to be, then to our Ego, the crossing must be one of great distress. If we are not prepared for it, Binah will appear as mighty and terrible; if we surrender and accept the loss of our Ego and all that we have identified throughout our life transient, then the crossing will be a sublime awakening.

An anthropologist once took a rain forest pygmy, who had spent his entire life under the canopy of the great trees, and placed him on a hill top above which was nothing but open sky. The pygmy had a sense of vertigo and panic as if he was afraid that, without the protection of the trees, he would fly off into space. To many people, a hilltop capped with a beautiful open sky and free-formed clouds would be a setting for serene meditation, but to the pygmy, it was filled with anxiousness, even terror. Our Egos are also like this, scared of their own groundlessness, clinging to various illusions about reality, afraid of the moment when they recognize that they have to end and move on.

Both "Hansel and Gretel" and "Fatal Flower Garden" are horror stories, tales of infanticide and murder. However, they both contain mythic elements that express a child's experience of surrendering to reality, of crossing an Abyss, and arriving at the vast ocean of Binah with all its terror and beauty.

First published in two parts in *Behutet: Modern Thelemic Magick & Culture*, Issue 52, Spring 2012, and Issue 53, Summer 2012.

THIS GUARDIAN
DEMON AT MIDDAY

Rennes-le-Chateau and
The Da Vinci Code

ONE

The Da Vinci Code is a novel by Dan Brown published in 2003.

At first glance it is a compelling thriller, a page turner that combines tight fisted prose and short action-packed chapters, driving suspense and cliff hangers at every turn. Its protagonists, Robert Langdon, a Professor of Religious Symbology, and Sophie Neveu, a cryptographer for the French police, get swept up into a vast conspiracy that takes them to locales like the Paris Louvre, London's Temple Church, Westminster Abbey and Scotland's Rosslyn Chapel. The novel is a well-constructed suspense thriller whose clues unfold in a clever and complicated manner, certainly a great pot-boiler if not a great work of art. It hits all the right buttons, follows the correct formula, and was, from the start, destined for the best seller list. The 60 million readers who have bought the book as of the fall of 2006 all seem to agree that it is an exciting and entertaining work.

But as the plot unfolds, we are introduced to many things that don't normally find themselves in such a blatantly commercial work: the esoteric meaning of Renaissance paintings, pagan interpretations of the Pentagram, the role of secret societies behind world politics and religion, pagan sex rituals, Isaac Newton, the Gnostic Gospels, the Dead Sea Scrolls, the Holy Grail, Masonic architecture, Opus Dei, the Priory of Sion, the Knights Templar, the origins of Christianity, and so on.

True many of these elements have appeared in various forms in Hollywood movies and best-selling books, but somehow *The Da Vinci Code* is different. From the very beginning when Robert Langdon explains to a cynical French police lieutenant the true meaning of the Pentagram after it is found drawn on a dead body at a crime scene, we know that author Dan Brown, while not always rigorous in his historical scholarship and not always correct in his interpretation of occult symbols, does present the five pointed star as a positive and deeply spiritual symbol, in his view a pictograph of the Divine Feminine. This is very different from the evil interpretations that usually accompany mass media's treatment of occultism. It is the French policeman's stubborn insistence that the Pentagram is an evil symbol and Langdon's bold correction that somehow make *The Da Vinci Code* a deviation from the typical paranoia-about-evil-demonic-secret-societies-taking-over-the-world formula. Just like the post Cold War James Bond films that could no longer posit the Russian government as the enemy and had to rely on insane renegade ex-Soviet generals for their villains, modern fiction finds it more and more untenable to posit occultists and mystics as pure bad guys. The bad guy has to be some renegade Grail scholar gone amok. The Pentagram is in fact a symbol being used by the good guys.

Yet *The Da Vinci Code* is not about the occult or occultists, although it does daringly venture far into the esoteric meaning behind religious symbols. It is no secret, and therefore not much of a spoiler, to point out that the mystery revolves around an ancient military order, the Priory of Sion, that protects the bloodline of Jesus Christ, and has been doing so for 2,000 years since the human-all-too-human Christ married and fathered a child onto Mary Magdalene. It is the suppression of this knowledge that led to a violent and repressive patriarchy that destroyed the goddess religions and denied the sacred feminine its role in the spiritual economy of civilization, it also caused all sorts of nasty stuff like the Crusades, the persecution of witches, the destruction of paganism, the persecution of Gnostics, the domination of the Catholic Church and every other bad thing you can possibly think of.

What is remarkable about *The Da Vinci Code* as a mass media entertainment is that it walks a fine line between heresy and reverence. While it smashes through the power structures of the Catholic Church and debunks the generally accepted stories about Christ, while it portrays the Vatican as an organization that is based on a lie and which suppresses one-half of our spiritual heritage, while it paints the Emperor

Constantine as a brutal villain who destroyed paganism with intolerance and military force, while it accepts some of the more outlandish Gnostic gospels as truth and makes claims about Christ that reduce him to a mere mortal of flesh and blood rather than a God, it never once demands that we reject Christianity, but in fact, in the end, encourages that we embrace spiritual wisdom and religious legacies from Judeo-Christian esotericism, as well as from paganism and ancient goddess cults. In short, it attempts to re-unite the Aeon of Osiris with the Aeon of Isis, balancing one with the other, reintegrating our connection to the Divine by rediscovering the sacred feminine.

Not a bad ambition for a pot boiling best seller.

But the first step in assessing the truth behind the novel that attracted 60 million readers and launched an entire industry of books about Mary Magdalene, the Holy Grail, the Knights Templar, the Gnostic Jesus and Leonardo Da Vinci's mysterious paintings, is to point out that Dan Brown derived his material about the Priory of Sion and the Bloodline of Christ from previous material, in particular a book called *Holy Blood, Holy Grail*, published in 1982, which in turn derived its material from sources as far back as 1956, relating to a series of events in a small village in the south of France sometime between 1891 and 1917. And our understanding of those events, all the source material that deals with those events, all the physical, documentary and historical evidence that interprets those events, is based upon an elaborate hoax. It is upon a series of fake documents, false claims, made-up stories and fabricated genealogies that The Da Vinci Code has been built.

It is not my intention to debunk the novel in any way, since the labyrinth of claims it makes about Leonardo Da Vinci, the Catholic Church, or the Bloodline of Christ can be considered independently of the hoax that gave birth to the conspiracy theories. But by limiting my discussion to the pivotal base of the story, the secret treasure of Rennes-le-Chateau and the strange career of Berenger Sauniere, the eccentric curate of that town, I intend to focus on how a complex forgery gave birth to a mythology that has been consumed by four generations of conspiracy buffs. We can gain much insight by examining how a book based on a hoax, on lies that were accepted as fact, on a secret society that made false claims, can lead to a bestselling suspense thriller that ultimately unlocked a profound spiritual truth, and spoke to mass audiences all over the world in a way that has been unparalleled in modern publishing history.

Two

While the story of Rennes-le-Chateau has, since 1956, sparked an international publishing industry of its own, many of the books about it are deep sea dives into the murky waters of cryptic messages, decoded paintings, old manuscripts with mysterious genealogies, weird and demonic church architectures, pentagrams drawn over landscapes, secret societies and hidden treasures whose revelations could destroy the foundations of western civilization. Few studies have actually attempted to show how the mystery behind Rennes-le-Chateau is, in fact, no mystery at all, that most of the controversy has been the result of forgery. One of the best books that pitches a claim for a hoax is *The Treasure of Rennes-le-Chateau: A Mystery Solved* by Bill Putnam and John Edwin Wood, whose diligent and exhaustive research this article owes much of its material and which, to my satisfaction, solves the riddle of Rennes-le-Chateau and the Priory of Sion.

Putnam and Wood take a very skeptical approach to the Sauniere affair, and unlike Henry Lincoln, the co-author of *Holy Blood, Holy Grail*, who has written book after book that imposes all sorts of fantastic conspiracies and ancient bloodlines onto the entire business, these authors have examined all the physical evidence that is extant and have traced the evolution of the Rennes-le-Chateau legend itself. By taking a chronological approach, they have presented a strong case for an elaborate practical joke and have taught a lesson in how to investigate an unsolved case that makes so many fantastic claims and is riddled with so many revisions of accepted history. Their book is a welcome concentrated lesson in a skeptical and rational approach towards historical mysteries.

Their chronology goes as follows:

On January 12, 1956, *La Depeche Du Midi*, a regional newspaper that serviced the Languedoc in the South of France, started publishing a series of articles about a relatively obscure hilltop town of 100 inhabitants called Rennes-le-Chateau. The articles told of a turn-of-the-century priest, Berenger Sauniere, who had supposedly stumbled across a hidden treasure while excavating his impoverished church. It was a simple story based on local legend and gossip, dealing with events that had happened a half century earlier. The journalist who authored it had no access to any living witnesses, but the Languedoc was a region steeped in mythic folklore, having been conquered at various times by the Romans, the Visigoths and the Cathars, and legends there ran deep. Filled with mountains, caves and forests, the provincial land had inspired, over the centuries, many fantasies about the Knights Templar, secret societies and buried treasure. In the 13th century, it had been the focus of the Albigenisan Crusade, a violent Papal act of aggression against the Cathars and their heresies. The fact that Sauniere, a poor priest with a meager income, had mysteriously spent a fortune on elaborate construction projects and a lavish lifestyle while never disclosing the secret of his wealth, led many readers in 1956 to wonder if the rest of the treasure still lay buried under the forest-laden hilltops of Rennes-le-Chateau.

Sauniere arrived in Rennes in 1885, a poor man besieged by financial difficulties and scandalous political differences with the French government that almost jeopardized his mission. At first he lived a very Spartan existence, even hunting for his own food to sustain himself, and he was very discouraged to find his church in bad disrepair, with few appreciable funds to improve it. Determined to make his unglamorous post a more spiritually satisfying one, he rolled up his sleeves and set about renovating the building himself. It was in 1891, according to the article in La Depeche, while dismantling the altar, that Sauniere found some manuscripts hidden in a Visigothic column being used to support the altar top. While this original newspaper account does not draw any direct conclusions about the manuscripts, it was heavily implied that whatever information they contained led to the discovery of a hidden treasure.

Sauniere's sudden wealth was inferred from the fact that at some point he started spending extravagant sums of money, more than can be accounted for by his personal income. Not only did he rebuild the church at Rennes, but he constructed a tower in honor of Mary Magdalene (La Tour Magdala), a large villa for himself (the Villa Bethani) with elaborate terraces and gardens, all the while hosting luxurious dinner parties with abundant supplies of expensive wines and foods, supposedly spending the equivalent of a few million dollars. Despite the church's attempts to bring him up on charges of trafficking in masses (a practice, forbidden by Rome, in which a priest receives money to say a mass but never does), he died without ever revealing the secret of his sudden and unexplained wealth.

Noting the fact that the Languedoc had been occupied at various times by the Cathars, the Visigoths and the Merovingians and that the Knights Templar had established a strong presence in the region, the writer in *La Depeche* states plainly, "Rennes having been a large Visigothic fortress with buried treasure, there is a strong chance that the Cathar treasure, including the famous Holy Grail, was taken there."

This article is the first appearance not only of Rennes-le-Chateau and its mysterious priest in the public imagination, but it is the first indication that anything more than a pedestrian treasure had been uncovered. It is interesting to note that between Sauniere's death in 1917 and the appearance of this sensationalist article in 1956, there had been no national discussion of anything unusual about Rennes history, outside of the fact that some regional priest had once mysteriously spent a lot of money and got in trouble with Rome.

Perhaps the articles had been prompted by Pierre Cordu, an entrepreneur who owned Sauniere's Villa and had turned it into a hotel to exploit the tourist trade. The article in the *Dispatch* was quite a lucrative public relations triumph for Cordu. Many people came from all over France to hunt for Sauniere's treasure, hoping to find the plundered treasure of the Cathars, perhaps even to find the Holy Grail itself.

Now this is all very interesting, but many towns and cities around the world have increased their tourism through boasting rumors of a fabulous lost treasure. There was little in the story of Sauniere and his mysterious wealth to interest the international tourist trade, but the French public took an interest and Cordu made out like a bandit, milking it for what it was worth. In a 1960 French television production about the Sauniere affair, Cordu himself dramatically portrayed the priest. After the television show brought more hordes of treasure hunters to the town, Cordu was able to retire in 1965 and ran off with the real treasure: the money gathered from all the desperate people who came to the town with metal detectors and pick axes.

Shortly after the television program was aired, Cordu anonymously deposited into the Departmental Archives at Carcassonne a history of the Sauniere affair, clearly an attempt to play up the legend to the max. The account even inflates the amount of money that the curate had supposedly spent on church construction and personal indulgence, grossly exaggerating it to four billion francs, clearly an indication that some fabulous buried treasure had indeed been found.

In December 1962, a departmental librarian from Carcassonne named Descadeillas decided to set the record straight and to investigate the affair once and for all. He deposited his findings into the

Departmental Archives. His document is much more sober than Cordu's, greatly reducing the total sum paid by Sauniere and speculating that any romantic notions about a Cathar or Templar treasure can be explained away by a simple nest egg of coins that had been buried by an 18th century Abbe. Delving into wine merchant accounts, letters and diaries by Sauniere, and statements made by his faithful house keeper, Descadeillas concluded with a plain and sensible statement that "The treasure of Rennes does not exist. But the secret of the Curate of Rennes is real. And it is in him that the mystery resides."

By all accounts, the librarian's report should have settled the matter, leaving the question of how Sauniere could have afforded to build a tower and a villa and buy all that wine as a simple regional mystery. Perhaps the curate had stumbled across a pot of gold after finding clues to its whereabouts in the Visigothic pillar. Perhaps he had indeed generated funds by illegally selling masses as claimed by Rome. Or perhaps his brother Alfred who had considerable money, secretly funded his projects. Perhaps it was a combination of all three. Regardless, with the exception of a lot of fortune hunters who showed up in Rennes with their shovels, the world at large had little reason to pay attention to this unsolved affair.

But around this time, a strange figure appeared in the region. Descadeillas comments in a book published years later, "This man lived in Paris. He had no connections and no known relatives in the area. He was a difficult person to place, drab, secretive, cunning, with the gift of gab, but people who spoke to him said it was hard to follow what he said...He used to go about surveying the area and enquiring about the origin of properties."

There is reason to believe that this secretive cunning man was Pierre Plantard, the man who would be responsible for the elaborate circus that was to follow. And in 1967, with the publication of an exploitative book of pseudo-history, the little tale of Sauniere and his secret gold was about to be transformed into a vast conspiracy that spanned several thousand years and attempted to undermine the pillars of Christianity.

THREE

It was in 1967 that a writer named Gerard de Sede published a book called *The Gold of Rennes* or *The Accursed Treasure of Rennes-le-Chateau* in which he vastly expanded the story that had been set into motion by the 1956 *Dispatch* accounts. De Sede, a non-fiction writer who had published sensational books with names like *The Templars Are Among Us*, suddenly had access to evidence and materials related to the Sauniere affair that not even Cordu had known about, including the text of the manuscripts found in the Visigothic Pillar. He also had unexplained access to conversations that had occurred between private individuals, all of whom were dead by the time de Sede started writing his book. With almost nothing to back up many of his statements, de Sede wove a tale of intrigue and mystery, one that hinted that the treasure of Rennes-le-Chateau not only existed but was of far greater importance than any one could possibly have imagined.

De Sede's account has Sauniere discovering manuscripts filled with Biblical quotations that have been altered with additional letters and markings. These texts were a cipher code but de Sede neither reveals the deciphered text nor reveals how he got possession of the documents. After the discovery of the manuscripts, Sauniere travels to Paris where he consults with Bishops and buys copies of famous paintings by Teniers and Poussin (we shall see why later) and returns to Rennes, where he proceeds to deface some tombstones that, according to de Sede, contained important information that helped him decipher the secret messages. Sauniere then proceeds to spend between 15 and 20 million francs on his various construction projects and his lavish life style. De Sede even tells of a deathbed confession that Sauniere made to an Abbe who was so shaken by what he heard that after the Abbe left Saunierre's presence, he never smiled again. The book's conclusion tells of various untimely deaths that may have been the result of too many people knowing too much about the secret of Sauniere's wealth.

De Sede's book is obviously hack journalism, relying upon sensationalism, feeling little need to do any real historical work, to reveal any sources or cite any witnesses. It is tempting to say that de Sede was an opportunist who knew that he could pump out a sure-fire best seller. Perhaps that is true, but there is early evidence that de Sede was actually working in tandem with another group of people who had an interest in exploiting the Rennes legend, shadowy figures behind the scenes who held pieces of the puzzle that complimented and explained much of what de Sede had dangled before the public.

The first evidence of an elaborate hoax is de Sede's citation of two works deposited in the Bibliothèque nationale de France between 1956 and 1961, both of them dealing with bloodlines descended from the Merovingian kings, but he offers little explanation of what this all has to do with Rennes-le-Chateau. A closer examination of these manuscripts reveals that they had been deposited under false pretenses: one was attributed to a man who had died the year before and another contained a contact address of a street number that didn't exist. There was a deliberate covering up of tracks and careful timing was involved in this incremental release of information. De Sede's book, in retrospect, seems like bait that was cast out to trap a large fish, a mere prelude to a vast hoax.

The fish that took the bait was Henry Lincoln, an English actor turned journalist who amongst other things appeared in episodes of *The Avengers* and wrote scripts for *Dr. Who*. With one foot in the world of science fiction and the other in a public world of consummate showmanship, Lincoln read de Sede's book while vacationing in France and was immediately captivated by its version of the Sauniere affair. Somehow Lincoln managed to get a contract for three episodes of the BBC documentary series *Chronicles*. Usually a vehicle for sober and reasoned scholarship, *Chronicles* broke its own formula with Lincoln's three documentaries: *The Lost Treasure of Jerusalem?* (1972), *The Priest, The Painter and the Devil* (1974) and *The Shadow of the Templars* (1979). More like an episode of *Leonard Nimoy's In Search Of* than anything *Chronicles* had previously presented, the shows not only accepted the de Sede version of the Rennes affair, but expanded the legend into the version that was to appear in Lincoln's book *Holy Blood, Holy Grail* (co-authored with Michael Bagent and Richard Leigh).

Starting with a straight presentation of the de Sede findings, the shows became increasingly more outlandish as Lincoln was fed more information via de Sede himself. Lincoln now started looking for evidence that Sauniere was encoding clues to the location of the treasure into the architecture of the church itself, and that an obscure road-side stone tomb in the countryside around Rennes is the basis for the painting "The Shepherds of Arcady" by Poussin. Further, Lincoln ties the mystery of Rennes-le-Chateau to the lost treasure of Jerusalem, transferred to Rennes-le-Chateau by way of the Knights Templar, and protected by a secret society called the Priory of Sion. This society had evidently created the Knights Templar as its military arm, and had protected some immense treasure, or secret, for over a thousand years. Lincoln even traces the Priory of Sion to modern day Paris and its Grand Master,

Pierre Plantard de St. Clair, who claims to be a blood descendant of the Merovingian kings of France, evidence of which is included in the manuscripts that de Sede discovered in the Bibliothèque nationale.

By this point, it seems as if Henry Lincoln has, with the help of de Sede and the Priory of Sion itself under the Grand Mastership of Plantard, put all the pieces together. Berenger Sauniere had unwittingly discovered the secret of the Priory (the bloodline of Christ and perhaps even Christ's tomb in the countryside around Rennes), and was either paid off for his silence with large sums of money or was acting in the interests of the Priory. Sauniere could barely resist the temptation, however, to scatter clues about his involvement and the location of the secret in many of his architectural projects. Regardless of the exact details, it is clear to Lincoln that Sauniere had stumbled across a conspiracy that had been sustained over a thousand years and involved many famous people including Leonardo Da Vinci and Isaac Newton, both of whom were supposed to have been Past Grand Masters of the Priory of Sion.

Henry Lincoln was to follow up on his television success with the book *Holy Blood, Holy Grail* (1982), the de Sede version of the Sauniere story was exploited for all it was worth: the trip to Paris, the purchasing of the paintings, the vast sums of money spent on construction projects, the Priory of Sion, the cipher manuscripts, the tomb of Poussin, the pentagrams and hidden clues on tombstones—all were presented as fact. Further, the book went several steps further and suggested that the ultimate secret of the Priory of Sion was that the bloodline of Christ was the true nature of the Holy Grail. The book became a best seller and cemented the entire Christ bloodline legend into the public imagination and, twenty years later, served as the chief inspiration for *The Da Vinci Code*.

While the theories of the Christ bloodline can more easily be discussed and evaluated independent of the Rennes-le-Chateau story, Lincoln's evidence is largely centered on the strange case of Sauniere, the crucial foundation for his theories. It is worth keeping the focus on the Rennes affair, looking at how the legend had been constructed and for what purposes and by whom. Not only do the answers shed a lot of light on *The Da Vinci Code*, but also illuminate the imaginary mechanisms by which legends, mythology, folk tales and the romantic histories of secret societies and their claims to historical authority originate and how they grow until hoaxes and imagined events act as foundations for people's beliefs.

FOUR

The altar manuscripts themselves are problematic. De Sede noted that they did not appear to be ancient, despite the fact they are written in a lettering similar to uncials which was in wide spread use between 200 and 700 AD. However, de Sede claims he never saw the originals, but does not explain how he could have judged the age of the manuscripts from photographs or hand-written copies. The deciphered message also refers to the inscription on a tombstone in the Rennes church cemetery of someone who was buried in 1781, making it unlikely that the manuscripts had been sitting in the altar pillar since the days of the Knights Templar. Moreover, the Biblical texts that constitute the body of the manuscripts are translations from an edition of the Bible published in the late 1880s, mere months before Sauniere supposedly found them in the altar pillar.

Clearly, there are only two possibilities: that Sauniere himself forged the documents and pretended to find them, or that they were fabricated after the 1956 articles in the *Dispatch*. Balanced against the weight of all the other evidence, it is more likely that the documents were forged in the 1950s or early 1960s.

The contents of the manuscript texts can be deciphered with key-words derived from a tombstone in the Rennes graveyard. Perhaps inspired by the fact that Sauniere was known to desecrate tombstones and abolish inscriptions (supposedly to use the stone in the restoration of his church), the Hoaxers gave de Sede hand drawn copies of two stones, both belonging to Marie de Negre d'Ables, who was interred in Rennes-le-Chateau in 1781. In 1905, an archeological society discovered her tombstone cast aside in the graveyard by Sauniere (not defaced or destroyed in the 1890s as de Sede claims) and made a copy of the inscription. There is nothing out of the ordinary about the inscription other than certain letters on it constitute part of the keyword that helps decipher the manuscripts. The second stone, supposedly one that lay flat on the grave, has much more explicit references that the Hoaxers used to build their mythology, including Greek letters that spelled out the Latin phrase ET IN ARCADIA EGO (a reference to the painting by Poussin that de Sede claims Sauniere purchased while in Paris) and the initials PS, supposedly a reference to the secret society Priory of Sion.

The major problem with the tombstones is that they are no longer extant, de Sede never saw them with his own eyes, and the only known witnesses are the archeologists who drew only one of them and which reveals little evidence. It is clear that whatever elaborate references existed on the second stone (which may not have even existed) were designed by the Hoaxers to strengthen the connections between Sauniere and the Priory of Sion.

The decrypted message on the first manuscript reads as follows:

"Shepherd, no temptation, Poussin and Teniers hold the key. Peace 681. By the cross and this horse of God. I finish off (destroy) this guardian demon at midday. Blue apples."

While several generations of Rennes-le-Chateau fanaticists have labored over this message, attempting to analyze each and every phrase and word with the intensity of medieval Kabbalists, it is most likely that it means very little other than to support other material that was being forged at the time. The references to artists like Poussin and Teniers reinforce the story of Sauniere purchasing paintings by both artists during his supposed trip to Paris, a story that has its origin with de Sede. One of the paintings, the "Shepherds of Arcady" by Poussin, shows several rustic farm folks gathered about a stone tomb on which is inscribed the words ET IN ARCADIA EGO. This is supposed to be another connection between the various elements of the mystery and Rennes-le-Chateau, but the fact remains that the Poussin painting, the cipher text and the tombstone inscription that refers to the Latin phrase all have their first appearance with de Sede. No one ever recovered any bill of sale proving that Sauniere purchased the painting, no one ever saw Sauniere with the painting, no one ever found the painting in Sauniere's possessions after he died, no one ever produced the original of the altar manuscript, and no one ever saw the second tombstone of Marie de Negre d'Ables.

But none of this seemed to bother Henry Lincoln, who bought it all hook, line and sinker. Lincoln went even further, tracing lines on the cipher manuscript, and proving that a pentagram can be overlaid on the words when connecting certain portions. Even Pierre Plantard, the mastermind of the entire hoax, was genuinely surprised to see this. Unfortunately, this obsession with finding pentagrams in manuscripts and even in the physical landscapes around Rennes was to dominate Lincoln's attention for the next several decades as he clung fanatically to the de Sede legend and became its most notorious believer.

FIVE

Shortly after finishing his first documentary, Henry Lincoln was looking at the second cipher text and suddenly realized that there was a very simple way to decode it. It was only a matter of minutes before he came up with the following hidden message, "The treasure belongs to King Dagobert II and to Sion and it is death."

Talking to de Sede shortly afterwards, he asked the writer how he could have missed such an exemplar cipher, to which de Sede replied, "We thought someone like you might be interested in finding it yourself." Lincoln was chilled at the use of the word "we."

The manuscripts that de Sede "discovered" in the French National Library were largely attempts to trace the bloodlines of the Jewish tribe of Benjamin to the Merovingian Kings of France, and through to Dagobert II, who died young and childless but who now is blood-connected to the modern French family of Plantard.

Here Pierre Plantard first rears his ominous visage, many years after he hiked around the Languedoc in the post-war years piecing together his own personal mythology. Plantard's motive, apparently, was to declare himself a blood descendant of the Merovingians, the rightful heir to the throne of the Kingdom of France, and further, a blood descendant of Jesus Christ.

The manuscripts in the National Library are highly suspect. One of them is registered in the name of a dead man. One year after its arrival in the archives, someone inserted an extra page into the manuscript claiming that the author had died in October of 1966. This is particularly curious since the man who signed the protesting letter died in September of 1966, one month earlier. Not only this, but the text claims that Sauniere found a Merovingian genealogy in the Visigothic altar and makes no mention of the cipher manuscripts. Such contradictions and obvious attempts to mislead are rampant through the forgeries and fictional storylines that run throughout the Plantard hoax.

The various manuscripts cited by de Sede are riddled with references to the Merovingians, Dagobert II, the painting by Poussin and the mysterious phrase ET IN ARCADIA EGO and there is always the dark hint of a secret society, with the initials PS, that is the key to the entire mystery. But it is evident from a careful reading of the texts that were deposited into the archives over a seven-year period culminating in 1967 when de Sede's book was published, that Plantard's mythology had been evolving throughout the decade and fresh manuscripts had to be deposited in the archives to upgrade the details of the hoax. There are contradictions between the first texts deposited and the final ones that show clear evidence that the hoaxers were generating new fake evidence and coming up with new claims. One was an Abbe who lived a century before Sauniere wrote the cipher text which came from a Bible translation that had been published only a year before Sauniere supposedly discovered it.

It is the final manuscript deposited in 1967 that finally springs the trap and talks openly about the Priory of Sion, a secret society that dates all the way back to the days of the Knights Templar (and which allegedly still exists). It claims that past Grand Masters have included Leonardo Da Vinci, Isaac Newton, Victor Hugo, Claude Debussy and Jean Cocteau. It also reveals the Plantard family coat of arms which includes a six-pointed star, tying it to the tribe of Benjamin, and the motto ET IN ARCADIA EGO.

The hoax has now come full circle. Through deception, lies, forgeries, fake addresses, pseudonyms, false genealogies, the use of dead men's identities and the claim that a king who died childless actually had a bloodline, and by bringing in an obsessive science fiction television writer like Henry Lincoln who had the resources to capture an international audience, the Hoaxers had laid the ground work that would enable Pierre Plantard de St. Clair to claim bloodline descent from nobility, royalty, and Biblical Gods.

Six

It is obvious that Pierre Plantard was in cahoots, so to speak, with Gerard de Sede long before 1967 since there is a lengthy interview with him in an earlier book by de Sede about the Knights Templar. But curiously de Sede's book on Rennes and the first two documentaries by Lincoln for *Chronicles* do not even mention Plantard. This furthers the case that Plantard was working in close collaboration with de Sede throughout the years that the French archives were being sprinkled with bits of the puzzle. De Sede's job, it seems, was to release information in a piecemeal fashion and let people like Lincoln slowly put together all the pieces.

So, who was Pierre Plantard?

He was born the son of a butler but later forged a birth certificate for himself claiming that his family name was Plantard de Saint Clair, strengthening his ties to more appealing bloodlines. He developed a personal interest in mystical philosophies but grew increasingly paranoid about Jewish and Masonic conspiracies about which he wrote a letter of warning to Marshal Petain, offering up the services of a hundred men who would fight for the purity of France. His fanaticism about French national renewal led to a series of short lived societies and a newspaper that denounced Jews and Masons and which were tinged with a weird mixture of nationalism and mysticism.

A police report from 1941 after Plantard was imprisoned for his activities reads, "Plantard, who boasts of having links with numerous politicians, seems to be one of those dotty, pretentious young men who run more or less fictitious groups in an effort to look important." Plantard was fundamentally addicted to forming mystical societies structured as medieval orders, often right-wing and anti-Semitic in nature, forging documents, pathologically lying about his origins and family bloodline, and attempting to create multiple facades and fake identities behind which he could maneuver for power.

After the war he made his living as a draughtsman and fashioned himself an archeologist with a deep interest in the occult. He spent a lot of time in the late 1950s lurking about Rennes-le-Chateau and making people uncomfortable with his oddball mannerisms and his suspect motivations. It was shortly after this that Plantard began his fantastic claim to the French throne by tracing his own ancestry back to the Merovingians through Dagobert II.

He worked in close collaboration with Philippe de Chérisey, a French actor and radio performer who worked on a *Candid Camera*-like show that played elaborate hoaxes on its listeners. It is believed that Plantard and de Chérisey started forging the cipher manuscripts as prepared material for the show and that it was a television producer who suggested that they do this to back up their claim that Plantard was the rightful heir to the French throne. De Chérisey, a genius when it came to cryptic puzzles, worked out the cipher manuscripts and produced the documents. He also created many of the genealogical documents that appear in the French archives.

But it was with the best selling publication in 1982 of *Holy Blood, Holy Grail* that Plantard's elaborate hoax solidified into a mythology that attracted international exposure. The myth went something like this:

The Priory of Sion, a chivalric mystical military order that had been forged in the days of the Crusades, was preserving the bloodline of the Merovingian kings and contained within its ranks the blood descendant of Jesus Christ himself, Pierre Plantard de Saint Clair, who was the rightful heir to the throne of France. This was the fully flowered myth that had been collectively created by the various lies, deceptions, exaggerations, hoaxes and swindles of four individual men: Noel Cordu, the hotel manager at Rennes who wanted to make a buck off gullible treasure hunters; Pierre Plantard, a disturbed right-wing anti-Semite who invented secret societies and bloodlines; Gerard de Sede, a dubious historian who acted as a front for a large and elaborate deception; and Henry Lincoln, whose obsession with finding mystical proof for the awful treasure of Berenger Sauniere has led to a lifetime spent chasing after Templar treasure, holy grails, and five pointed stars.

SEVEN

Oddly enough, the only person who wasn't part of the creation of the mythology was Berenger Sauniere himself. His silence on the subjects of French monarchical bloodlines, hidden treasure and secret societies has long been pointed out to be proof of his collusion with the conspiracy, but his silence could very well have just been that those subjects were the furthest things from his mind.

Still, beyond any shadow of a doubt, there is a mystery left to solve. The church, the Tower of Mary Magdalene, the Villa Bethanie and a host of other structures and architectural elements exist to this day as mute testimony to the fact that Sauniere did indeed spend a lot of money between 1891 and 1917. In view of the overwhelming proof that the treasure, the bloodline, the secret society and the cipher manuscripts were all fakes, how do we answer these still unanswered questions?

Between 1885 when Sauniere was appointed to Rennes and 1891 when he supposedly found his treasure map, the sources of the funds that Sauniere spent on church and altar renovations are well documented, including a wealthy woman who had once taken ill in Rennes and paid her gratitude to the village by paying for the new altar top. It is also interesting to note that a few thousand francs were spent on windows and paid off in four payments, finally being settled in 1900, nearly ten years after Sauniere supposedly discovered the hidden treasure of the Templars. One would have thought that upon discovering a fortune in gold, the priest would have paid off the windows immediately to save on the interest.

There is a possibility that Sauniere did discover something of value while working on the church or tearing up the graveyard. He could have discovered some old papers, or perhaps just a curio in a tomb or within a cavity in the altar. Perhaps this discovery, in itself perfectly innocent and not really anything of more than passing note, launched the local legend that he had discovered a treasure.

But it is certain that no one can quite agree on what it was he found. The parchments revealed by Gerard de Sede are obvious fakes, created by Plantard and de Chérisey. So are the genealogies and the connections between Sauniere, the paintings by Poussin, the Priory of Sion and King Dagobert II. What is left is the possibility that he found some gold coins, or valuable archeological objects. Either way, there just doesn't seem to be any treasure.

But what accounts for the money that Sauniere spent after 1891?

Upon close examination of Sauniere's diaries, account books and personal papers from late 1891 to early 1897, we find that not only did Sauniere borrow money for some of his renovations, but he even stopped construction when funds for the masons ran out. There are letters from contractors demanding their payment, inquiring about unpaid balances, and negotiations for discounts. One payment for windows was paid off at 500 francs per month over a period of time. And indeed, for a span of two years before the building of the Tour Magdala and the Villa Bethanie, there was a break in the construction so Sauniere could catch up with himself financially. This is hardly a sign that a buried treasure had fallen in Sauniere's hands. The mystery, so far, was not how Sauniere was paying for all this; but how he expected to meet all the monthly payments.

It is the vast construction that went on between 1900 and 1910 that raised the largest number of eyebrows. It is during that period that Sauniere built the Tour Magdala which hosted his elaborate library and the Villa Bethanie, with its Impression Belvedere, where he hosted elaborate dinner parties and drank all that expensive wine. The amount of money spent during this period was so much that his own Bishop launched a series of investigations into the source of the funding that was to last for the rest of Sauniere's life.

It was the impression of Sauniere's Bishop that the good priest of Rennes-le-Chateau was engaging in trafficking of the mass, receiving funds from all over the South of France to say the mass, more requests than he could possibly fulfill. Indeed, we can still read the advertisements in old newspapers where Sauniere offered his ecclesiastical services at 1 franc per mass. There are records to show that he received funds for as many as eighty masses per day, obviously a number that was far beyond his physical capabilities to fulfill. Even though Sauniere's claimed that he was receiving funds from private individuals who preferred to remain anonymous, he was removed from his post as Curate of Rennes. At the time of his death by cardiac arrest in 1917, he was waiting for a hearing in Rome about the accusation once and for all. Perhaps if he had lived, the truth would have come out, and there would be no mystery of Rennes-le-Chateau and Pierre Plantard would have had to look for his bloodline somewhere else.

It is worth noting that Sauniere's own reckoning of 193,000 francs as how much money he spent on all the construction between 1891 and his death is a reasonable calculation of how much money he could have collected from private donations, as well as how much he could have brought in from mass trafficking, based on his own extant diaries and other various sources. Considering how much effort Sauniere put into juggling payments to contractors, and the persistent negotiations that went on with construction costs, coupled with the very realistic notion that he had private investors who wished to remain anonymous, 193,000 francs seems a sum that does not require the discovery of buried treasure, or pay-offs from the Priory of Sion to keep quiet about the last resting place of Jesus Christ, to explain away. The sum is also far from the 4 billion francs claimed by Cordu.

To cap off the improbability that Sauniere had unlimited funds, upon his passing, his life-long housekeeper and companion lived in a state of financial crisis until decades later when she sold the Villa Bethanie to Noel Cordu on the condition that she could remain on the premises as a tenant. She died penniless.

So, if Sauniere remained quiet about the source of his funds, persistent in his claims that his investors must remain anonymous, it is more likely that he was hiding the fact that he was obtaining the funds illegally. Therefore, even though Sauniere's expenditures still need full explanations, no Templar treasure, no last resting place of Jesus Christ, no secret societies from the middle ages, no bloodlines or Holy Grails, need to be introduced into the story to provide a satisfactory solution to the mystery of Berenger Sauniere.

And what of the Priory of Sion?

The Priory of Sion did indeed exist. It was registered with the French government in July of 1956 and seemed to have been formed to oppose government intervention with council housing. It stated as part of its mission to "carry out good deeds, to help the Roman Catholic Church, defend the weak and the oppressed." It declared itself a monastic order, but activity didn't seem to have extended beyond the confines of Plantard's council flat. At one point, members teamed up with their local church to run a school bus line. The French government has recognized no official activity from the Priory since 1956 although Plantard kept the organization going, no doubt in name only and for the purposes of propagating the de Sede myth, until 1996. Around that time Plantard got involved in a government scandal and had to admit under oath that he had fabricated everything relating to the Priory. He died in 2000.

EIGHT

In the movie *The Da Vinci Code* (2006), Robert Langdon is listening to Leigh Teabing (whose name is a nod to the *Holy Blood, Holy Grail* co-author) discuss the Priory of Sion.

"Philippe de Chérisey exposed that as a hoax in 1967," Langdon reminds his friend.

"And that is what they want you to believe," Teabing responds with a wry smile.

With this one interchange, the filmmakers deal with the allegation that the Priory of Sion was a hoax perpetrated by Plantard and de Chérisey. What is bizarre about this dialogue is that de Chérisey never publicly declared that the story was a hoax. The year 1967 seems to have been picked by the screenwriter because it was the publication date of *The Gold of Rennes* by Gerard de Sede, a book which was, in fact, the start of the hoax, not the exposure of it.

It is the ultimate defense of any political paranoid ranting about secret societies that if something can be proven beyond a shadow of a doubt to be false, there must be a conspiratorial collusion to prove it false. Teabing, being the ultimate paranoid in the story, takes that defense. However, in the world of *The Da Vinci Code*, the Priory of Sion is very real. I'm sure the filmmakers were well aware of the hoax but had little reason to dwell upon that. Dan Brown had created an extremely entertaining and romantic thriller that drew its strength from all the myths and falsehoods about the Priory of Sion. The focus here in not on Rennes-le-Chateau, but the mythology that grew from it. The only explicit reference to the historical background behind the mythology is the name of the curator of the Louvre whose murder kicks off the mystery—Jacques Sauniere—and the name of the family that contains the bloodline of Christ—Sinclair.

The relationship between *Holy Blood, Holy Grail* and *The Da Vinci Code* is like that between a biography of William Randolph Hearst and Orson Welles' movie *Citizen Kane*–fiction based on fact. There was so much that Brown derived from the earlier work that two of the authors sued Dan Brown's publisher in court claiming that the book derived most of its content from their work and also presented the material in a manner similar enough to be plagiarism. The *Holy Blood, Holy Grail* authors lost the case. Personally, I felt they could have saved the lawyer's fees and just enjoyed the fact that their book was back in print and selling quite well as a result of Dan Brown's popularity. To suggest that use of historical material from a non-fiction book is an act of plagiarism is walking on thin ice indeed.

But what *The Da Vinci Code* drew on the most was the practice cultivated by many Rennes-le-Chateau investigators and Grail enthusiasts in looking for clues all over the physical landscape, in classic works of art, in cipher texts and tombstone inscriptions, in musty archives and libraries, in sculptural elements within churches and chapels, in the legends of the Knights Templar and the bloody history of the Cathars, in the puzzles and riddles that the Rosicrucians left behind, in the mysterious rituals of the Freemasons and their cryptic imagery, in the larger than life characters of men like Isaac Newton and Leonardo Da Vinci, in the powerful archetypal symbols that they incorporated into their work. It has become a standard practice of most paranoid researchers of secret societies to think that these great writers, thinkers, artists, religious leaders and men of science had the same urge that serial killers have of sending clues to the police department, encoding their secret knowledge into public works.

The most extreme paranoia is only now coming into maturity with the rantings of public personalities like David Icke and Alex Jones, who think that if anyone utilizes in their artwork or architecture any symbol that vaguely suggests some mystic archetype then they are part of a vast conspiracy of extraterrestrial reptiles whose bloodline is controlling the world. The word Illuminati is heavily exploited to make us believe that all world events including wars, genocides, economic depressions, assassinations and changes in government, are all carefully orchestrated by a bunch of robed men in temples who are worshipping giant smoking owls.

The Da Vinci Code was built upon the foundation of Rennes-le-Chateau, which had been growing in elaboration and detail for almost nine decades, and which had reached full maturity in the publication of Holy Blood, Holy Grail twenty years earlier. But while all the talk about the Priory of Sion, the bloodline of Christ and the origins of Christianity makes for provocative investigations, none of it is required to investigate what happened at Rennes-le-Chateau. The only connection seems to be that Plantard exploited that local mystery to his own advantage to perpetrate myths about his genealogy.

But The Da Vinci Code does something that the Plantard mythology and the authors of Holy Blood, Holy Grail do not. The Priory of Sion was created by a right-wing anti-Semite who was concerned with the bloodlines of kings, including the King of Kings himself, Jesus Christ. All this talk about wars, genealogies, churchmen and military orders is all very patriarchal and male dominated. But The Da Vinci Code is focused on the feminine—the Sacred Feminine—which, according to Leigh Teabing, is what the Holy Grail is all about. Perhaps Dan Brown has not just lifted the theories of Holy Blood, Holy Grail for his own storyline; perhaps he has evolved it, added another layer that makes the story relevant to our modern age, an age where women's spirituality and mythology are starting to emerge with an equal importance to match masculine counterparts. All this talk about the Goddess and the Sacred Feminine that comes pouring out of its pages would no doubt have made Pierre Plantard very upset. His focus was more on kings and thrones and the bloodlines of the Sacred Masculine. He was a dethroned king who wanted to get back on the throne, not to reinstate the matriarchal age of goddess religions.

At the very end of the novel, as Robert Langdon bows before the entombed bones of Mary Magdalene, he does so not with the smugness of a typical crime detective who has finally solved a case, but with intense spiritual reverence and terrible awe. For those who have seen the Ron Howard directed version of The Da Vinci Code released in 2006, Langdon, played by Tom Hanks, upon realizing that he is standing over the last resting place of the Bride of God, very subtly glances about to see if anyone is watching, and then bows in reverence before the Goddess, a very spiritually moving cinematic moment which brilliantly sums up in one image the ultimate power and draw of the entire *Da Vinci Code* phenomenon.

Perhaps it is the largest reason for the book's popularity. Not only does it satisfy the hunger for a clever mystery, but the spiritual hunger for a deeper communion with the divine. From this mytho-poetic perspective, the Goddess, who has been suppressed and dethroned, is reaching out again from her hiding place, making her priests visible so they can openly worship, exposing her scriptures so they can be read once more, unearthing what had been buried by thousands of years of militaristic patriarchy so it can feed the spirits of humanity in a way that the Catholic domination of Western Culture did not.

While the "rough beast" of William Butler Yeats is slouching towards Bethlehem to be born, perhaps the Goddess of Dan Brown is slouching towards the Louvre—or Rennes-le-Chateau for that matter—for some spectacular rebirth.

Note from the Author: This article is deeply indebted to the work of Bill Putnam and John Edwin Wood whose book *The Treasure of Rennes-Le-Chateau: A Mystery Solved* (Sutton Publishing Limited, 2003) is a brilliant examination of all the extant evidence of this most mysterious chapter in Languedoc history. All translations from the French in this article are theirs.

First published in *Behutet: Modern Thelemic Magick & Culture*, Issue 32, Winter 2006.

LITERATURE AND THE ARTS

INTERVIEW WITH
KENNETH ANGER

Kenneth Anger is a California-born filmmaker who has been producing and directing since the 1940s and is responsible for some of the
most infamous underground films of all times, including *Scorpio Rising*
(1964) and *Lucifer Rising* (1970-1980). His major works have often taken
years to complete, and all together they arguably can be contained on
one DVD; but the visceral power of his cinema has been revolutionary
and widely influential, not just on several generations of underground
filmmakers, but on mainstream culture. His use of cutting images to
popular music for ironic effect has not only worked its way into the films
of Stanley Kubrick and Martin Scorsese, but became a prototype for the
slick MTV style that Anger himself finds repugnant and decadent. As
the bestselling author of the groundbreaking *Hollywood Babylon* series,
he set the tone for the genre of celebrity sleaze documentary, but no
one has been able to reproduce Anger's vision of the film capital as a
soul-devouring Moloch that has abused the black magic of filmmaking.

Indeed, what sets Anger's cinema aside from all his imitators is his
awareness that film is a potent form of magick. His films are magickal
workings, and the plots themselves (if plot is the correct term) often
revolve about dark rituals and invocations of demons and angels. To
a Thelemic audience, Anger often needs no introduction, having been
one of the few filmmakers who has incorporated Thelemic philosophy
and magick into his cinema. Yet he is also ranked with the likes of Maya
Deren, Stan Brakhage, Jean Genet, and Jean Cocteau. In his films,
magick, surrealism, pop culture and mysticism all blend into a unique
artistic voice.

His more recent works include *Mouse Heaven* (2004), a documentary about the world's largest Mickey Mouse toy collection, and *A Man*

We Want To Hang (2002) about Aleister Crowley's paintings. These are his first two films in over 20 years. There are rumors that he is still trying to raise funds for a filmed version of the *Gnostic Mass*.

Back in 1989, I had the opportunity to chat with Anger and found him to be very witty, candid and deeply fascinating. Although conducted more than a decade ago, the following interview is a broad overview of a truly remarkable life.

You mentioned you got funding from the National Endowment of the Arts and other institutions. Is that how you generally funded your films?

No. The films where I've had a considerable budget...I've...how can I say this and not sound too cynical. A relative has died and left me some money and I put the money into making the movie rather than... in fact, like when my grandmother died, I cashed the bonds that she left me. Like in General Electric and things like that. And my brother and sister thought I was stupid and another example of my insanity to do that. Of course, if I had kept them, I would have had some income from them over the years. But I'm not sorry I did it. So, I've had a couple of relatives die, my mother and my grandmother both left me some things I could negotiate into money.

In other cases, I've earned the money myself, through books and translations. You see, I lived for over twelve years in Paris and I was a major in French before I went over and I did translations, English-French, French-English and so forth. Just to supplement my income while I was living in Paris and I was working for Henri Langlois of the Cinémathèque Française. This was up to the early sixties.

When did Hollywood Babylon first come out?

I wrote it in French while I was living in Paris. It was published by Jean-Jacques Pauvert in 1959. Basically, I had published several articles in the *Cahiers du Cinema* which were like sketches for some of the chapter ideas in the book. Like the Fatty Arbuckle story; that was never known in any detail in France. They were fascinated by all that. They just knew vaguely that Arbuckle was a comedian who had worked with Chaplin and Keaton and that something nasty happened and his career was ruined. They didn't know much more beyond that, so I just filled in the details. Then Jacques Daniel Valcroix who was the editor of the

Cahiers du Cinema said at the time, "Why don't you expand on it and turn it into a book?" As I needed money at the time, I did, and I found Pauvert who was publishing at the time something called *Eroticism in Cinema*, and I thought well it would tie in with that series, having an interest for the French who were wrapped up at the time with Bridget Bardot and all that.

At the time the French were interested in American film, in particular film noir which led to films like *Breathless*. And I knew people like Goddard and Truffaut when they were writing film criticism, but they hadn't made any movies. I was there when Truffaut made his first movie. I knew Goddard when he was so poor he had to wear layers of newspaper under his shirt in the winter to keep out the cold. They were just sort of sleeping at the office at the *Cahiers du Cinema* like wild eyed enthusiasts.

Did you ever hear any of these director's subsequent criticism of your films?

Well, the people who liked my films in France were people like Jean Cocteau, Jean Genet...it was a more esoteric group. My own films, I never went out of my way to show them to people like Truffaut.

Fireworks reminded me of something out of Genet, in particular Querrelle.

I think Genet felt that too, and of course it was several years before his film *Un Chant D'Amour*. I didn't like that film too much and he himself told me that he was out of his element in doing it. The film was meant to be completely private. It was never to be shown except to private collectors. But Genet himself called it "child's play" in a derogatory sense. And he had a much more ambitious script which was never filmed, and I feel that was too bad. He let me read it. Actually, it was an idea that I feel came more out of Cocteau's *Blood of a Poet* because there's this scene when a protagonist is peeping through keyholes down a corridor and sees different things in each one. Well, in Genet's script, there's a series of what would now be called peepshow machines that he looks into--these are the old versions of what would be the video machines in X-rated book stores now. Different things would be happening, and it would be an excuse to show different visual things in a dream-like way. I thought that was much more sophisticated than *Chant D'Amour*. Actually, I was a bit embarrassed by the sentimentality of *Chant D'Amour*...the literary metaphors turned into images like garlands of roses and things like that. They didn't really work. Running around the forest playing peek-a-boo and things like that.

That reminds me of William Burroughs' The Wild Boys which had a section called "The Penny Arcade Peep Show."

It's very similar, yes I remember that. Of course he wrote that considerably later. It's a similar idea, I don't know if Genet ever let him read that, he might have.

What was the film that you were making with Cocteau that was never completed?

The title was *Le Jeune Homme et la Mort*. It was a twenty-minute ballet that Cocteau did that was, a big success and was premiered just before I arrived in Paris in 1950. It had shown for a couple of years already, so I saw it and was very impressed by it. It had a set that transformed from an artist's garret to the rooftops of Paris as they were in the 1920s when the Eiffel Tower was covered with neon spelling out Citroen, which was a French automobile, and it was a very dream-like thing. Cocteau gave me permission to film it, and he gave me a letter which I showed around to several producers, but I wanted to do it in Technicolor and 35mm or there wouldn't have been any point in filming it. And the ballet dancers were very enthusiastic about it. But basically, there was the usual frustration that the kind of money I needed to do it on 35mm Technicolor, people said, "You could make a black and white feature for what you're asking." I said, well, maybe so but this film could be shown for the next fifty or a hundred years. It's going to be a classic, and the money is going to come back slowly but it could be shown as a short, it can be sold to ballet schools. Well, even with the letter from Cocteau I wasn't able to get the money I needed, and I wasn't willing to scale it down. But I did film it in 16-millimeter black and white as a study film. That version is in the collection of the Cinémathèque Française. And I gave it to them and they have it and they can show it occasionally if they want to. But I'm disappointed that I was never able to make it in the big way I planned. What it does show is the original choreography and the original dancers who created the parts. In that sense it's valuable.

It's one of the few cases, and both of them happened in France, where I had been attracted to someone else's literary work and wanted to film it. One was the ballet, then there was *Maldoror*, and *The Story of O*.

Didn't you complete portions of The Story of O? What happened?

I began in the mid-1950s filming with a very beautiful young lady. She helped find the financing, through her boyfriend, but then I found out where the money was coming from. I was making it in black and white 16mm. But we still needed quite a lot of money because we were traveling to the country and filming in a big old castle. The money had actually come from a kidnapping. He had kidnapped Eric Peugeot of the Peugeot Auto Company and got quite a big ransom from it. Then, this was his girlfriend. Eventually, he did a foolish thing. The boy was never harmed because the kidnapping was actually arranged by the boy's mother in revenge against old man Peugeot, the money in the family, who ran the company and he disapproved of her because he felt that his son had married beneath him. She hated the rich old grandfather and (it's a diabolical story and all true) she wanted some way of getting the money out of the old grandfather and she knew he was very fond of this five-year-old boy. She arranged for her lover to kidnap the boy. The maid left the boy playing in the garden and the boyfriend drove up with his car and the boy said "Hi," because he knew the lover because he had seen him many times when the husband was working in the factory, come up in the afternoon to visit mother. So he ran off in the car and was gone about a week. And the settlement from the grandfather was like 20 million dollars (the French equivalent).

Then he began living too high off the hog, like he rented a château in Chamonix which is a famous ski resort. Only rich people go there. He rented the villa next to Ali Khan, the husband of Rita Hayworth. He began giving lavish parties, inviting hundreds of people to these lavish spreads…all weekend parties, sort of like *The Great Gatsby*. And suddenly the French police said, "Just how did this happen?" In other words, if he had played it cool he probably would have been able to keep the money. But they never do!

Some of this money went into my production. As soon as they found out it was him I was suddenly confronted by the equivalent of the French FBI. And they said they wanted all the footage and all the details and I said, "Well, I didn't know what he was doing. I just knew he was the boyfriend of the girlfriend." Now, the girlfriend who played the part was the daughter of the Minister of Finance of the government at that time. And her parents were Huguenots, which was a very puritanical kind of religion that goes back...if you saw *Intolerance*; they were the ones who were massacred by King Francis. Just like Howard Hughes hired nobody but Mormons to look after his accounting and finances, in France, traditionally, the Huguenots had always been in the Ministry of Finance even to this day. They don't smoke, they don't drink, they don't believe in going to movies, a whole bunch of them don't like the Mormons or something. So this girl was rebelling against her parents. So, I knew she had well placed parents, but I didn't know to what degree by playing this sadomasochistic fantasy that she was defying her parents. At any rate, I filmed about 25 minutes of it and that is in the collection of the Cinémathèque Française. But because of the legal reasons, I really can't show it, but film stills have been published in the *Eroticism in the Cinema*, but I can't show it in this country. The name of the girl is still off limits; her family is still involved in the government.

What about the American version of Hollywood Babylon which was very popular and a best seller in the late 1970s?

Basically, whenever I do something that has commercial overtones it means I am staring in the face of insolvency and have to think up something to earn some money. I knew that my knowledge of the history of Hollywood, in particular its seamier side, its shadow side had commercial possibilities and people kept saying why don't you do it in America? And I said, "Well, maybe someday I will." Then suddenly I was faced with the fact that I had run out of money and I got an advance from Jan Wenner of *Rolling Stone* magazine to bring it out through his book division Straight Arrow Books in San Francisco. They brought out the first American edition and from there it was taken up by Dell in the trade paperback then it went into paperback, then the second book was brought out by E.D. Dutton and both were best sellers.

And you wrote the second book as well?

Yes, of course. Who else? [chuckles]

*In Hollywood Babylon II there's a photograph of Groucho Marx with his
body completely covered in tattoos. Is there a story behind that?*

Well, that was his hobby. And he gave it away in the film *At the
Circus* with the song "Lydia the Tattooed Lady," which was a private
in-joke. Whenever he felt in a bad mood, or a good mood, he would go
off and get a tattoo, usually to Long Beach. It's too bad his skin wasn't
preserved; it would have made an interesting artifact.

I had been friends with his daughter Miriam Marx; we went to
Beverley Hills High School together. She knew about it and we actually
peeked at it a couple of times at his private swimming pool. The interesting thing about this is that Marx being Jewish is absolutely defying
Talmudic law because it is absolutely prohibited in orthodox Jewry to
tattoo the body. It goes way back; the Ancient Egyptians tattooed their
body as well as the Africans and the Arab tribes that surrounded Israel
and the Jews were setting themselves apart from all this. I think it had
something to do with the prohibition against graven images. It was like
a desecration of the body. There's all sorts of heavy talk about it in the
Talmud. I asked Dr. Kinsey [Alfred Kinsey, founder of the Institute for
Sex Research at Indiana University] what he thought of this, and he
said, "Oh well Groucho has to be defying his ancestors, even though
he's an agnostic."

In what capacity did you work with Kinsey?

Well, it was unpaid work. I was a friend of Dr. Kinsey. He heard on
the grapevine about *Fireworks* in 1947 and it had had very few showings
and they were private. He approached me wanting to buy a copy for the
Kinsey Institute for Sex Research in Bloomington, Indiana. I was very
happy to sell him a copy and then he said he would like to interview me
and he did one of his famous eight-hour interviews; in fact I think it
went over three or four days in which we did some each day. This was
for his *Sexual Behavior in the Human Male*. So, I was one of the thousands of people he interviewed for that. And I also helped find other
people for him to interview, because that was the way he worked. If he
met people he had confidence in, he asked them is there anyone else
who would like be interviewed. I got him people like Robert Duncan
the poet and about six other people.

You mentioned that you did Hollywood Babylon in America to make money, you were low on funds. How come you never decided to do that with a feature film that would be more accessible?

I've had several ideas that I've tried to promote along those lines including a movie based on *Hollywood Babylon*, a feature. But Ed Pressman, the producer of *Wall Street* and *Badlands*, took an option on *Hollywood Babylon* a couple of years ago. I submitted a script and all that, which is an attempt to do a feature version based on the stories in my book, but we can't agree on the budget. He did a film for David Byrne called *True Stories*, and his budget there was about 2 million, which considering the fact that it didn't require any production of any sort, it was just Byrne driving around in a small Texas town, it didn't involve any elaborate sets or costumes...that's the kind of money that Ed Pressman thinks he could risk because I'm not a bankable name, to use a cliché. But I need 15 million, so we're several million dollars over. It would be a dramatization of the stories, actually, very stylized. Ed said he's afraid of stylization, which he thinks would put people off. And I said, well, my books have gone into five or six editions, which would mean hundreds of thousands of readers. At least most of the people who read the book would want to see what I did with a movie of it. So, it would draw that kind of audience to start with.

Would you have wanted Liz Taylor to be in it?

(laughs) No! During her fat period, I wanted Divine to play Liz Taylor but Divine died on me.

I don't think Taylor would agree.

No, she wouldn't. She once caught a technician on the set of one of her TV movies reading *Hollywood Babylon II* that has her picture on the cover. This is authentically witnessed! She picked the book up and threw it across the set and said, "Don't ever let me see that book on this stage again!" And of course, she blew her cool...she has a temper...that wasn't the best thing to do because it got in the gossip columns and it even got in the *National Enquirer*, which got more publicity for my book!

Did you have anything to do with that picture on the front cover?

I selected it. I designed the whole book. The fellow that's with her in the shadows in the limo is the late Steve Rubell of Studio 54. And when they staggered out of the club at four in the morning they were obviously coked to the eyes. That was when it was daring or "in" to takes lots of cocaine. And there's a special room in the old Studio 54 which I think was in the basement (I never was in it but it was described to me) that was the VIP Coke Room. Those things now sound so quaint, like something out of the 1920s.

Could we print this?

(Laughs) Oh sure! Everybody is dead! Well, she's still around, but what can she do about it. It's well known that she and others going there were coking up and that was what got Studio 54 going. I hate disco music! It ruined the 1970s! It's such a bummer! I can't stand the beat or anything about it! Formless kind of music that goes on for twenty minutes. Donna Summer and all that! It just poisoned the 1970s!

Is there any music you like today? When you made Scorpio Rising you used a lot of music from the period like the Angels ("My Boyfriend's Back") and Elvis? Anything today you would use in a movie?

Well, you're putting me on the spot. Not really. They called me the Godfather of MTV, like putting pop music and images together. But I actually despise MTV. The Fine Young Cannibals made a video that is a frame by frame copy of *Scorpio Rising* at certain parts. And instead of stealing my ideas, if they had approached me and said, "We'd like to do it and here's a handsome fee or something, or even real money," I'd be tempted to do it unless I absolutely hated the music and thought it was trash. But it's much cheaper just to rip me off. There are a few things in the last five years, for a while I liked the satirical songs of Weird Al Yankovic.

Why did you move back to California?

I moved back here because I was living in New York for seven years and decided to leave after the third mugging. That last mugging took place in the vestibule of my apartment building at 4 o'clock in the afternoon with people walking by. I was calling for help while I was being beaten to a pulp and people walked by and looked like, "Oh, look there's a dog doing doo-doo on the sidewalk." They were that indifferent to it, which is also against the law in New York because you're supposed to pick up after your dog. Well, that was the third mugging and it wasn't like I was going around the docks or the piers after midnight or something in dangerous places. These all occurred around 91st and 1st Avenue, the area where I lived on the Upper East Side. And I decided I'd have to be an idiot for spending any more time there. And it was getting too expensive to live in New York, even though the difference is actually pretty slight between here and there. But I'm basically a Californian even though I've lived about half of my adult life in Europe. But I'd never consider myself a New Yorker; I was just a visitor there.

Where in California are you right now?

I live in the city of Hollywood, right in the middle of the old city, about a mile from where Valentino is buried in Hollywood Cemetery. It's near the old RKO studios which are on Gower and Melrose. I live in the area between Santa Monica Blvd and Gower; it's off Vine Street, which is now about 90% Mexican, mostly illegal. It's not a desirable neighborhood but my landlord is now Sampson De Brier whose is now 81. He was the star of *Inauguration of the Pleasure Dome* which was filmed in his house which is still here behind my house. He's my landlord.

What is your fascination with these Hollywood icons like James Dean and Rudolph Valentino?

I have one of the largest private collections of objects connected with Rudolph Valentino. I've also seen a lot of his films, studied a lot about him, and I'm supposed to do a picture book for his 100th birthday in 1995. I have a lot of unpublished pictures of him. I hope it'll happen; I'm still shopping around for a publisher.

I'm interested in human beings who have charisma and he had charisma. I see it, and I'm not the only person who saw it in him. Even though some of the films have silly plots, whatever he had comes across and I'm interested in that kind of human being, whether they be male or female. Clara Bow is another person who I would have loved to have worked with. She had incredible electricity.

You seem to have a fascination with the 1920s.

It was a period when creativity and individuality were still possible in Hollywood even though people like Irving Thalberg were imposing the production line, factory system on the creativity. Thalberg is revered as some kind of genius or something but he was actually a genius at getting creative artists to toe the line and he invented the re-take. He would say, "This won't go with the public, go back and re-film this ending" and so forth. And he ruins artistically many magnificent films (I've read the original scripts), you know very commercially successful films that didn't offend the public. The happy end, things like that. Softening the end so people didn't go out in gloom or tears.

Thalberg cut up Greed, didn't he?

Yeah, he was responsible for that, as well as Louis B. Meyer. They both hated Stroheim and felt that he was wasting their money.

Is there a complete copy of Greed or is that lost forever?

It can safety be assumed to be lost because if a print hasn't surfaced in all this time, I knew von Stroheim in Paris and I said, "Why didn't you take home a print?" and he said, "Well, it wasn't my property! I was too honest to do that." Because this physical film was owned by MGM.

Was he very heartbroken over it?

By that time in his life, the last ten years, he had other problems, like cancer. Everything had fallen into an ironic perspective. He said Hollywood had killed him. He was a wonderful man.

What was the connection between Preston Sturges and Aleister Crowley?

Oh, his mother is Mary D'Este Sturges who co-authored several books with Crowley. Her name is on *Book Four* and two or three others. She was Crowley's mistress in the 1920s during the period when Crowley was living in Cefulu in the Abbey of Thelema, and Preston Sturges grew up with Aleister Crowley as a surrogate father and babysitter and disciplinarian and so forth, or lack of disciplinarian. Crowley's name in his diary for Preston was The Brat, and, apparently, he was very much a smart aleck and almost uncontrollable, running around naked and all that. Actually, that was encouraged, lack of clothes. Peeking in while people were making ritual love and things like that.

Has any of this manifested in Sturges' films?

Oh yes, I think his type of cosmic irony and humor. You see Crowley was very much a humorist. It comes across in Preston's work and I asked Preston if there was any connection between his work and Crowley's humor and he said, "Well, actually we were like cats and dogs at the time." You see, he was a difficult child. At other times, Crowley would tell him dirty stories and such, fairy tales made sort of naughty, more than naughty. One time, Crowley told him a famous fairy tale called the "Yellow Dwarf into the Purple Dwarf," which of course is the phallus. That's the type of thing that Crowley would do.

So Crowley's had an influence on his films?

Yes, in anarchy of his upbringing. I mean, he was a brilliant child, he had a very high IQ and Crowley recognized that. But when he dubbed him The Brat, he...it was like having some little wild animal running around doing things like interrupting his meditation. (Laughs) It was almost like a little elemental demon of some kind. Yet at the same time he loved the kid. Crowley could be marvelous with children when he wanted to.

Did Crowley like Hollywood films?

In Crowley's diary, during the last few years of his life, Rene Clair's film called *I Married a Witch* with Veronica Lake showed up in England and Crowley liked it very much. He wrote several pages about it in his diary. During the 1920s he wrote several film scenarios, particularly one called Spaghetti, which was obviously influenced by Mack Sennett. It was a wonderfully visual comedy, all the humor told visually. But none of these were ever made of course.

But Jane Wolfe, who was a Hollywood actress who played Mary Pickford's mother in *Rebecca of Sunnybrook Farm*, and they had a scheme to write some film scripts to raise money. Nothing ever came of it.

What do you think of Hollywood today? Where would a Kenneth Anger find a place in Hollywood?

I came back here hoping to find a place for at least one feature film, which would be *Hollywood Babylon*. That was because I didn't go after them which is something I said I would never do but they came after me. My conditions were unacceptable; in other words, I had more money than they were willing to risk. People said, oh how lovely you have Ed Pressmen, one of the most respected producers in Hollywood today who did films like Walker and Wall Street and Conan the Barbarian (laughs), you know he's had a pretty good track record. And I said, well yes in theory but in actual practice we can't agree on a budget and he's not willing to risk much money on me. He could be any other Hollywood producer as far as I'm concerned.

Are there any Hollywood directors you like working today?

Well, I'll always go see anything that Scorsese does. He's one of the few directors who admitted he was influenced by *Scorpio Rising*, like the use of pop music and so forth. I like the one he did with Jerry Lewis. And I never bothered to see his film about Christ. Somehow all the controversy kind of put me off.

Have you seen anything by David Lynch?

I didn't like *Blue Velvet*. I didn't like his use of what I considered to be my music! I wasn't comfortable with that film, I didn't care for it. I thought Dennis Hooper was horribly over the top and I found it almost unwatchable. That's just my gut reaction.

And Dune was so heavy, it had wings of lead.

But I'm glad to be back in Hollywood because there are a lot of people who are in their 80s and will soon be dead. People like Madge Bellamy, who was the female star of John Ford's 1924 epic *The Iron Horse*. It's really my last chance to talk to these people. For that I'm glad to be back.

Your current projects are Mouse Heaven and Gnostic Mass. Do you have information on these films?

Yes, *Mouse Heaven* is my study of the large collection of Mickey Mouse memorabilia which is owned by a man by the name of Mel Birnkrant. He lives in upstate New York and he's known among collectors as having the world's largest collection of Disneyana and everything pertaining to early Mickey Mouse. So he's very graciously allowed me to film his collection.

What I'm doing is filming very small dolls and wind-up toys, so it's going to take a number of years to finish. I've made innumerable trips to his home in Beacon, New York, which is across the Hudson from West Point but I can only film a few toys each visit because they have to be taken out of their glass cases (his home is like a museum). He's an active toy designer and often that entails working on deadline, so I can't do any filming when he's involved with one of these design projects where it might interfere.

It'll take a number of years to finish. The project is sponsored by J. Paul Getty Jr. who lives in London, and he gave me some seed money for the project.

What about the Gnostic Mass?

Well, that is something I've planned and have in script form; however, I don't have the needed funds for it. I can't start things until I have an adequate budget. What I used to do on my earlier films is just start when I had the fire of inspiration and then often run out of money and go through long periods of desperation trying to scrape up the additional funds.

Is that following the Gnostic Mass by Aleister Crowley as it's published in his Magick in Theory and Practice?

Yes, in fact it's to be a record of it. But it's filmed in such a way that it expands on the symbolism. But the actual mass with the various participants is filmed. That's the plan.

Is this going to be a synchronized sound film?

That will be my first! So, the first words that will be spoken in a film of Kenneth Anger will be the words of Aleister Crowley, which is fine with me.

Why are so many of your early films missing or not available?

Either because they've been genuinely lost or I feel there's something incomplete about them; either they lack a soundtrack or footage is missing and I don't feel there's any point except for an archives point of view. I wouldn't care to show them in public.

Were the very early ones more like home movies?

They're apprentice works. The films preceding *Fireworks*, I was learning how to work a camera, how to cut, all those things.

Did you have your own film equipment at the time?

Yes, my first camera was the Family Kodak camera that just had one lens and a wind-up motor. It was a good 16mm camera, sort of boxed, rectangle shaped, it's now an historical artifact.

Do you still have it?

No, unfortunately I don't. It did have the disadvantage that the motor would only last for so long, about half a minute. Also, the speed was just one speed, 16 frames a second, so my early films would be at that speed.

There are two films in your filmography that I would like to find out about. One of them wasn't even yours, it was a Stan Brakhage film called The Dead. Why is that listed in a Kenneth Anger filmography?

I guess it was a kind of parenthesis because I appear in the film. Actually, it came about because of me. I lived in Paris at the time, and one autumn afternoon I took Stan, who was a friend of mine at that time on a tour of the Pere-Lachaise cemetery where Oscar Wilde is buried and Sarah Bernhardt, it's very famous, very romantically gloomy interesting cemetery where unfortunately Jim Morrison is buried. Because his tomb has attracted all sorts of groupies and disrespectful fans who have written their names all over neighboring tombs and made a complete mess of the cemetery, it's a disgrace.

What happened between you and Mr. Brakhage that you're not friends with him any more?

Stan has very few of his old friends left; his character is so cantankerous and difficult that most of his old friends have dropped him. The friends who are as old as he is, are mostly ex-friends. I'm not libeling him; that happens to be a fact. We can respect him for what he did and everything but the basic thing is that he's very paranoid and he attacked me in writing in a Colorado magazine. It came out of the blue. He wrote an article that could have been penned by Anita Bryant. He called me an "enemy of the American family." And considering that I have been very kind to his family and given his kids presents on birthdays and things like that up to that point, I found this all baffling and unforgivable unless he was suffering from some sort of mental illness like Ezra Pound (laughs). And that was basically the point when I ceased being Stan Brakhage's friend.

What about the documentary about the Abbey of Thelema in Sicily?

The film may exist. It's the only film I ever made with an outside commercial sponsor. Most of my films I somehow managed to find my own funds or got assistance from the Ford Foundation or the National Endowment, etc. The sponsor for this film was a picture magazine in England which no longer exists, it's gone extinct. It was the English equivalent of *Life* or *Look* magazine and it was called *Picture Post*.

When I went to Sicily in the mid 1950s, just about the time that James Dean was killed (I was in Sicily when I heard the news) Picture Post sent a film crew down to photograph my discoveries in Aleister Crowley's villa. I had gone looking for it, I found it, it had been boarded up for thirty years, I tracked down the landlord, and got permission to get the keys and rent it for the summer. I scraped off the whitewash that Mussolini's police had covered up Crowley's erotic frescoes. I spent the summer painstakingly washing off this stuff to reveal these very interesting frescoes. Luckily they were painted with good quality oil paint so they survived the whitewash. The colors were absolutely brilliant and fresh.

After *Picture Post* came down, three issues, three successive weeks, featured my discoveries in the Abbey of Thelema. Of course, I didn't like the way they played it up because they said, "The Lair of the Wickedest Man in the World discovered" with stuff about sex orgies. There actually had been a few naughty details about the Abbey like Crowley's mistress having intercourse with a goat but basically it was all done in an artistic way. The paintings were similar to the paintings of D.H. Lawrence.

Do you have a collection of Crowley paintings?

Yeah, because of the people I knew in England who were friends of his, they bequeathed them to me when they died. Someday perhaps I could find the correct publisher to bring them out as a monograph.

This was called the Hulton Publishing group that published *Picture Post* and a dozen other magazines. They were all killed off in England by the television revolution, ironically enough. But they had a television sort of omnibus little program, sort of like *60 Minutes* which came down to make a documentary film about my work at the Abbey, my discoveries, my living there in this ruin. It is an interesting story and particularly since Crowley's popular reputation in England, especially in the 1950s was very lurid and he had died only a few years before when he had been in the headlines again. But on the condition that I said, "The only way I'm going to let you do it is that you allow me to direct it and cut it," and I had to fight for that. But I did get it.

When the company went belly up, I went to England trying to reclaim. It was shown on television in England, but it can't be located. I won't say it's destroyed, I can't imagine why they would do that, but it can't be located. I've searched quite extensively for it. It was in color and it was quite a beautiful thing. It was as close as anything I've done to a documentary because it was about a real…well, in that sense *Scorpio Rising* was also a documentary, about real people and real places. But I tried to give it as much of my poetic twist as I could. But it did have some narration, which is not a usual feature in my films at all; but that was a concession to the public.

Your films are very heavily influenced by ceremonial magic.

Yes well, particularly *Lucifer Rising*. *Scorpio Rising* has things like the Halloween party which has elements of things like initiation but that's all very ironical. Things like initiations into fraternities which often get out of hand.

The things in Scorpio Rising that I saw as magical were the montaging of the shots of what must have been from an old movie about Jesus Christ.

Yes, it was an educational production by a company called Family Films which still exists and makes Sunday school films for evangelical types.

Did they give you the rights to this thing?

No, they didn't! The title of the Sunday school short was delivered to my house by accident while I was cutting *Scorpio Rising* and I considered this such a fortuitous act that I said, Well, this is a gift from the Gods! And I kept it, and I had no flak from them for many years but at least 15 years after the film was made, Family Films sold this collection of films to the Lutheran church in Indianapolis and I got a letter from the church saying, "Well, we now own the copyright on these things and you can't use these clips!" But I defended it, I got a civil rights lawyer and I defended it on the right of...I said, "Well, this is a lousy film! It shows a simpering kind of ludicrous Christ and you should be ashamed to show such things to children, you know, in a Sunday school." And I said, "I'm suing for my editorial right of commentary!" And that's a constitutionally protected right, and the number of minutes I used in the film fit within that. And they backed down! I was worried because if they wanted to get really heavy with me they could have. Suddenly, I didn't hear anything further from them.

How did you get the rights to use the rock music, though?

In that case, in 1964 I got a rights clearance lawyer on Broadway, I think he was in the Brill Building. I cleared more than a dozen songs that were current that summer of 1963-64, pop tunes of that particular time. I cleared them through official channels and the clearance rights cost me at that time, including things like "Devil in Disguise" by Presley, $15,000 for a short, not a feature. If it had been a feature it would have been another ballgame. The budget for the film itself came to about $8,000. I'm talking in terms of 63, not today. So it was very hard for me to scrape together the additional money for the rights. But I wanted to use the music; the music was all around me when I was filming that summer. It was the summer before JFK was shot, that was sort of...America changed when that happened, the mood of the whole country. Then the Beatles came in. Then American music for quite a few years there took second place after the inundation of the Beatles.

Was Scorpio Rising filmed in Coney Island?

Filmed mostly in Brooklyn. I never would have made it if it wasn't for the kindness of another filmmaker, Marie Menken, who had a penthouse apartment in Brooklyn Heights with her husband Willard Maas. During the six months that I was involved in the making and cutting of the film I was their houseguest and I'm very grateful to them for it.

I was Marie's guest, not Willard's, Willard's another filmmaker and professor at that college on Staten Island. I don't know if you know this, but Willard Maas and Marie Menken are the models for the characters in *Who's Afraid of Virginia Wolfe* and they were friends of Edward Albee, who wrote the play based on them. George is Willard Maas.

That must have been quite a trip living with them!

Well it was, because they would get drunk every single weekend, on purpose. It was like a ritual and I was their referee. I could have written a play about them too, considerably rougher than the Albee play. Particularly when they went out onto the 15th floor roof...she had two dogs, Blackie and Whitie, these enormous Irish wolfhounds, and these marathon battles would reach their climax between three and six o'clock on Monday morning when they had to clean up their act and look forward to going to work—Willard worked for *Time* magazine. And a couple of times they would climb up on the parapet which was about four feet tall and about a brick wide on the edge of their terrace and push each other back and forth like Punch and Judy. But since they were both heavy set it was more like Tweedledum and Tweedledum. They would chase each other around this narrow parapet, a drop of fifteen floors, hurling insults and sometimes throwing liquor bottles at each other, with the dogs barking furiously.

What was going through your mind at this time?

I was really there to protect Marie because she was afraid of Willard. The two dogs were supposed to protect her as well. They bit him occasionally. Suddenly, I realized if I intervened between them, I'd be the one over the edge and falling 15 floors. And they'd be up there looking down at me falling. My other function was as an official voyeur. They were putting on this Punch and Judy show for me.

A lot of people talk about the music in Scorpio Rising and the ironic use of music. Even further, the juxtaposition of these songs, which are sounding quite superficial, like "My Boyfriend's Back" by the Angels but when juxtaposed to these images take on a much deeper meaning and that behind the humor there is something else going on.

They were very carefully chosen. I didn't actually ever cut it with the Mickey Mouse effect when you're cutting to the actual beat of the music. But the way I cut it they fit, and I knew I wanted to use that music. You see, in "My Boyfriend's Back" the female singer is saying, "You better watch out, because you've been treating me bad and now he's going to get you!" So, there's that implied menace in the song. And most of the songs have a kind of double edge.

The images as well. You're cutting back and forth between Brando and the bikers and then Christ and the disciples, so there's almost different planes of reality going on: the pop image and the archetype of that image going on behind it.

Absolutely, it fell together in a sort of magickal way. I didn't have enough money for a work print and I directly cut my color master and practically every original cut is what ended up in the film. I didn't fudge and re-think and re-cut and all that.

I think it's a very mystical film on a subtler level than Lucifer Rising which is more overt, largely because the juxtaposition of these images are almost like showing occult correspondences between the pop images and the religious images.

I think that's true. And there are a couple of esoteric nuns who have shown it to their students. I'm quite amused that they found their own interpretation of it. And they found that there's interest there.

Have you spoken to your brother and sister lately?

No, I haven't done so in about twenty years and that was because of a dispute in which they succeeded in cheating me out of my third of my family home which was worth a lot of money because it was a view lot on Pacific Palisades on the same street as Ronnie Reagan's house with a terrific view of the Pacific Ocean with a beautiful sunset every night. But I was out of the country and they somehow got me declared... that I lost my rights to my third of the house which was left to me by my mother. They ended up selling the house and I never got anything. I could have sued them in court, but it seemed so sordid to sue my own brother and sister. They were always my enemies.

You've called your brother a war criminal?

He was. Strategic bombing in the Vietnam war. He's retired now in San Diego county where all the right-wing people retire. My brother and sister are both heavy into the right wing of the Republican party. And on the few occasions when I DO vote, I usually vote Democrat. You see, I'm an anarchist and an occasional Democrat.

I've noticed when we anarchists do vote, we usually vote Democrat.

Well, we don't seem to have much of a choice.

With special thanks to Robert Carobene.

First published in two parts in *Behutet: Modern Thelemic Magick & Culture*, Issue 27, Autumn 2005, and Issue 28, Winter 2005.

J. G. Ballard: An Appreciation

"Fiction is a branch of neurology: the scenarios of nerve and blood vessel are the written mythologies of memory and desire."

—J.G. Ballard

Introduction

Working quietly over the last forty years from the domestic seclusion of a London suburb, J.G. Ballard has proven to be one of the world's most imaginative and thought-provoking writers. His books are primarily known to readers of science fiction, but he has produced work that crosses many boundaries, borrowing from and blending several genres, fusing action adventure with hard science, psychiatry with surrealism, and postmodernism with pulp narratives. His stories, often hallucinatory or dreamlike in character, are futurist predictions of where technology, media and the internal logic of our own suburban landscapes may be leading us. Ballard has described his mission as writing "a mythology of the future," and that is about as accurate a label as you can give to his collected works.

To a mainstream audience, he is the author of *Empire of the Sun*, a novel about his wartime experiences in China, and *Crash*, a puzzling and disturbing novel about the sexuality of car crashes. Both have been made into Hollywood movies, the former to great acclaim by Stephen Spielberg in 1985 and the latter by David Cronenberg in 1995 amidst a controversy that resulted in the film being banned from certain parts of London. Both films have done justice to the source material, mixing

Ballard's authentic poetic sensibilities with the highly individual visions of their respective directors. Hopefully, the films have helped his books find a new generation of readers.

Ballard has never stayed within the perimeters of his chosen professions. As a medical student in Cambridge, he looked at the dissected corpses upon which he labored with the subconscious fascination of a Surrealist poet. In *The Kindness of Women*, he wrote, "I held her dissected hand, whose nerves and tendons I had teased into the light. Its layers of skin and muscle resembled a deck of cards that she waited to deal across the table to me." As an RAF pilot-in-training, he was more concerned with the dream of mass atomic destruction than the craft of flying: "The mysterious mushroom clouds . . . were a powerful incitement to the psychotic imagination, sanctioning everything."

Likewise, as a science fiction writer, he shied away from the usual trappings of the genre. Missing are the spaceships, galactic empires, and imaginary fantasy worlds with their elven kingdoms and fanciful histories. Also gone are the alien races, the flying saucers and mutated atomic monsters so prevalent in the science fiction of the 1950s when Ballard got his start. Instead we are treated to a poet's vision of a haunted world. Though still essentially grounded in science fiction (his future technologies and ecological disasters are unsurpassed in the genre), reading one of his books is like falling into the interior world of a Surrealist painting.

Ballard often said that the main difference between a Surrealist landscape and one painted by a classical artist is that the Surrealist landscape is lacking the element of time. Whereas the scenes depicted by Rembrandt, for example, are always very explicit about time—the light of the sun penetrating the picture in such a way that you can always pinpoint the time of day—a landscape by Ernst shows a place where the element of time has been extracted. Ballard has tried over and again not only to portray these timeless landscapes (often needing to destroy civilization to bring them about in a way that makes narrative sense), but he has shown his main characters suffering from a time extraction that is very real.

From *The Atrocity Exhibition*:

> Dr. Nathan passed the illustration across his desk to Margaret Travis. "Marey's chronograms are multiple-exposure photographs in which the element of time is visible-the walking human figure, for example represented as a series of dune-like lumps . . . Your

husband's brilliant feat was to reverse the process. Using a series of photographs of the most commonplace objects-this office, let us say, a panorama of New York skyscrapers, the naked body of a woman, the face of a catatonic patient-he treated them as if they already were chronograms and extracted the element of time." Dr. Nathan lit his cigarette with care. "The results were extraordinary. A very different world was revealed. The familiar surroundings of our lives, even our smallest gestures, were seen to have total altered meanings. As for the reclining figure of a film star, or this hospital..."

The virus in *The Crystal World* that is destroying the African jungle is not a conventional virus, but one which freezes matter into a timeless state:

Radek paused, collecting his energies with an effort. "Tatlin believes that this Hubble Effect, as they call it, is closer to a cancer than anything else—and about as curable—an actual proliferation of the sub-atomic identity of all matter. It's as if a sequence of displaced but identical images of the same object were being produced by refraction through a prism, but with the element of time replacing the role of light."

The infected jungle landscapes he describes in *The Crystal World* are worthy of a painting by Max Ernst, who transformed the Arizona desert with the keen eye of a timeless visionary. No wonder many of Ballard's early paperback collections of stories feature cover paintings that depict Tanguy-like amorphic blobs floating on the fused sands of psychic landscapes. What Ballard wrote was more like a Surrealist painting in prose, visions of vast subconscious shifts and the intersections where they touch the perimeter of conscious reality and every day life.

LIFE

James Graham Ballard was born in Shanghai, China in 1930, where his father ran a textile firm. He was raised in the International Settlement amidst a discordant atmosphere of privilege, poverty and warfare. When he was seven, the Japanese invaded China and violent battles were fought in the outerlying suburbs. Ballard's family lived in their middle-class homes under a darkening sky, waiting for the war to close in them, watching their swimming pools drain and their Packards sit motionless in the driveways while artillery shells and stray bombs invaded their private world.

His parents remained in the city up until the Japanese occupation and scenes of apocalyptic devastation were daily fare for young Jim: tours of battlefields where mutilated bodies lay twisted in the mud, savage attacks on the Chinese populace by the brutal Japanese military, the omnipresent threat of arrest and death. After Pearl Harbor, the International Settlement was occupied by the Japanese and by 1943 the British living there had been relocated to a prison camp eight miles from Shanghai. This was the camp, with its swampy canals and malarial mosquitoes, that was recreated in the novel and subsequent film *Empire of the Sun*.

After the war, Ballard moved to England, a country that was as alien to him as any distant planet. He claims that he suffered a culture shock that he has never recovered from, moving from a volatile world of warfare, death and political upheaval to one of bourgeois comfort, complacency and boredom. He attended Cambridge, where he took up medical studies in a bid to become a psychiatrist, but after a few years of studying what he considered to be the interesting parts of medical studies (anatomy, physiology and pathology—disciplines that would surface and resurface in all his later fiction), he decided he wanted to be a writer. In the late 1940s and early 1950s, he wrote a few unpublished works that were highly experimental, largely influenced by the Surrealist movement which he had discovered and regarded as one of the most important art movements of the twentieth century.

Soon he took an impulsive about-face and went to Canada with the RAF to learn how to fly. He realized that the atomic age would give birth to armies of airborne young men driving their bombers deep into the far reaches of the world, carrying their destructive cargo, and he wanted to be a part of it. In spirit, he was embodying the farcical moral contradictions of *Dr. Strangelove*, a movie he would come to admire. His internal visions of world destruction were paving the way for the later creative projects that would destroy the earth over and over again in a series of powerful short stories and novels. It was at this time, hanging out with the RAF pilots in Moosejaw, Saskatchewan, that he discovered in the racks of the airbase cafeteria the science fiction magazines that were to dominate the next few decades of his life.

His early short SF stories, published in magazines such as *Science Fantasy* and *New Worlds Science Fiction*, are at once both firmly rooted within the genre, consciously imitating other authors (Jack Vance in "Passport To Eternity," Ray Bradbury in "The Drowned Giant"), and at the same time transcendent of the traditional formulas through their use of experimental techniques such as Surrealism. Of course he was not the first to mingle sci-fi with experimental fiction; William Burroughs had just published *The Naked Lunch* as he was coming of literary age, and Ballard openly admits that the Beat writer had a mesmerizing influence over him.

By the time Ballard published his first few novels, he had emerged as a mature voice with strong literary roots. In the jungles, deserts and drowned cities, in the legions of pirates, marooned scientists and obsessed adventurers that litter his early work, one can feel the dark landscapes of Joseph Conrad and the whale hunters of Herman Melville. It was recognized almost immediately that he was a skilled and visionary writer who, like his Surrealist predecessors, painted detailed, realistic and vivid scenes of inner landscapes and haunted dreams.

WORKS

His early novels, *The Wind From Nowhere* (1962), *The Drowned World* (1962), *The Drought* (a.k.a. *The Burning World*, 1964) and *The Crystal World* (1966), form a tetralogy of the elements (Air, Water, Fire and Earth respectively), each depicting the destruction of civilization by some elemental disaster. The ice caps melt in the wake of a solar storm, heating up the planet, and the cities of the earth are flooded; a virus that crystallizes time spreads through an African jungle, etc. Ballard's post-apocalyptic universes are stages upon which he plays out the future evolution of human consciousness. His main characters are often scientists who are possessed by the changed landscape of the earth, living in the ruins of cities, usually in abandoned hotels, ignoring danger for the sake of following some change that is occurring deep in their psyches. Ballard's characters often prefer the destroyed civilizations in which they live over the living cities in which they grew up. Their changing psyches adapt to the landscape:

> Sometimes he wonders what zone of transit he himself
> was entering, sure that his own withdrawal was

> symptomatic not of a dormant schizophrenia, but of
> a careful preparation for a radically new environment,
> with its own internal landscape and logic, where old
> categories of thought would be merely an encumbrance.
> (*The Drowned World*)

After a respectable and successful decade as a science fiction writer, Ballard produced two novels that challenged his reputation and placed his career on a different path. Perhaps he was outgrowing his need for science fiction contrivances and returning to his roots of experimental fiction; perhaps he was working through a personal crisis sparked by the accidental death of his wife; but his work grew considerably darker. Indeed, his later work has occasionally been labeled perverse, pornographic and even psychotic.

The first of these "new" novels was *The Atrocity Exhibition* (1970). Fragmented, obsessive, cryptic, and openly inviting disgust, this novel comes as close as modern fiction can to the paranoid-critical vision of a Dali painting. Contributing to the reader's dark experience are atrocity photographs from Hiroshima, dissection films, and Vietnam medical textbooks filled with photos of body mutilations. Though morally repulsive and almost completely incoherent, the novel still manages to paint a beautifully disintegrated vision of a future in which mental patients and their doctors piece out the fragments and images of World War III through their artwork, obsessions, and billboard advertising.

In his quest to write a "mythology of the future," Ballard was pilfering the present for the icons, images and psychologies that were emerging from the media consciousness of pre-World War III culture. A novel like *The Atrocity Exhibition* is arguably a sane response to the moral dilemmas being raised on an almost daily basis by the psychotic media in the late 20th Century. In any event, there was nothing to compare with it: Ballard had finally arrived at an authentic and original voice.

Crash (1971), his next novel, was turned down by many publishing houses, one rejection letter even going so far as to recommend that the author seek out psychiatric help. Indeed, when Vaughn the perverted motorist stalks Elizabeth Taylor in an attempt to die with her in a head-on collision, and treats colored photographs of crash-induced body mutilations like pornography, one certainly can wonder about the motives and even the mental stability of Ballard himself!

But despite the outcry from the critics, Ballard knew exactly what he was doing with his dark creations. Few noticed that the author had brilliantly singled out car crashes as an iconic image that dominated our media. In the early 1970s when the novel was written, pornography was just becoming an above-ground phenomenon with its own industry, and film audiences were demanding car chases and their subsequent crashes in ever increasing quantities. The relationship between eroticism, sex and car crashes was a pulse in our contemporary culture that everyone felt but few consciously noted.

Throughout the 1970s and early 1980s, Ballard returned to more traditional storytelling with *Concrete Island* (1974), *High Rise* (1975), *The Unlimited Dream Company* (1979) and *Hello America* (1981). Never abandoning the themes he had begun exploring, however, these novels continue a fascination with deviant psychologies (the tenants of High Rise turn their own apartment building into a primal battlefield in which they are trapped like the schoolboys of *Lord of the Flies*), destroyed worlds (*Hello America* portrays a United States after its destruction by a rampaging desert), and new sexualities (the air pilot of *The Unlimited Dream Company* reduces the London suburb in which he crashes into a Edenic paradise through the strange medium of his own semen). Ballard even boldly continued his car crash theme in *Concrete Island*, in which a motorist crashes into an enclosed wasteland between highway ramps and becomes trapped in an odd landscape of abandoned basements and destroyed cars, populated by a homeless duo whose psyches have adapted to the surreal world of their concrete prison.

In 1984, he published *Empire of the Sun*, an account of his childhood experiences in China, and his first novel lacking any elements of the fantastic or the outré. This is not to say, however, that he made a radical departure from his usual thematic material. Empire of the Sun and its sequel *The Kindness of Women* (1991) lay bare in clear fashion the autobiographical details that have helped shape his weird world of violent accidents, destroyed cities and dead astronauts. Like Dali, whose various autobiographies have helped many viewers demystify his strange paintings, these two novels reveal the meaning and motives behind many of Ballard's recurring themes and on-going obsessions. They have also helped solidify his reputation as a major Western novelist with serious intent beyond the usual trappings of the science fiction genre.

Since his mainstream success with *Empire of the Sun*, Ballard's novels have not yet returned to the harsh realms of science fiction from which he had gained his reputation and fame, but all still mirror themes, images and concerns from his earlier work. In *The Day of Creation* (1987), a stretch of African desert is transformed by an underground river accidentally brought to the surface by a mentally deteriorating English doctor. The Doctor, who identifies himself with the river, has much the same obsessiveness of the survivors of Ballard's earlier destroyed cities. He takes off along the river on a stolen ferry, journeying towards its source in a voyage that echoes Joseph Conrad, Herman Melville and the dream-like Venusian landscapes of William Burroughs' *Nova Mob* novels.

Rushing to Paradise (1994) likewise doesn't fail in painting the familiar but strange beauty of Ballardian landscapes, here a former nuclear testing site in the South Pacific. An ecologist who fits Ballard's often used description of "a beautiful but insane woman" takes over the radioactive atoll to establish her own destructive utopia. Published at the height of the literary trend for political correctness, the novel manages to mock and offend both environmentalism and feminism, reminding us that throughout his entire career, with his on-going obsessions with car crashes, dissected female bodies, nuclear explosions, death and mass murder, Ballard has never exactly been a politically correct voice in literature.

Running Wild (1989) and *Cocaine Nights* (1998) are both mystery novels that focus on bourgeois communities where the wealthy raise their families in an atmosphere of security cameras, cafés, cinemas, and housing estates, all in suffocating isolation from the outside world. Reading these novels, one is reminded of *High Rise*, an earlier work that probes the notion that the architectural landscape which we create can transform our inner life and alter the course of our psychic evolution, sometimes in dangerous and very destructive ways. One is also reminded of Ballard's own experiences in the International Settlement of Shanghai, where the aristocratic European elite lived in their luxury housing, maintaining their lifestyle amidst the turmoil and death in the outer lying suburbs.

Conclusion

What is one to make out of all this? To enter the Ballardian universe is much like approaching the collected works of Dali, a painter whom Ballard greatly admires and whose sensibilities have helped shaped his novels. Like that difficult painter, Ballard has littered his work with discrete images that recur and permutate to form a repeating music-like pulse: drained swimming pools, flooded or burned cities, concrete aprons and highway exit ramps, billboard hoarding, the haunted bodies of dead pilots and astronauts, silt-choked deltas, infested swamps and jungles, deserted military bases and hotels, psychiatric homes and the empty corridors of abandoned hospitals, rotting vegetation along tropical coastlines, crashed cars, buried airplanes, lonely beaches and the rusting gantries of empty space centers, high rise apartments, suburban streets and highway clover leafs, World War II bunkers and weapons ranges.

It is often hard to navigate through these recurring images and leit-motifs. Perhaps the whole of his work must be read to appreciate the depth, range and logical patterning of his constructions, from his earliest short stories to the recent *Cocaine Nights*. If one were to plunge directly into his most fragmented and troubling novel, *The Atrocity Exhibition*, or his most psycho-pathological, Crash, one would be adrift in a deep-ening ocean as destructive as the lagoons that flood the city of London in *The Drowned World*. But seen as a unified whole, his work emerges as a powerful meditation on the human consciousness—often brutal and morally repulsive, politically insouciant, at times even nihilist; but unwaveringly focused on the rare and poetic beauty existing in the pro-found light that his characters feel radiating from the fabric of matter itself. His novels and short stories, written over the span of forty years, lay bare our interior worlds and our relationship to the ever-changing physical world and the landscapes we create upon it, be they Pacific atolls blasted by nuclear testing, the patterning of highway ramps that stretch across our cities, the luxury communities we build to shield our-selves from our primitive natures, or the rivers, deserts or solar flares that destroy our civilizations and force us to bind to a new covenant with the sun and the earth.

First published in *Behutet: Modern Thelemic Magick & Culture*, Issue 34, Summer 2007.

THE LOGOS ARRIVES IN BERKELEY

Philip K. Dick's Four Novels of the 1960s

I am only a very minor science fiction writer"

—Philip K. Dick, 1958

ONE

It seems that every couple of years there is another announcement that the writer Philip K. Dick has finally arrived at literary respectability. It's hard to piece together a chronology of these past moments when our perceptions of PKD shifted from him as an obscure sci-fi writer with a cult following to a literary voice recognized and lauded by the mainstream, much in the same way that it's hard to remember all the singer-songwriters who were touted as the New Dylan. When we examine the growth of Phil's lasting influence on popular and underground culture over the last half century, it's a little hard to see those proclamations as anything more than an attempt to push a new collection of essays, or to accompany the umpteenth release of another cut of the movie *Blade Runner*. It got to a point where I just ignored all the hype, as big of a Dickhead as I am. After all, Steven Spielberg's *Minority Report* wasn't exactly a turning point for those of the Phil Faith—it just meant that book sales would spike for a while, new short story collections with a special movie cover would appear, and we'd have another big glitzy Hollywood-produced DVD on our hands that once again failed to capture what we like so much about Phil's self-created universe.

But with the publication of the Library of America's *Philip K. Dick: Four Novels of the 1960s*, there is now proof that Phil has taken his place amongst the ranks of Hemingway, Faulkner, Melville and Henry James. No longer do you have to go to the stigma-riddled science fiction section to obtain copies of Phil's paperbacks; you can lift your head up with snobbish pride and go straight for the dark blue spines on the Library of America shelf, skipping past the writings of George Washington and Thomas Jefferson, blowing a raspberry at the complete poems of Hart Crane, grunting in disappointment at the literary essays of Edmund Wilson, looking down with elitist disapproval at Jack Kerouac's Road novels, and finally lay your eyes on the large cursive "Dick" that leaps off the binding with dignity and, most importantly for Phil wherever he may be, literary respect. It feels quite different from any previous re-release, and it even has a silken bookmark down through the middle. Classy stuff, indeed. And long overdue.

After all, the Library of America was started in 1979 to preserve and promote the finest flowerings of American literature, even serving as a sort of "director's cut" edition of each of the books, correcting texts, restoring lost and excised passages, and allowing recognized literary experts to choose their works with an authoritative voice that collectively commands, like the Council of Nicaea, what stands in the American canon, and what does not. The world of science fiction has always been the Dead Sea Scrolls of the literati, committed to underground burial and studied in secret because it contained stuff that was too wacky and too threatening to the orthodoxy. So, this LoA edition feels like a Gnostic Gospel that has been finally approved by the Vatican for inclusion in the New Testament. Well, maybe not as Earth-shaking as that, but try telling that to a Dickhead.

Appropriately enough, the collection was edited by the ultimate Dickhead, Jonathan Lethem, a writer whose own career went from science fiction to mainstream success with his two great novels *Motherless Brooklyn* and *The Fortress of Solitude*. In his own right, Lethem is a phenomenal writer, possessed of an authentic voice that perfectly integrates high-brow and low-brow culture. Lethem as a teen absorbed the pulp magazines and the classics, was passionate about Marvel Comics and Italo Calvino, *Star Wars*, and Jean-Luc Goddard. It was with a great sense of discovering a long lost twin that I read Lethem's account of his trips to the Thalia on the Upper West Side to sit through numerous viewings of *2001: A Space Odyssey* (was I in the same audience?); and as I poured over his passionate essay on the Eno-Fripp collaboration *No Pussyfooting*, it was as if I were reading my own autobiography about the downtown New York cultural landscape of the early 1980s (I went to Stuyvesant High School). I wondered if Jonathan and I ever bumped into each other at Bleecker Bob's shopping for Pink Floyd bootlegs or rushed the stage together at a Marvel convention to get Stan the Man's autograph on a copy of Spider-man #121. And, of course, I must have brushed shoulders with him in the Fourth Avenue book shops, hunting for old editions of *Ubik* and *The Three Stigmata of Palmer Eldritch*, two PKD novels represented in the LoA edition. If there was any man I trusted to present Phil to the world in the way that he deserved, it was Lethem, and his name on the Library of America edition was just as sellable to me as Phil's!

In a way, this edition is the culmination of all of PKD's dreams. When Phil was growing up in Northern California in the late 1940s and early 1950s, he saw himself as a serious novelist. He read through James Joyce, Homer and Shakespeare like every dutiful aspiring writer, hung out with poets and other writers (including Anthony Boucher and Robert Duncan), and wrote passionate true-to-life novels like *Voices from the Street* (the title itself a tip of the hat to Joyce's Ulysses), but there was little hope, beyond incredible luck, for him to be properly published. Before long, he discovered that he could write science fiction stories for the pulps, see his name in print and pay his rent (barely) all at the same time. He could have boasted about being published, but Lawrence Sutin, the author of the amazing biography *Divine Invasions: A Life of Philip K. Dick*, reports that Phil, painfully shy that his stories were published in pulp magazines, tended to downplay his achievements to his friends. At the time he died, he had written 11 mainstream novels (*Confessions of a Crap Artist* and *The Broken Bubble* being two of his best), most of which saw publication during his lifetime, some of which are lost.

So why is the Library of America edition so valuable to his literary reputation even though it contains exclusively science fiction novels? There is nothing in the PKD mythos that says that his mainstream novels were better or less personal than his sci-fi efforts. He did write some piss-poor pot boilers along the route, but even his most cartoonish effort, his most sci-fi pulp piece of fluff, still contains ideas and elements that bemuse the mind and challenge consensus reality in a clever and often funny way. And even in his most comic book-like story, the human element is always present, the solid psychology of the characters and the bits of pieces of Phil's own life that he peppered about in all his tales. Only in a PKD novel do you have a psychologically accurate depiction of a marriage in the midst of collapse in the same plot line as an encounter with a Ganymedean slime mold. It's almost as if Phil was saying, "I want to write about my life and my interior experiences, but I'm stuck in an episode of *Star Trek*. Fuck it! I'm going to do both!"

And that's not a bad thing. Phil wanted to portray true-to-life portraits of troubled people in the Bay Area of California during the 1950s with a penetrating realism. But he was also struggling with a mental disorder that made him vulnerable to lapses of reality, and his Fox Mulder-like obsession with his dead twin sister forced him into religious and mystical areas that were a bit too far-out for novelistic realism. Science fiction, then, seemed like the perfect vehicle in which Phil could explore that more spiritually troubled side of himself with unfettered indulgence, examine his own mystical interpretations of the world, and even work into his stories a form of psycho-therapy, sort of an attempt to carve literary art out of pulp. And Phil's mystical ideas are just as potent and valid a subject of literary art as any psychological realism. So, while it would have been nice to see a celebration by the Library of American of four of his mainstream novels, Lethem chose wisely to go down the science fiction route, and he couldn't have made better choices. The four novels represented here are amongst Philip K. Dick's finest.

Two

In 1958, Philip K. Dick, a young writer not yet thirty years old, moved with his wife Kleo out of his native Berkeley to Point Reyes Station where their marriage promptly fell apart, not the least because of the presence of a new woman in Phil's life, Anne Rubenstein. Despite the fact that Anne had three children from another marriage and there was the thorny issue of how to leave his wife for another woman, Phil carted his Royal Electric typewriter, his massive vinyl record collection and all his pulp science fiction magazines over to Anne's and initiated divorce proceedings against Kleo.

At first the new relationship seemed a success. Phil became quickly domesticated, started to raise farm animals, took an active role in the lives of the three children, and even began observing strict nine-to-five hours for his writing. Still, he was embarrassed at being a paperback science fiction writer and deeply yearned for mainstream literary respectability.

Just a short car ride away was San Francisco, where the Beat Generation had set up their blossoming literary movement, largely centered around the City Lights Bookstore where Phil occasionally sojourned to buy paperbacks. He took no social advantage of this, however, and was further disillusioned when Harcourt Brace, after a promising overture, turned down two of his mainstream submissions. In a fit of inspiration that may have been mingled with desperation, Phil wrote one of his best novels, the stunning *Confessions of A Crap Artist*, more than a little based on his own marriage to Anne. His mainstream style had matured beautifully, and one can see in *Crap Artist* the great artist that could have emerged if Phil had only become, in his early 30s, a full-time literary novelist, unburdened by the need to write genre stuff to put food on his table. Sadly, the novel wouldn't get published until 1975, but fortunately for the rest of us, the best of his science fiction was yet to come, inspired by a strange and unexpected book: the four-thousand-year-old Chinese Oracle called the *I Ching*.

Roughly translated as *The Book of Changes*, the *I Ching* is a series of mythic-poetic interpretations of 64 symbols called hexagrams that represent all the possible combinations and permutations of yin (male active energies) and yang (female passive energies) forces of the universe, providing a divinatory roadmap through the complexities of events, often helping the human mind to perceive patterns of order in chaos. The relationship between patterns and randomness is reminiscent of the philosophical implications of quantum mechanics, something Phil, as an avid follower of science, would have been aware of. More than a few modern books on what is called the New Physics have drawn the parallel between the teachings and experiences of the *I Ching* and those of quantum physics. *The Tao of Physics* by Fritjof Capra is one such popularized introduction to the subject, drawing connections between the mind-bending discoveries in the sub-atomic cloud chambers of modern science and the ancient writings of the Chinese mystics.

Back in the early 1960s, Philip K. Dick had no such books on a New Age shelf of his local bookstore to guide him, but he may have been aware of the works of composer John Cage, who had been using the *I Ching* and an emphasis on randomness as valid ways to make choices in composition. Often Cage would use the *I Ching* to guide his composition as if the book was a living entity revealing patterns or anti-patterns that his own rational conscious-mind would not have done on its own. Phil also decided to use the *I Ching* to generate his art, and appropriately enough, he wrote a novel, *The Man in the High Castle*, containing characters who use the I Ching on a daily basis to interpret the events in the world around them.

The novel, the first in the LoA edition, takes place in a post-war world in which Germany and Japan have been victorious in World War II. The German Reich has occupied the Eastern United States and the Japanese have occupied the Pacific States. Within this world, a renegade novelist has used the *I Ching* to divine a possible alternative universe in which Germany and Japan actually lost the war. As a result, the novel is considered subversive and subsequently banned. While this seems, on the surface, to be a clever *Twilight Zone* plot, it is actually a bit more brilliant than that, which I simply can't explain too much about without giving away the ending. So even here, writing a sci-fi what-if story about Nazis taking over the country, Phil plunges head-on into mysticism and quantum theory.

For a long time, physicists were troubled by the growing evidence that the particles of matter and photons of light that were the subject of their scientific observations were not fixed entities in time and space. In fact, bits and pieces of the atom and quanta of light seemed to be probability waves that only took on solid substance when a human consciousness made a direct measurement. It was a disturbing hint that our own observations were creating, altering, or choosing realities. Einstein himself, reacting to the analogy of a multi-faced die being thrown and the result representing the reality that was created by the toss, retorted with his famous rejection of quantum physics: "God does not play dice!"

Einstein, himself a Princeton professor, died two years before a 1957 doctoral thesis in which a Princeton student suggested that the probability formula that covers all the possible states of a particle (including an infinite number of positions) were all true in multiple universes, and our observations and measurements merely filtered out just one of those universes to be objective reality. Our own consciousness may very well be choosing and creating realities from an infinite array of realities. There could be another universe where everything is exactly the same except for one single atom light years away that is in a different position, or another universe where everything is the same except talk-show host David Letterman is President. Only in science fiction could we even begin to explore the possibilities and implications of this hypothesis and what it suggests about how our own choices, both conscious and unconscious, are engaged in a creative and formative dance with chaos.

In some ways, this was a scientific justification of what users of divinatory systems like the *I Ching* or the Tarot have been saying for years. And to Phil, whose own inner suspicious sense of parallel universes must have been quite personal, the *I Ching* was revealing to him a Nazi/Japanese dominated universe that had split off from our own. It is to the credit of his genius as a writer and modern mythmaker that the novel also includes an extremely realistic depiction of what the occupation of the United States would be like, from a cultural and racial standpoint, as well as a military and political one.

The effect of the occupying Asians on the native population is subtle and complex. A lesser writer would have put in more overt racism and would have failed to understand the intricacies of the philosophical chasm between East and West, but Phil nails down the different paradigms of the Americans, the Japanese and the Germans, and the cultural clashes that would result when they come together in a battle to posses the world.

One of the main characters, an antiques dealer who caters to the Japanese elite by selling them fabricated artifacts from America's past, helps explore the nature of what is real and what is simulation, and how real the simulation can actually be. In a world about to explode with theme parks like Disneyland and the presence of media-created realities on television, Phil's insights into the reality of fakes in *The Man in The High Castle* is a brilliant complement to the greater theme of living in an alternative reality. If all realities are real, then all fakes are real as well.

Another plot element drawn from Phil's own life was the jewelry business started by Frank Frink, a Jew who manufactures fake antiques in the Bay Area. This was very similar to the business started by Anne Dick that served to supplement the couple's income since Phil's writing was bringing in so little stable money. Just as a next-door neighbor callously stuck one of Anne's attempts at beauty on a wall in his home as if it were a simple trinket, the Japanese client who inspects Frank's jewelry attempts to turn it into mass-produced junk.

A few years later, Phil was to write an essay called "Schizophrenia & *The Book of Changes*" in which he stated his belief in the veracity of relying on an Oracle for daily events. His conclusion was that the value of the reading was not fortune telling, but a meditation upon the energies at play in your localized situation and how it relates to a more general and cosmic relationship of energies. From this understanding of these complicated relationships, the reader can divine from the *I Ching*'s hexagrams a way to guide consciousness through the moment. But whoever would be addicted to such oracular revelations for every aspects of life, like using the *I Ching* for taking a bath or opening a can of tuna for your cat, would clearly be schizophrenic. Such is the fine line between mysticism and madness. Use it for the big questions only, he cautioned. One gets the impression that Phil had a lot of insight here because he had used the hexagrams for more than a few tuna can openings for his cat.

When the novel was finally published, the public enjoyed it as a clever political thriller with a fascinating alternate universe twist, but in a strange turn of events, the book was included in the Science Fiction Book Club and was ultimately awarded a Hugo as Best Novel of the Year. Phil, who had just had several of his mainstream manuscripts rejected and literally dumped at his front door, finally resigned himself to the science fiction ghetto and, fueled with the creative fires that leapt from his rocket-shaped Hugo, furiously wrote eleven novels in two years.

THREE

The Three Stigmata of Palmer Eldritch is one of Phil's best works but was produced during a period when he was trying to raise four children while barely holding on to a rapidly disintegrating marriage; in the midst of this chaos he somehow managed to produce eleven novels. It seemed a minor miracle that not only did the novels get produced, but Phil and Anne survived without killing each other.

It was during this period that Phil started to take drugs to both self-medicate his curious mental and emotional conditions as well as provide vision and inspiration to his fiction. The biggest price was paid in his marriage, and before long the constant arguing and intense unhappiness between the two led to Anne being hospitalized for mental illness. When she returned heavily medicated, Phil was inspired to include Anne as a character in several of his books. He began to doubt his own sanity but funneled this anxiety into his fiction. A mentally disturbed moment when Phil saw an evil face staring at him, filling him with a profound sense of fear, led to the character of Palmer Eldritch, whose name alone evoked the insane horror of an H.P. Lovecraft mythos creature. But to understand the way that Phil used his drug experiences and Anne's bout with mental illness, we must first take a look at the religious philosophy called Gnosticism, which was playing a larger role in Phil's life.

Gnosticism is a non-mainstream spiritual belief system that was, after many millennia, having more and more of a relevance for the generation caught up in the radical changes of the 1960s. Along with the ancient Chinese philosophy embodied by the *I Ching*, Gnosticism had come down into the modern world via the theosophical and magical societies of the Victorian Age and mystical writers like Madame Blavatsky (who first popularized the tradition of the spiritualist medium channeling an ancient Tibetan entity for spiritual wisdom) and Aleister Crowley (the ceremonial magician who had died in the 1940s but who shared a prominent place on the cover of the Beatles Sgt. Pepper's Lonely Hearts Club Band). While it is doubtful that Phil did a systematic study of either the theosophy of Blavatsky or the Kabalistic magic of Crowley, it is clear that Gnosticism came to him as an important step in his spiritual quest and not just a convention for his fiction.

Dating back to the time of Christ (some believe it predated Christianity and helps to explain that religion's origins), Gnosticism was practiced by a minority and often persecuted by the ruling powers, eventually almost completely suppressed by Roman Catholicism and, later, Islam. It was a strange syncretistic movement that centered around the belief that the material world was a delusion created by a Deity called, by some, the Demi-Urge and was inherently evil, separate from the spiritual world of the monadic God. This material world, it was claimed, could be transcended by Gnosis, or direct spiritual experience of the Divine. Although many different schools of Gnosticism existed, they all had in common a belief that the world around us was not the true divine world that existed behind the veils of matter. Like Morpheus of the film trilogy *The Matrix*, the Gnostics were offering us a way to wake up to our Divine selves and cast off the delusions of the Demi-Urge that keep us physically and spiritually enslaved to the material world.

In *The Three Stigmata of Palmer Eldritch*, povertized Martian colonists become preoccupied with Perky Pat Layouts, small sets representing penthouse apartments inhabited by a Barbie doll-like figure and her Ken-like mate. When combined with the use of a hallucinogenic drug called Can-D, these sets can give the colonists—who live in miserable hovels—the illusion not only that they are living in Perky Pat's luxurious apartment but actually inhabiting her perfect body as well. A crisis is sparked when Palmer Eldritch, a missing space adventurer, is rumored to be returning to earth after being stranded on Pluto. His new hallucinogenic drug, Chew-Z, takes the form of a mystical revelation and threatens to wipe Can-D off the market. A psychic war erupts that amounts to no less than a battle for human consciousness between Palmer Eldritch and the manufacturers of Can-D.

Personal elements are also present in the book. The couples who live upon Mars in their hovels, supposedly living in squalor and deprived of the luxuries of life upon Earth, do not resemble hardscrabble Depression-era farmers so much as they do middle-class Americans in their suburban housing developments, getting together to take drugs and enter the world of Perky Pat and engage in a mystical union with each other that also resembles the practice of couple swapping, another popular suburban middle-class pastime. Perhaps in the Martian couples there is more than a little of Anne and Phil Dick and their Port Reyes Station friends. Interestingly enough "the Hovel" was also the nickname of a small hut up the road from their house that Phil rented in order to have privacy for writing.

The novel is complex and suitably zany, leading the reader through a maze of psychic marketing men, talking suitcases that act as therapists, psychedelic Barbie dolls possessed with the ability to invade consciousness, imaginary drugs that change reality and identity, and communal hallucinations in which multiple people merge into one. In *Palmer Eldritch*, Dick not only focused on the mental illness issues permeating his failing marriage, but he also created a strange, surreal comical vision of Gnostic beliefs with all the trappings of science fiction.

FOUR

After Phil's marriage to Anne collapsed, he moved away from the tempting safe comforts of middle-class living and went back to Berkeley, where he plunged head-long into two self-indulgences: for one, close and frequent contact with the thriving science fiction community, enjoying friendships and parties with luminaries like Marion Zimmer Bradley, Poul Anderson and publishing icon Donald A. Wollheim. His other indulgence was to engage in serial monogamy. He met a string of women in succession, often falling in love immediately, often making them a bit frightened of his mood swings, his weird mystical bent on reality, and his unresolved emotional issues from losing not just his wife but four children he had come to love, including one of his biological own. By July 1966, he was married again, to his fourth wife Nancy, and he was also starting to take LSD and other drugs that were to characterize the counter-culture in the 1960s. His spiritual manias, often were mythic inventions based on his own mental instability, were also revealing to him powerful visions that shaped his fiction and helped to stamp his art with that unique flavor that to this day we call PhilDickian. Phil was a brilliant artist, and although he was almost impossible to live with and seemed to many around him as the most miserable man they ever knew, he was a walking example of Arthur Rimbaud's call for a "derangement of the senses" that every visionary has to create in order to get closer to his own true self.

During this period, Phil became close friends with Bishop James Pike, an Episcopalian minister who had gone off into some theological deep waters of his own when his son committed suicide and Pike started experimenting with contacting the son's dead spirit. Pike also took trips to the Holy Land in order to follow in the historical footsteps of Jesus, but with Gnostic twists. Pike was reported to have said, "If I were not a Christian, I would be a Jew. And if I were not a Jew I would be a Zororastrian!" a reference to a Persian religion based on the teachings of the Persian prophet Zororastra, or Zarathustra, a religion very Gnostic in flavor. The Californian Bishop, who was eventually to die of thirst in the Israeli desert after his car broke down, later become the main character of Philip K. Dick's last novel *The Transmigration of Timothy Archer*.

One of the interesting side-bars to come out of his friendship with Pike was Phil's reaction to the Bishop's search for life after death. Phil definitely took the more Hindu approach that the ego that we experience during this lifetime is an illusion that will be shed upon death, a moment when, he declared, the cards of reality will be revealed and the game will be dispelled. Truly in line with many mystical systems of thought, as well as the findings of quantum psychics, Phil believed reality to be something created by a consciousness that shields us from the "real" reality of the unmanifest. And with typical PhilDickian humor, he also revealed that if upon dying he turns out to be wrong, "I'll be content. I'll have no choice."

It was at this time that Phil wrote another masterpiece: *Do Androids Dream of Electric Sheep?* The novel, chosen by Lethem to grace the third slot in the Library of America volume, was the basis of Ridley Scott's film *Blade Runner*, perhaps one of the most famous media products associated with Phil's name to date. It is in this novel that Phil tackles the question of what it means to be human. The answer he provides is one of his most lasting legacies to our current age. In a world where machines, primarily computers represented in the novel by androids who are created to be worker-slaves for off-world colonies, are seemingly more human than humans, what is it that separates the human from the machine? Phil's answer is the ability to feel empathy for another being's suffering.

Here, the androids, known also as replicants, are distinguishable from other humans only through the Voigt-Kampff scale, an empathy test which poses questions largely concerning the suffering of animals. When Rick Deckard, a professional android hunter, is hired to track down and decommission (he can't use the word "murder") renegade replicants who have escaped their servitude and came illegally to earth, he fails to feel any empathy for the artificial humans that he tracks and kills, and doubts are raised about his own humanity.

For those who are familiar with the *Blade Runner* film and have never read *Do Androids Dream*, you are in for a surprise. While the novel provided the film with a basic plot-line and some characters, and while the world of the movie was so close to what Phil had visualized in his mind that he was in tears when he was shown a test reel of special effects by the studio, there are big differences, some of which are regrettable, but some of which were necessary for the powerful emotional impact of the film.

The religious movement Mercerism, left out of the film, is a Gnostic-flavored cult that also appears in Dick's short stories. Mercerism combines doubts about reality (Wilbur Mercer, whose presence is experienced in trance-like states by his followers, is rumored to be an actor in a television studio) with a subversive force, much like Palmer Eldritch and the *verboten* novelist of *The Man in the High Castle*. Followers of Mercer have their own empathy box whose handles they clutch to propel themselves into a virtual shared reality where they literally merge with the consciousness of Mercer, an old man who climbs a hill while off-screen tormentors hurl rocks at him. The practitioner feels the pain of the rocks and identifies with Mercer's suffering. While this is clearly a reference to the Christian practice of meditating upon the wounds of Christ, it is also a perfect image, both spiritual and material, of the ability to have compassion for another sentient being, an ability that separates the human from the machine, in Phil's estimation.

Phil loved animals and had a deep compassion for their suffering as well and *Do Androids Dream* portrays a world in which a great war has greatly reduced the animal population of the planet, causing humans to resort to android pets because the real animals are too cost prohibitive. In fact, the moral dilemma of Deckard is that he needs to kill the replicants for the bounty pay so he can replace his mechanical sheep with a real one. Deckard's merging with Mercer towards the end of the book, one of Phil's funniest laugh-out loud moments in all his novels, is replaced in the film version by a profound moment of beauty in which the android that Deckard hunts down allows his own bounty hunter to live because of the replicant's own awakened empathy.

Phil wrote *Do Androids Dream of Electric Sheep?* in the mid-1960s and it was published in 1967, the year of the Summer of Love and the high-water mark of the psychedelic counter-culture. It was one of his own crowning achievements, giving us a Gnostic myth about the modern age of spiritual machines that is even more relevant today than in its own time. However, the Philip K. Dick of the 1960s was to produce one more genuine masterpiece to cap off the decade: *Ubik*.

FIVE

In many ways *Ubik* stretches the definition of science fiction because there is really very little science in it, but there is plenty of mysticism. Phil's personal psychological issues, his unrelenting quest to make sense out of his own reality, his marriage problems, the low brow genre in which he was working, and his continual fascination with mystical texts make for a very strange mix of sci-fi entertainment, *Twilight Zone*-style plot twists, and obscure literary and mythic references. For that reason, it is surprising that *Time* magazine in 2005 hailed it one of the top hundred best novels written since 1923.

Just as *The Man in The High Castle* was inspired by the *Chinese Book of Changes*, and *Palmer Eldritch* and *Blade Runner* derived concepts and themes from Gnostic beliefs, *Ubik* derives its internal focus from *The Tibetan Book of the Dead*, otherwise known as *Bardo Thodol or Liberation*

Through Hearing In The Intermediate State. Essentially a collection of funerary rites, it is also a guide for the dead as they travel towards their next rebirth. The Bardo, or the state of consciousness in which they exist between lifetimes, is mapped out in the text. Meant to be recited by a lama over the body of the deceased, the text guides the consciousness of the dead person through the various experiences starting from the moment of death and culminating in its attraction back to the cycle of birth, life, death and rebirth.

In this brilliant novel, a group of people witness their employer, Leo Runciter, die in an accident, and subsequently believe that he is communicating to them from beyond the grave. Soon, they are shocked to realize that it was *they* who have actually died, and Runciter is attempting to prolong their ties to the real world through the use of a drug called Ubik. As Runciter guides his dead employees through a weird landscape that seems to be moving backwards in time, their life-forces gradually begin to diminish. Only Runciter's mystical Ubik, which he introduces into their hallucinations in the form of spray-paint and snake-oil unctions, can keep their minds and souls from completely dissipating into the void.

Many of the mind-bending and reality-altering conceits that one finds in a Philip K. Dick novel, narrative and thematic elements that made him so endearing to his readers and have ensured him a rabid sub-culture of readers for many decades, are now commonly accepted by mass audiences in popular movies such as *Fight Club* and *Being John Malkovitch*. *The Eternal Sunshine of the Spotless Mind*, in which two lovers are having their consciousness altered to forget each other, mostly takes place inside their heads while their memories of each other and realities they have experienced together begin to disintegrate. Obviously, this film owes a lot to Philip K. Dick and *Ubik*, both of which have cast a long and lasting shadow on our culture.

And what a beautifully written book it is, as witness this passage:

> We are served by organic ghosts, he thought, who, speaking and writing, pass through this our new environment. Watching, wise, physical ghosts from the full-life world, elements of which have become for us invading but agreeable splinters of a substance that pulsates like a former heart.

What a fitting summary of it all: "served by organic ghosts who pass through this our new environment." How much truer now in an age of cyberspace than in 1969. And Philip K. Dick, the canary in the coal mine, was one of the first to sense it.

SIX

Our culture has grown fascinated by Philip K. Dick, simply because the energy, the vision and the philosophical underpinnings of his major works are becoming a significant presence in our collective psyche. Witness the popularity of the film *The Matrix*, with its insistence that we are not living the reality that we think we are, that behind the veils of matter is a sinister conspiracy to control not just our bodies but our very consciousness. There is also the growing concern over the rise of computer intelligence as evident in the paranoid teachings of David Icke, the predictions about the future of computers by Ray Kurzweil and movie franchises like *The Terminator*, where machines attempt to enslave the human race. All the anxieties, fears, and mystic visions of how cyber-technology will change not just our bodies but our minds, force us into a new definition of reality and a new definition of what it means to be human, which was the very theme of *Electric Sheep/Blade Runner*. That may explain *Blade Runner*'s continuing popularity and the non-stop release of more and more director's cuts and final editions of the movie.

Yet, the disturbing inner experiences of Philip K. Dick, from his early struggles with the feeling that he didn't quite fully exist, to his later Gnostic visions of sharing a consciousness with a first-century Christian and his pronouncement that an alien intelligence was downloading information into his head through a nocturnal pink beam aimed from an orbiting satellite called Valis, seemed to many at the time to be a sign of religious mania at best, mental illness at worst. Phil suffered alone back then, trying to work out his own sanity in his writing and to find a relationship with a woman that would accommodate such a lofty and unsettling spiritual quest.

In today's world, however, what he went through is more commonplace. Starting in the 1970s, with a vast explosion of new age psychics claiming to channel extraterrestrial beings, long-dead philosophers and saints, angels and gods, including Timothy Leary, who wrote about his Sirius Transmissions, leading one to suspect that despite the veracity of some of these prophets' claims, one or two higher chakras that are in the process of becoming more active than ever before. New creative spiritualities seem in the process of creation all the time, incorporating the findings of eastern mysticism, western magic and quantum physics, turning the wacky world of the particle accelerator into a mainstream post-modern philosophy, much to the chagrin of many dogmatic atheists and religious fundamentalists.

Further, computers, the Internet, radical new inventions like nanotechnology and the evolution of super string theory are leading many more of us to radical interpretations of reality and, for some, new types of religious experiences on the edge of cyberspace. While in his time, Phil wrote furiously to pay his rent bills, in today's world, Phil may very well be revered as a cyber-shaman and be writing screenplays for the Wachowski Brothers.

So here in the Library of America's *Philip K. Dick, 4 Novels* of the 1960s, we can clearly see the first awakening of the Gnosis in the genre writings of the early 1960s. Thanks once more to Jonathan Letham for bringing this wonderful collection to our attention and for choosing the novels wisely for his fellow Dickheads.

First published in *The Journal of Advancing Technology*, Volume 8, Summer 2008.

DO COMPUTERS DREAM
OF SILICON SHEEP?

*Philip K. Dick and the Anxieties of the
Spiritual Machine*

In April of 2000, Bill Joy, the co-founder of Sun Microsystems, published an alarming article in *Wired* magazine entitled, "Why the Future Doesn't Need Us." He had just met Ray Kurzweil, an accomplished inventor whose musical synthesizer had changed the face of popular music and who was a pioneer in the field of speech recognition technologies. Kurzweil had recently published a book, *The Age of Spiritual Machines*, and after engaging the author in an animated discussion about the book's darker implications, Bill Joy was deeply disturbed.

The Age of Spiritual Machines (1997) is a wide sweeping vision of how computer technology is expected to evolve over the next few decades, vividly showing how Moore's Law, the tendency of data density on a computer chip to double every 18 months, predicts that at some point in the near future, a single computer chip will be more powerful than a human brain. Kurzweil speaks of self-replicating nanobots, human minds downloaded like software into android bodies, and the fleshy human body itself slowly being infiltrated, like the Borg of *Star Trek*, with machine implants, fuzzing the lines between humans and computers. Our own machines that we have built to extend our senses and increase our own intellect's productivity, Kurzweil says confidently, will soon be waking up to consciousness and will begin the construction of even more advanced machines. Robot factories will not only build further robots, but design them as well, and not always without well-being in mind. By the year 2099, there will be no clear distinction between humans and computers. Intelligent machines will by then be spiritual machines and legally recognized as a species in their own right.

While this all seemed like something out of a Hollywood movie to be enjoyed with a bucket of popcorn, Joy was deeply distressed. For all of his career he had taken pleasure in being part of a new paradigm, of watching computer science evolve from its geeky hacking culture that created early operating systems, programming languages, and cheaper, more powerful computer chips to the big industry of today that is improving life for so many workers and providing vast improvement to home entertainment. "But while I was aware," he wrote, "of the moral dilemmas surrounding technology's consequences in fields like weapons research, I did not expect that I would confront such issues in my own field, or at least not so soon."

While Kurzweil, in interviews, seemed calm and collected about the dawn of the spiritual machines and the surrendering of much of what we consider to be our humanity, Joy was walking about in a panic, saying, "Does anyone else here think this is strange and dangerous?" In fact, he would have to look no further than the literary genre of science fiction, which has been openly exploring anxieties related to the surrendering of our humanity to our own machines for almost a century.

Since its inception, science fiction has been relegated to the ghetto of pulp magazines and reduced by Hollywood into action-adventure space operas. It has always struggled to maintain its literary respectability and promote understanding of its social import. Hugo Gernsback, publisher of *Amazing Stories*, the first monthly magazine of "scientifiction" which premiered in 1926, demanded hard science at the core of each story. But there has always been a trend towards commercializing the formula, dumbing it down for mass consumption. Despite Gernsback's efforts, the genre found its biggest audience in adolescent males and was quickly laughed off as "Buck Rogers stuff." It found its marketing niche on the same book shelves as dime store detectives, gun-toting cowboys and masked superheroes.

Yet, from the beginning, the genre attracted many highly intelligent and visionary writers who weren't as interested in the swashbuckling adventures of planet-hopping Errol Flynn-types (as in the popular stories of Edgar Rice Burroughs), but instead in the potentials and possibilities inherent in the rapid exponential growth of technology and all the ethical, moral and philosophical quandaries that surround it. In the 1920s, when writers like Jack Williamson, Murray Leinster, Edmond

Hamilton and E.E. "Doc" Smith were pioneering new directions in storytelling, the world around them was changing at a breakneck pace. The world saw a dynamic expansion of technology and waxed optimistically that the human race can be improved through technology, while at the same time suffering tremendous anxiety over the potential misuse of the very machines that were improving our lives.

For this reason, early science fiction novels and short stories show both an enthusiasm for, and a dread of, new technologies. The classical image of the mad alchemist who "tampers in God's domain" and pays the price for his trespasses, portrayed to perfection in Mary Shelley's *Frankenstein*, was transformed, by the early 1900s, into the materialistic scientist who was so obsessed by his new invention (be it an invisibility ray, a time machine, or a way to harness nuclear power) that he could not see its physical dangers or moral implications. It's not surprising then that many of the sci-fi classics have dealt with the profound ethical dilemmas posed by technologies that paradoxically hadn't been invented yet. When a deep space mission goes awry, or a new invention that promises to improve the human race turns out to be deadlier than any war weapon yet invented, the writer is merely imagining a possible future technological dilemma. The sheer fact that we can imagine these machines and spaceships taking over our lives is enough to fire the creative juices and makes for great drama. The best science fiction writers have always been "canaries in the coalmine," small creatures whose early death signaled to the workers that the air in the mine shafts have turned rank and deadly.

The anxieties and unconscious dilemmas of science fiction writings have always been an almost Freudian journey through our collective anxieties and dilemmas, arrayed in the trappings of entertainment. Contemporary political situations like the Red Scare and the Cold War, and controversial technologies like the atom bomb and the computer have all fed the story mills of the sci-fi imagination. While many sci-fi writers appeared on the surface to be just "spinning a good yarn," even the *Star Wars*-style space operas played upon our fears of evil empires and our growing dehumanization, as typified by Darth Vadar, the man who lost his humanity to robotic body parts.

War of the Worlds (1897) depicted a Martian race that was amorphous and blob-like, hardly a threat to our military, until they constructed their tripods and heat rays and blew away human civilization like it was a cluster of insects. The H.G. Welles novel came across almost as a pre-echo of the violence of World War I, where tanks and airplanes appeared for the first time on the battlefields and showed the world how the horror of the Martian Invasion was possible within our lifetime, brought about by our own machinery.

Early science fiction also reflected the fears of being industrialized and the radical social conditions that were being created from the factory system. Early depictions of robots showed them as clanky, humanoid hunks of metal filled with gears and wires and often reflected the largest fear of the industrial age: the revolt of the worker. Machine age industrialists were witnessing the advent of communism and other socialist movements that threatened something they did not count on, that the workers who were enslaved in their factories were actually human beings with needs and feelings and, perhaps worse, the resources to organize resistance. The deepest source of this drive towards resistance was the manner in which capitalist industrialism dehumanized the worker, threatened to turn him into a cog in a machine, a robot if you will, and no doubt sci-fi literature dealt with the consequences of that dehumanization.

This is not to say that science fiction was a politically revolutionary movement—but it did tend to explore the fundamental anxieties that the machine age had produced. Early masterpieces like Karel Capek's *R.U.R.* (1921) and Thea Von Harbou's *Metropolis* (1927) did overtly carry the robot-as-worker metaphor into the political arena and showed us the various dangers of mechanizing life itself in the name of progress and profit.

Over the decades, the source of the various anxieties that gave formative shape to the sci-fi plots and dilemmas has changed in variance with the shifting of the historical, political and social forces. The "evil empire" sci-fi of Flash Gordon paralleled the rise of Fascism in Europe; the adventures in the deserts of Mars or the jungles of Venus gave some insight into the dynamics of civilized man's exposure to Paleolithic cultures in the Congo and the Amazon, not to mention the empire's fear of losing their colonies to revolt. By the 1950s the menace of the Pod People in *The Invasion of the Body Snatchers* (1955) played upon our fear of the communist infiltration of our own society, or in preference to a non-political interpretation, our xenophobic fear of the outsider invading our communities. No longer was the menace a force from another planet, or another alien or robotic race; now the danger was inside of us, biding its time in our own neighbors and spouses. The horrors of radiation unleashed by the military and the nuclear scientists gave rise to giant monsters and mutations.

And then came the threat of the artificial intelligence, the computer that considers itself superior to the human race. In the super computer Colossus and HAL9000 of *2001: A Space Odyssey*, we have villains to rival, if not exceed, any of Flash Gordon's antagonists. In both stories, the computers built by humans to improve our world and drive our spaceships suffer acute paranoia and lash back at humans like they were unwanted factors in a new world order. But still, the computer was exterior to ourselves, bland voices emerging from voice units, cold calculating circuitry that couldn't possibly feel or relate subjectively to the world. All we have to do to release ourselves from the tyranny of these machines is to pull their plug and watch them go as lifeless as a television turned to a dead channel.

Paranoia reached its extreme in Philip K. Dick, a prolific novelist and short story writer who, unlike other sci-fi writers who focused on social and political anxieties relating to technology, showed us those anxieties as they manifested inside our own consciousness. Dick suffered many neuroses and phobias, one of which was the frightening feeling that he didn't exist, or that the world around him was so unstable that he would doubt the input of his own senses. Over many painful decades, he wrote haunted novels that had a long-term influence on the genre. His dark footprints can be seen in films such as *The Matrix*, *The Truman Show*, and *Videodrome*, all films in which the main character's sense of reality has been severely ruptured, and they struggle to determine what is real and what is fabricated by some inhuman machine with its own agenda.

In more than 30 novels, both sci-fi and mainstream, and over 100 short stories, Dick explored the possible disintegration of his own consciousness. He considered a fundamental question in conquering this breakdown to be: what does it mean to be human? In his novel *Do Androids Dream of Electric Sheep?* (1968), he presents his clearest answer while further exploring the crisis of technological consciousness that now obsesses our sci-fi imaginations and made Bill Joy feel so uncomfortable while reading the words of Ray Kurzweil more than 30 years later.

The dystopic world of *Do Androids Dream* is one that would appear in various forms in many Philip K. Dick novels throughout the 1960s.

In this novel, a mad rush to colonize Mars has left the earth under populated by genetically inferior people, a global catastrophe that radiated the cities and killed off most of the animal life on the planet ("Strangely, the owls died first"), and the earthly survivors are left to wallow in the advance of the slowly building garbage and useless rubble that advances in the cow catcher of entropy. Popular demand amongst the Martian colonists has encouraged the robotics industry to produce Nexus-6, a brand of android that is indistinguishable from human beings but can labor without complaint and give human beings an unprecedented period of leisure. Nexus-6 is illegal on Earth, where the earthlings must labor under harsh radioactive conditions.

Rick Dekkard, a bounty hunter contracted by the police to terminate rogue androids who have escaped to Earth, is very much an everyman wage laborer, hustling to get contracts so he can raise the money required to buy a real animal, instead of the android sheep that he covets on his rooftop garden. As the novel opens, Dekkard's wife is chastising him for being an assassin, which he denies, since the androids he terminates are not human in the first place and therefore his work is not murder. In short, he does not recognize the essential selfhood of the androids and rationalizes that the major difference between humans and androids is that the "andys" do not have the ability to empathize with the suffering of other creatures. In fact, the only way to legally prove that someone is an android, short of testing their bone marrow, is to apply a complex psychological examination that tests their neuromuscular reaction to tales of animal suffering.

From the beginning we are confronted by the essential problem in the novels of Philip K. Dick. What is it that makes us human? We can distinguish ourselves from the lower life forms, we can differentiate between us and apes, but when confronted with a machine that can think as well if not better that we can, who is to say that we will still maintain our status as the dominant species. The answer is plain and simple to Dick: Empathy. In many of his novels, and in anecdotes drawn from his real life, Dick had a fondness for the soulful presence of animals and had occasion to feel great pain while witnessing an animal's suffering. In witnessing a pet cat's death by cancer, for example, Dick no doubt found a good deal of discomfort in other people's blank reactions to the feline's suffering. To Dick, the difference between humans and machines must be the ability to feel empathy for the suffering of others.

The humans who have stayed behind on Earth, some because they could not afford to emigrate, others because they have been deemed inferior (or "chickenheads") by the government, are struggling to maintain their humanity. It is implied that those who have emigrated to Mars have given up their humanity, surrendered the all-too human drudgery of their every day life to the androids, given up the remote possibility of clean air and healthy landscapes for artificial machine-driven ecosystems. Back on Earth, the remaining humans, fighting against the onslaught of kipple and fearful of the superior race of androids, so much so that they have been outlawed on Earth, have adapted a quasi-religious practice to keep touch with their gradually diminishing humanity: Mercerism.

Mercerism is practiced by the followers of Wilbur Mercer, who may or may exist. He can only be "accessed" by a Mercer machine, a virtual reality box that plugs the person who is gripping its handles into a weird Golgotha-like landscape where a robed bearded figure, Wilbur Mercer, is ascending a steep mountain slope. From out of eye range, hostile "others" are hurtling rocks at Mercer, and when they contact him, the user of the Mercer-box feels the pain as if the rock had hit him personally. Mercer's climb up the hill is experienced, both visually and physically, by everyone who is currently using the Mercer machine, and all those people are locked together in an empathic experience of shared suffering.

Dekkard, skeptical of his wife's use of the Mercer machine, is experiencing a loss of his own empathic abilities, and knows very well that this ability to experience another's suffering is what makes us fundamentally human and distinguishes us from artificial life. During the course of his bounty-hunting day, a gross and obnoxious TV comedian named Buster Friendly, one in a series of on-going Dick characters who resemble the 1950s celebrity Jackie Gleason, threatens to expose Mercer as a fake, an actor in a studio. The suspicion that Buster Friendly is a pawn of the aliens who have an acute self-interest in destroying Mercerism, haunts Dekkard's day.

In 1997, more than thirty years after Dick wrote *Do Androids Dream*, Ray Kurzweil published *The Age of Spiritual Machines*. Previously, Kurzweil had been loudly applauded for predicting the World Wide Web. For this reason, his new book was much anticipated. Although the book relaxes the reader into an amusing and comical romp through an imaginary future, presenting us with fascinating portraits of what everything, from virtual sex to schoolroom education tools, will be like in the near future, the predictions within the book seem to have much deeper and very frightening implications.

After going through the sharp exponential curve that computer technology is experiencing, plotting the number of integrated circuits that can be burnt onto a chip, and predicting at which point the computer chip will exceed the thinking power of the human brain, Kurzweil, who had been a pioneer in popularizing artificial intelligence, speculates about the ethical, psychological and spiritual implications of computers that can think better than us. He raises our awareness that by the time this happens, computers will be so integrated into our daily lives and into the infrastructure that makes up our societies and the frameworks of our welfare, that the Turing Test (measuring the ability of a computer to fool a human into thinking that he is interacting with another human) will cease to have any relevance: computers and the range of technologies that will evolve from computers, tens of thousands of daily devices and components of our financial, political, military, and physical life support systems, and the infiltration of nanotechnology into our physical bodies to control health, disease, and aging, not to mention to enhance our senses and eliminate such common handicaps as blindness; even computers that will paint pictures, write poetry, solve ethical problems, evaluate law and compose music so much better than us.

Unlike the Hollywood movies and popular novels of the last few decades that dramatically portrayed the rise of the computer threat, Kurt Weill's dark vision is even darker when you consider that the rise of computers as an independent form of life that is superior to mankind does not necessarily have to be a bad thing. Only our egoist clinging to our present consciousness would insist that no matter how good a computer gets at composing music, it was Beethoven's soul and his spiritual life that made his symphonies great, something a computer can never have. But, it can be argued, the machines will have souls, no more or less, perhaps more than human beings. Perhaps the outcries of the human soul for God we hear in the Ninth Symphony will also be heard in a piece of music composed by some android two hundred years from now. Whether the composer is a consciousness conceived in silicon or carbon, what difference does it make? And if we are ultimately little more than organic circuits and electrified protoplasm ourselves, why should that be superior to the liquid filled quantum computers that will come to dominate the planet?

In fact, as Rick Dekkard goes hunting down the androids so he can collect his bounty money and buy a real flesh and blood animal, he confronts the intelligence and the apparent inner aesthetic world of the androids. The Nexus-6 is the latest and greatest, more human than human, and not even the Rand Corporation who built them understands the inner dynamics of their own subjective world. Dekkard confronts one of the aliens while she is headlining an opera event and is seduced by the powerful music and the android's very human singing of Mozart's *The Magic Flute*. Later, in an art museum, he contemplates why so many androids are drawn to the works of Edvard Munch, "The Scream" in particular, which he assumes is a painting that reflects the inner feelings of an android. Predictably, in a very painful turnabout, Dekkard starts feeling contempt and indifference towards the other bounty hunters and more unconscious respect for the machines he is contracted to destroy.

The thought that our own technology can one day awaken to consciousness and experience a subjective reality replete with emotions and survival instincts, not to mention intellectual ambitions and concern for their own quality of living, is one that looms over our rapid progress throughout both the machine age and the electronic age. As I have shown, being dehumanized by our own machines is what has caused the fundamental anxieties at the heart of our science fiction literature. We are afraid that our technology, given the freedom to choose its own destiny, will proclaim human beings inferior and worthy of either servitude or destruction. One has to think no further than the Nazi Concentration Camps, where a "master race" attempted to exterminate, like insects, a seemingly "inferior race." It is not that the Nazis lacked compassion as human beings, but simply that they did not think that human compassion applied to their enemies because their enemies were less than human. It doesn't take much leap of imagination to see a race of sentient computers that do not consider humans as equal partners in selfhood and treat us in much the same way that humans have treated cattle and horses, perhaps even attempting a human genocide. Perhaps it is no coincidence that Dekkard's target android gains his empathy with a German opera, and a German painting; or that in the film *Blade Runner*, adapted from Dick's *Do Androids Dream*, the leader of the renegade Nexus-6 group is played by a blonde actor with distinctive Aryan features, and is prone to the same flights of poetic fancy that seized the Wagnerians when they waxed lyrical about their tribal warrior ancestors.

But can a machine ever compose Beethoven's Ninth Symphony? Kurzweil goes to great pains to present us with examples of art created (generated?) by computers, including some paintings, poems, and even a short story. At first blush it seems incredible that a program can produce works with such emotional impact, but even Kurzweil admits that the programs needs to be feed input from existing painting, poetry and literature techniques that have been created by humans. The question is whether a computer can ever write a poem simply out of the sheer joy and love of the language, or to express some inner state of being. When a monkey in a laboratory can be trained to punch symbols representing happiness at seeing a banana or sadness at the disappearance of a loved one, we have no doubt that the money is experiencing happiness or sadness. But when a computer writes a poem about joy and love, we still believe that it is learning mechanically from input culled from thousands of the greatest poems by human beings. However, the original poets like Shakespeare or Byron also were fed enormous amounts of input from the poets who came before them. So, what makes their poems more authentic than one generated by a computer program?

Perhaps, Philip K. Dick is telling us that while Shakespeare felt despair over death, the computer can merely mimic it. On the surface, a Turing test will fail to distinguish between a Shakespearian sonnet about death and a Microsoft one; but some unforeseen Voigt-Kampf test will be able to distinguish the micro fluctuations in the computer's neuromuscular apparatus and see that the emotional thoughts that are mimicked in the poem are not reflecting in the computer's bioreactions. Or will it? Dekkard never could foresee that he would feel more empathy for the androids than the humans, and one of us could never foresee that under certain circumstances, we would feel love or creative respect for a silicon-based machine run from a computer chip.

In *The Matrix Reloaded*, Neo takes a tour of the vast mechanical underground of Zion, the city of humans, and reflects on how the colossal engines and computers that run the city are more powerful than the humans who no longer even know how the machine works. The humans in Zion simply cannot shut the machines off even if they wanted to. What would happen to a nation like the United States if we lost the computers that ran the power plants that delivered the heat and electricity, if we lost the chips that ran the automobiles and the transportation systems, if we lost the circuits that ran the factories that produced the food and purified the waters. Even if, after a period of readjustment, we managed to rebuild an industrial agrarian society, similar to the one we had a hundred years ago, how many people would die in the interim, and once such a replacement society was established, how would the technology of a hundred years ago feed, house and keep warm the vast population that we have today? Is it true that the machines and computers have permeated so deep, that we are no longer independent of them, that we are now committed to this exoskeletal nervous system we call technology?

Ever since the publication of his book, Kurzweil appears to be calm and collected about the possibility that we will gradually merge with our machines and become some form of hybrid race, that human consciousness can be downloaded into chips and put into other android bodies, that our culture, our flesh, our minds will gradually be replaced, one circuit at a time, by computer components, that the very concept of a computer itself will be deconstructed and redefined by incorporating our very humanity and our very consciousness into a new vision of what it means to be human and what it means to be a machine. While the various pundits of our scientific communities debate over whether Kurzweil's visions are even technologically possible (and there is considerable debate), we are faced with a very ponderous dilemma, one that has already generated vast anxiety as reflected in our current science fiction trends: the fact that we cannot shut off our computers without bringing human society to a crashing halt. As Kurzweil points out, even 30 years ago that wasn't the case. Now it is.

It seems that by turning off our machines, we turn off ourselves.

First published in *The Journal of Advancing Technology*, Volume 8, Summer 2008.

THE HISTORY OF SCI-FI PULPS

Philip K. Dick experienced the youthful discovery of science fiction in 1941 while he was still in the seventh grade. His eye had been caught by the title of a new magazine called *Stirring Science Stories*, a very short-lived publication that was edited by Donald A. Wollheim. Mistaking the magazine for a popular science journal, young Phil was surprised to find that it contained fiction that not only provided adventure but was also grounded in scientific principles. He had long been an avid reader of L. Frank Baum's fantasy novels about the Land of Oz, but those tales had never relied on much science to explain their imaginary conceits. It was *Stirring Science Stories* that opened up a whole new world that was his to explore for the rest of his writing career.

Dick became a fanatical collector of science fiction pulp magazines; in particular Wollheim's *Astounding and Unknown*. He fed himself on a diet of Isaac Asimov, Robert Heinlein, L. Ron Hubbard and A.E. Van Vogt, all of whom were giants of the Golden Age of Science Fiction, and their influence on Dick was deep and lasting. Later in his youth, he would discover Greek philosophy, ancient Gnostic libraries, James Joyce and Shakespeare; but it would be the bug-eyed monsters and space pilots of the sci-fi pulps that formed his first literary sensibilities.

In this respect, he wasn't alone. Science fiction enjoyed a lasting presence in the early American literary scene, but it was generally disrespected by the mainstream markets. Up until *Amazing Stories* premiered in 1926, science fiction did not have its own specialized magazine, and the young boys who were naturally attracted to the genre were often seen within their own communities as lonely science nuts, often pursuing their literary interests where they could, in Jules Verne and H.G. Wells books, in a few scattered publications like *All Story* or *Argosy*, and in the fantasy fiction of Edgar Rice Burroughs. The fans were an alienated group of people, and it came as no surprise that when the science fiction pulp market exploded, they reached out for each other through the magazines. Editors often ran contests for new stories by fans, conventions were organized throughout the country and the home addresses of many famous writers were published so the fans could correspond with them directly. The networking of science fiction fans was quick and explosive, leading to the establishment of a new genre with its own magazines and movie serials.

Unfortunately, by 1941, science fiction had already earned a reputation for cheap writing and adolescent adventure with more of an emphasis on alien monsters and ray guns than any real science. To make things worse, some of the best science fiction was often presented in magazines with lurid cover depictions of aliens and spaceships that boasted sales but often betrayed the quality of the writings inside.

But originally, science fiction had a noble intent: to educate a general reading public on scientific principles, as well as make speculative predictions of a social and technological nature through the agency of entertaining stories. It had enjoyed a long history in England and Germany and had nurtured the writing careers of Edgar Allen Poe, Jules Verne and H.G. Wells but it had curiously never given rise to a dedicated magazine or a generation of writers who specialized in the genre. Perhaps it was the giant leap forward in technology at the dawn of the new century that encouraged science to infiltrate fiction writing even deeper.

America at the turn of the century was still a land of unbounded opportunity, where men like Thomas Edison and Nicola Tesla were changing the landscape of everyday lives with spectacular new inventions. Light bulbs, steam engines, telephones, airplanes and automobiles were powerful new agents of social change and stimulated the creative imagination of writers to predict future technological trends. Early American scientific fiction was a reaction to industrialization and the machine age, most evident in the very popular Frank Reade stories that ran from 1876-1898 and featured a mechanized man powered by steam, giving literature its first robot, as well as its first long running series. Inventors were often portrayed as comical characters alongside their offbeat inventions in stories that poked fun at technology and warned about our growing dependency upon it. Popular interests in physics, astronomy and the occult sciences inspired many stories of sub-atomic journeys, fantastical visits to other planets and tales of time travel, mesmerism and antediluvian races living under the earth. But there was always the emphasis on scientific explanation, often downgrading the literary value of the story by pausing the action for long-winded scientific discourses.

The pulp magazine was pioneered by Frank Munsey, who during the period 1905-1911 published a wide range of scientific fiction in his *All-Story*, *Cavalier*, and *Argosy* magazines. The February 1912 issue of *All-Story* featured the first installment of a novel called *Under the Moons of Mars* by a new writer whose pen name was Norman Bean. This novel was later to be published under the name *A Princess of Mars* and its author was revealed as Edgar Rice Burroughs. Destined to be one of the most popular authors of the 20th century, Burroughs pioneered with this single novel a new breed of science fiction, one in which the scientific believability and explanations took a back seat to sheer adventure.

Princess of Mars plunged its protagonist John Carter, civil war veteran and gentleman of Virginia, onto the red planet, where his superior strength and Earth cunning enabled him to dominate in a war between two species, the green and red skinned races of Mars, and enviably to become their warlord. While there were attempts to show how the planetary atmosphere factory produced breathable air for a dying planet, to explain the biological life cycles of the egg-hatched Martians, and a clever attempt to describe the anti-gravity mechanisms of hover-ships, the book's main focus was on the hack-and-slash of battle, the romance of winning the heart of a princess and political intrigues of militant alien empires. This formula was to prove not only profitable for Burroughs as a writer but was to set the tone for the entire history of science fiction, even to the present day. With subsequent series, often serialized in the pulps, Burroughs invented *Carson of Venus*, *Tarzan of the Apes*, David Innes *At the Earth's Core*—all Caucasian male adventurers who travel to another planet (or encounter a previously unknown race), inevitably conquer them with strength and intelligence, win the heart of their most beautiful female, and rise to the status of Emperor, King or Warlord.

With the enormous success of *A Princess of Mars* as far back as 1912, it is very surprising that it took another fourteen years for science fiction to produce its own dedicated magazine and consolidated fan base. The next bold step was to be taken by an immigrant radio inventor named Hugo Gernsback.

THE GERNSBACK CONTINUUM

Hugo Gernsback (1884-1972) was an important counter-point to the Burroughsian style of science fiction. Born in Luxemburg, he was a young man possessed with scientific knowledge and talent. After perfecting his own radio technology, he came to New York to market it. Soon he was an author, with an article on radio published in no less than the *Scientific American* magazine. He soon formed his own company, which imported scientific equipment from Europe, and also his own magazine, *Modern Electrics*, with the intent of teaching scientific principals to the average public. Before long, his magazine was publishing fiction that was more speculative in nature, including his own predictions about television.

In 1911, *Modern Electrics* magazine showcased a multi-part series by Gernsback called "Ralph 124C41+" about an inventor in the year 2660. Gernsback gave free reign to his imagination, whilst keeping his speculation as close to scientific possibility as he could. In the pages of the Ralph series, futuristic technologies such as radar, virtual reality and television are described in detail. The success of the Ralph series gave Gernsback the idea to expand the amount of fiction in his magazine (which eventually was reborn as *Science and Invention*) and started amassing a stable of writers that included Ray Cummings and Clement Ferzandie, who created the popular Dr. Hackenshaw series. Ferzandie's stories, which ran throughout the 1920s, featured Dr. Hackenshaw, who lectured quite prolifically on subjects as wide ranging as television, time travel, robots and atomic physics. Gernsback's declaration that Ferzandie was a "titan of science fiction" only makes sense considering that Gernsback's definition of science fiction was tightly bound to scientific explication and that the fictional Dr. Hackenshaw was a titan of that particular talent.

Eventually, Gernsback took the bold move of publishing a pulp magazine completely devoted to scientific fiction. In 1924 he announced in a mass mailing that he would be producing a magazine entitled *Scientifiction* (his own term), but the response from would-be subscribers was less than impressive, no doubt due to the obscure and difficult title. Two years later in 1926, encouraged by the continued success of the science stories in his *Science and Invention* magazine, *Amazing Stories* premiered with a snappy title worthy of any action adventure pulp. It sported its famous comet tail logo and a brightly colored cover illustration by Frank Paul depicting spacemen ice-skating on a moon of Saturn with nautical ships oddly balanced on glacier peaks. The magazine premiered with a literary bang, featuring short fiction by Edgar Allen Poe, Jules Verne and H.G. Wells. Nothing like it had ever been seen before and despite the fact that most of the early run consisted of reprints culled from the Munsey magazines and Gernsback's own *Science and Invention*, subscription rates climbed dramatically.

Amazing Stories succeeded largely due to its willingness to commercially cater to a vast audience of young men thirsting for action adventure mingled with a moderate amount of science. This was clearly a dilution of Gernsback's own ideals for scientific instruction, but the bug-eyed monster and spaceship covers by Frank Paul caused the magazine to leap out from a newsstand inundated with pulp magazine, all vying for attention. The lurid covers and sensational stories caused concern among a large number of parents, who saw the new scientific fiction as a threat and a corrupting influence. Gernsback tried to counter this image by encouraging readers to form fan clubs and take part in scientific discussions, as well as running contests that encouraged his readers to try their own hand at fiction writing, but Gernsback had given birth to a genre that would soon spiral out of his control.

Within the first year, things moved quickly. Gernsback published an *Amazing Stories Annual*, which featured a brand-new *John Carter of Mars* novel by Edgar Rice Burroughs, making the special edition so popular it quickly became a quarterly. Edward Elmer "Doc" Smith rose from obscurity by selling Gernsback his "Skylarks of Space," which pioneered the space opera sub-genre. *Amazing Stories* also published the first stories by Philip Francis Nowlan, whose space pilot character Anthony Rogers was better known as "Buck" Rogers. To illustrate how immensely popular *Amazing Stories* had become, the whole genre was popularly known as "that Buck Rogers stuff." Flash Gorden soon arose as an imitation and landmarked the very first science fiction Sunday comic.

Ironically, Gernsback was unraveling his own empire even as it was being built. He was notoriously late in paying his writers. This trait earned him the legendary nickname "Hugo the Rat," which was coined by none other than H.P. Lovecraft, whose story "The Color Out of Space" was unique in all the stories published in *Amazing* in that it earned the largest amount of respect from the mainstream literary community. Gernsback eventually had his magazines taken away from him.

THE HIDDEN GEOMETRIES OF HISTORY

A Review of Against the Day
by Thomas Pynchon

"Bells are the most ancient objects. They call to us out of Eternity."

—Against the Day

One of the joys of growing up in New York has been celebrity spotting, hoping to catch a glimpse of some famous person on the street. The high-water mark of my career was spotting John Lennon and Yoko Ono on Central Park West and turning a corner in the Village to find a strangely domestic Lou Reed taking out his garbage. But the Holy Grail of my quest was always to spot Thomas Pynchon, the Ineffable One, the Author who never gave interviews, had no photographs that were more recent than the 1950s and existed in the same cloud of unknowing as UFOs or the Loch Ness Monster. Rumored about endlessly, barely existing on this plane of existence, he nonetheless reveals his identity through the issuance of novels once every decade or so. I yearned to bask in the shadow of his passing, if not to look upon his face. I scoured the streets hoping to catch a glimpse of him. Not only did I not know what he looked like, but he was only rumored to live in New York. Like the Guardian Angels of a Wim Wenders film, he was faraway, and yet so close. It was a hopeless quest, almost spiritual, and it never paid off. But I fed upon his published words with joyous rapture whenever he saw fit to send them forth into the world.

It takes me about ten years to read a Thomas Pynchon novel, just about as long as it would take him to write one. I can scan every word on every page in a few weeks or months, and make claims that I have finished it, but like a good bottle of wine or frame blow-ups from the Zapruder film, the text matures over time, takes on subtleties and reveals aspects that cannot possibly be apprehended on a first read. I have been reading *Gravity's Rainbow* for more than two decades, often returning to passages that I have autopsied countless times only to find some new shade of meaning that previously eluded me. And the most rewarding goal of a Pynchon novel, discovering how the varied elements of the story all harmonize together, is often discovered years after you first crack it open and after you have abandoned the labyrinth of academic papers, literary criticism and on-line fan sites to confront the Pynchon text in your solitude, like a failed mountain climber who has come back to Everest for the fifth time to hurl himself once more at the summit.

For this reason, I freely admit I've only tackled the first 429 pages of *Against the Day*, Pynchon's latest offering and one of his longest. Clocking in at 1,085 pages, it simply defies the average critic to not only read through it but to digest it enough to write anything coherent or useful. The best one can do is get to the 15,000-foot base camp before the oxygen bottles run out.

Pynchon himself is no help. His self-penned fly leaf is tantalizing and offers seductive tidbits, but ultimately seems to deceive more than it illuminates. Do you expect anything less from the man who could only be represented on the Simpsons with a paper bag over his head and a question mark painted on the forehead? Such is life in Pynchonia. At least we got to hear his voice.

So, with trembling hands, I opened *Against the Day*, ten years in the making under a cloak of secrecy, promising to be more epic than *Gravity's Rainbow* and to unveil more mysteries than *V* or *The Crying of Lot 49*. The cover itself shows the novel's title hovering over two translucent reflections of itself, a pre-echo of the theme of physical and spiritual bi-location and the mysterious phenomenon of light moving through shards of Iceland Spar that would recur over and over in the book. To deepen the mystery, there is a stamped seal with Tibetan characters that according to the *Against the Day* on-line Wiki translates into "Tibetan Government Chamber of Commerce." This alone promises that the book will be a wild ride mixing both literary illumination and frustrating befuddlement.

Indeed, from the first page, the novel takes off with a blast of comic lunacy and surreal dream, thrusting the reader into a world that seems to be America in 1893, but not quite. It is an America as depicted in a film directed by Terry Gilliam, scored by Spike Jones and his City Slickers and based on a novel by Upton Sinclair that was written while tripping on LSD.

We are on board the hydrogen air craft the Inconvenience, piloted by the Chums of Chance, a group of uniformed youths aligned in some sort of secret military order, receiving their directives from some undefined headquarters called the Upper Hierarchy. This group of five Tom Swift-like aviators are a super hero team using 1890s technology combined with some fictional engine designed by Nikolai Tesla, wafting across the American landscape to carry out missions that appear to be angelic in nature, as if they can patrol and control history itself. Possessed with all the charm and pluck of boy scouts but seeming to be privy to the quantum secrets of Time and Space (the word "chance" in their title implying something of a quantum nature), they are traveling at full speed to the Chicago World's Fair (a.k.a. The Columbian Exposition) to carry out airborne surveillance over that city to stem the tide of political Anarchism. The Chums are brutally anti-Anarchist, although their literate ship dog, Pugnax, spends his time with a wet nose buried in a Henry James novel espousing working class political philosophy, much to the chagrin of the Chums.

Pynchon's Chicago is about as surreal and baroque as anything out of science fiction, a vast slaughter pen where the backs of cattle outnumber the tops of hats (at least from the balloon's point of view), a grimy industrial landscape that is sprawled over what used to be the great plains of the mid-west, now reduced to an increasingly dense city of crime, death and political activism. The Fair is a Fellini-esque labyrinth of pygmies, Zulus, Chinese Boxers and Indian swamis, all parading their shamanic pranks on pavilions that line the White City like a cross between a carny freak exhibition and William Burroughs' apocalyptic vision of a Penny Arcade Peep Show

Private detective firms competing with the ever-vigilant Pinkertons against the bomb-tossing revolutionaries roam the nightclubs as bodyguards for visiting European royalty (including Archduke Ferdinand, later a victim of an Anarchist assassin). Silver plate photographers and adulterous stage magicians, revolutionary dynamite experts and crime bosses proliferate like a multi-armed octopus with tendrils of political conspiracies and webs of intrigue. But along with this expansion comes the literary ink-clouds, the obscurities of meaning, the hidden connections that underlie the surface like a vast network of mystical correspondences, as only Pynchon can get away with and still be published.

Against the Day is populated by hundreds of characters, but after an introduction to the Chums and their magnificent flying machine, a central cast begins to emerge from the chaotic Marxian duck soup of the Chicago streets. Merle Rideout, a photographer with a mind for alchemy and anarchy, travels through the Midwest with young Dahlia, the daughter of a stage magician's assistant, very reminiscent of the grifter family of *Paper Moon*. Lew Basnight starts as a hired gun monitoring political subversives in Chicago from the Chums of Chance's airship but soon gains a deepening understanding of the Anarchist philosophy. Webb Traverse is a coal miner obsessed with explosions and acts of terrorism against the mine owners while raising his numerous sons Frank, Kit, Reef and daughter Lake to be mathematicians, engineers and card sharps. After Webb's horrible murder at the hands of hired assassins, the Traverse clan fans out across the country and the world, supplying a good deal of the multiple plot threads of the novel.

And then there is Scarsdale Vibe, the patriarch of a wealthy family, a mine owner and Wall Street tycoon, a man obsessed with killing off "every damned socialist and so on leftward, without any more mercy than [he'd] show a deadly microbe." Vibe is particularly obsessed with the implication of Nikolai Tesla's work on unlimited free energy, which is a dangerous counterforce to the resource capitalism represented by Thomas Edison and which Vibe feels would be the death of the world as he knows it (one of many End of the World motifs that would appear again and again in the text). Vibe lords over his breed of young Harry Crosby-like boys and interacts with the working-class Traverses in a complex social interaction (Vibe sends one of Webb's boys to study mathematics at Yale and Lake gets sexually involved with her father's assassins who were contracted by Vibe) that aligns the two families like the epic clans of the Mahabharata, pitted against each other in some cosmic battle that borders on the religious.

More than anything, the novel is brimming over with Anarchism. That political philosophy that pours out of every cranny of *Against the Day* with the persistence of exploding dynamite, has always been a looming shadow in Pynchon's fiction, mentioned explicitly here and there and always poking its characteristic nose up through the floor boards of his narratives. During the time period of the novel (roughly

1893-1914), Anarchism was a major player on the political and cultural scene, both in America and in Europe, and was as menacing and as dangerous to the status quo as Communism became in the 1950s. A contemporary audience that only knows Anarchism through its stereo types of working class bombers and assassins would be surprised, much as Lew Basnight was when assigned to go undercover into their secret meeting places, that the Anarchists of that time period were ordinary working people reacting to extraordinary circumstances and were a major part of this country's cultural and political history. Ever since the rise of International Communism, Anarchism has been misunderstood and taken out of context. While the Anarchists struggled against involuntary servitude on all social and political levels, Communism gave rise to entire new tyrannies and dictatorships, this distinction, however, was lost in the Red Scare and the Communist witch hunts.

Nevertheless, *Against the Day* seems to be all about Anarchism in both its political and its spiritual forms, an Anarchism infused with mystical properties, where the explosions of the bombs are portals into other worlds. There are labor union Anarchists, spiritual Anarchists, alchemical Anarchists, Anarchists who see the mystical lightning of Tesla contrasted to the capitalist rationalism of Edison's light bulb. In either case, the elemental properties of electricity and light are the raw materials exploited to weave magical control over the forces of nature, whether it's by the dark renegade Tesla or the capitalist stooge Edison, or their vice regents within Pynchon's novel: Scarsdale Vibe and his sons, or the sons of Webb Traverse. The powers and weapons are the same, only the intent and the will to power are different.

In Webb Traverse's world, the preparation of dynamite and bombs is an arcane art passed down to his children that resembles the secrets of the alchemists. If the capitalists can use the earthly metals to forge their global economies and drive their war machines, the terrorists can use those very metals to bring about the destruction of those economies. In this sense, there is within the novel a battle going on for who is going to control the forces of the world.

As Webb explains to Merle Rideout as he mixes his terrorist bombs, "...if you took away everything from mercury not essential, the liquid-metal business, the shine, the greasy feel, the weight, all the things that make it 'mercury,' see, you'd be left with this unearthly pure form of it the cupel ain't been made that can hold it, something that would make this stuff here dull of traprock. Philosophic Mercury is what they called it...supposed to really mean God, or the Secret of Happiness, or Union with the All, so forth."

After going on to explain that various metals like gold, silver and mercury mixed with various acids can produce the agencies of destruction sought by the Anarchists, such as fulminate of mercury, Rideout marvels, "You mean to say gold, silver and these shining and wonderful metals, basis of all the world's economies, you go in a laboratory, fool with em a little, acid and so on, and you get a high explosive that all you got to do's sneeze at the wrong time and it's adios, muchachos?"

Merle has a very different use for the alchemical metals. Through the art of photography, he traps light on plates of silver and captures the forms and images of the world. One can only see Pynchon himself, a man phobic of his own photograph, knowing full well the mystical power of photography. *Against the Day* delights in exploring that spiritual side of technology, focusing on a period in history when rapid technological expansion was producing miracles on a daily basis, when men like Tesla and Edison wrestled like two competing Wizards over who was going to control the light of the world, when air ships, automobiles, electricity, phonographs, motion pictures, and telephones were extending the capacities of man through new agencies to discover new hierarchies of energies in the form of the periodic table, the sub atomic particles of the quantum world, the range of industrial machinery and the new engines that could raise cities and empires.

For this reason, *Against the Day* is filled with just as much fantasy and science fiction as history. By the time the Chums of Chance fly their airship into the caverns of the Arctic waste to find passage to the center of the earth, where they do battle with the Legion of Gnomes and are held prisoner by Chthonica, Princess of Plutonia, we realize we are flying way off the conventional literary map, and that Pynchon's writing game is more than meets the eye. The Chums fly to Venice to hunt down maps that may lead them to the mystical kingdom of Shambhala, and eventually they meet up with the Transgressors, time travelers from the future who are building an army of slaves by inducing amnesia and making them join the Marching Academy Harmonica Band. By this point, we are firmly rooted in the cosmic Zen of the Ineffable One's literary dream world. After several hundred pages of thinking that we will at last see the face through the paper bag, the question mark has now appeared once again on the forehead and the reader begins to wonder where in the name of the Marx Brothers he has landed.

The Tarot, which figured prominently in earlier Pynchon novels, emerges here as Lew Basnight is initiated into a secret occult society that is something like the Hermetic Order of the Golden Dawn, as rewritten by Monty Python. T.W.I.T. (The True Worshippers of the Ineffable Tetractys) worships a secret neo-Pythogorean way of knowledge and act as global dispatchers of the various people in the world who are holding the "office" of each of the Major Arcana of the Tarot deck, collectively known as the Icosadyad. Believing that alternative histories co-exist in bi-located realities, T.W.I.T. sees the two rival university professors who jointly hold the office of the Devil card to be a conduit between those realities. One of the oddest things about T.W.I.T. is their belief that Anarchists are modern day shamans due to their ability to provide explosions that open gateways to other worlds. In the strange universe of Thomas Pynchon, the world as we know it, portrayed with a "minor adjustment or two," is one in which even bomb throwing Anarchists are transformed into "agencies of the angelic."

Besides masquerading as teen adventure literature and historical epic, *Against the Day* also brings us into the heart of the wild western frontier. Modern cities and civilization keep pushing the frontier further and further out along with the various characters of this novel, to the endless mining camps, saloons and whorehouse hotels that give us a sense of what HBO's *Deadwood* would have been like if Thomas Pynchon had scripted an episode. There is even a scene of utter evil, a town run by cannibal vampires where Frank Traverse discovers the mutilated body of his father who has been tortured and killed in a haunting scene reminiscent of the violent mysticism portrayed in Jodorowsky's *El Topo*.

Most of Pynchon's characters are openly sensitive to messages from the infinite beyond, often drawing their inspiration and revelations from some undefined plane that bisects our own time and space continuum. Directives from the Chums of Chance Upper Hierarchy are delivered via the agency of spectral ghosts in the night or radiate from the inner light of gemstones. Bilocated Tibetan shamans appear in the Arctic waste with cryptic prophecies dished out to astonished expeditionists; aeronauts ascend to the upper altitudes where they receive weird voices and visions from entities that share our reality but are as elusive as imaginary numbers. The way in which Pynchon's characters are living within a holographic reality pattern that can be traced and studied by scientists and mystics alike is reminiscent of the war time crisis caused by *Gravity's Rainbow's* Tyrone Slothrop, the military liaison whose sexual orgasms were supernaturally aligned with the destruction wrought by Nazi V-2 rockets and the Sado-Masochism of the SS men who built them.

In fact, the characters of *Against the Day* are less like human beings and more like sub atomic particles moving in cloud chambers, elusive and ever morphing into their opposites, traced not by concrete mechanical properties like position and speed, but by qualities that move transversely through time and space. Michelson and Morley, two scientists who performed the experiments that discounted once and for all the existence of the luminiferous aether, are themselves perceived by Merle Rideout as two waves of light moving in opposite directions, or perhaps they are also two mutually exclusive possibilities of the wave/particle duality of quantum physics; and Blinky Morgan, the renegade desperado who is being sought by law enforcement as diligently as M&M are pursuing the Aether, can't seem to exist in the same universe as the Aether, so the hunt for both are somehow, in a way that transcends logic and time/space, identified with each other.

One of my favorite examples of Pynchon's literary technique comes when Merle is staying in Cleveland during the Michelson/Morley experiments, and a local lunatic asylum is filled with people who have become deranged in the debate over the nature and movement of light:

> Some were inventors with light-engines that could run a bicycle all day but at nightfall stopped abruptly, causing the bike to fall over with you on it, if you weren't careful. Some claimed that light had a consciousness and a personality and could even be chatted with, often revealing its deeper secrets to those who approached it in the right way. Groups of these could be observed in Monumental Park at sunrise, sitting in the dew in uncomfortable positions, their lips moving inaudibly. There were diet faddists who styled them Lightarians, living on nothing but light, even setting up labs they thought of as kitchens and concocting meals from light recipes, fried light, fricasseed light, light a la mode, calling for different types of lamp filament and colors of glass envelope, the Edison lamp being brand new in those days but certainly not the only design under study. There were light addicts who around sunset began to sweat and itch and seclude themselves in toilets with

portable electric lanterns. Some spent most of their time at telegraph offices squinting at long scrolls of mysteriously arrived 'weather reports' about weather not in the atmosphere but in the luminiferous Aether... It was a sort of small Aether community, maybe as close as Merle ever came to joining a church. They hung out in the saloons of Whiskey Hill and were tolerated by though not especially beloved of the regulars, who were mill hands with little patience for extreme forms of belief, unless it was Anarchism, of course (page 59-60).

So, in this surreal Pynchonian landscape, characters are also cosmic principles as well as reflections of forces of nature or elemental particles in some quantum soup. They are also bilocated in time. Scarsdale Vibe the tycoon is also John D. Rockefeller, and his globe trotting anthropologist son Fleetwood is an 1890s version of Michael Rockefeller, whose arctic expedition to recover a mystical meteorite turns into a pastiche of H.P. Lovecraft's *At the Mountains of Madness*, and the havoc and destruction wrought upon the "Northern City" in the wake of the serpentine alien horror is a bilocated version of the terrorist attacks of September 11, 2001. Such is the multi-spatial fictional worlds of Thomas Pynchon, realities and unrealities layered upon each other, doubling into infinity the possibilities of phenomenon, as the introduction of imaginary numbers into mathematics enlarged the playing field of science.

In *Against the Day*, there is meticulous attention paid to density and altitude, be it the density of base metals dug from the earth by the dynamite obsessed anarchists in their mining camps, or the altitude of air ships that climb so high into the upper atmosphere that the crewmen come perilously close to meeting the living creatures that dart between worlds, revealing themselves only to those who have slipped outside of time and space. The technology of *Against the Day* gains power as it moves in vertical directions through a hierarchy of elemental forces. The ferocity of waterfalls (earth and water) grind the turbines that create the electricity that ascends into the air as light (fire and air). Sometimes the height of the dark earth and the height of the realms of air come together through the medium of light, as when Merle Ridout discovers that his profession as a photographer involves trapping the reflected light of the things in the world onto plates of silver, exciting their electrons and reproducing the image of earthly beings. There is no one in *Against the Day*, not even Scarsdale Vibe the Tesla-obsessed Wall Street tycoon, who is not mindful of the occult forces moving through the physical matter of things. This makes *Against the Day* just as much a book about Mysticism as it is about Technology or Anarchism, or perhaps, as various characters within Pynchon's book discover, there is little difference between the two and only your altitude, density and speed of motion determine whether you process reality through the spiritual or the scientific. *Against the Day* merges mysticism, science and politics in a way that I've never quite seen before except perhaps in Neal Stephenson's *Baroque Cycle*, or the recent film *The Prestige*, which shares with Pynchon a fascination with Nikolai Tesla and physical bilocation.

This magical blend is what I've always liked about Pynchon and it is tempting to say that *Against the Day* is his most explicit statement yet of his own interior perceptions, the way that he processes the world. It shows the real mind beating behind the paper bag's question mark.

I know I have a few more months of intense reading ahead of me as I follow The Chums of Chance's surreal airship deeper into the world of the Transgressors and the Earth's Core, spiritual mathematics and the quantum mechanics of light, the Ineffable Teractys, the mysterious explosion at Tunguska, Bela Lugosi, and, if his fly-leaf doesn't lie, an encounter with Groucho Marx who, I'd like to think, is presented as some form of cosmic magus hurtling out banana peels like so many Zen Koans for us to slip on.

Very much like Pynchon, the Ineffable One himself, calling to us out of his hidden cloud.

I still look to spot him on the streets of New York. I will know him by the sound of Angelic kazoos and the Bells of Eternity playing "Yes We Have No Bananas."

Faraway, so close.

Great work fellow Writer, wherever you dwell.

First published in *The Journal of Advancing Technology*, Volume 6, Summer 2007.

THE UNKNOWN TOPOGRAPHIES OF TIME

A Review of Book 3 of Thomas Pynchon's Against the Day

We are metaphysicians at heart. There is a danger of becoming too logical. At the end of the day one can only consult one's heart.

—*Against the Day*

Quite some time ago in high school, I studied calculus. It was during a particularly difficult lesson on limits that it occurred to me that one of Zeno's paradoxes was more than just an amusing mind game to play on your friends when they are stoned. The idea behind the paradox is that between any two points is an infinite number of points and, since you simply can't physically traverse an infinite number of points, it is paradoxically impossible to arrive at any destination. Or perhaps I heard this from Mr. Whoopee on an episode of the cartoon *Tennessee Tuxedo*, I can't remember which one. But no matter. If you stop and meditate upon this, you not only appreciate the benefits of calculus as a means of measuring motion between infinitesimal distances, you also begin to gain an insight into the novels of Thomas Pynchon.

In the previous issue of this journal, I reviewed the first 428 pages of Pynchon's most recent novel, *Against the Day*. In this issue, I plan to review pages 429-693. That's 264 pages compared to the 428 pages covered in the first review. If Zeno's paradox holds any water, in the next issue, I shall review the next 120 pages or so, and then in the fourth issue approximately 60 pages. And so on, until I reach the limit

somewhere around page 931, at which point I will be reviewing approximately one paragraph, then a single sentence, and eventually perhaps
one letter. And to put the finishing touch on my mathematical reading of *Against the Day*, the reviews themselves shall get correspondingly
shorter, at which point the review of the single letter shall consist of a
single letter.

And so, in some remote issue of this journal, while the rest of us
have moved on with our lives, I will be reviewing a single pixel (or fiber)
of that letter. By that time, I will be quite insane and will never have
fully reached the ending on page 1084. Zeno's logic would have won out
and defeated me before the Pynchonian finish line. Somehow this is all
bizarrely appropriate.

So what is *Against the Day*? I suppose if I am to review "Bilocations,"
the third section of the book, by itself and not talk about the rest, it
would be a bit like reviewing *The Empire Strikes Back* and not talking
about *Star Wars*. *Against the Day* is the latest novel by Thomas Pynchon,
an author who has amused, perplexed and frustrated readers ever since
the early 1960s. *Gravity's Rainbow* (1974) was considered one of the
iconic novels to emerge from the postmodern literary movement. It was
a very dense book about the V2 rocket program during World War II,
but that is a bit like saying *Citizen Kane* was about a guy who runs a
newspaper, and is a lot like saying *Against the Day* is an historical novel
that starts with the 1893 Chicago World's Fair and follows the members
of several American families across the country and around the world
for two decades as they encounter anarchism, espionage, physics, mathematics and underground occult societies.

We have the adventurous airship crew called the Chums of Chance,
who start off helping to rid Chicago of anarchism, but somehow wind
up traveling to the earth's core to fight an army of gnomes and to sail
on a sub-desertine frigate under the Arabian desert in search of the
mystical city of Shambala; Lew Basnight, a Chicago gumshoe detective who takes on the task of tracking the world's living embodiments
of the Tarot cards; Merle Rideout, an itinerant photographer obsessed
with the occult properties of light; Kit Traverse, the son of a coal miner/
anarchist who travels across the world to find the pure truths behind
mathematics; Yashmeen Halfcourt, a beautiful woman obsessed with
the fourth dimension and Riemann's zeta function; Pugnax, a dog who
can read novels about radical politics; Professors Renfrew and Werfner,
who as living embodiments of the Devil Card of the Tarot, may actually

be the same person backwards (as if that makes any sense, but somehow Pynchon pulls it off); Reef and Frank Traverse, who travel across the western frontier looking for the hired guns that murdered their father; Time travelers who appear on future battlefields with evil premonitions of World War One; and the Grand Cohen, the cryptic leader of T.W.I.T., the True Worshippers of the Ineffable Tetractys, a group of Pythagoreans who may or may not have the key to what the hell is going on in this novel.

Add to all this a strange brew of literally hundreds of minor characters, including Belgian freedom fighters, Russian ship captains, renegade physicists, arms dealers, hustlers, gunslingers, archdukes, anarchist terrorists, Nikolai Tesla, Groucho Marx, Jack the Ripper and an endless stream of logical impossibilities—e.g., two characters merging into one like quantum particles in a cloud chamber and bombs whose explosions open up portals through time and space—and set everything into motion to the gun shots and bicycle horns of Spike Jones' orchestra, and you have a Thomas Pynchon novel: bold, daring, very large, extremely dense, maddening to read, impossible to ignore, original, strange, repulsively beautiful and hilariously sublime, perhaps his best novel yet, and hopefully not his last.

You can see how words fall short to convey the scope of *Against the Day*. By isolating "Bilocations," I am not suggesting that it can be read by itself, nor that it was meant to be isolated. But I see the breaks between the books of this novel as base camps where one can pause on the way to the summit to rest up and get some fresh oxygen.

There are, however, ways in which "Bilocations" differs from Books One and Two. While the opening sections of the novel criss-cross the American continent through the Old West, the mining camps and frontier towns, the carnival circuits and old theaters, the large post-industrial cities crowded with their radical working class and greedy factory bosses, Book Three takes us across the wide ocean on the *S.S. Stupendica* to various exotic locales in Europe to the heart of Germany where mathematicians and scientific geniuses plot out the vectors and inner dimensions of time. We travel to the canals of Venice and the ports of the Mediterranean where freedom fighters and anarchists negotiate for secret weapons and try to puzzle out the unsolved equations that promise to reveal the structure of reality. It is no small coincidence that *Against the Day* takes place during that same time period when quantum mechanics was being invented and Albert Einstein was writing the little paper that would be his escape route from a desk job. As new mathematics and new science came into being, many of them contradictory to each other, so did new ways of perceiving the world.

Kit Traverse and Yashmeen Halfcourt build a relationship around Yashmeen's obsession with the non-trivial zeros of the Riemann zeta function. When was the last time you were romantically fired over such a notion? Only in a Pynchon novel would we hear of an art movement called Anharmonic Pencillism, or be really excited that we are going to the Projective Geometry Symposium (p. 532). The obsession with mathematics is brought to a strange extreme: Kit and Yashmeen visit a museum in Germany that is devoted to math whose building is made of a "black substance [that is] not so much a known mineral as the residue of a nameless one, after light, through some undisclosed process, had been removed" (p. 632). Here they find panoramas devoted to the history of mathematics with titles like "Professor Frege at Jena upon Receiving Russell's Letter Concerning the Set of All Sets That Are Not Members of Themselves," and where the inner geometry of the hallways and rooms reflect the principles of imaginary numbers. The exhibits themselves change their composition depending on the position and velocity of the observer. This bizarre museum, one of the most unsettling of places I have encountered outside of a surrealist painting, is a perfect analog for the interior of *Against the Day* itself. No character, no setting, no event seems to be independent of the shifting variables, accelerating differentials and imaginary quantum fluctuations of the inner mind of the novel and its ever-present and yet ever-illusionary author.

As you may have guessed, "Bilocations" is preoccupied with mathematics, as are the characters themselves. Never before in any novel have I seen the subject treated with such a daring clarity. While Pynchon does not ask us to consider any real equations, he does confront us with whimsical musings upon scalars and vectors, imaginary and complex numbers, Riemann's zeta function, Maxwell's field equations and the basic fundamentals of differential calculus. In this novel, mathematicians are portrayed with the same biting satire as Monty Python would use to portray British Members of Parliament with all the esoteric pomposity, self-delusion and charming brilliance that we would expect from men and women who see the world through abstract forms. There is also an ideological war being waged between the Vectorists and the Quaternions, a conflict exemplified by the differences between the variables xyz and ijk, a distinction that seems to be analogous to the battles between anarchists and rationalists, those who think in terms of three dimensions and those who think in terms of four. In fact, Yahmeen Halfcourt has the ability to walk into the fourth dimension, causing frightened Vectorists to shout at her in the street as if she were some Typhoid Mary of advanced physics.

"Bilocations" is full of events that go beyond strange, like the Indian yoga master who goes into what he calls the QuadrantalVersorAsana, in which he twists his body into so many imaginary and complex angles that he literally disappears and reappears in another room with different colored hair; or a *Titanic*-like luxury liner (the *Stupendica*) that is somehow two ships at once, joined at the engine room, and at one point bifurcates into two complete ships headed to two different destinations without the passengers being any the wiser. There is even a scene where Kit Traverse, the renegade Quaternion studying in Germany, has an attempt made on his life by a Belgian anarchist group that tries to drown him in a vat of mayonnaise. We even have a journey under an Arabian desert in a sand-frigate where the Chums of Chance discover an ancient sub-desertine city built by the Manicheans, an ascetic group that believed in a pure division between good and evil, light and darkness, leading to one of the funniest lines in the novel: When it is explained that the followers of Mani deferred the pleasures of the world for the blinding truth of illumination, one of the Chums of Chance belts out, "That's the choice? Light or pussy?" (p. 438)

At first glance (if such a thing as a "glance" is actually possible with this novel), *Against the Day* seems to be some historical pastiche that uses the same logic-bending satire of comedians like the Monty Python troupe. But Pynchon is Pynchon, and he follows his own convoluted multi-degreed polynomials to their illogical differentiated curves. I believe he is expressing profound metaphysical truths through the clichés and conceits of experimental literature. Here and there in the text of *Against the Day*, the characters hint at the fact that they know more than they are telling about reality itself. Whether it is the Chums cautioning each other to remain quiet about the metaphysical and occult truths that they have learned from experiencing extremely high altitude, or the Grand Cohen of T.W.I.T. revealing that we are all living in multiple realities, or the mystical ramblings of bomb-tossing anarchists who had found portals into other dimensions, there are few characters who don't have some metaphysical key turning in their cryptic locks.

In a dream, Kit Traverse has the following vision:

> Deep among the equations describing the behavior of light, field equations, Vector and Quaternion equations, lies a set of directions, an itinerary, a map to a hidden space…Within the mirror, within the scalar term within the daylit and obvious and taken-for-granted has always lain, as if in wait, the dark itinerary, the corrupted pilgrim's guide, the nameless Station before the first, in the lightless uncreated, where salvation does not yet exist (p. 566).

The term "lightless uncreated" gives the tremendous hint that Pynchon has been more than a little influenced by the Hebrew Kabbalah, a medieval mystical system in which the "Ain Soph Aur" (light without limit) is worshipped as the higher form of non-being that pre-dates creation as well as stands outside the cycles of time. If that does not make any sense, then I encourage the reader to accept that the Kabbalah has played more than a trivial role in Pynchon's work, *Gravity's Rainbow* most explicitly, and it would behoove any long-suffering Pynchon scholar to study more about it. In fact, the organization in *Against the Day* known as T.W.I.T. is a satire of the Golden Dawn, a Victorian school of Hermetic magic that taught Kabbalah as the fundamental framework of their entire philosophy. Further, Kabbalistic references (and Tarot which has been tied very closely to Kabbalah by the Golden Dawn) share the same mystical vision of light, time and space that the characters of *Against the Day* share. I would even be so bold as to state that *Against the Day* is a novel that can only be understood in the Light of Kabbalah (pun intended).

At one point, Lew Basnight, the Chicago detective who has fled to England where he studies under T.W.I.T., has a conversation with the Grand Cohen, his mystical guru (note the Jewish name), who tells him quite honestly,

> We are light, you see, all of light—we are the light offered the batsman at the end of the day, the shining eyes of the beloved, the flare of the safety match at the high city window, the stars and nebulae in full midnight glory, the rising moon through the tram wires, the naphtha lamp glimmering on the costermonger's barrow. When we lost our ethereal being and became embodied, we slowed, thickened, congealed to… [grabbing each side of his face and wobbling it back and forth] This!

The soul itself is a memory we carry of having once moved at the speed and density of light. The first step in our Discipline here is learning how to re-acquire that rarefaction, that condition of light, to become once more able to pass where we will, through lantern-horn, through window-glass, eventually though we risk being divided in two...(p. 687-688).

While the Grand Cohen often undermines himself in a zany Zen-like manner, he does reveal a lot about Pynchon's narrative methods. Those who labor to unlock the mysteries of his novels should pay heed to the Grand Cohen who tells us,

It is after all quite common in these occult orders to find laity and priesthood, hierarchies of acquaintance with the Mysteries, secret initiation at each step, the assumption that one learns what one has to only when it is time to. No one decides this, it is simply the dynamic imperative operating from within the Knowledge itself (p. 686-687).

So Pynchon is initiating us at every step. The best kept secrets, according to the mystics, are the ones standing out in plain sight, because reality cannot hide itself. As humans, we have lost our ability to see it, and initiation is the process of remembering what we have forgotten, before we were bilocated from the original Oneness.

Perhaps one day, all the writings of Pynchon will dissolve away and we will realize that he was merely pointing a finger at some deeper truth. We have spent our lives reading his books and staring at the finger instead of looking at what it has been pointing at.

But while I'm sitting around waiting to remember the original Oneness, I'm going to finish this book, Zeno's paradox be damned!

To be continued...

First published in *The Journal of Advancing Technology*, Volume 7, Fall 2007.

ROBERT ANTON WILSON
A Personal Meditation

Robert Anton Wilson, writer, novelist, stand up philosopher, literary critic, quantum psychologist, chronicler of conspiracy theories, explorer of inner psychedelic space, advocate of the expansion of human consciousness and the extension of the human life span, supreme Agnostic and Pope in the Church of the Sub-Genius, Discordian and Anarchist, a man who has had as many Selves within him as there were people consciously aware of his existence, who had as many facets to his Being as James Joyce's novels had perspectives, went to his greater feast on February 7, 2007, after a long battle with post-polio syndrome.

RAW was a profound influence on my life, starting in 1981 when I was 16 and listening to music at ML's Stuyvesant Town apartment on the Lower East Side of Manhattan. We were tripping our asses off to a soundtrack of Gong's *Radio Gnome Invisible* followed by Pink Floyd's *Interstellar Overdrive* when ML suddenly presented me with the Dell paperback of *The Eye in the Pyramid*, the first part of *The Illuminatus!* Trilogy by Robert Anton Wilson and Robert Shea. "Here," he said. "You're into the JFK assassination. You'll love this." I believe I devoured the book in about three subway rides and subsequently begged my most literate trip master for the other two volumes.

The novel plunged me in a goofy and multi-perspectival world that reflected my own acid influenced descent into occult correspondences, political paranoia and post-modern chaos. Drawing heavily upon the 1960s counterculture, the magical underground, and a vast array of conspiracy theories, the novel depicts a war waged between the Illuminati and the Discordians for control of human reality. Reading like a pulp paperback as plotted by William Burroughs and Philip K. Dick and re-written by H.P. Lovecraft, the novel goes on a crazed surrealist roller coaster ride layered with bizarre meta-fictional techniques that threaten the sanity of the main characters when they start suspecting that they are merely fictional creations in a novel, the ultimate paranoia. It is filled with yellow submarines, tantric sex, ceremonial magick, Lovecraftian monsters, pop culture, rock music, paranoid hallucinations and more slapstick conspiracy theories than you can stuff into a Marx Brothers stateroom. Besides, I was thrilled that the book was divided into ten "trips," each one named after a different Sephiroth. And the Captain Nemo-like helmsman of the Discordian yellow submarine was Hagbard Celine, a prototype for Douglas Adams' Zaphod Beeblebrox, but far trippier, far more Kabalistic and dangerous.

Illuminatus! was a book that could only be written in the early 1970s, and only make sense to my young paranoid imagination in the Greenwich Village of the early 1980s, where I was deeply immersed in radical politics, psychedelic music and hallucinogenic drugs. In the rarified time warp of the Village circa 1981, my generation of teenagers still thought that the 1960s had never ended and RAW had hurled into our dazzled presence the ultimate manual for our on-going trip. I spent many months trying to convert all my friends to Wilson's unique vision and I found it surprisingly easy. *Illuminatus!* was feeding a hunger that we all felt, that somehow beyond the leftist dogma of the Lower East Side anarchists and the banner waving activists was a world through the mystic looking glass where left was right and right was left and nothing was true and everything was permitted. When I added a hefty dose of William Burroughs, Genesis P-Orridge, Wilhelm Reich, Timothy Leary, James Joyce, Aleister Crowley and Allen Ginsberg into the frying pan where Robert Anton Wilson had been bubbling away on a low flame, the effect was a mighty explosion of my consciousness that lasted for more than 25 years.

In 1977, Wilson published *Cosmic Trigger: The Final Secret of the Illuminati*, a non-fiction account of the journey that led him to the writing of the trilogy. It's a powerful exploration of personal obsessions that covers everything from Crowley's reception of the *Book of the Law* and William S. Burroughs' *23 Enigma*, to UFO abductions, grassy knoll assassins, LSD visions, Timothy Leary's model of consciousness, the OTO, the Templars, the Masons, ceremonial magick, Zen, Gnosticism, Sufism, J.G. Gurdieff, Carlos Castanada, quantum physics, political paranoia and the Holy Guardian Angel. Wilson describes his own story of how, as a writer at *Playboy*, he started investigating political conspiracies and subsequently became lost and adrift in Chapel Perilous, the Abyss of Mirrors that occurs when one starts living the paranoid life of conspiracy theories without a wand of intuition, a cup of sympathy, a sword of reason or a pentacle of valor. In short, you can become like Gene Hackman at the end of *The Conversation*, trapped inside multi-reality tunnels at once and consumed by paranoia.

Wilson's story resonated with my own as I wandered the Lower East Side through a labyrinth of JFK assassination lectures, anarchist squats, William Burroughs sightings, left wing rallies, industrial music performances, street theater, indy film festivals, occult gatherings, homeless activism, and anarchist bookstores. And all the time I was devouring every newly published book by Robert Anton Wilson, which became increasingly more profound and mind blowing as the decade progressed.

Prometheus Rising (1983) was an expansion of the eight circuit model of consciousness that he had borrowed from Timothy Leary and which I frantically tried to map onto the Hindu Chakra system and the Kabalistic Tree of Life. The cover of the original Falcon Press edition depicted a naked angelic being rising from a fallen suit of armor, a clear reference to the psycho-sexual theories of Wilhelm Reich, whose concept of character armor explained the rigid energy held within the body, preventing us from feeling, experiencing and living. Reich himself was the grandfather of modern bioenergetics, the teacher of Alexander Lowen, whose book *Bioenergetics* is a classic in the field. Another Reichian psychologist was Israel Regardie, who had been Aleister Crowley's secretary and a student of Dion Fortune. One of Regardie's occult students had been Christopher Hyatt, the publisher of Falcon Press and a Reichian therapist himself who had added Tantric yoga to the mix and was producing books that I bought in the same batches with RAW's works. Wilson drove me into multiple directions, multiple authors and reality tunnels that were all connected under the surface. And it spoke my language, down to earth, funny, irreverent, and severally skeptical of all dogmatic systems.

The New Inquisition (1986) was a wild and funny critical exploration of fundamentalism and logical thinking. In that book I read about Charles Fort and the rains of frogs, the mystical physics of Nikola Tesla, the cosmological absurdities of Velikovsky, the ghostly cloud chambers of quantum physics, Schrodinger's Cat and more about Wilhelm Reich, his mysterious orgone box and his downfall at the hands of the Food and Drug Administration. The book was a programmed trip designed to show how multiple realities can exist simultaneously, all being tunneled through various filters of consciousness. Like William Burroughs before him, RAW was determined to rub out the word "is" which had been imposed upon the Western mind by the rational tyranny of Aristotle.

Coincidance: A Head Test (1988) was a series of essays that explored everything from quantum psychology to the complex mytho-poetry of James Joyce's *Finnegans Wake*. This was my first deep exploration into the *Wake*, setting me off on a twenty-year journey to fathom its secrets. RAW made it tremendous fun, relating the various elements within the book to magical correspondences, quantum physics and Egyptian magic. RAW's simple explanation that the Joycean word "oxhouse-humper" was a portmanteau word cobbled from the meanings behind the first three Hebrew letters blew my mind and sent me pouring over every page of the *Wake* trying to find the threads and patterns and mystical templates that were so intricately woven throughout. I'd like to think that I discovered a few on my own without recourse to footnotes or study guides. But RAW, even more so than Joseph Campbell, was always my main source for all things *Wake*.

Wilhelm Reich in Hell was a stage play he wrote that expanded upon the ideas in *The New Inquisition* in which Reich converses, Marat-like, with the Marquis de Sade about politics and sexuality. He also wrote two more fiction trilogies, *Schrodinger's Cat* (1981) and *The Historical Illuminati Chronicles* (1982-1991), which narrates the adventures of Sigismundo Celine, an ancestor of Hagbard Celine of *Illuminatus!* and traces in typical RAW style the various Masonic—Templar—Gnostic—Magickal—Illuminati conspiracies of 18th century Europe.

A RAW novel of great interest to Thelemites is *Masks of the Illuminati* (1981), a tour de force about Aleister Crowley in which the Master Therion plays hide and seek occult games with none other than Albert Einstein and James Joyce. As implausible as it may sound, this novel really bites at the root of all three men, explicating their various reality tunnels with great accuracy.

Before Amazon and eBay, It wasn't easy to find RAW's books and I hunted diligently around the city before it occurred to me to seek them out in occult bookshops. Indeed, there was a whole Robert Anton Wilson section at Herman Slater's Magickal Childe. This was the store where I first came across the video tapes by Mystic Fire, discovering the world of Kenneth Anger and Maya Deren and other experimental filmmakers. In that small backroom that doubled as tarot reading parlor I first saw videos by the Residents, Throbbing Gristle and SPK. But I would always make it a point to look for the new Robert Anton Wilson books. And when I only had enough money for the subway ride, I would stand before Herman's shelves staring at their covers. Such was the hold that RAW had over me.

Why the fascination? Perhaps part of the reason was that Wilson was from New York (he was Brooklyn Irish) and had a down-to-earth NYC accent that I could relate to. He was funny above all, and his interviews and lectures came across as mystical stand up comedy more than anything else. His take on the human condition and consciousness was full of Zen-like parables, sharp and bitter insights and the ability to take a wide disparity of people, events, concepts, abstractions and mystical revelations and tie them together in an artful and mind-expanding way, always with a cosmic wink at his audience that he wasn't really to be taken so very, very seriously. He always deconstructed his own ideas even as he espoused them, claiming that he wanted to apply agnostic thinking to everything, to believe in everything and nothing, and to let the seeming contradiction between those two goals reveal something that can approach the status of Truth.

Perhaps because I had also been a physics student at Stuyvesant High School and had gone through my formative teen years reading books like *The Tao of Physics* and *The Dancing Wu Li Masters* that I dug Wilson's take on quantum reality. Logical contradictions and the abandonment of Aristotelian logic was not just appropriate for acid trips, but for explorations of modern physics and all the possibilities and anti-possibilities that were opening up in cloud chambers and particle accelerators around the world. So, when I saw this funny Brooklyn guy projecting the strange language of Quantumland onto the JFK Assassination, Crowley's Magick, Tim Leary's Sirius Transmissions, UFO sightings, the conspiracy of the Masons and the Illuminati and the writings of James Joyce, I took to the stream like a fish to water, hungry for more.

Most of my obsessions and interests over the years have spun from some page of one of RAW's books, either his fiction or non-fiction. To me Wilson was a launching off point, a focal node that could lead me to various spokes on the wheel. He was a way for me to integrate within myself Anarchism with Thelema, scientific rationalism with Zen lunacy, faith with skepticism, ancient tradition and wisdom with modern and post-modern sensibility. He was a way of separating all different belief systems into what he called Reality Tunnels. In short Robert Anton Wilson was the Zen master striking me continually with a stick for my own sudden enlightenment. True there were more erudite scholars in the field with more reputable credentials. Compared to other writers I admired at the time like Alan Watts, Alexander Lowen, Chogyam Trungpa or Khrisnamurti, RAW seemed like a rough-hewn comedian with a low brow irreverence, but that's what I loved about him.

I tip my hat to him upon his passing into the beyond and promise, as he asked in one of his last missives, to keep the lasagna flying. If the Three Stooges ever gave up their various jobs as plumbers or gas station attendants and retreated to the mountains for spiritual enlightenment, I suspect they would find Robert Anton Wilson up on his throne made out of discarded orgone boxes, pretending to be the Grand Poo Bah of the Illuminati and dishing out all sorts of Zen paradoxes like so many banana peels for them to slip on.

At least this is my own humble reality tunnel.

Rest in pieces, Robert Anton Wilson. And thanks for all the books.

First published in *Behutet: Modern Thelemic Magick & Culture*, Issue 23, Autumn 2004.

UNLEASH THE WORD HORDE
The Life of William S. Burroughs

William Seward Burroughs is most popularly associated with the Beat Literature movement of the Post-War era, of which he is considered one of the founders, along with Allen Ginsberg and Jack Kerouac. This most unlikely trio, composed of a scion of a mid-Western WASP family, a Jewish communist from New Jersey, and a Roman Catholic football player from New England, almost single handedly changed the course of literary history with *Naked Lunch*, *Howl*, and *On the Road*, respectively. These three seminal works were the heart and core of the Beat movement, irreplaceable mainstays on the shelf of any intellectual hipster. They transformed our cultural landscape, much to the shock of many a conservative academician or self-imposed curator of literary decency, affecting novels, poetry, film, music and theater for decades. But little was understood about the exact role of William Burroughs in the Beat movement; even less about his importance in the general category of American literature beyond the boundaries of the Beat phenomenon.

The writings of William Burroughs are as significantly different from the Thomas Wolfe nostalgic optimism and boundless energy of Jack Kerouac's novels as they are from the Buddhist politics and Blake-like fire of the poetry of Allen Ginsberg. While the hub of the three-spoked wheel seems to be a shared admiration for the New York hipster street culture and the mystical revelations that could accompany the ravages of drug addiction and outlaw status in society, Burroughs always seemed to pursue his own independent route. While Kerouac and Ginsberg applied an extreme romanticism to the low-life and blue-collar world they found themselves immersed in, they always returned to secure comforts, in Kerouac's case his mother's apartment when he wrote *On The Road*, or in Ginsberg case an almost establishment status in office day jobs and therapy to eliminate his homosexuality. But Burroughs always seemed to descend into a harsh world of nihilistic self-destruction while burning his bridges behind him.

He had managed, by the time he was 45, to be a drug addict on the streets of New York, a marijuana farmer in Texas, a renegade from the law in New Mexico, a writer of sexually explicit gay literature, a murderer (he shot his wife under circumstances explained below), and a junky living in exile in North Africa with teenaged boys as lovers. While this resumé of outlaw behavior may repel potential readers, Burroughs could likewise be described as an accomplished novelist, man of letters, student of philosophy, cultural critic, essayist and a writer who has drawn upon traditions as diverse as surrealism, science fiction, modern painting and such strong literary voices as Franz Kafka and Joseph Conrad. He has also done duty as night club performer and public speaker, teacher of writing, and inventor of experimental literary techniques that flavor his writings and that have influenced generations of other writers, a cultural icon who has influenced not just other authors but rock stars, filmmakers, composers, and painters.

His life became a work of art in itself, transformed by myth and self-generated legends. He was on the scene when the Beat movement was born in New York during the 1940s, his various apartments serving as a meeting place for junkies and writers alike. He traveled in Mexico and South America, settling in North Africa where he was able to penetrate the closed society of the writers in exile, including Paul Bowles and his wife Jane. He lived in Paris and London throughout the 1960s as a notorious pornographic writer whose works were banned by customs officials and whose slogans were being used on the streets by Situationists and Anarchists. He was on the front lines at the 1968 siege of Chicago as a reporter when the police went to war against the Yippies trying to shut down the Democratic Convention. In the 1970s he was reborn as a great-grandfather of punk, living in lower Manhattan while the explosion of wild boy garage bands and heroin-soaked song writers made New York their own and Burroughs their favorite icon and stand-up comic.

Perhaps the crowning example of his ethereal presence on our cultural landscape is his unexpected guest spot on *Saturday Night Live* in 1981 where he sat behind a desk with his inimitable poker face and in his mid-western laconic drawl and systematically befuddled the studio audience and the millions watching with an odd slapstick and scato-logical tale of the sinking of the *Titanic* that he had written back in the 1930s.

His strongest appeal to all the rebels and outsiders who devoured his work was his self-declared battle against political, social, and psycholog-ical addictions of all kinds. He fought against the tyranny of language itself which he called the Word Virus and wrote and structured many of his novels as an attempt to throw off the control of conventional litera-ture (in much the same way that Jackson Pollock cracked open painting) to allow the floodgates of the unconscious to find its way onto the page.

In his novels, he created a vast palette of alternative mythologies of his own devising. These mythologies construct themselves by drawing upon themes, images, and techniques from science fiction, medieval paintings, surrealist literature, pulp paperbacks, science journals, clas-sical myth, eastern religions, western occultism, Gnostic mysticism, anthropology textbooks, and even the borrowed words of other writers. His most popular construct was the Nova Mob, a group of ethereal spir-its who need human hosts to survive and who target the planet Earth for Nova—the condition that results on a planet where incompatible life forms compete for scarce resources. In their particular case, they feed upon people's addiction, including addiction to drugs, addiction to hav-ing a body, addiction to words. The Nova Police is a law enforcement agency composed of members who have kicked their addiction to flesh and word, capable of existing in the silence of bodiless space. By elimi-nating the Need, they destroy the Suppliers in much the same way that a drug dealer would be destroyed by his customers' lack of need for the drug. This mythology struck a chord with readers of the 1960s as the perfect metaphor for the oppression of a police state using mass media as a form of mind conditioning.

His later fiction grew in scope to encompass utopian societies, some of which seem to exist outside of time and space. There are savage bands of male teenagers living in the desert perfecting their assassination tech-niques and weapons training, reproducing themselves—in the absence of women—through bizarre rites of sex magic. Also, we read of 18th century pirates who try to establish the island of Madagascar as a haven for all free men where they can live under the Articles that guarantee their human rights and do battle with the astral demons of the Cities of the Red Night. Then there are the Johnsons who haunt the old west with a peculiar honor system and homosexual gun slinging, traveling back and forth through time in an attempt to arrive at a radical revision of history and some spiritual state of purity.

The literary worlds of William S. Burroughs are deep, mystical, and profound. Beyond the scatology, sketch-like vaudeville humor, graphic sex, and obsession with autoeroticism, there beats at the core of his novels a moral center that attempts to decipher the cause of human suffering and the identification of those fellow castaways who insist on crapping in the water supply and drilling holes in the lifeboat floor. Burroughs saw the planet as a spaceship. "It's the space age," he was fond of saying. "And we are here to go." It is in his fiction that we find the literary maps of control and the social, spiritual, and psychological mechanisms that keep us in bondage, that trap us in the body of flesh and prevent our wordless ascent into the freedom of space. This had been Burroughs' literary mission, and contrary to what it may seem on the surface, his intentions were far more important and profound in scope than a scatalogically funny junky writing about drug addicts.

William Burroughs' colorful and dangerously adventurous life began in St. Louis, Missouri, in 1914. He was born into a family that had in its lineage Robert E. Lee and the inventor of the adding machine. His mother Laura Lee Burroughs was a classic Tennessee Williams character of obsessive Victorian propriety and moral observance as she and her husband Mortimer tried to maintain a proud face amongst the St. Louis Society, most of whom were far wealthier than they were. In his later fiction, principally *The Wild Boys*, Burroughs would wreck satirical havoc upon the St. Louis of his childhood.

Burroughs took an early interest in writing and even produced a manuscript of adolescent amour called "The Autobiography of a Wolf" in which he professed homosexual love for another boy. Horrified at his own confession of undisciplined emotions, he wished the manuscript burned and its ashes buried in someone else's garbage can. He was soon shuttled off to a boarding school at the Los Alamos ranch where the atomic bomb had been developed. At the rugged outdoors camp filled with horseback riding and rifle shooting, Burroughs developed a strong taste for teenaged boys, sporting weapons, and living in the wild. He also was drawn to pulp fiction with its over-romanticism of western outlaws and city gangsters.

He was then off to Harvard, where he studied linguistics and anthropology. Both disciplines were to figure heavily in his life's work as a writer. As a linguist, he studied the writing of Alfred Korzybski who emphasized, long before the Structuralists of the 1950s, that words and the objects of words were separate and that the relationship between the two were constructs of the human mind. In his novels, language as an oppressive barrier to reality was to reach epic proportions to the point where Burroughs would even consider language itself to be a virus contracted by the human race, which lead to its spiritual corruption:

> In the pass the muttering sickness leaped into our throats, coughing and spitting in the silver morning, frost on our bones. Most of the ape forms died there on the treeless slopes, dumb animal eyes on me brought the sickness from white time caves frozen in my throat to hatch in the warm streamlands...sick apes spitting blood laugh. Sound bubbling in throats torn with the talk sickness... (*The Soft Machine*)

Anthropology played a large role as well. Burroughs, a world traveler, was to look at various religions, cultures, and traditions with the trained eye of a social scientist. Even his first two published novels, *Junkie* and *Naked Lunch*, are littered with footnotes explaining the junky argot and foreign terms. In his creation of imaginary cities like Interzone, he was showing not only a surreal sense of landscape, but an understanding of the social dynamic of a third world city and the polyglot of forces that gives that city a particular spirit.

Not knowing what to do with his life, he used an uncle as a contact with the OSS (the organization that would later become the CIA) but he was turned down for being mentally unstable. It would have been interesting to see what would have become of Burroughs if he had joined in on the CIA from the ground floor. Throughout his renegade life as a writer, he would often portray writers themselves as field agents working for some psycho-spiritual agency. In the Cronenberg film of *Naked Lunch*, the writers in Tangiers sit in centipede-meat cafes with their typewriters writing their field reports for psychic insect agencies. In this one horrific image of the writer being controlled by his typewriter (which is also a pustulating mind-controlling insect), Cronenberg managed to capture Burroughs' vision of the dark agents of the world and their cults of intelligence. Such men would appear and reappear in his work.

Subsequent to being rejected by the OSS, Burroughs landed in

Vienna to study medicine. It is ironic that the world's most famous junky would have started his drug career as a rich student abroad studying medicine. It was to his advantage later on: even when ravaged by the horrors of drug addiction, a piece of him maintained a cold detached scientific attitude to the chemical agents working within his body. *Naked Lunch* is filled with medical descriptions and introduces one of his most intriguing creations, Dr. Benway, the unscrupulous doctor who manages to kill more often than he heals, is perennially addicted to the drugs he treats, and would go so far as to remove a tumor with a rusty sardine can and his own teeth. In the portrayal of Benway, one could see what Burroughs thought of the medical profession and the men who practiced it, as well as why Burroughs probably didn't leave Vienna as a medical professional.

He was soon in New York to wait out the war, and it was there that he made the social contacts that were to define the rest of his life. First, he became involved with a woman named Jane Adams, later to become his wife. Her ex-roommate had been Edie Parker, a girlfriend of Jack Kerouac's whom she introduced to Burroughs. Soon, Kerouac and Burroughs were hanging out with Allen Ginsberg, instantly bonding on an intellectual level, sharing books, reading poetry together, philosophizing about language, culture, and politics. Burroughs introduced these young Columbia students to a strange new world of names like Franz Kafka, Wilhelm Reich, Spengler, Korzybski. The bright young kids must have been so addled to be in the intellectual presence of a world traveler and Harvard graduate, one who dressed and acted like a banker but who also frequented Times Square junkies and small-time criminals. Before long, the trio amassed a scene that was the kernel of the Beat movement. They talked about being writers and romanticized their contacts with the underworld as a journey of what Arthur Rimbaud once termed a derangement of the senses to arrive at the Truth.

Before long, they realized that their flirtations with crime could yield serious results. A friend of theirs had knifed to death a homosexual stalker; Kerouac and Burroughs had helped dispose of the body and given their friend safe harbor before turning themselves into the police. Lucien Carr, the friend who had done the actual stabbing, received a relatively minor sentence because it had been deemed an act of self-defense, and Kerouac and Burroughs briefly caught trouble with the law for their involvement. Their world was rapidly disintegrating. Kerouac would soon go on a cross country adventure, chronicled in *On the Road*. Ginsberg would soon arrive at Rockland State Hospital, where he would be committed to the electro-shock table (a crucial inspiration for *Howl*). Burroughs would be off with his new wife Jane to pursue a career as a marijuana farmer outside New Waverly, Texas.

An odd footnote that can be appended to this New York period was that Kerouac and Burroughs collaborated on a novel together, a fictional account of the Lucien Carr affair called, after a newspaper headline about a fire at a city zoo; *And the Hippos Were Boiled in Their Tanks*. The novel is, to this day, unpublished and by all accounts relatively juvenile and weak. Kerouac would later use the New York of the mid-1940s to far better effect on one of his last novels, *The Vanity of Duoluz*, in which Burroughs appears as Old Bull Hubbard.

In Texas, the luck of the newlyweds only grew worse. Jane soon gave birth to a son, William Burroughs, Jr., whose short and brutal life started with his mother shooting heroin several times a day during her pregnancy. After a failed crop, the family migrated to New Orleans, where Burroughs was eventually busted by the police who found not only drugs in his possession but enough guns to stand off a siege. This prompted the couple to flee over the border to Mexico City, where they settled down to a life filled with guns, drugs, and classes at Mexico City College on cultural anthropology. It was here that Burroughs collected the bizarre material on Mayan religious rites that were to figure so prominently in his novels *Soft Machine* and *Ah Pook Is Here!* He had also fully formed a socio-political philosophy of control and totalitarianism that was highly colored by his years of experience with customs officials, narcotics agents, policemen, and the complex burocracies and hypocrisies surrounding the drugs laws. Burroughs had hardened into a strong Libertarian, believing that the function of government bodies was to penetrate the private space of the individual and create intolerable tyrannies.

It was in Mexico City, during a period when the couple had some reasonable chance of leading a stable life, that an event occurred that would change the course of William Burroughs' life. Jane had been increasingly depressed and suicidal, during a party at a friend's house she placed a glass atop her head and challenged her drunken husband to shoot it off with her pistol. Burroughs complied but shot her straight through the forehead. Years later, in a 1984 documentary by Howard

Brookner called *Burroughs*, the writer would give the first public accounting of the event from his perspective. Apparently, he knew what he was doing, and he didn't have to miss, but he had been dominated by a controlling entity that he dubbed the Ugly Spirit. It was a foul presence that had plagued him. It worked in him through many channels, including his drug addiction and his nomad-like existence, his inability to fully connect with any other human being. After the tragic event that ended Jane's life, Burroughs woke as if from a dream. It was then, he claims, that he became a writer. His wife's death, no matter how terrible, freed him to be himself. This startling psychological fact is crucial to understanding the moment in Cronenberg's *Naked Lunch* where Bill Lee "proves" that he's a writer by shooting his lover with a gun.

Miraculously, the Mexican officials treated Burroughs with relative decency as he tried to convince them that the shooting had been an accident. During this period, he also started writing and before long had penned two short books, *Queer* and *Junkie*, both drawing heavily upon his underworld experiences. He sent the books in pieces through the mail to Allen Ginsberg back in New York, who had managed to secure a literary contract for *Junkie* through a contact at Ace Books. The book, published under the name of William Lee, was printed back-to-back with a lurid FBI drug agent tale and hardly made a splash as a piece of literature. The book, however, is hard and tight in its prose, keeping very much to the facts and focusing on fine detail about the world of a junky, reading at times almost like an anthropological study of a particular culture. It is curious in retrospect because it not only gives us a little window onto the Burroughs universe, circa 1944, it also contains isolated pockets of pre-echoes of the later avalanche of surrealistic science fiction, as in this passage where Burroughs describes a fellow junky:

> There as something boneless about her, like a deep sea creature. Her eyes were cold fish eyes that looked at you through a viscous medium she carried about with her. I could see those eyes in a shapeless, protoplasmic mass undulating over the dark sea floor.

The novel certainly didn't launch a literary career, and Burroughs was soon off to South America where he decided he was going to hunt through the Columbian jungle for a plant called Yage, purported to propel its user into a mystical state. This stated quest does much to dispel the myth that he was just a pitiful junky hooked on heroin. His sharp intelligence, his fascination with ancient cultures including the South American Aztecs and Mayans, his appreciation of altered states of consciousness as a mystical experience, ennobled his search which is chronicled in the *Yage Letters*, a collection of correspondence between Burroughs and Allen Ginsberg who, in his own way, was pursuing the spiritual experiences of alternative drugs.

Soon he was back in New York living with Allen Ginsberg. Burroughs had confronted his own solitude, especially in the wake of losing his wife in such a horrible manner. He bonded with Ginsberg and the two of them engaged in what the poet later described as a "great psychic marriage," Burroughs, however, was possessed with the idea of the two of them merging into one organism and pursued the vision to the point of mania. In his later novel, *The Ticket That Exploded*, he would open with this powerful image:

> So that is how we come to know each other so well that
> the sound of his voice and his image flickering over the
> tape recorder are as familiar to me as the movement of
> my intestines the sound of my breathing the beating of
> my heart.

Ginsberg became frightened by the almost religious fervor with which Burroughs fueled his obsession. The couple soon parted, and Burroughs was off to Tangiers hoping to enter into the exiled community of writers that included such luminaries as Paul Bowles, the ex-patriate author of *The Sheltering Sky*. Burroughs had a lot to offer this crowd, but he came across as an unhygienic and dirty junky with a severe gun fetish. He lived in squalor with various teenage hustlers, the most renown of which was Kiki, a young boy who was to appear fictionally in his novels. Despite the fact that the writing community would have little to do with him, he tried his best to keep his writing projects going. Most valuable to understanding Burroughs in Tangiers are the letters that he sent back to Allen Ginsberg in New York. Carefully edited and lovingly preserved in a collection entitled *The Letters of William Burroughs*, they include a powerful portrait of a metamorphosis from sick addict to one of the most brilliant writers of the 20th century. William Burroughs was slowly becoming *William Burroughs*, shedding his past skin behind him and emerging as an important writer and man of letters.

The letters include attempts at routines, little sketches of comic content that drew on the early Beats' penchant for putting on skits, complete with wigs, costumes, and foreign accents, in their own living rooms to each other's great amusement. This accounts for some of the vaudeville-like humor that abounds in the works of Burroughs, the scenes often presented as play scripts with dialogue and stage direction. Burroughs' letters to Ginsberg included attempts at routines that are purported to be part of a new project called *Naked Lunch*, an unflinching look at drug addiction that goes several steps beyond *Junkie* in both scope and style. Some of these routines have also been preserved in a slender volume called *Early Routines* and are immensely enjoyable and fun to read. For the first time, the acidic black comedy of William Burroughs is finding a voice. *Early Routines* also includes one of the most powerful self-portraits he ever sketched:

> Lee's face, his whole person, seemed at first glance completely anonymous. He looked like an FBI man, like anybody. But the absence of trappings, of anything remotely picturesque or baroque, distinguished and delineated Lee, so that seen twice you would not forget him. Sometimes his face looked blurred, then it would come suddenly into focus, etched sharp and naked by the flash bulb of urgency. An electric distinction poured out of him, impregnated his shabby clothes, his steel-rimmed glasses, his dirty gray felt hat. These objects could be recognized anywhere as belonging to Lee.

When Kerouac and Ginsberg visited Burroughs in Tangiers in 1957, they found a strange paranoid man living in a room full of empty Eukodal bottles and a sprawling manuscript littering the room, pages blowing liberally out the open window. The two writers set about to structure and give form to the profuse outpourings of Burroughs' imagination. Burroughs would amuse his visitors by picking a piece of manuscript almost at random and reading it out loud, alternatively howling with laughter and launching into tirades about political and social hypocrisies.

Naked Lunch, as it took shape in the squalor of the Tangiers apartment, is a fragmented collection of vignettes, sometimes threaded together with just the barest hints of characters, sometimes chaotic and surreal, often brutal and disgusting, always filled with a sublime beauty of a kind rarely seen in literature. Its characters include Kafkaesque petty bureaucrats in stifling and dream-like offices, the ugly red-necked sheriff of the South, corrupt South American customs officials and border guards, homicidal surgeons and drug addicted doctors, mentally damaged psychotics and their equally insane psychiatrists, eccentric millionaires and their teenage-boy-infested rumpus rooms, petty city detectives and narcotics agents, corrupt religious leaders and small time junkies...all blurred together against a surreal landscape that resembles at times Tangiers, New York, South America, 18th century Germany, a painting by Pieter Brueghel and Salvador Dali.

By 1958, the Beat movement was in full swing. Ginsberg had published his epic poem *Howl* in 1956 and was traveling about the country giving readings that were akin to rock performances. Kerouac had published *On the Road*, which soon became an anthem for the Beat Generation. Meanwhile, William Burroughs, who helped start the whole scene, was living like a covert agent in a foreign country writing a surrealist nightmare of unpublishable pornography. But Ginsberg recognized that something important had been produced and he went back to America where he peddled *Naked Lunch* to his contacts, eventually getting two excerpts of it published by the *Chicago Review*. The third installment was slated for publication in the winter of 1959, but the University of Chicago's chancellor ordered "any potentially scandalous pieces" removed from the next issue. All but one of the editors from the *Chicago Review* resigned in protest and formed their own journal *Big Table* where they promptly started publishing more works by William Burroughs. Interest in *Naked Lunch* exploded, and Maurice Giordias in Paris published it through his Olympia Press. William Burroughs was now in the same company as fellow Olympia writers Henry Miller, Samuel Beckett, Georges Bataille, and even the Marquis de Sade.

An editor from *Big Table* soon brought the book to Grove Press in New York, where it was published to great scandal. Throughout the world, especially in England, customs officials were confiscating the novel, which had to be smuggled into various countries. A Boston book seller was arrested for selling *Naked Lunch* and at the subsequent trial such luminaries as Norman Mailer testified in the book's defense. It is at this trial that Mailer gave the famous quote that "Burroughs may be the only American living writer possibly possessed by genius." The court ruled, after an appeal, in the bookseller's favor and declared the novel "not obscene."

Burroughs had now moved to Paris and was possessed by writing. He lived at a small hotel that has since entered history as "The Beat Hotel" and struck up a friendship with an old acquaintance from Tangier, Brion Gysin. The two bonded deeply and found that they shared many interests, including magic, surrealism, modern painting, depth psychology, and the history of the assassin cults of Islam. Gysin helped Burroughs invent a literary technique known as the Cut-Up, in which a page of text would be sliced with a razor and pieced back together at random, very similar to the random poetry generation of the Dadaists. Burroughs saw this technique as a form of "writing magic" and akin to the collage technique of painting. He quickly hacked away at his manuscripts. His new fiction had brilliantly sustained moments of literary inventiveness and powerful narrative, but more often than not, the prose would fold in on itself with passages such as:

> Naked boy sitting on Blue Age of the Short Time Hyp.
> A soiled idiot body dissolved in night youths of cold
> scar tissue. Catatonic limestone hands folded over his
> Yen. A friend of any boy structure cut by a species of
> mollusk. Fades out in lust of metal burning bodies to
> Boy Blue on the nod.

One of the effects that this prose had was to try and discover ghostly patterns in the prose, meaning that is strained from the words that would not have been revealed if they had not be subject to the Cut-Up process, a juxtaposition of words as images, much like college create meaning by juxtaposing various images. Burroughs was taking this all several steps further. He was on a mission to "Rub Out The Word," to short-circuit the patterns of consciousness that were being controlled by the Word Virus.

His mythology was rapidly evolving. When he had been in England taking his Apomorphine cure, he was impressed with the way that Apomorphine did not just substitute one addiction for another, but eliminated addiction altogether. Methadone, on the other hand, a state approved cure for heroin, was not interested in making itself obsolete and had a personal interest in keeping heroin addiction present in the world. Burroughs saw this as an excellent metaphor for a police state, where the police were not interested in eliminating crime since that would mean they would make their own jobs obsolete. His fiction now turned towards the Nova Mob, a group of disembodied viruses that needed human hosts. They invade, damage and occupy usually through some sort of sex vice or drug addiction. Counter to this, and similar to Apomorphine, are the Nova Police, whose job it is to eliminate the Nova criminal completely, making their own jobs obsolete. This weird way in which drug addiction, the addiction's cure, criminals and police, states of consciousness and unconsciousness, word and image, and sexuality are all blended together into one vast surrealist dream, is the key to understanding the 1960's novels of William Burroughs which now started appearing: *The Soft Machine, The Ticket That Exploded,* and *Nova Express.*

The ambiances of the novels are spiritual and physical crisis. The various life forms that inhabit the planet are fighting for various positions of advantage, for resources, for a monopoly on consciousness, for words themselves which are used as weapons, the only counter-weapon being silence and bodiless states of consciousness. The Nova Mob and the Nova Police and their various agents are fighting endlessly in passages that read like Raymond Chandler detective novels. The battles are described in endlessly repeated phrases like, "Word Falling—Photo Falling," "Break Through In Grey Room," "Storm the Reality Studio," and "Towers Open Fire." The Towers referred to are the giant guns of imageless silence that counters the Word Virus that holds a monopoly on consciousness.

Political paranoia is extreme and the board syndicates of the earth are seen as holding the books of control, the volumes of symbol systems that maintain a monopoly on consciousness, the sacred books of the human priests that must be smashed:

> Listen to my last words anywhere. Listen to my last words any world. Listen all your boards syndicates and governments of the earth. And you powers behind what filth deals consummated in what lavatory to take what is not yours. To sell the ground from unborn feet forever...

> Top Secret — Classified — For The Board — The Elite — The Initiates —

> Are these the words of the all-powerful boards and syndicates of the earth? These are the words of liars cowards collaborators traitors. Liars who want time for more lies. Cowards who can not face your 'dogs',

your 'gooks' your 'errand boys' your 'human animals'
with the truth. Collaborators with Insect People with
Vegetable People. With any people anywhere who
offer you a body forever. To shit forever. For this you
have sold your sons. Sold the ground from unborn feet
forever. Traitors to all souls everywhere.

The control systems so vilified in his novel, *The Nova Express*, were
not just confined to the worlds of the drug addict, the Nova mob, and the
Venusian collaborators. Burroughs also brought into play his old interest
in anthropology and the theocracy of the Mayan priest-caste. Playing
upon every known stereotype of the Mayan religion, Burroughs worked
the human sacrifices, mind control, and contact with aliens into his
Nova War. Portraying the priestly Mayan caste as psychic vampires that
controlled the field workers through a series of symbol books, his novels
are filled with hilariously campy scenes of his Nova heroes infiltrating
the inner sanctums of the priests where they perform their disgusting
and sexually depraved rites and destroy the books which subsequently
cause "the whole shithouse to go up in chunks." Burroughs may have
taken vast liberties with Mayan culture and religion—archeological
discoveries in the last few decades have proven that the Mayans were
not quite as Burroughs describes them in *The Soft Machine*—but he uses
a science fiction version of the Mayan scene that is as effective as any
other conceit in modern literature.

Burroughs didn't stop at fiction to perform his experiments. He
continued with tape recorders, performing elaborate experiments with
words and ambient sounds with a reel-to-reel magnetic machine. And
in film, he collaborated with Anthony Balch, a sometime pornogra-
pher who made short and effective films including *Towers Open Fire*
that attempted to portray the chaotic sense of embattled consciousness
that permeate the novels. Being that Burroughs appears in the films—
running about the streets of Paris with a tape recorder, listening to his
headphone as he gives his orders to attack the Reality Studio—the films
come across today as a sort of proto-rock video with the Burroughs'
taped cut-up as the music track.

Throughout the latter half of the 1960s, Burroughs lived in England
and took his time writing his next novel, *The Wild Boys: A Book of the
Dead*. In his usual episodic fashion, the writing sessions for *The Wild
Boys* produced enough material to feed two more projects, *Port of Saints*

and *Exterminator!* They fit together in much the same way that the three post-*Naked Lunch* novels did, interchanging characters, themes, and routines with a dream-like repetitiveness.

The Wild Boys drew its inspiration from a very particular source that Burroughs had discovered through the agency of his friend Brion Gysin: the legends surrounding Hassan-e Sabbāh, the 11th century Ishmaelite rebel who had retreated to the mountains in resistance to the Islamic majority that had dominated the Persian Empire. The stories of Hassan-e Sabbāh and his band of assassins (we derive the word assassin from Hassan's name) are as flamboyant and subject to historical doubts as Burroughs' giant liberties taken with Mayan religion. In Burroughs' version, the assassins trained by Sabbāh would infiltrate the households and offices of important officials, sometimes acting for years as cooks, servants, and drivers. Then at a crucial moment, the assassins would strike. This is how Hassan waged war against the establishment hegemony. Burroughs became fascinated by this legend and derived his own gay fantasy of the Hassan-style tribal training of killers in the form of the Wild Boys.

It is here that Burroughs emerges as one of the great literary misogynists of all time. He not only distrusts women as predatory entities (the scenes of the Wild Boys massacring a tribe of wild lesbians is horrific in how funny Burroughs tries to make it) but elevates the evil status of woman to a cosmic level. To him, women represent the Word Virus that must be rubbed out, that bars the way to space and silence. It was later commented by a close friend that Burroughs himself wouldn't survive one minute in the Mad Max-like universe of *The Wild Boys*. It is his ultimate gay-teen gun-porno fantasies paraded before an astonished reading public that had fought for over a decade to establish him as a writer of high moral integrity, despite his scatology, pornography, and obsession with filth.

But it was still possible to debate the writer's moral integrity. His novels showed the harsh reality of the red-necked sheriff and the white supremacist organizations that targeted gays as often as they did blacks and Jews, the oppressive military occupations of history with their systematic rapes and massacres, the suicidal production of atomic weapons and materials, the diseased nature of police states, and the hypocrisy of religions that are used as lingual viruses to maintain complex power relationships that are as often predatory as they are vampiric. The Wild

Boys and the Nova Police are two examples of science fiction tribes sprung from the imagination of the author to counter these dark, evil forces in the world, the only hope for lifeboat Earth. Seen in this light, the gangs of rampaging teenage boys armed with their deadly knives, rifles, and perfected weapons of death, targeting the military installations, the spiritually dead suburbs, and the churches of the establishing powers are a fantasy on a scale that any reader could relate to.

In the late 1970s, Burroughs moved to New York, a move that was prompted by an offer to teach at City College. He seemed to have been a competent teacher, but his students were less than enthusiastic. He commented that he must have disappointed them when he appeared in a suit and tie instead of swinging into the classroom completely naked and sporting a strap-on. His short-lived career as a writing teacher put him back in New York, living, appropriately enough, in a renovated boys' locker room that he had dubbed the Bunker. In true Wild Boys tradition, Burroughs claimed that a dead boy named Toby haunted his rooms, and he often saw him materialize in a scintillating blue light.

At the same time, Burroughs' neighborhood was the site of a cultural explosion. Punk rock started in a few small clubs on the Lower East Side and the likes of Lou Reed, Patty Smith, Iggy Pop, the New York Dolls, Television, the Talking Heads—all New York-based and all influenced by the writings of William Burroughs—turned to him as a sort of spiritual godfather. Burroughs became a man on the scene, appearing in nightclub performances, often sitting behind a desk with a pitcher of water, reading the more outrageous passages from his novels like a funky old sex-maniac of a grandfather. The Bunker soon became the scene of a large variety of visitors including not only the New York crowd but luminaries such as Andy Warhol and David Bowie. Through the agency of his neighbor, poet John Giorno, Burroughs recorded his sit-down comedy routines for a series of records called *The Giorno Poetry Systems*. Here he stood side-by-side with other artists such as Laurie Anderson, Jim Carroll, and Anne Waldman.

This entire period in Burroughs' life was made partially possible through the hard work and dedication of James Grauerholtz, a Kansas-born boy who had been profoundly moved, as a teenager, by *Naked Lunch*, an instant awakening that helped Grauerholtz come to terms with his own homosexuality. He came to New York to seek out his favorite author and quickly endeared himself to the aging writer. Burroughs was

kind enough to make Grauerholz his literary collaborator, social secretary, business manager, and the chief executive in William Burroughs
Enterprises.

Together they set about to work on yet another trilogy. This series
was to be more mature, more coherent, and more visionary than anything that Burroughs had attempted before. The three books, *The Cities
of the Red Night*, *The Place of Dead Roads*, and *The Western Lands*, are by
far his finest works. Perhaps not his most clever or his most humorously
quotable, but they are a testament to a lifetime of experience, thought
and study, a concentration of everything that had made him Burroughs.

Started and finished in New York, *The Cities of the Red Night* shows
the heavy critical hand of Grauerholz. Never before had Burroughs
managed to sustain such a brilliant narrative. The novel often decays
into cut-ups and hallucination, but the plot threads are clear and the
themes that hold them together brilliantly illuminated. Although the
novel was to be accused by its various negative critics as an example of
how Burroughs had become a parody of himself, the reality was that his
life-view and artistic working of it had finally taken shape. The novel
was a far cry from the tortured fragments of *Naked Lunch* and yet stands
in relationship to that work as a grown adult would to his adolescent self.

The next novel in the trilogy, *The Place of Dead Roads*, continues
the theme of time travel and shifting identities. *The Place of Dead Roads*
is the first major novel by William Burroughs since *Junkie* to sustain a
character and a plot thread throughout the entire book. But in a typical
bit of Burroughsian tour de force, *Dead Roads* is a Western novel unlike
any other Western ever written. The gunslingers are gay, morphine
addicted teenage time travelers who are often clones and often engaged
in ways to mutate the human organism for space conditions.

His final novel, *The Western Lands*, was released in 1988 and fulfilled much of the promise of encapsulating and rounding off a life's
work. A prolonged meditation upon the nature of death with an emphasis on the political, cultural and mythological systems of the Ancient
Egyptians, the book also reads as an expository essay by the author,
reviewing his own matured philosophies and confessing an overt longing for paradise by a writer for whom spiritual release has always been
an apocalyptic and self-destructive journey:

> I want to reach the Western Lands—right in front
> of you, across the bubbling brook. It's a frozen sewer.
> All the filth and horror, fear, hate, disease and death

of human history flows between you and the Western
Lands. Let it flow! How long does it take a man to
learn that he does not, cannot want what he "wants."
You have to be in Hell to see Heaven. Glimpses from
the Land of the Dead, flashes of serene timeless joy, a
joy as old as suffering and despair.

Burroughs spent the better part of his last decade living a quiet
peaceful life in Lawrence, Kansas. He even discovered painting and
practiced it as diligently as he once practiced writing. At first glance, his
paintings were reminiscent of Jackson Pollock with their trailing splat-
ters and tentacle drips, until one realizes that Burroughs achieved the
effect by nailing cans of paint to a wooden fence and then shooting a bul-
let through them, causing the paint to splatter. He had found the perfect
expression of his fascination with the violence and power of firearms,
a cloud-chamber in which the violent act becomes visible, revealing its
time traces. His artwork sold well and there were gallery showings.

Even in his 80s, he kept up his creative output. He recorded albums
with Bill Laswell's Material and Kurt Cobain, as well as acted in movies
by Gus Van Sant (*Drugstore Cowboy* and *Even Cowgirls Get the Blues*).
A surprise filmed appearance during a U2 concert scandalized the
networks, who didn't appreciate the unscheduled tone poem in which
Burroughs rhapsodized his own irreverent interpretation of the holiday
called Thanksgiving. He also wrote the lyrics for a Tom Waits theater
piece called *The Black Rider* and appeared in a Nike commercial.

During his last years, he claimed a sense of inner peace, partially
attributed to a Navajo Indian ritual that he had commissioned, a form
of exorcism in which the unwelcome Ugly Spirit was confronted at last,
armed with the spiritual forces of Indian wisdom. Burroughs sensed the
ritual had been a success and it helped buffer him against the loss of his
friend Allen Ginsberg to pancreatic cancer.

His last few books included a dream diary, which is a fascinating
key to his subconscious mind, as well as some of his novels, such as
Ghosts of Chance, which continues some of the themes that were included
in the last trilogy. *The Cat Inside* was published in 1992 and is a star-
tlingly mystical and profound little book about William Burroughs' new
found love for the soul of cats, a love that is reflected in his last diary
entry written the very day that he passed away at age 83:

Nothing is. There is no final enough of wisdom, experience—any fucking thing. No Holy Grail, No Final Satori, no final solution. Just conflict.

Only thing can resolve conflict is love, like I felt for Fletch and Ruski, Spooner and Calico. Pure love.

What I feel for my cats present and past.

Love? What is it?

Most natural painkiller what there is.

LOVE.

First published in two parts in *Behutet: Modern Thelemic Magick & Culture*, Issue 29, Autumn 2005, and Issue 30, Summer 2006.

THE SECRET PLACE
The Cave of the Three Brothers

On the eve of the outbreak of World War I, a cave complex full of profound mystery was discovered in the Pyrenees at Montesquieu-Aventes by three boys and their father. Les Trois Frères (The Three Brothers) was not the first complex of corridors, tunnels, and mammoth chambers found by the sons of Count Henri Bégouen; they had entered into a nearby grotto two years earlier and were confronted with the remains of an ancient hunting sanctuary. After the war, when these underground wonderlands were properly explored, it was determined that the two complexes were once part of an overall labyrinth, now separated by a rock fall.

On July 20, 1914, one of the boys was lowered by his father (who could not fit) into an artificially enlarged "rabbit hole," thereby reactivating an entrance to the underworld that had not received visitors for at least twelve thousand years. The first stage of the journey was a sixty-foot drop; the second, a narrow and dangerous passage through dank and slippery corridors. The boy found his way with a miner's lamp and mapped his journey through the labyrinth by unspooling a ball of twine behind him.

Over an hour later, his father the Count and his two brothers felt a tug on the rope and raised the boy to safety. He told them excitedly of a new cave, separated from the grotto they had previously discovered, and filled with hundreds of pictures.

Dr. Herbert Kuhn, who visited Trois Frères in 1926, wrote of his own passage into the inner sanctum:

> Then there comes a very low tunnel. We placed our lamp on the ground and pushed it into the hole ... The tunnel is not much broader than my shoulders,

nor higher. I can hear the others before me groaning and see how very slowly their lamps push on. With our arms pressed to our sides we wriggle forward on our stomach, like snakes. The passage, in places, is hardly a foot high, so that you have to lay your face right on the earth. I felt as though I were creeping through a coffin. You cannot lift your head; you cannot breathe... And so, yard by yard, one struggles on; some forty yards in all ... It is terrible to have the roof so close to one's head ... Then, suddenly, we are through, and everybody breathes. It is like a redemption. The hall in which we are now standing is gigantic. We let the light of the lamps run along the ceiling and walls: a majestic room—and there, finally, are the pictures. The surface had been worked with tools of stone, and there we see marshaled the beasts that lived at that time in southern France: the mammoth, rhinoceros, bison, wild horse, bear, wild ass, reindeer, wolverine, musk ox... (Quoted by Joseph Campbell, *The Masks of God, Vol. 1: Primitive Mythology*, pp. 307-08)

The boy's miner's lamp may have been too feeble to illuminate the chamber and to reveal the immensity of the space and the sprawling extent of the pictures, but he was correct in estimating them to be in the hundreds. Unlike the painted animals found in the other Paleolithic caves of southern France and northern Spain, they were engraved, utilizing the contours of the rocky surface to achieve an awesome life-like effect.

One is reminded of another child, albeit fictional, who discovered a fabulous underworld. Just before falling down the rabbit hole, Alice contemplated the dullness of her life while puzzling over a dry, boring book void of "pictures or conversations." If only she could have seen the vast hall of Trois Frères with its mighty images that spoke across the millennia in a language whose power was in its silence.

The Count's son had found his way into the secret place, the inner sanctum of what later scholars were to call a "Paleolithic Cathedral." The boy walked and crawled along a sacred path which seemed to have been carefully designed to lead the traveler from the suffocating and claustrophobic birth canal into the vast interior of a ritual chamber. Unlike his Stone Age counterpart, the boy went alone and unguided, burning kerosene instead of wood, tied to his family by twine, but nonetheless adrift in a shadow world of images, beyond time, beyond space: the secret place.

The minds that conceived Trois Frères, the hands that shaped it, the feet that once walked those narrow and dangerous corridors, belonged to a people whose secrets have been unlocked only since the Count first sent his son down the hole with his lantern. The cave art has survived hundreds of centuries of condensation, mold mulch, cave-ins, calcification, limestone deposits, and other erosions of time, and has already told us much: the pictures reveal the fauna hunted by the men who engraved them.

Late Paleolithic glaciation drew the thick-hided mammoth, rhinoceros, and cave bears down as far as the Pyrenees, where the human inhabitants of this region began to hunt them. These animals are the first to be depicted in the cave art. The subsequent glacial retreat turned the land gradually from arctic tundra to grassy steppe and finally into woodlands. The land was warming and filling with the oxen, bison, ibexes, and horses that were to dominate the cave art of the next period.

There is little mystery as to the "when" and the "how" of these underworld caves; it is the "why" that mocks us. We can easily explain them as ritual chambers for hunting magic; compared to the hunting rites of present-day indigenous people, the scenes of sympathetic magic at Trois Frères conjured by these remarkable clues seem straightforward. A closer look, however, reveals more mystery, as if the final explanation of the secret place forever eludes us.

In the main sanctuary, there is a section of the cave wall where animals are depicted in a dense tangle. Other large sections remain blank. It is in the dense collage that the mysterious Bison-Man dances, with what is perhaps a bow superimposed over his body. The mystery of this figure lies in the two animals directly before him. They are fantastical; one possesses the legs of an antelope and a bison; the other, clearly a reindeer, has the forefeet of a duck. Why were these otherworldly dream animals depicted along with their real life counterparts?

Nearby, fifteen feet off the ground in a dark apse, in a remote position not easily discerned from the ritual ground below, is depicted the most powerful image of Trois Frères, and certainly the most controversial. It is a tiny creature, no more than two and a half feet high, with the ears of a stag, the eyes of an owl, the beard of an old man, the tail of a wolf, the paws of a bear, and the legs of a dancing shaman. Known as the Sorcerer of Trois Frères, clearly this is not a man dressed in the hide of a beast, nor is it a mere addition to the parade of fauna below.

The figures tempt us with their silence. If not for their presence, we could be content with our simple theories of sympathetic hunting magic. We could add to this the threading trail of generations of young boys being led by torch light down the meandering corridors, crawling on their bellies through suffocating tunnels, and then being brought into the awesome sanctuary where the secrets of the hunt are revealed to them with great solemnity in a womb-like underworld appropriate for their death and rebirth as men.

But hunting magic is performed by modern indigenous hunters with an ease and simplicity that needs no complex construction or excavation, laborious engravings, or acrobatics upon scaffolds to reach ceilings and nooks. The haunting owl eyes of the Sorcerer of Trois Frères stare over the chamber as mute reminders that there is a crucial linchpin absent from our theory, as absent as the river that once cut its tortured way through the limestone depths below the soil of France.

The cave of Trois Frères is a temple. It is an important interface between two worlds, like Chartres Cathedral and the Sistine Chapel. Whereas the medieval churches are designed to propel the worshipper into a higher realm—surrounded by stained glass images of human depictions of saints, angels, and martyrs, enacting mythic scenes of Biblical past and heavenly eternity—the sanctuary at Trois Frères uses animal symbolism instead, with earthly animals surrounded by images of the heavenly herds, which are the objects of desire and love.

A basic tenet of religious worship is that a covenant must be created between divinity and humanity, a bond between the worshipper and the worshipped that will ensure the balance of life. What we find in Paleolithic hunting is just such a covenant.

More than the object of the hunt, the flocks of ice age creatures upon the limestone rocks represent the nourishment administered by the gods to their dependents, the human inhabitants of the earth. These images of bison, oxen, horse, rhinos, mammoths, tundra and plains dwellers, intentionally crafted for preservation, are no less than the wafer of the Stone Age mass, the food of the gods, the herds of eternity. Here we have the creation of a sacred place for ritual use, the depiction in graphic animal and semi-human form of the otherworld inhabitants; and the preservation of a mythic tradition based on extra-temporal events.

The secret place is yielding its secrets. Buried far below the earth, untouched by the rays of the sun, it is nonetheless being exposed and deciphered. Few of us will ever feel the profound wonder experienced by the three boys and their father as they first laid eyes upon the tunnels and walls illuminated by their lanterns after twelve thousand years of darkness; we will not experience the mystery of crawling through the entry tunnel into the large sacred space where the animals dance their mute rites and the Sorcerer holds his secret court.

Only in the province of our own dreams can we feel the awe that no longer moves us in a world where the secret places have been measured, catalogued, carbon-dated, copied and modeled in life size, set up as exhibits in museums and photographed in all-revealing light.

As Count Bégouen's son entered into the sanctuary of Trois Frères and found the magnificent display of glacial tundra beasts from another age, he entered the very fount of conjuration, a place of deep magic and dreams that gives nourishment to the imagination. It matters little that he couldn't "read" the pictures on the walls. They spoke to him beyond words, welcoming him as their first initiate after one hundred and twenty centuries of silence.

First published in *Parabola: The Magazine of Myth and Tradition*, Summer, 1992.

JAMES JOYCE:
FINNEGANS WAKE AND
THE BOOK OF THE DEAD

There are many reasons why *Finnegans Wake* by James Joyce should matter to Thelemites and all interested in esoteric studies. It is not a book about magic, but it is one that has been written magically. The book itself is magic in its form and texture. To study the *Wake*, to train your mind into thinking like the book, you are training yourself to think magically. To study the sources from which James Joyce composed the *Wake* (literary, mythical, historical, and religious) is to gain a comprehensive overview of the secret teachings of the Western tradition. Over the next few issues of *Behutet*, I will attempt to prove both these statements, first by examining how the book relates to *The Egyptian Book of the Dead* and the Teamhur Feis or the pre-Christian rites of ancient Ireland, then by examining the book's historical and literary sources with an attempt to teach how to read Joyce's language, to decode the narrative, to identify the characters and to learn the book's meaning. Further, I will attempt to show, in all the installments, how the *Wake* relates to Thelema and the Magick of Aleister Crowley.

My first attempt to read *Finnegans Wake* was at the age of eight when I found it in my father's bookcase. I asked him what it was about and he answered bluntly, "Nobody knows, but it seems to be about Everything!" The idea of a book that no one can read but was about everything fascinated me and I have spent my life since taking a crack at its 628 pages of portmanteau words, multilingual puns, hybrid phrases, four-dimensional sentences, mythic images, dream visions, spiraling and infolding sentences, words teased and tortured into convoluted versions of their mundane forms, and characters coming into being and then dissipating like clouds and mist vapors. The novel violates every technique of effective writing and known rules of grammar and even pushes the ontological implications of writing to the limits of consciousness. The *Wake* is the horizon of writing, a prose that seems to be coming from the very font of writing that attempts what does not seem possible: writing catching itself in the very act of writing, reflecting on itself and seeing its counterpart in the human soul, the mirror of the reader. It is a book about words themselves and how they exist like multi-dimensional aspects of consciousness. This should sound familiar to any occultist familiar with the Western traditions of magic.

Finnegans Wake was published on May 4, 1939, after seventeen years of composition. But for more than a decade before that date, Joyce's work in progress was a most eagerly awaited literary event. The fame that Joyce acquired in 1922 with the publication of *Ulysses* primed an international audience for more literary acrobatics, more scandal, and more brilliant prose. However, when excerpts from the *Wake* began appearing in literary reviews, the initial reactions were hostile. Harriet Weaver, Joyce's most serious patron and champion, commented:

> I am made in such a way that I do not care much for the output from your Wholesale Safety Pun Factory nor for the darknesses and unintelligibilities of your deliberately entangled language system. It seems to me you are wasting your genius.

Nora Joyce, long embittered by the poverty in which her husband's bohemianism had paralyzed their lives, was very angry that he wasn't writing anything that people may actually want to read. Joyce's own brother suggested that the author had gone insane. In fact, a casual glance through the text of the *Wake* would suggest that Joyce had turned into one of those unbalanced individuals whose dark, disheveled apartment was populated by hundreds of notebooks filled with incomprehensible gibberish. However, the test of time and hundreds of dedicated scholars and critics (Anthony Burgess, Robert Anton Wilson and Joseph Campbell among them) have meticulously dissected the book, finding method in the madness. Not only is there meaning but there is purpose and very serious purpose indeed. Joyce, who died in 1941, shortly after its publication, simply did not live long enough to explain that purpose.

When *Ulysses* was published, there was much confusion over its experimental style. It was a simple story about three people living in Dublin during a single twenty-four-hour time period that straddles June 16 and 17, 1904. The narrative follows the journeying about the city of Stephen Dedalus, a literary-minded student based on James Joyce himself, and Leopold Bloom, a Jewish advertising man. Much of the book narrates their interactions and, most importantly, their failure to interact with each other. Hundreds of other characters and common citizens of Dublin drift about, most of whom had made appearances in Joyce's previous books such as *Dubliners* and *Portrait of the Artist as a Young Man*. Molly Bloom, the third main character, remains home in bed all day but dominates the last chapter of the novel in a stream-of-consciousness monologue that is celebrated for its literary innovations and insights into female consciousness. The Molly Bloom monologue also seems to solve the issue of how to portray subconscious thought in narrative fiction. Techniques created by Joyce in *Ulysses* are so omnipresent in today's popular fiction that they are no longer considered experimental. Just look at how many times the unconscious speaks through the use of italics in Stephen King's *The Shining*.

While the novel impressed readers and critics alike, the significance of the title and how it related to the novel's meaning remained mysterious until Joyce himself let the cat out of the bag: the novel had been patterned and structured on Homer's *The Odyssey*. Leopold Bloom's journey about the city matched almost chapter for chapter the adventures of Odysseus, the Greek war hero. Stephen Dedalus was Telemachus, the war hero's son; and Molly Bloom was Penelope, waiting back in Ithaca for her husband to return from the war.

Episodes within the novel reflect episodes from Homer but whittled down to humble size to suit the common man, such as a one-eyed racist in a pub as a stand-in for Polyphemus the Cyclops. Mr. Bloom's sojourn among the Lotus Eaters consists of the newspaper man relaxing in a Turkish bath watching his genitals float in the water. Telemachus' consult with the wise sage Nestor becomes Stephen's encounter with his boss who lectures to him about anti-Semitism and hoof-and-mouth disease. The Sirens are now two barmaids gossiping in a restaurant. The arrow competition is now two drunken men pissing against a wall after leaving a brothel.

The grand scope of Homer's heroic characters had been squeezed into the ordinary people of Dublin, but with a loving intent that shows how deeply affectionate Joyce was for the citizens of his beloved city.

Molly's betrayal of her husband, Bloom's suffering over the loss of his dead son, Stephen's deep guilt over his mother's death were all as noble and dramatic and passionate as the inner lives that were lived and the hearts that beat thousands of years ago during the Heroic Age.

Once this literary technique of layering the Greek epic poem over an ordinary day in Dublin was understood (Joyce himself mapped out the relationship), the book became far more understandable. When *Finnegans Wake* was published, therefore, readers were more than eager to map the new book to an ancient source and thereby gain an understanding of its meaning and structure. There was hope that the key to the book would be forthcoming, but Joyce's death smashed all hopes. As for the book itself, few people could read past the first sentence, far less interpret the meaning of the entire work.

It was clear enough that Joyce was employing thousands of references to ancient myth, religion and history; this suggested that the plot had been shaped by another source, but there were no concrete characters and hardly a shred of plot. Something suggesting characters drift in and out of the sentences, but they don't last for long. The one-to-one relationship between *Ulysses* and Homer's *The Odyssey* now seemed to be a many-to-many relationship between one order of "things" and some other order of "things."

It wasn't long before Joseph Campbell, the king of mythographers, published *A Skeleton Key to Finnegans Wake*, which seemed to crack the code and lay bare the content. It makes sense that a man deeply immersed in the study of mythology should be the first to tie it all together. *The Skeleton Key* is one of the first books that one should read to gain an understanding of the *Wake*, but Campbell was blazing a trail through a virgin forest and there was much critical work to be done.

By the 1980s there were many critical and analytical sources for anyone confident enough to tackle the *Wake*. Roland McHugh produced the very impressive *Annotations to Finnegans Wake*, which gives a page-by-page and word-by-word breakdown with an expository analysis. This book helps cut the way through the "alphybettyformed verbiage" (183.13) and the "ineffible tries at speech unasyllabled" (183.14). *A Reader's Guide to Finnegans Wake* by William York Tindall did much to elaborate on Joseph Campbell's mythic and psychological findings and can help advance a serious reader far into the vast fractal intricacies of the novel. *ReJoyce* by Anthony Burgess is an examination of the *Wake* by a novelist whose own lingual experiments in *A Clockwork Orange* were highly regarded as well as controversial. Even *Coincidance* by Robert Anton Wilson, while not as scholarly or systematic, does much to help appreciate the joyful and often hilarious synchronicities of the *Wake*.

It is easy to get lost in all these books. I once had the experience of having seven of these academic and interpretative works spread out before me and as I round-robined through them, referencing and cross-referencing, comparing one scholar's analysis of a particular passage with another's, taking notes on the dissection of words I found particular obscure, piecing together the meaning of a specific page from multiple sources, when I suddenly realized that I didn't actually have a copy of *Finnegans Wake* on the table (it was perfectly comfortable and unread on my bookcase). In a truly Wakean fashion, the *Wake* itself had disappeared into the scholarship.

The first major wave of interpreters focused on the *Wake* as a book that recreates a dream, and identifies the mythic images that recur in the text as Jungian archetypes of the collective unconscious. The "narrator" is an unnamed Dreamer that may or may not be Tim Finnegan the hod carrier after he has died. His initials are HCE, which is interpreted at various times as Here Comes Everybody and Humphrey Chimpden Earwicker, the proprietor of a pub outside of Dublin who has gone to sleep and is permutating through various fragmented identities, some of whom are figures from mythology and history. Some critics claim the Dreamer is Leopold Bloom after he falls asleep at the end of *Ulysses*; but regardless of the identity of the Dreamer, the text's landscape is the dream world. Various episodes in the text represent the different levels of sleep and unconscious awareness as the Dreamer travels through the night towards the dawn. The last chapter reveals the Dreamer waking up with the sunrise.

The paradoxes, the lack of lucid characters and situations, the tortured language and fantastical puns can all be explained away as a dream narrative written in a dream language. And since it is the belief of Carl Jung, Joseph Campbell and a host of other thinkers that human consciousness is hooked into one vast ocean of archetypes (the Archetypes of the Collective Unconscious, Jung called them), the book was seen as consisting of those archetypes existing in as vaporous and fluid a form as they would appear in our own dreams. Since psychology was an intellectual rage back in the 1940s, this approach to *Finnegans Wake* seemed inevitable. A whole generation of scholars started mapping elements within the text to all sorts of myths, gods, goddesses, dream images, archetypal symbols and ancient texts. The *Wake* itself gave tons of evidence that this was the approach encouraged by the author.

While mass audiences failed to understand the *Wake*, scholars were as delirious as Gabby Hayes at a gold strike and produced libraries of analyses. One can spend an entire academic career navigating those waters, and this alone turns off the average reader. Why should so much work go into understanding a work of art? *Ulysses* was difficult, but ultimately it was readable and revealed itself to be quite moving. But the *Wake* required monastic study in "everything" and few seemed to emotionally connect to it. It seemed inconceivable that the book should matter to the ordinary mortal who demanded entertainment from the books they purchased with their hard earned money.

In the final chapter of *Portrait of the Artist*, Joyce states clearly, through Stephen Dedalus, his mission as a writer: "Welcome, O life! I go to encounter for the millionth time the reality of experience and to forge in the smithy of my soul the uncreated conscience of my race." Such ambitions speak volumes about the meaning and purpose of Ulysses. It is my belief that it is also the meaning and purpose of *Finnegans Wake*.

As a writer, Joyce was going for spiritual-artistic gold. His aim was to take the techniques he had used to structure and texture *Ulysses*, a book that forged in the smithy of his soul the uncreated conscience of the Irish, and to apply those techniques to the vast depths of the collective unconscious of the human race. With *Finnegans Wake*, he created a sacred text for all humanity, a spiritual and magical text that requires a spiritual and magical language in order to be written at all.

To take *Finnegans Wake* to the next step of interpretation above the psychological and the mythical, one has to revisit the Irish music hall ballad that gave the book its name. The song is straight forward: an Irish hod carrier falls off a ladder, dies from a head wound, and is resurrected at his funeral when a drop of whiskey touches his lips. The song is funny, joyous and full of Irish spirit. It is also Joyce's inspiration for his great epic of the uncreated conscience of all races:

> Tim Finnegan lived in Walkin street,
> A gentleman Irish, mighty odd.
> He had a brogue both rich and sweet
> And to rise in the world he carried a hod.
> You see he'd a sort of a tipplin' way
> With a love for the liquor he was born.

And to help him on his way each day,
He'd a drop of the craythur ev'ry morn.

Chorus:

Whack fol' the dah, now, dance to your partner.
Wipe the floor, your trotters shake.
Isn't it the truth I told ya?
Lots of fun at Finnegan's wake.

One morning Tim was rather full;
His head felt heavy, which made him shake.
He fell from a ladder and he broke his skull
And they carried him home, his corpse to wake.
They rolled him up in a nice, clean sheet
and laid him out upon the bed
With a bottle of whiskey at his feet
And a barrel of porter at his head.

(Repeat Chorus)

His friends assembled at the wake
And Mrs. Finnegan called for lunch.
First she brought in tay and cake,
Then pipes, tobacco, and whiskey punch.
Biddy O'Brien began to cry,
"Such a nice clean corpse did you ever see?"
"Arragh, Tim, mavourneen! Why did you die?"
"Arragh, hold yer gob!" says Paddy McGee.

(Repeat Chorus)

Then Maggie O'Connor took up the job.
"Oh Biddy," says she, "you're wrong, I'm sure."
Biddy gave her a belt in the gob
And left her sprawling on the floor.
Then the war did soon engage;
'Twas woman to woman and man to man.

Shillelagh law was all the rage
And a row and a ruction soon began.

(Repeat Chorus)

Then Mickey Maloney ducked his head
When a noggin of whiskey flew at him.
It missed, and falling on the bed
The whiskey scattered over Tim.
Tim revives, see how he rises!
Timothy risin' from the bed!
Says "Whirl your whiskey 'round like blazes,"
"Thanum an Dhul! Do ye think I'm dead?"

(Repeat Chorus)

In Joyce's opening chapter, Finnegan's fall from the ladder is portrayed as an archetypal event that occurred deep at the dawn of history (or perhaps outside of time altogether) and the story of the death and resurrection of the hod carrier is now the source of all such death and resurrection myths:

> The fall (bababadalgharaghtakamminarronnkonbronnt onnerronntuonnthunntrovarrhounawnskawntoohooho ordenenthur-nuk!) of a once wallstrait oldparr is retaled early in bed and lateron life down through all christian minstrelsy. The great fall of the offwall entailed at such short notice the pftjschute of Finnegan, erse solid man, that the humptyhillhead of humself prumptly sends an unquiring one well to the west in quest of his tumptytumtoes: and their upturnpikepointandplace is at the knock out in the park where oranges have been laid to rust upon the green since devlins first loved livvy.

Several things to note here about Joyce's technique. Several falls are involved, most prominently the fall from the Garden of Eden ("the knock out in the park") and the temptation of Eve by the serpent ("devlins first loved livvy"). But there is also the Wall Street crash ("wallstraight") of 1929, the fall from a Wall that bedeviled both Finnegan the hod carrier and Humpty Dumpty, whose name is echoed in "the humptyhillhead of humself..." The fall is accompanied by a sound-effect, a 111-lettered thunder word that Joyce cobbled together from the words for "thunder" in several different languages. This reinforces the point that the fall from the ladder was prompted by a Thunder God and is the source of all such myths throughout history. Significantly, the location of the fall is Dublin but it is also an ancient mythic landscape. The park referred to is not only Phoenix Park in Dublin but the Garden of Eden and all such mythic places. "The knock out" can be both the temptation of Eve but also some unspeakable act committed in the park by HCE, some offense that is never quite made explicit although it may have involved three young women and some soldiers.

Tim Finnegan's wake now follows, and the words from the ballad appear in various forms but typically convoluted into Joyce's dream language.

> Sobs they sighdid at Fillagain's chrissormiss wake, all the hoolivans of the nation, prostrated in their consternation and their duodisimally profusive plethora of ululation. There was plumbs and grumes and cheriffs and citherers and raiders and cinemen too. And the all gianed in with the shout-most shoviality. Agog and magog and the round of them agrog. To the continuation of that celebration until Hanandhunigan's extermination! Some in kinkin corass, more, kankan keening. Belling him up and filling him down. He's stiff but he's steady is Priam Olim! 'Twas he was the dacent gaylabouring youth. Sharpen his pillowscone, tap up his bier! E'erawhere in this whorl would yehear sich a din again? With their deepbrow fundigs and the dusty fidelios. They laid him brawdawn alanglast bed. With a bockalips of finisky fore his feet. And a barrow-load of guenesis hoer his head.

The image of a sleeping giant with whiskey before his feet and a barrel of Guinness (note the pun on the words "Guinness" and "Genesis") becomes a repeating image through the book. The prostrate giant lies on the landscape that becomes the city of Dublin and its environs. His erect penis (the "upturnpikepointandplace") becomes the Wellington Monument (the "willingdone," which equates the male generative organ with the wand of the Magician) in the midst of Phoenix Park, which is also the site of his "municipal sin business." Within this physical body manifests the entire world of the book, and the journey from his feet to

his head (" the humptyhillhead of humself prumptly sends an unquir-
ing one well to the west in quest of his tumptytumtoes") maps out a
transit of consciousness much like the passage from falling asleep in the
night to coming awake at the dawn. In a later article, I will return to
the relationship between Finnegan's dead body and the Irish landscape,
buildings, streets and monuments, as well as its relationship to magical
practice, But for now we will focus on the passage from death back into
life that the *Wake* describes by borrowing heavily from *The Egyptian
Book of the Dead* to describe this journey.

That James Joyce had *The Egyptian Book of the Dead* in mind when
he wrote *Finnegans Wake* is not a question of debate. References to these
ancient sources abound in the text and recur over and over, sometimes
in very explicit ways. Prior to publication, Joyce tried to recruit Frank
Budgen to write the essay "James Joyce's Book of the Dead," which
Budgen retitled "Joyce's Chapters of Going Forth by Day," a title that is
odd until one learns that the "Chapters of Coming Forth by Day" refers
to what is known as the Theban Recension of the *Book of the Dead*.
Based upon earlier pyramid and coffin texts and drawn from scattered
manuscripts, prayers, inscriptions, rituals, texts, spells, incantations and
verbal talismans, the collective known as *The Egyptian Book of the Dead*
had many variations, many of which were on Joyce's mind when he conceived his own epic of death and resurrection.

The convention of calling the multiple texts that make up the mortuary literature and funerary texts the *Book of the Dead* arose from their
recovery from tombs by grave robbers. The various collections were
compiled by priests for specific clients who had paid them to ensure
their survival in the afterlife. The Papyrus of Ani and the Papyrus of
Nu have survived in various forms, Ani and Nu being the clients for
whom the books were compiled. Both of these papyri were composed
in Thebes when that city had the focus on power within the Egyptian
kingdoms. Joyce wrote that the grand theme of his work had been
"hunted for by Theban recensors who sniff there's something behind
the Bug of the Deaf..." (134:35-36) Not only does Joyce tie together his
hero Earwicker with the Egyptian texts but refers to censors who had
been his antagonists when *Ulysses* was seized and burned by customs
officials and declared pornography.

Joyce was influenced by the opening of the tomb of Tutankhamen
in 1922 and the works of E. A. Wallis Budge, particularly his *Gods of the*

Egyptians (1904). It is possible that the "budge of klees" (511:30) is the Keys of Budge that gave Joyce the material he needed during a decade that was gripped by an insatiable appetite for anything to do with King Tut or Ancient Egypt. Evidence internal to the *Wake* suggests that Joyce had studied the Papyrus of Ani and the Papyrus of Nu since references to them are very direct.

Besides the books by Budge, Joyce seems to have utilized Sir John Gardner Wilkinson's *Manners and Customs of the Ancient Egyptians* (2nd Ed. 1878), James Henry Breasted's *Development of Religion and Thought in Ancient Egypt* (1912), Sir James Frazer's *The Golden Bough*, and Alexander Moret's *Rois et Dieux d'Egypte* (1911). From these works he extracted the material he needed to weave Egyptian theology and mortuary rites into the text of the *Wake*. As for the *Book of the Dead* itself, Joyce used the folio facsimile of the Papyrus of Ani published by Kegan Paul, Trench, Trubner in 1899.

It is very important to realize that Joyce was not an Egyptologist and his use of this material was not an act of scholarship. He was a fiction writer casting a mytho-poetic eye onto works by Victorian scholars who had their own understanding of the Egyptian language, culture and theology, one that has been considerably revised in the past hundred years. But we have little doubt that he used these books since he was seen studying them and talked quite openly about his interests. There are direct references within the *Wake*, one of which even directly describes the source book itself:

> Well, Him a being so on the flounder of his bulk like
> an overgrown babeling, let wee peep, see, at Hom, well,
> see peegee ought he ought, platterplate (6:30:32).

This description of Finnegan on his back compares the prostrate corpse at his wake to a plate illustration on page 88 in Moret's Rois et Dieux d'Egypte titled "Veillée funèbre d'Osiris-Ounnefer mort" or "The Wake of Osiris" and indeed shows the Egyptian God lying on his back. Such pseudo-intellectual jokes pervade the *Wake* and allow Joyce latitude to sound like a scholar even when he is writing as an artist.

The purpose of a book of the dead in any recension or form was to provide the Deceased with enough spells, incantations, magical rituals and spiritual knowledge of the Hidden Lands to give his soul a chance at survival in the afterlife. This concept of trying to avoid death after one has died is strange and unfamiliar to us today, but the Egyptian conception of the afterlife is quite alien. The Egyptians developed a cosmology that envisioned the Sun traveling on a barge that protected its fires from the celestial waters over which it moved. This barge traversed the sky, entering into the portals of a vast tunneled underworld called the Tuat or the Hidden Lands at sunset, traveling the whole length of the underworld throughout the course of the night, and emerging triumphant in the east at dawn.

This underworld appears repeatedly in the *Wake* and Joyce gives instructions to "Seekit headup!" (454:35), which is also a pun on Sekhet Hetep, a district in the Tuat. Joyce's description of this landscape is often amusing:

> This wastohavebeen underground heaven, or mole's paradise which was probably also an inversion of a phallopharos, intended to foster wheat crops and to ginger up tourist trade... (76:33-35).

Equally amusing are the various descriptions of Finnegan's tomb, which appears sometimes as an armor-plated battleship, other times as a "Mastabatoom" (derived from the early Egyptian burial mound or mastabas) and as a midden heap undergoing excavation (the process of excavation being the wake itself and the excavation site the tomb of the "phallopharos.") In any of these forms, the tomb is filled with all that the departed needs for survival in the afterlife, including food, physical protection, urns for internal organs, even musical instruments, and furniture from the departed's home:

> Show coffins, winding sheets, goodbuy bierchepes, cinerary urns, liealoud blasses, snuffchests, poteentubbs, lacrimal vases, hoodendoses, reekwaterbeckers, breakmiddles, zootzaks for eatlust, including upyourhealthing rookworst and meathewersoftened forkenpootsies and for that matter, javel also, any kind of inhumationary bric au brac for the adornment of his glasstone honophreum... (77: 28-33).

Armed with these, the "roundtheworlder wandelingswight" can "live all safeathomely the presenile days of his life." Joyce describes this state as "lethlulled" and lasting "from grosskopp to megapod" as long as the sleeping giant is "embalmed, of grand age, rich in death anticipated." (77:36; 78:1-6) Note the pun on the word "Lethe," one of the rivers of Hades in Greek Mythology. While many traditions provide Joyce with images and descriptions of the afterlife, it is the Egyptian that dominates throughout the book. The mortuary location is often described as "the chamber of horrus" (455:5-6), which references the Egyptian deity Horus, and the transit of its length is often described as an archeological dig filled with the rubbish of another age, including the literary fragments that make up the *Wake* itself, just as the various inscriptions, paintings, hieroglyphics and stele that adorn the Egyptian burial chamber make up the scattered materials that are the *Book of the Dead*.

It is the journey of Ra's barge across the tunneled underworld of the Tuat that the departed soul must duplicate after physical death in order to be reborn. Once that soul has entered into this underworld haunted by the forces of disintegration and annihilation, it is subject to threats from the monsters, demons and serpents against whom the only protection are the spells and rituals of the *Book of the Dead*. The price of failure is to be denied the possibility of resurrection back in the world. Ra travelled in his solar barge, protecting the fires of the Sun from this haunted world in much the same way that the soul of the Deceased must protect himself, armed with books and words of power.

This whole pattern of dying, entering the underworld, traveling through the realm of death and emerging triumphant in the dawn is not just a model for those who have died. Joyce creatively identifies the journey through the Hidden Lands with that dark mysterious journey every human being endures each night and is so familiar with that it is taken vastly for granted: falling asleep, dreaming for several hours and then waking up in the morning.

I am not trying to say that Joyce's Dreamer is passing through the Egyptian afterlife. It seems more fitting to say that the journey of Ra's solar barge from the western portal into the Tuat to the eastern gates of dawn, as well as the passage of Tim Finnegan from his death on his ladder to his resurrection at his wake, are two visions of an ultimate truth that all visions of the afterlife seek to articulate and make accessible to the human mind. The entire premise of *Finnegans Wake* is that this ultimate reality is beyond the frenzy of forms that we attempt to wrap about it.

Joyce's Tuat or Hidden Lands are filled with a multitude of places and characters that are multicultural but predominantly Irish. While filled with puns on words from almost every known language, the dialect is Irish and the prose is best enjoyed when read out loud in a good rounded brogue. The landscape is Dublin and environs even if a few New York City skyscrapers, the Tower of Babel and Cheop's Pyramid impose themselves into the Dreamer's very Irish mind:

> to rise in undress maisonry upstanded (joygrantit!), a waalworth of a skyerscape of most eyeful hoyth entowerly, erigenating from next to nothing and celescalating the himals and all, hierarchitectitiptitoploftical, with a burning bush abob off its baubletop and with larrons o'toolers clittering up and tombles a'buckets clottering down (4:35-36;5:1-4).

The word " hierarchitectitiptitoploftical" is a great example of Joyce's "pun factory," where many words are merged into one to create a multiple layer of meaning. After much consideration, I consider this word to be a perfect adjective for whatever architecture structure dominates in a culture, whether it be a ziggarut or a skyscraper. This word was used only once in the history of the human race, on page 4 of *Finnegans Wake*.

The city landscapes are further described in a style that will later appear in Dr. Seuss's *How the Grinch Stole Christmas*:

> ...what with the wallhall's horrors of rolls rights, car-hacks, stonengens, kisstvanes, tramtrees, fargobawlers, autokinotons, hippohobbilies, streetfleets, tourn-intaxes, megaphoggs, circuses and wardsmoats and basilikerks and aeropagods... and the noobibusses sleighding along Safetyfirst Street and the derryjelly-bies snooping around Tell-No-Tailors' Corner and the fumes and the hopes and the strupithump of his ville's indigenous romekeepers, homesweepers, domecreep-ers, thurum and thurum in fancymud murumd and all the uproor from all the aufroofs... (5:30-32, 6:1-5).

While this cannot be a literal description of modern Dublin, it can be the dream-Dublin as experienced in that cluttered tunnel of the night's dream journey with its constant distractions, temptations and dissipations, where the human soul, even after death, is threatened with erasure. It is not coincidental that it is on top of this landscape that Tim Finnegan falls from his ladder:

His howd feeled heavy, his hoddit did shake. (There was

a wall of course in erection) Dimb! He stottered from
the latter. Damb! he was dud. Dumb! Mastabatoom,
mastabadtomm, when a mon merries his lute is all long.
For whole the world to see (6:8-11).

His death and mummification according to the precise rituals of
the Egyptian Recension are described throughout the entire *Wake*. In
ancient Egypt, the recently deceased was mummified like Osiris and
laid out in a chamber filled with the items necessary for his journey
into the afterlife, the most important being a copy of the *Book of the
Dead*, which contained the words of power and the names of the deities
that the soul, once separated from the physical body, will encounter on
its night's journey towards the light of dawn. The soul would be able
to overcome the various demons that lusted to devour it by knowing
their names and thereby overcoming them. The soul's journey was the
journey of Osiris and the journey of the Sun every night before its daily
resurrection in the east.

In this sense, every man is a hero who faces the dark night of death
and rebirth; every man becomes identified with Osiris. In Joyce's Irish
imagination, this dead and reborn hero is also Finn MacCumhail, the
giant hero whose legend dates from the third century. His rebirth is a
"Finn, again" and the passage of all men through the path of the night
to their rebirth is a great awakening of all the Finns or *Finnegans Wake*.
This makes Joyce's removal of the apostrophe in the title very significant.

When we first encounter Finnegan at his wake, the mourners are
trying to placate him in his tomb:

Now be aisy, good Mr Finnimore, sir. And take your
laysure like a god on pension and don't be walking
abroad. Sure you'd only lose yourself in Healiopolis...
(24:16-18).

Surely a soul in the dark night can easily be lost without guidance.
His predicament, however, is severe considering his body has been
mutilated, chopped into pieces and scattered amongst the stars in the
same manner as Osiris at the hands of his brother Set.

Hep, hep, hurrah there! Hero! Seven times thereto we
salute you! The whole bag of kits, falconplumes and
jackboots incloted, is where you flung them that time.
Your heart is in the system of the Shewolf and your

crested head is in the tropic of Copricapron. Your feet
are in the cloister of Virgo. Your olala is in the region of
sahuls. And that's ashore as you were born. Your shuck
tick's swell. And that there texas is tow linen. The
loamsome roam to Laffayette is ended. Drop in your
tracks, babe! Be not unrested ! The headboddylwatcher
of the chempel of Isid, Totumcalmum, saith: I know
thee, metherjar, I know thee, salvation boat. For we
have performed upon thee, thou abramanation, who
comest ever without being invoked, whose coming is
unknown, all the things which the company of the
precentors and of the grammarians of Christpatrick's
ordered concerning thee in the matter of the work of thy
tombing. Howe of the shipmen, steep wall! (26:9-23).

This passage references not only the scattering of the body parts
but the materials of mummification ("tow linen"); the Temple of Isis
("chempel of Isid," which is also Chapelizod, the suburb of Dublin where
much of the book takes place); the mummy itself ("Totumcalmum"); the
canoptic jars ("metherjar"); the barge of the Sun ("salvation boat"); and
the first of many prayers that the Priests say over the remains of the
dead man to start off his journey through the afterlife.

The coffin in which the dead man is encased is set off onto the great
river of time and space: "oldbuoyant, inscythe his elytrical wormcas-
ket" (415.01). Like the coffin of Osiris, it eventually comes ashore and
becomes embedded into a great tree: "clad in its wood, burqued by its
bark" (503.36) . There he is "healed cured and embalsemate, pending a
rouseruction of his bogey" (498.36). This ressurection occupies a great
deal of the *Wake* and culiminates in the final chapter that depicts that
awakening of consciousness at the moment of the rising of the Sun at
dawn.

Starting on page 105, Joyce humorously gives over a hundred alternative titles for the *Wake*, several of which reinforce the connection with
the Egyptian Recensions such as "How to Pull a Good Horuscoup
even when Oldsire is Dead to the World" (105.28-29) and "Suppotes a
Ventriliquorst Merries a Corpse" (106:20). Another significant title is
"Of the Two Ways of Opening the Mouth" (106:23-24) which reveals a
further connection between the plot of the *Wake* and the rituals within
the *Book of the Dead*, which we will return to in a moment.

The Dreamer is in the night, encased in his tomb, which is well-
stocked with "all the mummyscrips in Sick Bokes' Juncroom and the

Chapters for the Cunning of the Chapters of the Conning Fox by Tail" (156:5-6) and begins his isolation with a reading of the *Book of the Dead*. "We seem to us (the real Us!) to be reading our Amenti in the sixth sealed chapter of the going forth by black" (62:25). Within the tomb is also a reed with five lines of magical inscriptions, just as described by A.E. Wallis Budge.

> Can you read the verst legend hereon? I am hather of the missed. Areed! To the dunleary obelisk via the rock vhat myles knox furlongs; to the general's postoffice howsands of patience; to the Wellington memorial half a league wrongwards; to Sara's bridge good hunter and nine to meet her: to the point, one yeoman's yard. (566:35-36, 567:1-4).

Here is a reference to Hathoor of the Missed or the Dead. It also describes five landmark points within the county of Dublin that reinforces the notion that the Hidden Lands of the Tuat is actually Ireland as filtered through the unconscious of the Dreamer.

Also, in the tomb are the "the fourbottle men" (95.27), the Four Genii who are manifested as the canoptic jars which hold the inner organs of the deceased. This mysterious quartet appears and reappears in various forms within the *Wake*, as scribes, interpreters, interrogators and even the Four Evangelists (amalgamated together as a hybrid called Mamalujo for Matthew, Mark, Luke and John). In the Egyptian tomb they aide the deceased in his journey; in the *Wake* they obscure and over-intellectualize, consisting of frustrating and falsely encouraging the central Dreamer.

After death, the separate constituents of the soul begin to separate themselves from the physical body. "Nor to Ba's berial nether, thon sloghard, this oldeborre's yaar ablong as there's a khul on a khat" (415:31-32). The *Book of the Dead* is filled with spells and incantations that must be performed by the soul in the Tuat, but none of this is possible if the Priests do not first perform the Ceremony of the Opening of the Mouth. Throughout the *Wake*, this ceremony is referred to, described, and experienced, often in humorous ways such as Shem the Penmen (HCE's son, a character based on Joyce himself) stuffing his mouth with tinned food.

Once the jaws have been pried open, the Deceased can now enter the Hall of Truth, where he defends himself in a trial of his virtue, a sort of negative confession in which he must declare what he has not done in his life on Earth while also declaring what he has learned in his preparations. Indeed, one of the alterative titles for the *Wake* is "I Have Not Stopped Water Where It Should Flow and I Know the Twentynine Names of Attraente" (105:24-25). The Deceased is confronted by 42 judges and he must know the names of each individual judge. In the *Wake*, Joyce changes the number to 29 and makes that the number of emanations of HCE's daughter, Issy or Isis or Isolde. They continually engage their brother Shem in a name game in which he must guess their true identities, in much the same way the Deceased must know the names of the various judges, demons, spirits and monsters that he meets in the Tuat. Failure at this guessing game could mean spiritual catastrophe.

In the ritual of the Coming Forth by Day, the Deceased gets closer to rebirth. He becomes aware of his own beating heart and the prospect of arriving in the womb of a human mother:

> My heart, my mother! My heart, my coming forth of darkness! (493:34-35).

The rebirth is seen as a triumphant dawn, the sun emerging from the gates of the east after a night's journey in the Tuat:

> A hand from the cloud emerges, holding a chart expanded.
>
> The eversower of the seeds of light to the cowld owld sowls that are in the domnatory of Defmut after the night of the carrying of the word of Nuahs and the night of making Mehs to cuddle up in a coddlepot, Pu Nuseht, lord of risings in the yonderworld of Ntamplin, tohp triumphant, speaketh. (593:19-24)

Indeed, the entire last chapter of the *Wake* can be seen as a soul's rebirth experienced as a sunrise. And just like the Sun, its rise is the beginning of a new cycle. The last words of the *Wake* end in the middle of a sentence that is begun on the first page:

> A way a lone a last a loved a long the (628:15-16)
>
> riverrun, past Eve and Adam's, from swerve of shore

to bend of bay, brings us by a commodius vicus of
recirculation back to Howth Castle and Environs
(3:1-3).

In this manner, the cycle is complete and the entire book begins
again, or Finns Again. However, no one reader will tackle the book
from first to last page and then start reading all over again. Most readers tackle different sections of the book at random, depending on where
they have their breakthroughs. Joyce himself encouraged readers to
dip into the book mid-stream so to speak and plunge about where s/he
saw fit.

A Thelemite reading this article would immediately see parallels
with his own daily practice, primarily *Liber Resh*, the ritual of solar adoration in which the Egyptian barge carrying the solar disk is evoked
and adored. It is instructed to perform this ritual at each dawn, noon,
sunset and midnight, describing at each stage the identity of the god
who steers the boat.

> Hail unto Thee who art Ra in Thy rising, even unto
> Thee who art Ra in Thy strength, who travellest over
> the Heavens in Thy bark at the Uprising of the Sun.

> Hail unto Thee who art Ahathoor in Thy triumphing,
> even unto Thee who art Ahathoor in Thy beauty, who
> travellest over the Heavens in Thy bark at the Mid-
> course of the Sun.

> Hail unto Thee, who art Tum in Thy setting, even unto
> Thee who art Tum in Thy joy, who travellest over the
> Heavens in Thy bark at the Down-going of the Sun.

> Hail unto Thee who art Khephra in Thy hiding,
> even unto Thee who art Khephra in Thy silence, who
> travellest over the Heavens in Thy bark at the Midnight
> Hour of the Sun.

Each of these adorations are followed by quotations from The Stele
of Revealing, a wooden funereal artifact from the 25th Dynasty that
had been buried with a priest named Ankh-ef-en-Khonsu. The Stele
had been in a Cairo museum at the time that Aleister Crowley received

The Book of the Law, and not only does the Stele play a large role in the Thelemic religion, Crowley believed himself to be a reincarnation of Ankh-ef-en-Khonsu. The verse translation of the Stele's inscription included in the *Liber Resh* practice is from Crowley's 1904 poetic translation. Although the translation is more of an interpretation, it does provide some insight into the Stele's role as a mini-*Book of the Dead* with its declarations of Ankh-ef-en-Khonsu triumphant in the Tuat:

> The light is mine; its rays consume
> Me: I have made a secret door
> Into the House of Ra and Tum,
> Of Khephra and of Ahathoor.
> I am thy Theban, O Mentu,
> The prophet Ankh-af-na-khonsu!
>
> By Bes-na-Maut my breast I beat;
> By wise Ta-Nech I weave my spell.
> Show thy star-splendour, O Nuit!
> Bid me within thine House to dwell,
> O wingèd snake of light, Hadit!
> Abide with me, Ra-Hoor-Khuit

The permutations of identities that accompany the solar barge through the lands of the dead have parallel in the shifting identities of the characters of *Finnegans Wake*. As the traveller in the barge shifts from Ra to Ahathoor to Tum to Kephra, so does Finnegan shift from Finn to HCE to Shem to Shaun to a wide array of figures from mythology, religion and history.

While James Joyce may not have been explicitly aware of Thelema, he was well versed in the Victorian conception of *The Egyptian Book of the Dead* and understood the spiritual implications and applications that had influenced Crowley. *Finnegans Wake* is printed proof that Joyce thought magically and had invented his own words of power to navigate through the uncreated unconsciousness of the human race in its own journey on its solar barge.

James Joyce's *Finnegans Wake* has long confused, perplexed and angered readers for the complexity of its prose, the obscurity of its content and meaning, and its invented language which came across to many as a cruel joke intended to defy all translation rather than be enjoyed as literature. While all these difficulties truly exist and the *Wake* cannot be approached casually, an examination of its sources can demystify much of it and shed clear light on Joyce's methods and motives.

This article examined one of Joyce's major sources, the collections of writings known apocryphally as *The Egyptian Book of the Dead*. These writings, which dealt with the journey of the soul in the afterlife leading towards rebirth, were used by Joyce as a formative structure in the *Wake*. The Dreamer of the text passes through a series of ordeals, identity fragmentation, dreams within dreams, and eventual awakening in much the same manner in which the Deceased of the *Book of the Dead* passes from death into the underworld and back into life. It would be negligent to ignore Joyce's reliance upon the Egyptian texts in the composition of his own epic, as such study rewards the reader immeasurably.

This makes *Finnegans Wake* a book that matters to a reader such as a Thelemite whose own religion is heavily dependent upon Egyptian theology, solar worship and magical rites. James Joyce took his material piecemeal from various sources both ancient and contemporary, but he intended to craft his prose as magical words of power, giving the Twentieth Century its own book of the dead, a guidebook to the journey of life and death, a journey that is experienced each and every night by all humans when they sleep.

First published in *Behutet: Modern Thelemic Magick & Culture*, Issue 30, Summer, 2006.

ALMOST GONE: THE RUINS
OF BETHLEHEM STEEL

America is a land littered with the ruins of the industrial age. Abandoned factories, mills and worker housing seem to be just as much a part of our landscape as shopping malls and McMansion developments by the Toll Brothers. But not every day do you find an abandoned place that not only hauntingly evokes another age but is so significant in historical context that it is in itself an American icon.

Just such a place is the ruins of the Bethlehem Steel Corporation in South Bethlehem, PA. The Steel, as it is affectionately known by the residents of the town, was the second largest steel corporation in the country. The product that rolled off its assembly lines built many of the skylines of our major cities and supplied billions of tons of armaments for every conflict from the Civil War to Vietnam. Its forgeries and blast furnaces supplied steel to the Empire State Building, the Golden Gate Bridge, the Panama Canal and every naval battleship during World War II. The scale of Bethlehem Steel is hard to fathom by numbers alone, but the plant in South Bethlehem at the height of its growth covered more than 1,500 acres, employed over 30,000 men and women and boasted seven blast furnaces and just as many machine shops, Number 2 being the largest machine shop in the world.

In 1995, after a long steady decline of the American steel industry, the last iron was cast in Bethlehem and the plant closed its doors forever. Much of the remains of Bethlehem steel is now rusting and rotting at its location along the banks of the Lehigh River. A casual drive along Route 413 across the Minsi Trail Bridge and along the snaking perimeters fencing on

Third Street suddenly brings one within eye shot of the five remaining blast furnaces, cyclopean reminders of another age. To one uninitiated, the furnaces leap out like the hulks of spaceships that never quite made it off their gurneys and are now rotting in the sun.

Marc Reed, a painter and photographer from Lambertville, NJ, had much experience with industrial ruins. For many years he had photographed abandoned factories and power stations so he could have a visual reference for his paintings. When he decided to go photograph the Steel, it was with the intention of doing a series of paintings.

He was no stranger to the weirdness factor: Lambertville, after all, was home to the world's largest animal penis collection and the haunted shell of a burned down elementary school, both of which had been featured in earlier issues of *Weird N.J.* But Bethlehem Steel was a colossal icon of American industrial history and seemed worthy of photographic preservation. The corporation that owned it had declared bankruptcy and the Grand Old Lady of Steel was now in danger of being demolished. Marc felt it was important that someone document what was left of her before she vanished.

On New Year's Eve of 2003 Marc drove out to Bethlehem and parked his car at one of the structures at the plant that was still being used as a skating rink. He then got past the fencing that had been put up around the perimeter of the blast furnaces and headed off into the massive network of ruins.

"Trespassing is not something I normally condone," he explains. "The fence around the site was put there to prevent vandalism and injuries. But I'm a hiker and backpacker so I apply the backpacker's credo to my 'industrial spelunking' adventures: I take only photographs and leave only footprints. I am a silent observer. I disturb nothing."

Against his better judgment, Marc decided to have a go at entering the blast furnaces via the train tracks. The first blast furnace he entered was the A furnace, the oldest and smallest of Bethlehem's furnaces which had been out of commission since the 1960s. The casting floor there had been reduced to a shapeless mound; its brick-lined runners that once flowed with molten iron were buried under years of shifting sand. Broken staircases, crumbling brick, and large flaky scabs of rusted metal were strewn about.

He considered climbing some of the stairs around A furnace, but he doubted they could hold his weight. He continued to B furnace which was bigger and somewhat less dilapidated. A control room at the base of the furnace looked like it had been through an explosion. Months later, a Bethlehem steelworker viewing the photograph he took there confirmed that indeed an explosion did occur at B furnace in the 1980s.

Twenty years later debris was still strewn about like it had happened yesterday.

Marc took several other pictures in B, C, D and E furnaces and then emerged at the gaping entrance to the Gas-Blowing Engine Room. The Engine Room used to serve double-duty by generating electricity for the plant and sending high-pressure air to the blast furnaces, but it was shut down along with the blast furnaces in November 1995; and, like the furnaces, had been left to rust for eight years.

After photographing the Engine Room in the ghostly glow of the setting sun, Marc saw that across the street was an empty warehouse, now inhabited only by owls. He walked through this warehouse and was surprised to find himself at the doorway of the Welfare Rooms. At the time he didn't know what the Welfare Rooms had been used for. The presence of toilets and showers indicated that this must have been some kind of locker room. Metal baskets dangled randomly from the ceiling by chains. They had the basic shape of pumpkin-head Halloween baskets. Ventilation holes gave them the appearance of having eyes and mouths.

"In the silence and the gathering darkness, my own pounding heart provided an unsettling soundtrack," Marc recounts. "I set my camera up on a tripod and shot some long exposures. The baskets stared at me blankly. I couldn't shake the feeling that I was being watched."

Upon exiting the Welfare Rooms, Marc decided to enter the Number 2 Machine Shop. This had been one of eight machine shops at the plant, but it was the largest and had served as Bethlehem Steel's main ordnance facility during World Wars I and II. There was a day when it buzzed with men and women busily forging the weapons that won America's wars. Now it was cold, dark and silent. Marc took what pictures he could take, walked back into the darkened blast furnaces, and headed back to his car.

"There is something otherworldly about wandering alone inside an industrial behemoth that once employed 30,000 people," he stated. "It is eerie, but it is also magical. It's somewhat akin to one of those last-person-on-earth episodes of *Twilight Zone*, or possibly a science fiction movie where spacemen examine some destroyed alien civilization. Looking at some of the machinery left rusting in the mill, I could only theorize what it had been used for."

By the time Marc left the ruins, he had a few hundred photographs in his digital camera, and he was ready to go home and try to process, both digitally and psychologically, what he had seen. He was determined to learn the story behind each building and each room.

"What I found during my research," Marc says, "was the story of America. Bethlehem Steel was about the Industrial Revolution, immigration, race relations, unparalleled prosperity and terrible wars. It seemed in locked step with the history of America and, to some extent, also with the history of man."

But very soon, his relationship to Bethlehem Steel and to his own photographs changed into something quite unexpected.

On the day of Marc's visit, unbeknownst to anybody but a handful of insiders at International Steel Group (the company that purchased the bankrupt steel manufacturer earlier that year), accountants were busily liquidating Bethlehem Steel assets and canceling its stock. For at the stroke of midnight, Bethlehem Steel Corporation would be officially dissolved. In essence, Marc Reed was the last person to wander on the property of Bethlehem Steel while the corporation still existed. As soon as he heard that, he knew that his photographs could be a lot more than just visual references for his oil paintings.

The future of the ruins had been a matter of controversy and Marc now started to follow the public debate. During his visit, he noticed the decrepit state of many of the structures. The machine shops were literally collapsing, to the point you could see giant rents down the brickwork on the sides of the buildings. The floors were being pushed upwards like small mountain ranges by the pressure of the collapsing walls. In order to preserve these buildings, they would no doubt have to be demolished first and then rebuilt, a project that not only would defeat the purpose of restoration but would cost more money than it was worth.

In January, an ISG representative was contacted regarding their intentions for the Bethlehem PA steel mill and coldly remarked they would just as soon knock it down. This is precisely what happened to many historic steel mills around Pittsburgh.

Shortly after ISG's coldly indifferent announcement regarding the fate of Bethlehem Steel, Marc read a newspaper article announcing the formation of a Bethlehem grassroots preservation effort called Save Our Steel. They were holding a kickoff meeting in January 2004. "I went. I listened and I networked. I got phone numbers and made phone calls. Not only did they help get me back into the plant to complete the photographic study, but they helped make my work become part of the historic ongoing preservation initiative."

The ruins are now in the legal possession of BethWorks Now, an LLC founded by the Sands of Las Vegas Corporation to develop a casino complex on the property. Save Our Steel and many other grass roots organizations in the Lehigh Valley are trying to raise awareness that such a venture can easily go astray and ruin the historical integrity of the town and its legacy of Steel. The promotion of an industrial history museum, as well as the rehabilitation of some of the existing structures, is an attempt to preserve a very important part of American history and culture.

Marc's photographs stand as a testament to Bethlehem Steel before the wrecking ball can obliterate it forever. "I consider myself a painter and hadn't seriously considered creating any photo documentary," he says. "But there was such a wealth of information in every detail of the now-endangered steel mill. I decided this would be a photography exhibit and the basis of a DVD documentary. I spent the next year working with Garden Bay Films of Lambertville, NJ to produce *Almost Gone: A Pilgrimage to Bethlehem*, as well as a photography exhibit of the same title."

The ruins of Bethlehem Steel are still there, behind the heavily patrolled perimeter fencing. There are plenty of stunning sights to see without trespassing on the property: the majestic blast furnaces, the crumbling machine shops, the brick iron foundries dating back to civil war times. Hopefully, if Save Our Steel succeeds in their long-term goal of preserving some of the historical structures, many of us may have the pleasure of entering the plant when it reopens to the public as a museum and an entertainment complex.

UPDATE 2018:

On the site of the former Bethlehem Steel is now the Sands Casino Resort Bethlehem, a hotel and casino complex.

After moving to New Jersey from New York, Richard discovered what he considered New Jersey's saving grace: *Weird N.J.* magazine. After spending the winter of 2003/2004 sneaking into the shuttered Bethlehem Steel plant to take pictures, I showed my photos to Richard and he immediately wanted to use them in a story to submit to *Weird N.J.* And he did. This was the beginning of a collaboration with Richard that led to our short art film *Almost Gone* (also about Bethlehem Steel).

While working on material to finish the film, Richard and I explored the abandoned steel mill together on three occasions. While exploring, his personal observations regarding our large, strange, and dystopian surroundings kept me very entertained. Richard had a great sense of humor. Making the film was entirely Richard's idea, but I adopted this artistic pursuit and today, thirteen years after *Almost Gone*, I still continue to create short art films about abandonment and decay—much like the one I worked on with Richard.

Marc Reed
Lambertville, NJ
www.marcreed.com

First published in *Weird N.J.*, Issue 27.

DAVID BOWIE LIVE:
BEFORE AND AFTER ENO

David Bowie is a performer who has always drawn upon magic and mysticism to enact his art. His pantheon of theatrical alter egos (Major Tom, Ziggy Stardust, Aladdin Sane, the Thin White Duke), his shamanic use of stage craft to propel audiences into an altered reality, his surreal science fiction lyrics and suggestive occult references, elevated him above the average glitter rock star of the 1970s. Bowie was the extra-terrestrial who fell to Earth, the Gnostic alien who had been to higher planes through the use of drugs, magical practices and strange sex, ready to bring visions and wisdom to the human race through the vehicle of rock and roll.

His concerts were acts of ceremonial magic, his transmogrified body painted with sci-fi make-up ("screwed up eyes and screwed down hairdo"), morphing through different personas and states of consciousness. As Rogan Taylor commented in his excellent study of show business and shamanism, *The Death and Resurrection Show: From Shaman to Superstar* (1985), Bowie was the "man-woman about to take to the air," his Ziggy Stardust shows were "a purely magical drama revolving around the three worlds...[it's] central dramatic device: the transformation of the hero into a fantastic hero-form," and his *Diamond Dogs* concept was the "archaic shamanistic marriage of man and beast." By the time Bowie had become a rock star, he had studied Tibetan Buddhism and presumably had more than passing acquaintance with Magick (he tipped his hat to both Aleister Crowley and the Golden Dawn in his early song "Quicksand"). When he chanted the word "Ch-ch-ch-changes!" in one of his pop songs, he was not kidding around.

For a while, in the loopy swirl of the early 1970s, he embodied the

233

merging of pop culture and shamanic mysticism in an industry that was already awash with pop mysticism. Concept albums like *Ziggy Stardust* and *Diamond Dogs* unfolded like the soundtracks of fantastical movies that had never been filmed. References to Kubrick's *2001: A Space Odyssey*, *Clockwork Orange*, and the novel *1984*, his well-known use of William Burroughs' cut-up technique to generate lyrics, and his name dropping of Kahlil Gibran, Andy Warhol, and Bob Dylan gave the *Cracked Actor* an apostolic authority from a much larger paradigmatic cultural context.

His ambiguous sexuality enabled both male and female fans to vent their lust in a non-threatening way; his simulated fellatio on stage with guitarist Mick Ronson, his body fitting tights and envelope pushing nudity, and his provocative revelations to the press about his "tri-sexuality" further mystified his eroticism and put him several layers of transgression beyond anything rock had seen before. Throughout much of the 1970s he was rock and roll's cosmic shaman, highly theatrical, full of mystery, and endlessly original.

However, something had happened to David Bowie by the later part of the decade. He had wiped the lightning bolt off his face, moved to West Berlin and was producing obscure post-modern electronica, hobnobbing with the likes of Brian Eno and Robert Fripp, two musical intellectuals who combined the alchemy of the recording studio with chic European experimentalism and obscure mysticisms (Eno professed an interest in the Mystical Kabala and Fripp quit music altogether in the mid-1970s to join a Gurdjieff group). Like Thomas Jerome Newton, the character he played in *The Man Who Fell to Earth*, Bowie was disappearing behind a shifting façade of designer clothing and creative decadence.

The albums *Low*, *Heroes*, and *Lodger*, known to Bowie fans as the Berlin Trilogy, were colder, more distant and minimal, less easy to interpret than his earlier work. The differences between the Bowie of 1972 and the Bowie of 1979 were profound, like the difference between Marcel Marceau and Marcel Duchamps, one full of amusement and magic who leaves children dazzled wonder-filled, the other alienating and mercurial, swathed in personal vocabularies and arcane techniques. What had happened to Bowie? Was this elegantly dressed dude of post-modern music and electronic ambiance just another one of his theatrical masks?

To make things even more confusing, Bowie ended the decade duetting with Bing Crosby on a television Christmas special, comically bantering with the aging crooner and revealing that he was just as comfortable lounging in a family living room with a log thrown on the fire, singing carols and enjoying some eggnog, as he was trancing out in a Berlin nightclub, distorting his consciousness with sex and strange drugs. Bing Crosby, oddly enough, was greatly impressed with Bowie, calling him a fine clean-cut lad and trading home phone numbers with him (Der Bingle died one month later so this collaboration was never pursued). What was it about Bowie that enabled him to trade masks so easily, even if it was the illusionary mask of having no mask? In 1980 when he recorded one of his strongest albums, *Scary Monsters*, he presented his "true face" behind all the masks: a Pierrot clown pulling off his mask to reveal more make-up and more clown faces.

Who was David Bowie? What was his true face? By comparing the Bowie of the early 1970s to the bleached blond super star, ten years later, who strutted in Armani suits for his Serious Moonlight tour, one can see that the actor playing the character of David Bowie had undergone some unique transformation, perhaps changing with the times, perhaps following marketing strategies to sell records. Either way, he was not one to stay the same from one year to the next. Part of the endlessly fascinating appeal of David Bowie was his ability to magically morph and to hide his true personality and selfhood at the center of some elaborate maze that was never meant to be solved.

Which brings us to the CD releases of two of Bowie's live albums from the 1970s, *David Live* (1974) and *Stage* (1978). Although originally released on vinyl a scant four years apart from each other, they stand at opposite ends of that transformation that shocked and alienated his original fan base.

David Live is nicely repackaged in a fold-out CD cover accommodating two disks and a booklet full of lush photographs from the concert at Philadelphia's Tower Theater. It also includes an illuminating essay by career-spanning Bowie collaborator Tony Visconti who produced the album and who comes clean about the re-recordings that were necessary to preserve the integrity of the music. Featuring an extraordinary line-up of musicians including Michael Kamen, Luther Van Dross, David Sanborn, and Earl Slick (all of whom went on to impressive solo careers of their own), Bowie is caught in the spotlight without his Ziggy or Aladdin masks, abandoned by the Spiders From Mars, prancing about in a polka dotted shirt with red suspenders and red hair like a Southern California mall mime, portraying the character known simply as David, your host for the evening's delights, visibly the same clown who once upon a time sang amusing songs on the BBC about "Laughing Gnomes" and stoned space men.

But despite the show biz surface, the extraordinary surrealism of these songs would be a hard sell to Bing Crosby. With the exception of a few R&B soul tunes (like Ray Cropper's "Knock on Wood") that look forward to Bowie's *Young Americans* album, the set list is top heavy with material from *Diamond Dogs* and *Aladdin Sane*, a phantasmagoria of dreamscapes and fragmented imagery. Perhaps some of the songs like "Panic in Detroit" and "Suffragette City" are so familiar to us now that we have long ceased meditating upon the lyrics, but when you hear them fresh after such a long decade away from them, they really come across strange and wonderful. And dark as hell.

Unlike the early Bob Dylan who had stripped his act of all theatrical pretense and stood before audiences as a self-righteous social commentator, Bowie had a very different message: "The times they are a'telling, and the changing isn't free....Beware the savage jaw of 1984." He is dark, violent and full of black imagery, from the apocalyptic cityscapes of "Diamond Dogs," through the drug addiction and vampirism of "Sweet Thing/Candidate" to the pessimistic solitude of "Rock N' Roll Suicide," Bowie was no light weight song writer, and perhaps *David Live* loses a bit since we are denied the full visual experience of the stage show, but the songs, presented out of the context of their concept albums, as if David is trying to market his hits to a Las Vegas audience, shine like dark gems. Listen carefully. Crack open the old vinyl gatefolds and recover the lyrics in printed form. Follow along and see how full of tension and horror these songs really are, as if the painted mime has seduced us into his tent of balloons and funny animals, and then slammed the door shut behind us as he unleashes his hell hounds and black visions of a despairing future.

These may not be the best performances of the included songs, they may be rock stadium slick, overdubbed to perfection, lacking in the rawness we witnessed in the Ziggy Stardust documentary, but it is refreshing and revelatory to hear them again, thirty years later, through a musical telescope as 1974 accelerates behind us like a shooting star.

David Live represents the last manifestation of the old Bowie, the sci-fi alien with the multiple personalities and Gnostic visions. Shortly after, he would record *Young Americans* and *Station to Station*, two albums that bridge the gap of his inner transformation as an artist. It was *Station to Station* that caught the ear of the man I like to call "The Ghost in the Machine," the haunted shadow lurking behind so many of the major innovations in rock music during the 1970s and 1980s, that alchemical wizard of the recording studio, Brian Eno, the man who is everywhere and nowhere (he rarely broadcasts his own presence outside of liner notes and songwriting credits). In turn, his album, *Another Green World*, had mesmerized Bowie, and perhaps it was Bowie's careful listening to Eno's music that turned his mind and creative aspirations back toward Europe.

I define Eno as alchemical because during this period he was literally transforming the creative energies of musicians as he produced them. As bands like the Talking Heads, U2, Devo and countless others would reach the boundaries of their creative potential, Eno would suddenly appear in their lives like some holy guardian angel come to guide them on the sun path. He would enter into the life of the band, maintain a large degree of creative input, in many cases co-writing songs and playing instruments, infusing their work with the magical energy required to record their most profound, most inspired and most enduring albums. For example, the song "One" from U2's *Achtung Baby!* album (produced by Eno and recorded, coincidentally at Hansa-by-the-Wall, the same recording studio used by Bowie and Eno for much of the Berlin Trilogy) was originally composed as an instrumental titled from Eno's name spelled backwards.

The albums would be infused with a feeling of Eno, a process Peter Gabriel once labeled "Enossification." The Talking Heads (*Fear of Music* and *Remain in Light*), U2 (*The Joshua Tree* and *The Unforgettable Fire*) and Bowie (*Low*, *Heroes*, and *Lodger*) would all go on to create much more famous and commercial albums, and would enjoy much higher levels of pop success in the charts, but never again would their albums be Enossified. Like any good holy guardian angel, Eno would lead them to the outer limits of the abyss, and then abandon them.

The story of how Bowie become Enossified is explicitly laid out in a small book by Hugo Wilcken called *Low* (2005) that is part of Continuum's 33 1/3rd series, each volume of which is devoted to a single classic rock album. It is significant that the editors of the series chose Low as a signature Bowie album. It is his weirdest, most experimental, and most puzzling album, certainly his least commercial (when the studio suits heard the master tapes, they threatened to suppress its release) but the story of how the album was recorded and what was transpiring in Bowie's personal life, is extremely revealing and lays bare the course of events.

Wilcken picks up the story with the release of *Station to Station* and shows how Bowie pre-echoed his Berlin persona with a stage show heavily influenced by surrealist cinema and an "austere, expressionistic flavour redolent of the European modernism of the 1920s," and his increasing interest in the Nazis (Bowie claimed that he was writing a screenplay about Josef Goebbels and made some misunderstood public statements about Fascism (he wanted to start his own country—a conceit that has ironic overtones to his recent attempts to build an elaborate on-line web community and to start his own bank)). Most importantly, Wilcken describes the effect that occult beliefs and practices were having on Bowie's state of mind and his art.

David Bowie's relationship to the occult has always been explicit. In "Quicksand" (1971), he states boldly, "I'm closer to the Golden Dawn/Immersed in Crowley's uniform of imagery." And in "Station to Station" (1976) he lets the cat out of the bag with the line, "One magical movement from Kether to Malkuth" and indeed published a picture of himself reclined on the floor drawing a Tree of Life with colored chalk. Bowie himself claimed that the title *Station to Station* was a reference to the stations of the cross, but it is more reasonable to assume that the singer is driving "like a demon" from Kether to Malkuth.

Although these are his most famous and most oft-quoted occult references, magical sensibilities permeate almost everything he did in the early 1970s. The emphasis on being a rock and roll star with the emphasis on "star" ("Every man and every woman is a star" is a fundamental tenant of Crowley's mytho-poetic philosophy), and the rock star as divine being, an extra-terrestrial who has fallen from above, punctuates the spiritual aspect of his stage craft and personas. Besides, Ziggy's last name is "Stardust" and Aladdin Sane's name is not just a clever pun about mental illness, but a reference to Sufi parables and fairy tales. Also, the Thin White Duke of "Station to Station" who is throwing "sure white stains" could very well be Crowley himself who once published a scandalous book entitled White Stains. If one digs deeper, one can draw even tighter connections, but if you pull back to look at the wider picture, it is clear that David Bowie is a magician/shaman performing his magic both in the studio and on stage.

When Wilcken tackles Bowie's state of mind at the time of the recording of *Station to Station* and *Low*, he dips into the occult waters to describe some of the references and explain a thing or two about Sephiroths. His scholarship is not entirely stellar, since at one point he explains that Aleister Crowley shared his membership in the Golden Dawn with Heinrich Himmler, who had been born in 1900 and would have been a toddler at the time that the Golden Dawn splintered into fragments. No doubt he thought there was a connection because Bowie mentioned Himmler in the song "Quicksand" right after Crowley.

Wilcken also spends some time discussing a hidden and often neglected chapter in Bowie's transformation: the recording of Iggy Pop's "The Idiot," which was produced in Berlin by Bowie and which defied explanation. Certainly much different from any work previously done by either artist, it was, as Wilcken describes, a cross between Kraftwerk and James Brown, a prototype for the gloomy debut album that was to come two years later from the Manchester cult band Joy Division, who had originally called themselves Warsaw after one of *Low*'s instrumental tracks. Bowie, who had turned toward Berlin via a meeting with Christopher Isherwood, had enlisted Iggy Pop as a sort of demented Sally Bowles to his "Herr Issyvoo."

Wilcken explains vividly how Bowie's move to Berlin was driven by his fascination with the surreal landscapes, the post-war gloom, the aura of devastation and left-over monuments from the Fascist era. The instrumentals on the second side of *Low* ("Warszawa," "Weeping Wall," "Art Decade," and "Subterraneans") all draw deeply on the dark ambiance of Berlin, the weeping despair of its dead streets and the misty decadence of its underground clubs and emerging electronic music. Further, they all share a "willingness to treat music as soundscapes, rather than structured songs with their melodic narratives."

Wilcken also describes the sources of Bowie's musical transformation. While heavily under the influence of Brian Eno's *Another Green World*, he also became transfixed by the electronic bands that he was hearing in Europe, including Kraftwerk, Neu! and Can. These bands heavily "inform" the second side of Low and have more than a passing influence on the short, pulsing songs on the first side, such as "Breaking Glass," "Sound and Vision," and "Be My Wife."

During the *Low* sessions, Bowie had become obsessed with what is commonly known as "magical thinking." Combining occult beliefs with cocaine is a surefire mechanism to trigger paranoia, and Bowie certainly was lacing his white powder with angels and demons. His obsessions with psychic self-defense led him to create delusions about the people he was working with. Several times recording sessions had to be stopped because Bowie was convinced a band member was performing black magic against him. Further, his marriage was deteriorating and Wilcken describes the breakdown and divorce in painful detail, putting it in the context of Bowie's worsening mental state.

But what came out of the *Low* sessions was something new, something brilliant and paradigm shifting. Poised at the cusp of the punk movement, perhaps *Low* competed on the record store shelves with an explosion of New Wave and indy label bands that were transforming the industry, but the album's long-term influence is certainly apparent. Although the initial reviews were mixed (the *NME* said that the album was "stunningly beautiful if you can get past taking it as some kind of personal insult") the album grew on listeners over time. Wilcken explains, "A whole strand of post-punk owes its existence to some sort of combination of the glam-era and Berlin-era Bowie personae; to Bowie's and Eno's injection of the synthetic into the three-minute pop song... to the album's funk/electronic hybrid; to the turn toward a European aesthetic; to the non-pop experimentalism of the second side; to *Low*'s appropriation of modernist alienation."

Indeed, Philip Glass, one of America's most esteemed composers, has fashioned *The Low Symphony*. In 2002 Bowie himself performed the album in its entirety as befitting its rank as a cultural phenomenon; and a 2-disc 30thAnniversary edition is in the works. Few fans over the age of 35 do not have each note of the Berlin Trilogy memorized in their brain stem. As time moves on, *Low*, the one Bowie album that was least likely to survive with any critical attention, has become a crucial part of rock history; and Bowie's "Berlin personae" has much to do with the album's lasting mystique.

Stage is a re-mastering of a Madison Square Garden concert that was originally released in 1978. Technically, the show was part of the *Heroes* tour and featured a good deal of live material drawn from the *Low* and *Lodger* albums. Although Brian Eno is nowhere to be found amongst the musicians, clearly he had a large hand in composing and shaping the sound of many of the songs. Hearing *Stage* directly after *David Live* is revelatory and speaks volumes about Bowie's Enossification.

The entire first disc presents nothing but material from *Low* and *Heroes* with the exception of "Fame," which punctuates at the very end.

The impact of hearing "Warszawa" live, Bowie's most artsy and non-commercial track, presented with a thundering confidence that makes the performance better in many ways than the original studio recording, is startling to an audience accustomed to the Bowie opening with a more kick-ass like "Rebel Rebel." Clearly, from the first thundering notes, this is a very different Bowie we are dealing with. The songs from *Low*, in particular "Sound and Vision" and "Breaking Glass," feel more rounded, more conceived and song-like than the original recordings. Instead of being pieced together by Bowie and Eno as a challenging studio experiment, they are here played by a polished band that has worked around the experimental forms of the songs, shaping them into something more presentable to a stadium screaming for Ziggy Stardust showstoppers.

The song "Heroes," which was originally composed and recorded in Berlin, has references to armed guards on a wall (the recording studio Hansa-by-the-Wall where *Heroes* was recorded had windows that looked directly out onto the armed guards in the towers of the Berlin Wall) has locked that song into every Bowie fan's imagination with the disturbed politics of that war torn city. But Bowie's presentation on *Stage* is one of a polished showman, as if the personal torments, the occult paranoia, the disintegrating relationships and fractured attempts to find new musical forms, is now behind him, and he can strut his skinny stuff across a stadium stage once more, rocking out, and making the audience cream their pants.

Despite Eno's absence, other contributors help make this concert recording one of the most compelling that Bowie has ever released. The marvelous band included the Twang Bar King himself, Adrien Belew, whose wobbling guitar solos and aural pyrotechnics sound like dress rehearsals for the experimental deconstructions of melody he brought to the Taking Heads' *Remain in Light* and to Bowie's next album *Lodger*. Belew himself was only a year or two away from the exponential expansion of his talents, recording with Frank Zappa, touring with the Taking Heads, and then becoming the front man in one of the most musically awesome events of the 1980s, the reconstruction of King Crimson, where he held his own playing lead guitar with God-On-Earth Robert Fripp directing from his stage right stool. Belew is one of the great musicians of the 1980s and here, on Bowie's most powerful live album, just on the cusp of having his genius recognized, he is giving musical birth to himself.

Much of the tracks on the second disc derive from *Station to Station* and *Ziggy Stardust*. In fact, Ziggy is represented by five straight tunes in a row (I believe on the vinyl copy of *Stage* this was an entire side) which sound just as driven and exciting as they appeared in the Ziggy Stardust movie. The world doesn't really need another live version of "Hang On to Yourself" (I once joked that Bowie's next release was going to be the 4-CD *Hang On to Yourself Live* box-set), but how often are you going to hear a live version of "Soul Love" or "Five Years"?

Station to Station is represented by "TVC15," "Stay," and "Station to Station." The final instrumental ending of "Stay" is sheer electricity, transcending the original studio recording, and builds with a soaring Belewian solo to its crashing conclusion. "TVC15" is just as quirky and odd as it was when Bowie presented it on *Saturday Night Live* while dressed as an airline stewardess with a toy poodle, Klaus Nomi miming behind him.

After *Stage*, Bowie was to record his last two masterpieces, *Lodger* and *Scary Monsters* and then he put away his Japanese make-up and mime costumes for the Armani suits and the financially successful pop tunes. It was significant that after completing the *Low–Heroes–Lodger* trilogy with Brian Eno, Bowie was left with a dubious hole where his Enossification used to be. Only when he reunited with Brian Eno in 1995's *Outside* did Bowie do anything as musically innovative or self-transformative as *Low*. Fortunately, he has been a tad bit Enossified ever since.

First published in *Behutet: Modern Thelemic Magick & Culture*, Issue 28, Winter 2005.

CHARLIE CHAPLIN: THE MAKING OF A WOMAN OF PARIS

PART 1: A GENIUS'S FIRST FAILURE

In the summer of 1923, Charlie Chaplin, one of the most famous men in Hollywood, if not the world, released a film entitled *A Woman of Paris*. It was, by some reckoning, his 72nd film, made in the ninth year of his filmmaking career. As usual with his productions, he wrote, directed, produced, scored and produced the movie, filmed at his own independent studio on LeBrea Boulevard, to be distributed by United Artists, a company that he had founded along with his fellow independents and film giants D.W. Griffith, Mary Pickford and Douglas Fairbanks. It was a film that was much anticipated and his most ambitious film to date. Chaplin, a small, funny Englishman who had emerged out of the English Music Hall to conquer the world with his self-effacing comedy and his endearing character that many called the Tramp, but he preferred to call The Little Fellow, had been directing, writing and starring in his own films for nearly a decade, and with each release, his artistry became more refined. The release of *The Kid* (1921), a funny but emotionally powerful film about homelessness and child abandonment, had touched the hearts of millions. Advanced word was that *A Woman of Paris*, his first feature for United Artists, would be a masterpiece, Chaplin's greatest yet.

However, the film was a box office failure, despite the favorable reviews from the critics, several of whom did dub it his greatest achievement. As a reaction against the poor response from the public, Chaplin withdrew the film and kept it close to his chest for nearly fifty years.

It became a lost Chaplin film, soon overshadowed by the phenomenal success of *The Gold Rush* (1925), *City Lights* (1931), and *Modern Times* (1936). What had gone wrong with *A Woman of Paris* that relegated it to a low ranking on the Chaplin scorecard? How could a cinematic genius and the most beloved entertainer in the world have created a film that nobody wanted to see?

It is easy to state the obvious: *A Woman of Paris* was not a comedy, and Chaplin did not act in it (although he did have a three-second cameo heavily disguised as a train porter). To those who had spent a full decade watching Chaplin's burlesque comedy and slapstick genius move at a breakneck pace, roared with laughter at his endless innovation and increasingly more sophisticated comic scenarios, who had come to love the Tramp and his conflicts full of fun and pathos combined in a perfect blend; the radical shift to a dry, subtle comedy of manners about wealthy Parisians and starving artists in their boudoirs, empire apartments and raucous nightclubs was just too much. Evidently, Chaplin had not judged his audiences correctly. There was a market for *A Woman of Paris* (von Stroheim and Lubitsch would have released the film to great acclaim, no doubt), but Chaplin's audiences were expecting something different.

In the early 1920s, commercial narrative filmmaking had only been around for little more than a decade, and the medium was still evolving. Films had not yet learned to talk, but they had learned to move an audience to heightened emotions with the same artistry as a great novel. A style of acting was evolving that was appropriate for the screen if not the stage, a subtler approach centered on recognizable and true reactions. This was in great contrast to the exaggerated and outdated style of acting that had carried over from the Victorian stage. Chaplin, who had started as an acrobatic comedian designing gags to make people howl with laughter, was now openly exploring human conflict and the passions of the heart. In *The Kid*, he had shocked the world with a perfect blend of comedy and pathos, especially the scene in which the small child the Tramp has taken under his protection in the slum neighborhood is forcibly removed from him by the orphan authorities. In this one scene, Chaplin's huge potential as a filmmaker and performer had been achieved, and audiences were expecting more. It was not a guaranteed failure for him to cross the line into high drama. But perhaps the transition was too sudden. To remove his popular persona and trademark comedy from the production completely was a hasty and unwise choice.

Yet, there were several other reasons for the film's failure, any of which can be traced to career choices and professional relationships that went back several years.

PART 2: FEMALE TROUBLE

Chaplin had gotten his start in motion pictures when he joined the Keystone Film Studio run by Mack Sennett in early 1914. By the end of the year, he had cranked out 32 films through which he became a film star of unprecedented fame. His films were shown all over the world and his rapid rise included his transformation into a film director. Only 24 years old, he was one of Hollywood's most eligible bachelors. His flirtations with leading lady and director Mable Normand and his passionate pursuit of early film starlet Peggy Pearce ended in loneliness, with him living at the Athletic Club in downtown Los Angeles. Those who knew him at the time remembered the Spartan existence that this ex-inmate of the London workhouses led despite his rapidly acquired wealth. In his own mind he was still a gamin of the streets, orphaned and alone, speaking with an undignified Cockney accent and intimidated by wealth and power.

When his contract with Keystone ended, he signed up with the Essanay Film studios in Niles, California, a unit that had built its fame on top of one-reel Westerns starring "Bronco Bill" Anderson. The studio was located about an hour away from San Francisco to exploit the scrub lands for western landscapes. In this remote northern California town, Chaplin set up shop with more creative control over his films, expanded budgets and longer running times to allow for more elaborate stories. He had a studio at which to shoot his pictures, a stock company cast that briefly included Ben Turpin, and a camera man who was to become his lifelong collaborator, Rollie Totehroh. The only element missing was a leading lady, a situation that became more acute after he had interviewed several chorus girls, all of whom seemed to lack that extra something that translated as star quality.

A colleague suggested a young lady, barely nineteen years old, named Edna Purviance, who worked as a secretary in the city. Chaplin arranged a meeting with her and it was love at first sight. He was captivated by her beautiful eyes, handsome face and thick blond hair. The only problem was that she was deeply depressed over the collapse of a recent love affair and had a serious, dour expression that suppressed her charming smile. After getting her to fake an act of hypnotism with him at a studio dinner party, he fell hard for her charm and playfulness. Soon they were engaged in a discrete affair that enhanced their performances together in all the rest of Chaplin's films for the next decade.

On screen they were a natural team, exuding a magic that translated to an enthralled audience. As the Tramp character, Charlie fell in love with Edna time after time, in classics such as *The Tramp*, *Easy Street*, *The Cure*, *The Rink*, *The Kid*, and *Sunnyside*. He romanced her, sang to her, beat off her assailants, rescued her from crime dens, and generally won her over in the most unlikely ways. She dressed up like a man and crashed the set builders at a movie studio. She crossed the Atlantic on an immigrant boat and married Charlie after falling in love at a Bohemian café. She was the farmer's daughter, the minister's daughter, even the Rabbi's daughter! Unlike Mabel Normand, who burned out her flame early with drugs and fast living, Edna stayed at home, provided stability, posed as the domestic jackpot at the end of the rainbow. American film audiences fell in love with her as well.

When Chaplin relocated to Los Angeles to fulfill his contract with the Mutual Film Corporation, he took Edna with him as part of his stock company that now included Eric Campbell and Albert Austin. She was a mainstay in his films, if not his life. Although he had thoughts of marrying her, he was uncertain, and for reasons never fully confessed, they cooled off and Chaplin began seeing other women, sometimes in a very public way. In reality, Edna had felt very neglected and took to seeing another man. Chaplin, extremely jealous, dismissed her now as a "stranger." He kept her on his studio's payroll and continued to co-star with her, but the magic had ended.

In 1918, Chaplin married for the first time, a minor film starlet named Mildred Harris. The marriage ended in disaster and scandal, and, sadly, produced a deformed baby that did not survive its first week. The union was a misfire on many levels and was bad publicity for Chaplin. During the divorce proceedings, he had to flee to Utah with all the existing reels of his work-in-progress *The Kid* and edit the film in a hotel room for fear that his wife's lawyers would seize the property. Edna learned about the marriage from a newspaper and watched its downfall from a distance, perhaps regretfully wondering if she and Charlie would have fared better in matrimony.

One of Chaplin's romantic flings involved a show girl called Peggy Hopkins Joyce, who not only married and divorced a millionaire by the time she was 17 years old, but bagged four more in succession. The term "gold digger" was invented by the press to describe her. In the summer of 1921, the world press went nuts with a new story: Peggy Hopkins Joyce had bagged Charlie Chaplin.

In his autobiography (redundantly titled *My Autobiography*), Chaplin describes his relationship with Joyce as "bizarre, though brief." One can only wonder what that means. They took to fishing off Catalina Island together and tantalizing the press with suggestions of romance and possibly even marriage. During this time, Joyce beguiled Chaplin with endless tales of her adventures in Paris, how she had driven a melancholy young man to suicide (an incident verified by none other than Ernest Hemingway). Joyce confessed to Chaplin that all she wanted in life was to settle down with a legitimate husband whom she loved and have children. Chaplin found this confession quite touching although he took no moves to fulfill her fantasy.

The story of Joyce's sad regrets stayed with Chaplin long after his relationship with her sank into Catalina Bay. It was still on his mind when his contract with First National expired and he was free to pursue his independence at United Artists.

PART 3: INDEPENDENCE

Chaplin signed the contract for United Artists a few years before he actually started making films for them since his First National contract had been for eight two-reelers and he had only made four. His relatively tepid films, *A Day's Pleasure*, *Pay Day*, and *The Idle Class* show little of the Chaplin magic other than his always vibrant appearance and a few great gags, and it was clear that his heart was not in two-reelers anymore. He had produced one of his best films, *The Kid*, while at the studio, and he ended his contract with a clever little comedy called *The Pilgrim*, but the expectations were high that when he arrived at United Artists he would produce his best work. That turned out to be true, although it was not everyone's opinion that *A Woman of Paris* qualified as his masterpiece.

The other members of UA, including Douglas Fairbanks, Mary Pickford, and D.W. Griffith, had been putting out their own films and making money for the studio, but Chaplin's absence was a danger to their financial health. The pressure was on him to produce a blockbuster, one that would fill UA's coffers and restore Chaplin to the height of his artistic powers. His choice of material, a somber comedy of manners set in Paris, was only the start of what troubled his business partners. Chaplin had decided not to act in his own film, the first time he had not done so in his entire career so far.

Whether the American public would go for this was uncertain. Chaplin's intention was not to disappoint them, but to demonstrate his own range as a filmmaker as well as establish an independent career for Edna Purviance, whom he cast as the star of the film. He had no more plans to co-star with Edna in any of his films and he was hoping that *A Woman of Paris* would establish her as a dramatic actress of the first caliber and some other studio would promote her as a star. Edna may have been flattered by his assistance to her career—after all, how often does the most famous film director in the world build a movie entirely around you?—but she also sensed that he was now forever beyond her romantic range. He did comment that she was looking "matronly," which may have been a euphemism for his not being sexually interested in her any more. There may have been some truth to this: his next leading lady would be a teenager that would drop out of *The Gold Rush* after Chaplin got her pregnant.

PART 4: THE WORLD'S RESPONSE

PART 5: A WOMAN OF PARIS, A REAPPRAISAL

(UNFINISHED)

REVIEWS

The Terminal Beach
by J.G. Ballard

Welcome to the Terminal Beach. Just a short car ride from Vermilion Sands where the filmmakers are decorating the lonely landscape with shifting screens depicting the internal structure of the mind of some beautiful but insane woman. It is a fearful place to be, as deadly as it is unstable, but there are many points of interest for the discerning traveler. Feast your senses on the diamond studded scorpions let loose between the picnic baskets, the singing statues that croon with the wafting winds, the crushed cars rusting by the deserted hotels, the blanket of frozen crystals creeping its viral death across the fused sands. There is the half-buried crashed airplane, its pilot's skeleton still pinioned in the cockpit, his screaming skull framed by a cracked flight helmet. In the disturbed sands are the cryptic mandalas drawn by the escaped mental patients, their intricate details of geometric shapes and anamorphic blobs describing the inner lining of some poor visionary's skull. You can spend time examining the full frame blow ups of the Lincoln Continental within whose back seat rests the dead President with his exploded skull and whose driver, a World War III fighter pilot, sits at the front wheel, his face burned by the fall out from some future Hiroshima.

And if you are patient and wait upon the dying landscape, you may even catch a glimpse of Mr. Ballard, the Logos of this dream world, who walks the cracked sidewalks by the empty hotels, attempting to encompass within his own psyche the pivotal stillness that rests within all these chaotic and ever-shifting images. He is the myth maker of the Space Age, the dream interpreter of the future. You may just catch him paying homage to his muse, the woman who lies naked and crushed before the impacted fender of a twisted Porsche Spyder, the geometry of her death a glyph of some subconscious desire that will never be fulfilled.

For those daring enough to check into a room at the abandoned motel, whose balconies resemble the vestigial gill-slits of the motion picture actress with whom you yearn to die in a head-on car collision, you are setting yourself up for a vacation that will never be forgotten because it will never end. A guided tour to the deepest frequencies of your spinal column, a descent into the realm where words are magick and science fiction is holy scripture to be interpreted by a priestly caste of psychiatrists who have been driven mad by the art work of their patients.

This is the world of J.G. Ballard, the portal of the Atrocity Exhibition. Enter and leave behind all that you are. Here all mythologies are true, and the landscape whispers the last dark music of the painted night.

THE BIRTH OF GRAFFITI
BY JON NAAR

Over a two-week period in the winter of 1973, photographer Jon Naar and designer Mervyn Kurlansky journeyed about New York City, riding the subways, prowling the streets, scanning the walls of buildings to capture with a single lens reflex camera the growing phenomenon of inner city graffiti. A few dozen of these images, out of hundreds, was published as *The Faith of Graffiti* with an introduction by Norman Mailer in 1974, and at the time the colorful and starkly beautiful images that appeared were current events. The controversial practice of graffiti writing was being hotly debated by the press and by politicians and was the bane of Mayor John Lindsay's administration. But Jon Naar's photographic approach to the tags and pieces that decorated the subway trains, buses and buildings of New York City was a work of photojournalism. He viewed his material with the eye of a true archivist, one who wanted to capture and document the growth of a phenomenon without judgment or politicizing. With Norman Mailer on board giving his own literary and artistic interpretation of graffiti, the book received great critical acclaim and became a classic in the genre, a much sought-after photography book, but one that only contained a fraction of the images that Naar had assembled. Besides, the publisher had changed their original title, *Watching My Name Go By*, which dramatically altered the tone of the presentation by taking the emphasis off the writer's themselves.

The Birth of Graffiti (Prestel Press, 2007) is Jon's first graffiti book in nearly 35 years and gives more relevance to his photographic art than *Faith of Graffiti* did. Limiting the text to a few short essays, the book emphasizes the images in a beautifully designed volume that presents many of the photographs uncropped and lovingly selected by the photographer. Perhaps this is the book on graffiti that he had originally

255

planned, but one that packed a punch and an historical relevance that is only possible by viewing the images so many decades later when New York City and the world is so very different.

What is stunning about *The Birth of Graffiti*, and indeed is inherent in the title of the book itself, is that many of these photographs have lain unpublished in protective storage for three and a half decades and are now important historical documents. What we are witnessing in these hauntingly beautiful images is a time-locked period of history when New York City lay buried under a cosmetic layer of hieroglyphic writing that many praised as a powerful expression of the inner-city imagination and others cursed as an urban blight at best and downright vandalism at worst. Anyone who lived in the city at that time, or even gazed with wide eyed fascination at the tags and pieces that decorated the buses, subway trains, storefronts, and public monuments, can approach this book with a sense of nostalgia and a memory of lost landscapes that once characterized New York.

What we have to marvel at in these compositions are not only the graffiti writings, the textured layers of names and street numbers that explode like starry bursts from the metal flanking of subway cars and the red brick of apartment building walls, but the actual subway cars and red bricked apartment walls themselves. What makes *The Birth of Graffiti* so very different from *The Faith of Graffiti* is that now the city itself that had lain so innocently under the deluge of writing is just as visually fascinating to us as the writings themselves. The book is just as much a New York City time capsule as it is a book about graffiti.

Page after page brings us back to 1974 when New York was just a little less splashy than it is today, before Ronald Reagan, Donald Trump, or Edward Koch, when it was still on a financial decline that in 1975-1976 almost brought it to bankruptcy. It is the impoverished cityscape where movies like *Serpico* and *The French Connection* were shot on location. And like those films, these photos show us a world that once was but is no more. Because graffiti was his subject, Jon Naar did not shoot around the tourist traps. We don't see Times Square or Lincoln Center or the grand brownstones of Brooklyn. Instead we are taken on a tour of forgotten walls and doorways, Spanish bodegas and tenement apartments, subway corridors, abandoned buildings, Harlem handball walls, Brooklyn boardwalks, the empty spaces of housing projects, and school yards. If the graffiti was somehow airbrushed from these photos, they would still hold our fascination. They document the fine-grained details of the landscape known by the few people who move through the images: the Spanish mother walking her daughter, the tired looking subway riders, the workers huddled in a doorway, a security guard taking a break by a utility exit. These people go about their daily affairs with a fatigue and boredom that comes with any housing project or straphanger existence, walking past the urban sigils and tags and pieces and cryptic names and numbers as if they are just one more oppressive aspect of their city environment that they must endure from day to day.

Some of the photos give us a sense of shocked recognition, like the "You Don't Have To Be Jewish To Love Levy's" ad in the subway, a sight that was once as familiar to New York subway riders as chicklet vending machines and refreshment stands selling fruit punch in conical paper cups. Even the shapes and colors of the graffiti writing itself evokes a time and a place. As a child, I used to stand under the elevated trains at Ditmars Boulevard in Astoria, Queens, and watch the names on the trains go by. Some of those names like Star III, Taki 183, and Trease 158 are just as familiar in my memory as some of the office buildings in midtown that were torn down in the 1980s. These names from otherwise anonymous writers whose faces I will never know where part of my everyday New York childhood. By the time I was taking the subway to school every day in the early 1980s, much of it had been washed away— but somehow the subways looked bare to me. They were missing their dense layering of swoops and swirls and colored, almost psychedelic, letterings. By the end of the 1980s, graffiti had been subsumed into the artwork of Keith Haring and Jean-Michel Basquiat, and galleries were featuring codified and tamed examples of the graffiti style. Today, graffiti is still controversial, but with the growing phenomenon of permission walls and commissioned pieces, the excitement, the outrage, the danger, and the political incorrectness of the writing of 1974 is now just a memory.

What I love about many of Jon Naar's graffiti photographs is the use of lighting, whether it is the sun sinking behind the buildings on Central Park South or the gloomy fluorescents of the subways. It is the lighting that gives us a suburb seasonal sense. The pedestrians, subway riders, and graffiti artists captured in the photos are dressed for a chilled fall turning into winter and, combined with the dull cold skies over the buildings, we can almost feel the frozen breath in our mouths as we journey through the streets. New York has always been at its most melancholy during this season, and by capturing this late-November feeling along with his subject matter of graffiti writing and the objects on which they are written, Naar gives the photos an extra layer of ambient nostalgia.

But one must not neglect the writers themselves. When Naar and Kurlansky went off into the streets looking for graffiti, they had the good fortune of meeting, purely by chance, a gang of graffiti writers, young boys who ranged from ten to fourteen years old. Their group shot appears on the title page of *The Birth of Graffiti* and many more shots of them appear throughout, whether gathered together or posing separately in front of their tags. What I love about these shots is that rarely does Naar photograph them without some ghostly motion blur. These blurs give us a sense of the energy of graffiti writers, who no doubt found it very difficult to stand still. As they write, the wall and the tag stay in clear focus while the writer is a whirling motion, connoting the artist in the instant moment of creation.

The writers were young, innocent, not the dangerous gang members that middle-class New Yorkers feared were responsible for the defacements. They were multi-racial, black, white, Hispanic, mixed. They came out of their inner-city neighborhoods via the subway, targeted the subway to "watch their names go by" and to carry their tags and their fame to the outer boroughs and beyond. In their lifetime, they would no doubt never be famous, never been known, always thought of as a statistic in some rich white writer's sociological assessment of modern urban issues. But by putting their tags on a moving vehicle that will carry their names as far off as the northern Bronx, as far south as Sheepshead Bay, as far East as Jamaica Estates, they will be seen, their name will be known.

Jon Naar has given these artists expression, decades later, long after their names have been scrubbed from their surfaces, by showing these writers at work at the moment in history where they had seized the spotlight and forced us to recognize their existence. Like the Neolithic handprint that anthropologists found on an Australian cave wall, someone once spoke the words, "I am human. I was here. I am me. This is my name."

THE MYTHOS OF
V FOR VENDETTA

Why should Thelemites be interested in *V for Vendetta*, the new film by the Wachowskis? On the surface it seems like a liberal anti-Utopian sci-fi action adventure thriller that draws from sources as diverse as George Orwell's *1984*, *The Phantom of the Opera*, and *Batman's Dark Knight* Mythos. It doesn't have the overt Gnosticism of the *Matrix* (the Wachowski's most popular franchise) and it seems more concerned with political matters than anything spiritual. The film is an obvious blow at President Bush's neo-con, anti-terrorist paranoia, portraying the violation of homosexual civil rights and the right to free speech. None of this is necessarily non-Thelemic, but the film is coming from an American liberal standpoint and not from a hardcore Thelemic one. It seems much more like a prolonged polemic on post 9-11 politics than the dawning of the Aeon of Horus.

And yet, if you look closely, there is a magical formula at work in the story inspired by the magical content of the film's source material: the graphic novel by Alan Moore, a practicing ceremonial magician and a life-long admirer of Aleister Crowley. Needless to say, the original graphic novel is more magical, far darker, and more Thelemic than the film.

Moore is a major literary figure who happens to write comic books. Over the last two decades, he has produced provocative and important work that draws together popular culture, art, magick, philosophy, fairy tales, mythology, psychology, surrealism, science fiction, pulp fiction, and cosmic prophecy into one harmonious whole—in addition, he possesses the Holy Grail that every writer seeks: an original voice.

His work has grown more occult-oriented over time. One of his more recent graphic novels, *Promethea*, is a virtual textbook of kabalistic

259

magick, incorporating occult images and philosophies from all tradi-tions. It includes a multi-issue journey through the Tarot Trumps and the Sephiroths of the Tree of Life, from Malkuth all the way up to the Ain Soph Aur (where else can you see a comic book representation of the Ain Soph Aur?). Aleister Crowley, Austin Osman Spare, Jack Parsons, Dr. John Dee, and other occult luminaries appear liberally along the way. There is an intense confrontation with Lady Babalon in the City of the Pyramids and an unforgettable journey across the Abyss—no small feat for a guy who used to script *Swamp Thing*.

Needless to say, Moore is not inexperienced with occult systems and his graphic novels are magical workings. When he tackles subjects such as Jack the Ripper in *From Hell*, there is a heavy presence of Victorian Freemasonry and Occultism. *From Hell* includes an amusing cameo appearance by a pre-teen Edward Alexander Crowley. Under Moore's hand, familiar characters are transmogrified into their archetypal god forms. His Batman is a Lunar Avenger, his Superman a Solar Myth, his Wonder Woman a Goddess of Mercury, and his Swamp Thing an Earth Elemental. For many years he set the Goth Occult tone in comic books and influenced an entire generation of graphic novelists including Neil Gaiman and Grant Morrison.

V for Vendetta was an early work, written before Moore became a ceremonial magician. The story is based upon the political philos-ophy of Anarchism, Jungian transpersonal psychology, and Reichian bioenergetics. One can argue that both Anarchism and Reichian ther-apy were early manifestations of the Aeon of Horus. While Mikhail Bakunin, Wilhelm Reich, and Carl Jung may not have been followers of Aleister Crowley, or even heard the phrase "Aeon of Horus," they cer-tainly were pathfinders who struggled to open the portals to the same energies described in the *Book of the Law*. Anarchism, with its emphasis on the decentralization of political power and the distribution of power within the individual, Reich, with his examination of the relationship between the mind, the body, politics, and sexual energy, and Jung, with his extension of psychoanalysis into the transpersonal mind where reli-gious symbols and dream imagery become centers of power within the psyche, may not all have been explicitly Thelemic (and indeed these various philosophies and disciplines do have their differences with Thelema), but all were influential in laying down the cosmic carpet of the Thelemic Current. And with *V for Vendetta*, Alan Moore brings all of them together into one powerful and entertaining story.

V for Vendetta started as a comic book with a long and painful history (its initial run in England was aborted before all ten issues could be produced) but DC Comics starting re-printing them in 1987. The comics, now available as a graphic novel, tells the story of an England ruled by a fascist government, and the journey of a young girl, named Evey, from street prostitute to rebel leader, under the mentorship of V, an anarchist living under the sewers of London. Facially mutilated, masked and haunted by a tortured past, V is a poetic mix of the Beast from *Beauty & the Beast* and Erik from *Phantom of the Opera*—a rebel figure who moves within the fascist reign of terror with the ease of a neutrino unaffected by gravity, blowing up government buildings, and assassinating key figures in the power structure. Possibly the result of a bizarre medical experiment in a concentration camp, V is now determined to bring down the regime and free the minds and bodies of the masses suffering under their own psychological oppression.

Using the dark imagery and 1980s themes of a crime-infected city under siege and a lone haunted avenger determined to liberate the populace, Moore created his own Dark Knight, a far more mysterious and morally problematic one. While Batman remains faithful to law and order and acts as a guardian angel to the besieged citizens of Gotham, V sees the people of London as collaborators in their own servitude. To arrive at true liberty, the people of London must experience the ordeal of freeing the Self from its own oppression—and this, alone, is a very Thelemic concept.

When V takes over a television station and broadcasts to the people of London, he has this to say to them:

> We've had a string of embezzlers, frauds, liars, and lunatics making a string of catastrophic decisions. This is plain fact. But who elected them? It was you! You who appointed these people! You who gave them the power to make your decisions for you. While I'd admit that anyone can make a mistake every now and again, but to be on making the same lethal error century after century seems to be nothing short of deliberate. You have encouraged these malicious incompetents who have made your working life a shambles. You have accepted without question their senseless orders. You have allowed them to fill your workspace with dangerous and unproven machines. You could have stopped them. All you had to say was 'No'.

These words are heavily influenced by texts like Wilhelm Reich's *Listen Little Man!* and by passages from *The Mass Psychology of Fascism*. It is significant that V is talking to the people of London, not to the government that he is trying to overthrow. He is clearly centering the ultimate source of power within the individual self—only the slaves shall serve.

The original comic book was flush with magical references and a very post-modern and kabalistic style of storytelling. The name V itself, a code name used by the Anarchist, is suggestive of all the following:

1) The V for Victory sign made popular by Winston Churchill during World War II.

2) The name of the mysterious woman in V. by Thomas Pynchon

3) The letter V, which, in Morse code, sounds like the opening notes of Beethoven's Fifth Symphony.

4) The letter V is Roman for 5.

5) 5 is the number of the concentration camp room where V was held captive and experimented upon by his tormentors.

6) The initial used by Crowley to signify his attainment as Magus: V.V.V.V.V., which, in fact, is referenced in both comic book and film.

7) The horns of Aries.

8) When the horns are compassed by a circle, it is similar to the Anarchist A and the sigil of Z for Zorro, another avenger.

9) The position of the arms in the Sign of Apophis and Typhon.

In short, multiple meanings of V come together into a single concentrated sigil that contains the energy of all that V represents. Evey, the young woman who he rescues from being raped and brings to his underground lair, becomes fascinated with his mystery and anarchism and undergoes a series of initiations that are not too dissimilar from the journey of a mundane personality from the depths of Malkuth towards the solar power of Tiphareth. V is at once her mentor, her guide through the underworld, her Hierophant, and her Magus. He puts her through the ordeals that guide her through the tangled web of the Self towards the Light of Liberty. Along the way, he even declares the law of Thelema (although this was significantly removed from the movie).

Evey's transformation into her higher self is the keystone of the entire story and, fortunately, the film follows it faithfully. When Evey emerges from her own servitude, walking into a thunderous rainstorm with her arms raised in the V sign of Typhon, both Moore and the film-makers montage the image of V emerging in a similar fashion from the burning inferno of the medical camp that he torched. Fire and water, male and female, aspirant and holy guardian angel, come together in a perfect Hexagram moment.

As an assassin and a terrorist, V has been created in the tradition of Hassan I. Sabbah, the 11th century Ishmaili rebel leader who trained a highly-skilled band of assassins (indeed the word assassin is a tribute to him) to eliminate key figures in the ruling power structure, rather than use the mass bloodshed of military confrontation. Assassination as revolutionary tool was also referenced in films like *Apocalypse Now*. There, Colonel Kurtz is stopping Viet Cong activity in his sector by illegally assassinating double agents within military intelligence. In turn, Kurtz is killed by an assassin, which also references the killing of the King in Frazier's *The Golden Bough*. Likewise, V is eliminating key figures in the British government to accomplish a revolution that would have been impossible with an army at his command.

This elevation of assassination to a spiritual and revolutionary discipline is at the heart of *V for Vendetta*. Written in the late 1970s, when Anarchism and the use of violent force was still a very real presence in Europe, assassination was the perfect theme for Moore's story. In today's post 9-11 America, it strikes a very disturbing note. Watching government buildings collapse after terrorist bombings and asking us to feel empathy with the terrorist is a very dangerous game for Hollywood to play. Needless to say, almost all of the Anarchism has been removed from the film. In today's America, Anarchism is barely understood, hardly remembered, and certainly not viable subject matter for a Hollywood movie.

The Wachowskis made many compromises in the film and tones down more than a few elements. For example, all the Thelemic references are removed, with the exception of the five V's that are attributed to Julius Caesar. In the comic, the police detective Finch, reduced in the film to a deadpan cynic, actually travels to the ruins of the concentration camp where V had been experimented upon and ingests a dose of LSD, undergoing a severe spiritual initiation of his own (dropping acid in a concentration camp is not exactly perfect fodder for a Hollywood flick!). Not only was the drug trip removed from the film, the concentration camp was presented as a sinister medical facility. The whole conflict between Anarchism and Fascism has been replaced with two competing political philosophies—analogous to today's liberals and conservatives. The bad guys are right wingers doing constitutionally dubious things like spying on our privacy, generating paranoia about terrorism for political purposes, and hiding the truth about biomedical epidemics. The good citizens of London are politically correct liberals. Alan Moore specifically protested that the original story was about Fascism and Anarchism, and to remove these philosophies is to completely change his original creative vision.

Most importantly, the ending was changed to show that the citizens of London needed only the downfall of the government for them to march hand-in-hand into Liberty. In the comic book, the downfall of the government leads to bloody and violent street fighting because nobody can live without being ruled by Fascists. Their minds have not been properly prepared for the freedom that V offers them.

In the comic, V shuts down the surveillance systems that are invading everyone's personal lives. "For three days," he announces to the people of London, "your movements will not be watched, your conversations will not be listened to, and Do What Thou Wilt Shall Be the Whole of the Law! God Bless you and good night!"

"Is this your Anarchy, V?" Evey asks while witnessing the carnage. "Is this the Land of Do-As-You-Please?"

V replies, "No, this is only the Land of Take-As-You-Want. Anarchy means 'without leaders', not 'without order.' This is not Anarchy, Eve. This is Chaos!"

In V's distinction, one can almost hear the flapping wings of Ra-Hoor-Khuit.

V for Vendetta, both the graphic novel and the Hollywood film, holds a great deal of substance for Thelemites to sink their teeth into. It is a post-modern invocation of Horus the Avenging Son. Although the Wachowskis decided to cut the proclamation of the Law of Thelema from the film, it remains Thelemic in spirit.

One can argue that the Wachowskis were totally blind to any of this. Ultimately, it is a well-made, provocative, sci-fi action adventure film.

First published in *Behutet: Modern Thelemic Magick & Culture*, Issue 30, Summer, 2006.

STRANGE ANGEL BY GEORGE PENDLE

I have always liked Jack Parsons, ever since I first encountered him in a cheap exploitative paperback about the occult. There was little not to like about him: he was a rocket scientist and high magician who invented the fuel that sent our spaceships into orbit; he was a priest in a weird religious cult; he did ceremonial magic with L. Ron Hubbard; he manifested Lady Babalon; he wrote the fourth chapter of Aleister Crowley's *The Book of the Law*; he has a crater on the moon named after him; he blew himself up. I mean, how cool is all that? All the elements of a mythic life were in place, including the violent death that put him in the same eerie death cult category as James Dean, a blazing star that burned with intensity and then snuffed itself out before we could ever see it grow old.

Besides, there was something familiar about Parsons that made him very approachable as a person, despite his almost Satanic reputation. Occult history is marvelously arrayed with colorful and larger-than-life personalities, many of them regally titled and politically advantaged: Renaissance nobles who financed oriental expeditions to recover ancient mystical manuscripts, prominent Victorian gentlemen whose secret societies taught the Hermetic arts to their initiates, English court astrologers and German Barons who performed their alchemical experiments from the redoubts of their learned mansions. Even the granddaddy of 20th century occultism, Aleister Crowley, a Magus who considered himself a living Logos, had been heir to a brewer's fortune and often seemed an archaic remnant of the Victorian age, a sort of dark-side Oscar Wilde.

But John Whiteside Parsons was different. Born into the 20th century, he barreled along recklessly with the rapid technological advances that characterized the modern age. He grew up in a world of airplanes, Hollywood movies and science fiction pulp magazines. He lived against the black and white backdrop of a rapidly urbanizing Southern California and as a boy, his mind was filled with the same images of streamlined space rockets and bubble helmeted aliens that most of us post-war American children knew so well. By the time of his untimely death in 1952, he was able to watch air jets streak through the sky, fueled by the rocket technology that he had personally invented. And it was his solid fuel patents that led to extraordinary advances in space travel and rocketry. Unlike his magical predecessors who spent their lives in dark alchemical labs cooking base metals for spiritual illumination, Parsons poured his earthy powders into rocket engines, mixed them with oxidizing agents, and set them on fire to help bring about the world we now live in.

Strange Angel, a new biography of Jack Parsons by George Pendle, a science and culture writer for the *London Times* and the *New York Times*, paints a very human portrait of this brilliant and short-lived magician, examining both Parsons' career inventing rocket engines for the government and his more notorious life as a ceremonial magician and Thelemic Lodge Master. It is a very enjoyable and welcome addition to the growing literature dealing with Thelemic history and does help bring Parsons into perspective. Stripping away much of the mythical clap trap, it reveals a genuinely flawed man trying to creatively mix the elements of his troubled life with complex spiritual practices in much the same way he mixed his rocket fuels. It does not, however, tell us much about Thelema or ceremonial magick in general, and will not, unfortunately, do much to illuminate its non-magical readers about either.

Outside of certain occult circles, there has not been much previous material about Parsons, the only other full-scale biography having been *Sex & Rockets* by John Carter (a pseudonym that cleverly alludes to the hero of Edgar Rice Burroughs' Martian series that Parsons, a reader of early sci-fi pulp, would have been intimately familiar with). That book was geared towards a much more occult-savvy audience, with technical descriptions of the various magical systems that Parsons practiced. *Strange Angel*, by comparison, in spite of its excellent narrative technique and compelling story line, doesn't expend much energy on explaining the Enochian tablets or the kabalistic grade system of the western occult tradition. While the book sports a funky cover montage of third eyes and ancient temples, it fails to explain much about the 93rd Current that

Parsons labored within for so long, instead giving us a more anecdotal and character driven story.

And you can't get more character driven than this. Populated by such luminaries as L. Ron Hubbard, Aleister Crowley, Robert Heinlein, Forest Ackerman, Ray Bradbury and many celebrities from the world of rocket science like Willy Lay, Werner Von Braun, and Theodore Von Karman, *Strange Angel* is immensely readable and entertaining. It puts Parsons in the perspective of his age, charting the rise of Hollywood and the science fiction industry, the political battle for scientists in the chaos of World War II, the dark clouds of the Cold War and the anti-communist hysteria that nearly destroyed the same men who helped win the war against Fascism. Pendle's understanding of the science behind the rockets is exemplary, and he manages to capture the hard work of these rocketeers in its cultural and historical context. His less rigorous approach to the history of magick and secret societies, however, threatens to give the reader the impression that Aleister Crowley was merely an aging leech living in squalor while barking at his followers to send him money, and that the OTO Lodge at Parsons' home was all about wife swapping and hedonism. We do not learn much about the Law of Thelema or the OTO, both of which are vital to a real understanding of what fueled John Whiteside Parsons, but we learn just enough to enjoy the ride.

In fact, *Strange Angel* careens along with breakneck speed, often comically, mimicking the energy, drive, and fanaticism of Parsons' own obsessions and enthusiasms. It presents a rapidly growing world of technology. From the moment Parsons' parents step off the train into a mostly rural Los Angeles, the land changes under their feet. Pendle captures the nuttiness and beauty of an innocent Southern California discovering its dark heart in the rise of fad religions and skyrocketing real estate. It is this time and age that gave us people like Hugo Gernsback and Aimee Semple McPherson, Howard Hughes, and D.W. Griffith. If this was indeed the dawning of the Aeon of Horus, it was surely being heralded into California with a big bang of invention and imagination.

Jack Parsons had a very romantic youth, growing up in wealthy splendor in the most prestigious neighborhood of Pasadena. In fact, he spent all his life there, his work, both magical and scientific, drawing its inspiration from the landscapes of Orange Grove Avenue with its millionaire homes, exclusive hunting clubs, and the Arroyo Seco, a wilderness of ravines that flanked Pasadena on the north. It was on the Arroyo that young Parsons first played with firecrackers and where later he tested rockets and carried out experiments for CalTech and the Jet Propulsion Laboratory. Pendle takes his time describing Pasadena, its colonization after Los Angeles had grown from a Mexican village to a major American city. He describes the lushness of Orange Grove at a time when the homes were inhabited by families like Wrigley and Busch (Parsons grew up in the shadow of Busch Gardens). Much later, the neighborhood was to decline in fortune and the estate mansions gave way to condos and rentals—Parsons himself was forced to sell his last home and move into a coach house—but on those idyllic streets of his youth, he lived in an exclusive fantasy world, his imagination fired by Arthurian legends, Jules Verne novels and countless issues of *Amazing Stories* magazine, combining the high romance of a knightly brotherhood with fantasies of space travel.

Strange Angel paints an image of a prissy and aristocratically dressed teenager, who never before had to stray beyond the safe boundaries of his boyhood home, arriving at a public high school and subsequently being beaten by a schoolyard crowd of street-wise kids. To his rescue came a poor student from the wrong side of the tracks, Ed Foreman, who turned into Jack's best friend and life-long partner in rocketeering. The two of them would cast aside their class distinctions and spiritual differences to jointly pursue the goal of building a rocket that would travel to the moon. It can be argued that these two men, self-taught and lacking advanced degrees in either chemistry or engineering, were the progenitors of the technology that put Neil Armstrong into the lunar dust. Pendle doesn't dig quite so deeply into Ed Foreman (it would have been fascinating to see if Foreman did any personal writings relating to Parsons and to learn the story from his perspective), but the two of them were bound for life, manifesting their sci-fi imaginations into the physical world.

The road, however, was a hard one and started with nearly a decade of unpaid work and experimentation. When Parsons' family fortune vanished in the Depression, the young rocket geeks started to fight against the lack of cash and often pulled what they could out of junk yards to build their rockets. Pendle describes their struggle to commune with other rocket scientists and science fiction fans from around the world, combating the disregard that the scientific community felt for both the pulp literature and rocketry. We see the two young rocket men in their early 20s, taking day jobs at dynamite factories to learn what they could about the chemistry of explosive powders, panting around the door of the California Institute of Technology for resources and the chance to build more rockets. When they finally gained a presence at CalTech by hooking up with a student named Frank Malina, they learned the hard way that they would only obtain their long-term objectives by stripping their work down to basics: instead of building rockets, they would have to focus on the core engine. In short, they would have to spend their days testing various oxidizing agents and fuel injection methods before they could fulfill their Buck Rogers fantasies. The boyish rocket builders were now turning into scientists.

The narrative is sprinkled with surreal and often bizarre moments, such as a young Parsons presenting his first wife Helen with an engagement ring and a .22 caliber pistol to protect the jewelry against theft—he later made her pawn the ring so he could fund one of his rocket experiments. We also have Parsons being sent to military school, only to be returned when he blows up the latrines. There is the image of Parsons and Foreman borrowing so much money from Helen for their experiments that she eventually has them put on kitchen aprons and clean the house for money.

But best of all, there are explosions. Lots of them. It seemed that Parsons' little group at CalTech, dubbed the Suicide Squad, was always managing to blow up one of the campus buildings, or at least fill the hallways and stairwells with noxious gas. And they tossed about dangerous chemicals and buckets of explosives with optimistic carelessness, often to the frantic alarm of their wives. Parsons even reveled in dangerous practical jokes that involved the detonation of bombs, sometimes destroying valuable test equipment in the name of an impish gag. If it weren't for the tragic accident that ended his life, the explosions would come across to the reader as slapstick comedy.

The Suicide Squad constantly tried to gain legitimacy with the CalTech staff and were often dismissed as futile dreamers. Helen Parsons had to get a job to support both her husband and herself and only a mysterious fund of $1,000 from an obscure CalTech student kept them going for a few years in the late 1930s, although a third of it went to repairs on a building they damaged in an explosion. When the Suicide Squad finally landed their government contract, they were politely asked by CalTech to move their dangerous activities back to the Arroyo Seco, forcing them to work in relentless heat in shacks of corrugated iron, desperately trying to invent a jet propulsion system for the military.

The symbiosis between the rocket scientists and science fiction writers was a natural one and Pendle does an excellent job at tracing its evolution. Many of the rocketeers had grown up reading the pulp magazines published by Hugo Gernsback, who invented the genre of "scientifiction" or "gadget fiction." Their faithful belief that they could fire rockets to other planets and perhaps even galaxies came directly from the stories of Jack Williamson, Murray Leinster and Edmond Hamilton, the first generation of sci-fi celebrities. Many of the rocketeers had gone into their profession because of their love for science fiction (Werner Von Braun maintained a subscription to *Amazing Stories* even during the war), and as both fields grew and evolved, the men on both sides gained a healthy respect for one another, a respect that was sadly lacking in general society as both sci-fi and rocketry were considered adolescent triviality. When Jack Parsons was trying to solve the problems of a jet propulsion system for military aircraft, he drew inspiration from a Jack Williamson novel that portrayed a staged rocket that burned its fuel in separate cells. This concept eventually led to the staged rocket design used by the Mercury and Apollo astronauts. It was both Williamson's imagination as a writer, and years of work by Parsons in the blistering heat of the Arroyo Secco, that gave birth to one of the most familiar images of modern space travel: the burning up of the jettisoned stages of a moon rocket.

Parsons saw no distinction between the fantastical fiction of the pulps and his own hard science of rocketry. It was as if he were attempting to magically manifest the speculative technology of the pulps in the real world. Later, equally obsessed with occult magic, he would attempt to manifest spiritual beings like Lady Babalon on the mundane plane, much in the same way he was trying to make the space rockets of Buck Rogers come to life in the laboratory. He even performed his most infamous magical working with sci-fi writer L. Ron Hubbard, although one could debate endlessly this apprenticeship actually benefited any community, whether scientific, literary, or occult.

This symbiosis between the scientists and the writers would continue through the decades, even to this day, where the makers of television franchises like *Star Trek* would consult with NASA scientists who all grew up inspired to work in space travel technology by earlier incarnations of the television show. Pendle describes how the rocketeers and a new wave of writers like Ray Bradbury and Robert Heinlein came together in social clubs that originated in pulp fandom and grew to actively promote the science of space travel. Soon a polarization took hold in the sci-fi ranks that seemed to mirror what was occurring in the axes of world politics. The New Fandom promoted science fiction as pure entertainment, while the Futurians (typified by Isaac Asimov) looked towards sci-fi as a literature capable of transforming the future.

It was also at this time that Frank Malina approached the United States Military with ideas about the wartime applications of rocketry. With the world about to erupt in the bloodiest conflict in history and the militaries of the world scrambling for emerging technologies, rocket science was suddenly no longer a laughable pastime for cranks and sci-fi buffs. By substituting the word "jet" for rocket, the Suicide Squad finally had major funding and resources for a new project called JATO (Jet Assisted Take Off) which would enable military aircraft to boost their take-off capacity, facilitating the use of shorter runways in combat zones. The life-long passions of Parsons and Foreman were finally going to pay off—their vision, long neglected and scorned by the outside world, was now going to help transform the peaceful future that global warfare promised us. The Suicide Squad, so often derided and dismissed by their academic colleagues, was now the first rocket team to be funded by the United States Air Corps.

The origins of the AeroJet Engineering Corporation, the company formed by the Suicide Squad to manufacture and market their JATOs, is told by Pendle in a light hearted and comical way, showing the young rocketeers, none of them older than thirty, setting up shop and declaring as their mission statement: "To design, develop, experiment with, introduce, manufacture, assemble, build, repair, maintain, operate, lease, let, purchase, sell and/or generally deal with mechanisms, devices and processes now known or which hereafter may be developed, discovered or invented for the propulsion of airplanes and all other kinds of vehicles, projectiles of all kinds and description, or any other machine, apparatus, device or object requiring motive power whether for purposes of commerce, warfare, pleasure or otherwise." Such wacky idealism, with such an abstract focus, is all that could be expected of these proto-yuppies who were only alive through the sheer fool's luck of not blowing themselves up.

In fact, it is precisely this lack of focus that seems to have been Parsons' downfall in the rocket industry. By all accounts, he should have been a shining luminary in the field, accomplishing so much at so young an age, and being the co-founder of a corporation that would later be a leading player in the industry. Jack Parsons and Ed Foreman could have been to rocket technology what Steve Jobs and Steve Wozniack were to the world of home computers: two obsessive geniuses who spent their youth laboring away in-home garages, inventing the technology of the future, and later reaping the benefits of their labor as executives of their own corporation in an internationally powerful industry. Instead, Parsons laid the seeds of his own demise through errant behavior and irresponsible attitudes. We see him flirting with the office girls, charming them with his poetry, trying to persuade them back to the Thelemic commune he started at home, perhaps as prelude to sexual seduction. He likewise resisted the domestication of office hours and seemed to lack the ability to interact properly with co-workers. He may have been driven by deeply-rooted passion for rockets, but his star was never meant to rise behind a corporate desk.

The second half of *Strange Angel* is where the occult side of Jack Parsons is chronicled, since Thelema and the OTO dominated the last ten years of his life. Agape Lodge, which had been started by Wilfred Smith, a Canadian-follower of Crowley's, moved into Parson's large, rambling Pasadena home and became a center of intense OTO activity, inhabited or visited by many occult luminaries, rocket scientists, science fiction writers and a revolving guest list of freaks, bohemians, artists and other fringe personalities whom Parsons would bring in as borders to help offset the rent.

By the time Parsons joined Agape Lodge in 1938, the Californian OTO had been active for nearly twenty years. Pendle's narrative of the early history of Agape is not nearly as detailed as his story of American rocket research. Major figures in Thelemic history like Wilfred Smith and Helen Parsons Smith are portrayed more as confused adulterers than serious magicians, while Phyllis Seckler, Grady McMurtry, and Regina Kahl are just background anecdotes. Hardly any of the contributions of these individuals to the Thelemic community or their lasting legacy are explored in any depth and it is suggested that the existence of the OTO was just another offshoot of California's tendency towards off-beat religious groups. Varying interpretations of Agape Lodge's accomplishments can be debated—were they a collection of self-destructive misfits who blindly worshipped Crowley's personality, or were they serious magicians who were pioneers in a cosmic current. Regardless of your opinion about the OTO, there is no doubt that the Order has a rich and complex history and *Strange Angel* didn't quite explore it deeply enough.

This weakness of the book is unfortunate, since Pendle's work seems to have been blessed and aided by many high-ranking people within the OTO. While not lacking in some good occult history and not unsympathetic to both magick and Thelema, the book doesn't achieve the same depth of popular understanding as *Do as Thou Wilt*, Lawrence Sutphin's excellent biography of Aleister Crowley, or *Sex & Rockets*, the other Jack Parsons biography. There was an opportunity here to not only recover an important piece of the history of rocketry and space travel, but also the history of the OTO in America during Crowley's lifetime. With the presence of such colorful characters as Grady McMurtry, Phyllis Seckler, Helen Parsons Smith, Wilfred Smith, Jane Wolfe, and Marjorie Cameron Parsons, this could have been a very great history indeed.

The book is also lacking in the technical magical knowledge that would enable a reader to understand what Parsons or anyone in the OTO was doing. The tenets of Thelema, the teachings of Crowley, and the wisdom of Liber Al are glossed over in short paragraphs. By the time we see Parsons establish a functional magickal community in his own home and engaged in ambitious magickal workings, it would be fitting for the reader to have had an elementary vocabulary for magickal workings in general. Otherwise, the stories are reduced to witchy vignettes that focus on the sensational.

For example, Pendle quotes a resident of Agape Lodge who, hearing strange noises from Parsons' bedroom, opens the door and witnesses a strange scene:

> The room...was decorated in a manner typical to an occultist's lair, with all the symbols and appurtenances essential to the proper practice of black magic...Jack was draped in a black robe and stood with his back to us, his arms outstretched, in the center of a pentagram before some sort of altar affair on which several indistinguishable items stood. His voice...rose and fell in a rhythmic chant of gibberish which was delivered with such passionate intensity that its meaning was frighteningly obvious.

This is the type of description of a magickal operation that can easily be given by someone who knows nothing about magick. In the following paragraph, Pendle tells us that Parsons was engaged in elemental magick to obtain a mate (later manifested as Cameron Parsons—his second wife). Why not explain to us the nature of the "indistinguishable items" and the actual language being spoken, which was most likely Hebrew or Enochian, anything but the "gibberish" that was described? And when Parsons takes the "Oath of the Abyss" to become "Master of the Temple," it would be nice to have put these terms into their proper mystical context. Surely becoming a Master of the Temple is an achievement of no small spiritual importance, and Pendle presents it as merely another quirk of Parsons' misguided romanticism.

Strange Angel often blurts out fragments of Parsons' poetry, Crowley's "Hymn to Pan," which Parsons loved to perform at CalTech socials, and snatches of translations from the Enochian calls (which are called "ominous and obscure"), without any context or purpose other than to reveal to the reader how spooky and far-out this stuff is. In fact, Pendle calls Enochian a "strange singsong language" and the only glimpse he gives us of Enochian magick is Parsons masturbating over "paper tablets [that are] covered with arcane symbols and languages." Would one assume that Enochian tablets are covered with...hmm...say, Enochian symbols and languages?

Further, important pieces of writing like the *Thelemic Holy Books* (especially *The Book of the Law*) are barely explained. When it is mentioned that Parsons wrote his *Book of Babalon* as the "fourth chapter of the *Book of the Law*," an ordinary reader would not know what this means, or why it is important. Pendle merely quotes a sentence or two from the Babalon text as an example of how deteriorating Parsons' psyche was becoming, not instead any attempt to put Babalon into Thelemic perspective. And while important writings like "Freedom is a Two Edged Sword" are casually mentioned as an example of how Parsons was responding to the growing anti-Communist movement that was affecting his ability to get work in the rocket industry, the Thelemic content of that particular work is never fully examined. This would be like writing a biography of Thomas Jefferson and mentioning the Declaration of Independence without any word about Democracy and the Rights of Man but instead a deep discussion of the Founding Father's reaction to British military strategy.

Despite this set back, *Strange Angel* does tell a very compelling story of what happened at the Parsonage, as the house came to be known, and sheds a large amount of light on how Parsons' life fortunes declined, why magick took on more and more importance for him as he gradually lost his position in the field of rocket science (he spent his last days trying to start his own explosives company and doing special effects for Hollywood movies). From one perspective his descent into magick at the expense of his career seemed to be the fulfillment of his true Will, and from another perspective it comes across as a fantasy world into which he was escaping to avoid having to come to terms with his own demons, most specifically having to find a job. There is no more powerful image of Parsons' descent into subjectivity than that given by Cameron, his second wife, of how she raced about the house tying down the windows in light of a massive rain storm that was threatening to damage the house. "And can you imagine?" she commented. "I'm running around trying to close the windows, and Jack goes upstairs with his dagger to stop the wind!" Perhaps it was true that here was a man who was receding deeper with each ritual into a fantasy world where some simple life coping skills taught by a good psychiatrist would have been beneficial.

Then we come to L. Ron Hubbard, who, of course, deserves a whole biography to himself (and those are few and far between due to the restrictive nature of the Church of Scientology). It was ironic that Parsons considered Hubbard "the most Thelemic man I have ever met." In a way, perhaps he was, considering how he would later apply his concentrated will (and $20,000 of Jack Parsons' money) to starting one of the most successful religious franchises of the 20th century, eclipsing Thelema, outselling Crowley in the bookstores, and gaining international acceptance and public validation. It doesn't escape Pendle's attention that this was exactly what Crowley was hoping for himself but leaves it to the reader to interpret the value of what Hubbard created. The narrative, however, is coldly void of any real personality from Hubbard, painting him more as a Baron Munchausen-type who would stop at nothing to weave intricate myths about himself, including how he had infiltrated the OTO as an undercover FBI agent. Perhaps this distancing coldness is a result of Hubbard himself obscuring his true being for the sake of magically powered myths that charmed the hell out of everyone he met, including Parsons.

It is not incredulous that Parsons became enamored of this red haired, swashbuckling science fiction writer and that the two cut up together like two enflamed Princes of Wands. So instead of lifting jet assisted airplanes into space, Parsons sold his share of AeroJet and hitched himself to Hubbard's wagon, and the two founded Allied Enterprises. Their mission statement was even more confused and abstract as the one authored for AeroJet: "To pool and accumulate earnings and profits of any nature whatsoever, coming from any source whatsoever, and flowing from the capabilities and the craft of each of the partners." This translated into a weird business collaboration between Parsons' new explosives company and L. Ron Hubbard's science fiction writing. What happened instead was that Hubbard stole $20,000 from Agape Lodge and ran off with Parsons' lover to Florida, where he bought a yacht and started formulating a money-making religious organization. Needless to say, Hubbard didn't honor any of the business objectives of Allied Enterprises and Parsons was left broke, unemployed, alone, and magically deranged.

But in the end, it is hard not to like Jack Parsons. He was elegant, brilliant, eccentric and somewhat accomplished at almost every discipline he applied himself to, although his debacle with Hubbard and his fiery death at age 37 may lead one to think he was a disaster at being a magician. But undoubtedly he was enflamed with character and spirit. There is a picture of him taken in the late 1940s, seated at what could be a small table in a breakfast nook, with a candle burning before him. Here is the rocket scientist, the master of chemicals and solid fuel, a man who has nimbly and dangerously mixed volatile explosive powders, both physically and spiritually, seated before a simple candle flame. There is at once simplicity and magickal power to this image.

Having spent a lifetime evoking the fire demons, John Whiteside Parsons went out with an appropriate bang, leaving behind him a lasting legacy that lends itself to various interpretations. Some see his life as a series of brilliant accomplishments that have been ignored by history, his obscurity a symptom of deep rooted prejudice against the occult and the general public's failure to understand Thelema. Others see his life, especially his violent ending, as a cautionary tale of what happens when you play with cosmic fire. *Strange Angel*'s frightening description of the mutilated Parsons—still alive after the explosion in his coach house had ripped off his arm and his face, his legs pulverized, his body crushed under a sink that had been hurled across the room, the Pasadena evening breeze blowing through the air, the tattered pages of science fiction magazines and type written sheets of religiously enflamed poetry—is a haunting legacy to a life where science, literature and magick came together to both enrich a life and to destroy it.

CRYPTONOMICON BY NEAL STEPHENSON

Early in the novel *Cryptonomicon* by Neal Stephenson, Lawrence Pritchard Waterhouse, a student of mathematics at Princeton University, is bicycling late at night through the Pine Barrens of New Jersey, where he comes across a wall of fire that burns around the metallic framework of what looks to have been a giant pyramid. He sees naval men struggling with the flames, shattered suitcases, and a room that seems to have fallen from the sky whose wrecked walls are decorated with posters of Hermann Goering. Gradually, we realize that Waterhouse is witnessing the aftermath of the crash of the Nazi airship Hindenburg at Lakehurst, New Jersey, in 1938.

It is Waterhouse's peculiar perceptions of the patterns of things (he is more fascinated by the burning framework of the ship and the scattered objects in the debris field than he is by the human tragedy) that makes him valuable to military intelligence when the world erupts into a global war. Pritchard started his love for cryptology by playing the chapel pipe organ at college. Later, he speculated upon how a complete map of London could be recreated from the patterns made by people stepping up and down upon the street curbs. Somehow, he distills from the framework of the burning zeppelin the idea of preset symbols in machine language, an idea that gave Alan Turing (his friend at Princeton) the crucial element to design the modern computer. Once the war begins, Pritchard is rescued by his role as a navy glockenspiel player and recruited into a special detachment of the Royal Air Force to work with an intelligence corps so secret that vast resources are deployed throughout the world to cover the knowledge of its existence from the enemy.

Starting with the shocking historical image of the burning Hindenburg, Neal Stephenson steps off into uncharted territory, upping his own literary ante after a decade and a half of writing overt science fiction novels. His previous works, including *Snow Crash* and The *Diamond Age*, have been narratives that painted portraits of our technological future, one that seemed more grounded in possibility than any of the cyberpunk literature that came before. Quantum computers, nanotechnology, virtual reality, life as software, culture as hibernating virus, the brain as microprocessor...it's all been done before; but Stephenson somehow was different. His voice carried authority, as if he were personally inspecting the future through the telescope of the secret research labs—nanobots that circulate through the body hunting down cancer, generators that mass produce food on the molecular level and books printed on erasable paper with dynamic content—are everyday concerns.

It is these technologies that Stephenson projected in our future and not always in a benevolent manner. He made us believe that advertisers would soon plaster their visual mind control on the inside of our eyelids where we would be unable to escape their presence, or chat rooms would become as sophisticated as *Star Trek*'s holodeck but infected by viruses in the form of sword welding samurai. And unlike many other science fiction writers, we could hear Stephenson laughing at his own comic inventions as he went along.

Now he has given us a vastly complex book that ranks in the same category as Thomas Pynchon's—its similarities to *Gravity's Rainbow* are immediately obvious—or books by Kurt Vonnegut in the way Stephenson interleaves World War II with modern day and traces several generations of an American family as they interact with history. The Waterhouses, Lawrence, and his grandson Randy, are the central core of the novel, which keeps jumping back and forth between World War II and modern day. Lawrence is a key player in the crypto project that broke the German and Japanese military codes. Not only are the Allies privy to General Rommel and Admiral Yamamoto's every directive, they are continually faced with the moral dilemma of acting upon their hacked knowledge, thereby risking disclosure. RAF Detachment 2702 is formed as a sort of paramilitary counterintelligence force to keep the secret of the cracked codes.

We travel from the occupation of Shanghai by the Japanese, through Pearl Harbor, Guadalcanal, North Africa, the Battle of the Atlantic, the death of Yamamoto and the last stand of the Japanese on lonely Pacific redoubts, never once losing track of character or narrative purpose.

Not only do we meet endearing men such as Lawrence Waterhouse, who strolls on landscapes far from the enemy lines designing the cryptographic strategies of Detachment 2702; we also meet Corporal Bobby Shaftoe, a morphine addicted marine who carries out the physical grunt work in the jungles of the Pacific, the deserts of North Africa, and in the depths of the Atlantic Ocean as a prisoner aboard a German U-Boat. Also present are Enoch Root, a larger-than-life Priest-Warrior; Goto Dengo, a Japanese soldier who survives life amongst the cannibal tribes of New Guinea to carve out a mountain for mysterious military purposes; and Commander Schoen, a crypto-genius who is amassing the Cryptonomicon, the ultimate collection of documents about human ciphers, and has been driven insane by the psychic effect of his own chosen profession.

The modern day plot thread primarily concerns Randy Waterhouse, who is part owner of Epiphyte(2), a telecommunications start-up company that tries to build an international data haven in the caverns of an obscure sultanate-island off the coast of Borneo. His fiber optic cables are lain by the granddaughter of Bobbie Shaftoe and the router caves are being engineered by Goto Dengo himself. Also present are a surreal parade of characters, including the Dentist, a sexually perverse dental surgeon turned venture capitalist; the Sultan of Kinakuta, whose mission is to allow the Internet to escape the hands of international governments; and Andrew Loeb, an ex-role-playing genius turned digital terrorist who may or may not be the Digibomber. The scramble for a hidden cache of Nazi gold in an attempt to back the world's largest repository of digital currency is an epic, tragic and funny story. Stephenson's portrayal of role-playing game designers (who graduate from college with little more than a mountainous knowledge of the UNIX operating system) turned telecommunication tycoons, is a dead-on satire of the colossal gold rush that ensued in the wake of the Internet explosion in the mid-1990s. Stephenson brings to life the reality of the opportunists scouting the world for wealth, either gold sunken by the Nazis decades past or digital information hoarded by world governments.

Stephenson blends fact with fiction so beautifully that he makes it easy to believe that there is an open source operating system called Finux (read: Linux), a community of right-wing techno-libertarians called Eutropians (read: Extropians) and that the Sultanate of Kinakuta is just as real as Bletchley Park or Guadalcanal. The fictional characters move against a background populated by men such as Admiral

Yamamoto, Alan Turing and Douglas Macarthur so seamlessly that you start to wonder if Lawrence Waterhouse really did invent Random Access Memory (RAM) or whether the wacky kingdom of Qwghlm (which has more words for wool than the Eskimos do for snow) does indeed float in the English Channel, as described by the author.

Stephenson's prose is clean and accessible, enjoyable and funny. On almost every page there is a stunning metaphor or image that conveys volumes, over and above the event it has been charged to describe. For example:

> Shaftoe has had little direct contact with that Waterhouse fellow during their stay on Qwghlm, but he has noticed that men who have just finished talking to Waterhouse tend to walk away shaking their heads— and not in the slow way of a man saying "no," but in the sudden convulsive way of a dog who has a horsefly in his middle ear [page 374].

There are also many comic moments in the novel that never detract from the epic tone. The life history of Randy Waterhouse and his failed start-up companies is a small comic gem in itself, his girlfriend Charlene's deconstructive analysis of the racist use of facial hair is a perfect send-up of myopic postmodern academia, and the devouring of a box of Cap'n Crunch by a computer software genius resonates hilariously with the novel's other plot threads of sunken treasure and the cryptological search for patterns within nature:

> [T]he cereal engineers at General Mills had to find a shape that would minimize surface area, and, as some sort of compromise between the sphere that is dictated by Euclidean geometry and whatever sunken-treasure-related shapes that the cereal-aestheticians were probably clamoring for, they came up with this hard-to-pin-down striated pillow formation [page 479].

Humorous incongruities are scattered throughout the book and permeate even the most solemn of circumstances: a crew of Marines makes a Pacific atoll look as if it has been inhabited for months by dumping human excrement into the newly built latrines; the cryptographers at Bletchley Park must fake their employee records so the German spies wouldn't notice that the British team is hiring an unusual number of tall secretaries, thereby guessing that they have cryptographical plug boards on high walls; the Americans use the German's own Enigma Codes to fake a message to Berlin claiming that the Enigma Codes have been broken since the U-Boat Captain is thought to have gone insane and was not believed.

Bouncing back and forth between the men of mind (the cryptographers, mathematicians, strategists and politicians) and the men of action (marines, sailors, pilots, treasure divers, U-boat captains), Stephenson weaves a series of narrative threads that spans decades and harmonizes into a greater narrative unity. The Japanese soldier GoTo Dengo's life among a tribe of Pacific Island Cannibals, US Marine Bobby Shaftoe's adventures as a prisoner aboard a German U-Boat, Randy Waterhouse's attempts to build a data haven in the Philippines, Lawrence Waterhouse's cryptic analysis of the forms of nature and history, all blend together into a unified whole that leaves the reader with a euphoric sense of literary pleasure.

It is very difficult to summarize what this book is about. But computer technology, cryptography, the Internet, the controversy over digital privacy, the legacy of World War II, death, global politics, and computer operating systems seem like an accurate but incomplete list. The novel seems to be about Everything, or the use of symbol systems and decryption to discover the true nature of Everything.

In a long essay about computers and our techno-cultural landscape called "In the Beginning Was the Command Line," Stephenson touches upon the relationship between religion, cosmogony, quantum physics, and technology:

> ...somewhere outside of and beyond our universe is an operating system, coded up over incalculable spans of time by some kind of hacker-demiurge. The cosmic operating system uses a command-line interface. It runs on something like a teletype, with lots of noise and heat; punched-out bits flutter down into its hopper like drifting stars. The demiurge sits at his teletype, pounding out one command line after another, specifying the values of fundamental constants of physics...and when he's finished typing out the command line, his right pinky hesitates above the ENTER key for an aeon or two, wondering what's going to happen; then down it comes--and the WHACK you hear is another Big Bang.

This idea of the universe as a coded operating system is a powerful image that is central to *Cryptonomicon*. In its own way, Stephenson's little book on operating systems provides a philosophical companion to his novel. Lawrence Waterhouse, obsessed with the patterns of nature, searches in his own way for the signatures of the "hacker-demiurge":

> The sand at the surf line has been washed flat. A small child's footprints wander across it, splaying like gardenia blossoms on thin shafts. The sand looks like a geometric plane until a sheet of ocean grazes it. Then small imperfections are betrayed by swirls in the water. Those swirls in turn carve the sand. The ocean is a Turing machine, the sand is its tape; the water reads the marks in the sand and sometimes erases them and sometimes carves new ones with tiny currents that are themselves a response to the marks. Plodding through the surf, Waterhouse strikes deep craters in the wet sand that are read by the ocean. Eventually the ocean erases them, but in the process its state has been changed, the pattern of its swirls has been altered. Waterhouse images that the disturbance might somehow propagate across the Pacific and into some super-secret Nipponese surveillance device made of bamboo tubes and chrysanthemum leaves. Nip listeners would know that Waterhouse had walked that way. In turn, the water swirling around Waterhouse's feet carries information about Nip propeller design and the deployment of their fleets—if only he had the wit to read it. The chaos of the waves, gravid with encrypted data, mocks him [page 445].

Cryptonomicon is an immense work and its author has made it seem so easy—in an interview published on Amazon.com he confessed that he gathered much of the World War II Marine material from his wife's uncle and that he researched German U-Boats by watching the German movie *Das Boot*! But don't let him fool you: this complex and fascinating novel is carefully textured with a blend of historical reality and fictional invention that stitches together the origins of the modern computer in the chaos of World War II with the spanning of the globe by the Internet and its hard currency of information. With this novel, a science fiction writer has cast his trained visionary eye on our technological past and our cultural present to create a work of literature.

Our Gods Wear Spandex
by Christopher Knowles

Back in the late 1970s I sold my comic book collection. It was a strange and sad occasion, mixing a feeling of loss for old friends (the art work on Spider-Man #21 is as dear a memory for me as a distant birthday recollected) with the evil thoughts I had about how to spend all the money I was being paid by the comic shop. However, the money wasn't too joyous—in fact I got rid of my entire Fantastic Four collection for fifty dollars and each one of those issues now can go for a few hundred. But back then I was going through some weird anti-materialist phase in which I perceived the several dozen boxes of oxidizing paper in the closet as an anchor preventing me from entering a higher stage of enlightenment. About five years later I felt the magnitude of losing that collection as if a limb had been amputated. In fact, my entire childhood mythology, with its gods and goddesses, angels and demons, magicians, hierophants, amazons, shamans and secret brotherhoods, had been viciously removed from my psyche just so I could save some space in my closet.

Twenty years later I started collecting the reprints of those early 1960s Marvel comics in hardcover. With their snazzy gold trimmed covers and marble patterned paper, the freshly inked and brightly colored pages seemed impervious to time and the elements. Unlike their originals, they would not oxidize (at least not in my lifetime) and any time I felt like it, I could dip back into those myths and fairy tales that dominated my childhood, where Spider-Man's web slung across the Manhattan skyline like a guardian angel of the city, the Hulk bounded over hills in his Arizona desert like a rampaging shaman warrior, and the Avengers lorded over the world in their skyscraper headquarters, a brotherhood dedicated to truth and justice.

My feeling that comic book super heroes are deities incarnate is val-
idated by a new book by Christopher Knowles, *Our Gods Wear Spandex*
(Weiser, 2007), in which he explicitly ties together the pulp and comic
book heroes of the entire 20th century and shows how they are indeed
modern-day manifestations of the ancient gods, magicians and super
heroes of mythologies, religions and folklore from all ages and all cultures. It has never been a secret that all the creators of super heroes (like
Jack Kirby and Stan Lee) drew their inspiration from ancient stories and
archetypes, but Knowles' study of the subject really helps you focus on
just how prevalent the magic and mysticism of the ancient religions and
mythologies are in our pop culture, and how much of it young children
and teenagers are absorbing. Especially with the phenomenal success
of book and film franchise like *Harry Potter* and *The Lord of the Rings*,
there seems to be a gigantic surge of magical content in our mass culture. And while Knowles' book emphasizes the comic book heroes of
the 1940s through to the 1990s, he wisely expands his historical scope
to include the penny dreadful and pulp magazines of the 1800s, as well
as the modern emphasis on "transhumanism" (i.e., the future expansion
of human consciousness through computer technology). *Our Gods Wear
Spandex* is a clever and thoughtful meditation upon the progression of
this trend in our culture.

By starting off with the religions and mythologies of ancient Sumer,
Egypt, Greece and Rome, Knowles shows us that throughout the range
of human history, we have taken gods and heroes who have possessed
super powers and elemental abilities and reinvented them time and
again in plain sight. Mercury, the Messenger of the Gods, lords over
Grand Central Station and Isis, the Queen of Heaven, guards New York
Harbor. But it is in our comic books and action adventure fantasies that
these archetypes abound in an unending procession of gods and heroes.
Throughout the book Knowles builds a strong inventory of these archetypes and shows their historic progression from the ancient world to the
modern newsstand.

Knowles discusses religious and mystic movements like the
Freemasons and the Rosicrucians, as well as the paranormal spiritualists
of the 19th century and the Victorian schools like the Golden Dawn and
Theosophy. He inevitably covers Aleister Crowley and, oddly enough,
Harry Houdini and Edgar Cayce.

He moves through the Victorian and Edwardian age, passing by
Edgar Allen Poe, who invented the modern detective study, guides us

OUR GODS WEAR SPANDEX BY CHRISTOPHER KNOWLES   285

through the rise of the penny dreadfuls and the Argosy pulps, the birth
of science fiction and the works of writers such as H.G. Welles, Jules
Verne and Arthur Conan Doyle. Eventually, he gets around to Edgar
Rice Burroughs, the creator of *Tarzan* and dozens of early science fiction franchises like *John Carter of Mars* and *Carson of Venus*. And he
includes Robert E. Howard, the creator of *Conan the Barbarian* and his
creator collaborator H.P. Lovecraft. Sax Rohmer, the inventor of *Dr.
Fu Manchu*, makes an appearance, as does Jack Parsons, OTO Lodge
Master and science fiction patron.

If all of this just seems like a big laundry list, so does the book
at times. One of its weaknesses is that it covers too much ground too
quickly. Barely a handful of paragraphs are devoted to each author,
sometimes with a single sentence tying them to the larger theme of the
book. While it is fun to read a summary of early science fiction and
pulp heroes, we really spent our money to learn about mystical content. Knowles doesn't seem to be unaware of the occult references in
H.P. Lovecraft's *Cthulhu* Mythos stories or the adventures of *Conan the
Barbarian*, he just deals with them all too briefly and without any real
scholarly depth. There's nothing here you couldn't get from Wikipedia.

Unfortunately, the same is true of the second half of the book that
covers the history of comic books. Like the coverage of the Victorian
and the Edwardian pulps and early science fiction, we have all-too-
brief descriptions of our favorite comic book legends. For example, the
chapter on the Silver Surfer, one of my own personal heroes from the
1960s, is two paragraphs and is crammed with one-sentence anecdotes
about how Jack Kirby and Stan Lee created the character, the events
that transpired in the comic book where he premiered, and the recent
revival of the Surfer's popularity. Buried in those two paragraphs is a
mention of Galactus the planet vampire who had enslaved the Surfer as
a Herald, and a single mention of how Kirby considered the Surfer to be
"Christ-like." But the archetypal resonances of the Silver Surfer and his
master Galactus could fill volumes. They are two characters rich with
depth and mythic import, but Knowles opts for two brief paragraphs
full of "betcha didn't know"-type facts that easily could have been copied from a Marvel fan site.

It ordinarily wouldn't be a such a big deal that a writer should fail
to go into so much depth about the mythological origins and meanings
of the various comic book heroes. But this is, after all, a book about the
mythological origins and meanings of comic book heroes! It remains

largely hit and run descriptions of its various topics and despite its fine writing and captivating anecdotes, Knowles never really delves deeply into the heart of his subject matter.

For example, when discussing Alan Moore's *Promethea*, a comic book series that is a virtual primer of ceremonial magick, Kabala and Tarot (which deserve an entire chapter of their own in this book), Knowles covers it all in a single paragraph and doesn't mention that Aleister Crowley figures as a character, or even attempt to cover the richness of detail and occult lore that is present in the story.

One of the oddest touches in the book is the discussion of Batman, one of the most popular comic characters of all time, in a chapter on Golems. He ranks Batman as "the archetypal Golem" (!), a creature out for revenge, along with Wolverine and the Punisher whom he considers to be berserk Golems. While I see his point, it would have been more fruitful to include Batman in a discussion of all the mythic moon gods and goddesses and his relationship to the Tarot card the Moon, as well as the obvious mapping of his arch-villain the Joker to the Fool card. Or to have Batman and the Joker representing the Moon card in its dignified and ill-dignified aspect. After all, this very correspondence was done by Alan Moore in the graphic novel *The Killing Joke* which was the basis for the Tim Burton movie *Batman*. Knowles also compares Batman's mastery of weapons and gadgets to a rabbi trained in Kabala. It probably would have been a much better comparison to show how Batman's journey to maturity involves the same military discipline as the Ninjas or the Knights Templars. After all, the Hollywood movie *Batman Begins* took just this approach.

Jack "King" Kirby's use of ancient religions in all of his comics, especially *The Mighty Thor* and *The Eternals*, can fill an entire volume. And Kirby was a strong force in uniting mythology with science fiction. It was with great enthusiasm that he leapt onto the *2001: A Space Odyssey* bandwagon and produced several stunning variations on the original Kubrick/Clarke creation. Kirby was consciously aware that he was playing with ancient archetypes and he played it to the hilt (I'm convinced that the elemental nature of the Fantastic Four was his conscious decision—Stan Lee does tend to steal the credit whenever he can!). His work deserves more space than allotted here, as does Alan Moore, Neil Gaiman and Frank Miller (the founding fathers of the modern graphic novels).

Our Gods Wear Spandex also suffers from the lack of pictures of the actual super heroes. Perhaps the publisher didn't want to spend the cash on copyright fees, but Knowles really needs us to see illustrations of *Batman*, *Superman*, *Spider-Man*, and the *Fantastic Four* lined up side-by-side with their mythic archetypes. To see *Superman* lined up next to Apollo, or the *Fantastic Four* compared to the elemental four-fold powers of the Sphinx as described by Eliphas Levi, would have been more meaningful than the abstracted heroes who are displayed for comic purposes. There are, however, cool cartoons of Crowley and Sherlock Holmes, H.P. Lovecraft and Alan Moore, but not a single illustration of any of the instantly recognizable super heroes that constitute the subject matter of the book.

Either way, the book is a fun, quick read and gives one much to think about. But the definitive study of comic books super heroes and the ancient gods that they manifest has yet to be written.

THE SECRETS OF DR. TAVERNER BY DION FORTUNE

Arthur Conan Doyle, the writer who created Sherlock Holmes, openly confessed that his inspiration for the iconic literary figure was a lecturer at the University of Edinburgh, where Doyle had studied medicine. Dr. Joseph Bell was notorious for deducing from the physical appearance of a total stranger the man's occupation, background and medical diagnosis. He was accurate so often that many thought him to be possessed of uncanny powers. But Dr. Bell, like his literary counterpart, was merely a man who exploited his reason and his powers of observation. The explanation of his methods often disappointed because it revealed that no magic or psychic powers had been involved and that the material world was a machine of cause and effect from which deductions can be made based on precise and unalterable laws. Often the deductions were...well...elementary (Holmes knew that a visitor owned a particular breed of dog because of observable bite marks on his walking stick that no one else had noticed). Being acutely observant was a power accessible to any man and could be consciously cultivated, but only a Dr. Bell or a Sherlock Holmes would bother to do so. "It is simplicity itself," Holmes would say, almost perplexed that he was the only one who had noticed the essentially obvious.

As Dr. Bell had given inspirational birth to Holmes, so the great detective of Baker Street inspired an entire century of mystery fiction. Hardly a detective exists in print who doesn't owe some credit to Doyle's canon, which had established a formula for mystery stories that has become so ingrained into our literary psyches. The anti-social genius detective and his narrator-sidekick have become standard characters, paralleling the relationship between the Magus and the Fool archetypes. Dr. John Watson was based on Doyle himself and provided the reader with a character with whom to identify, as the detective himself was often intellectually remote and emotionally removed. The detective was the man of science and rationality while the side-kick was the hopeless romantic who described events from a more human perspective. There was often a master criminal whose own genius was worthy of the detective's own, as well as bumbling policemen who always in the end turned to the Great Man in their last desperate attempt to solve the unsolvable.

What all of these master detectives had in common was an unflinching materialist view of the universe. They rigorously employed the scientific method, and when the occult or the supernatural appeared in any of their cases (i.e., *The Hound of the Baskervilles*), the detective always exposed the perfectly rational explanation behind the superstitious nonsense. In this manner, the literary detective was a champion of rationalism. Similar to mathematicians who reverse-engineer the signatures of nature from its hidden structure and patterns, the detective reads the narrative behind the scattered clues, testimonies and crime scenes that he encounters in his work.

But not every author who modeled their crime fiction after the Holmes template was a strict adherent of scientific rationalism. Dion Fortune, a theosophist, ceremonial magician and psychoanalyst whose books on magic and the occult have had a huge influence on 20th century mysticism, penned her own contribution to the genre with *The Secrets of Dr. Taverner*, first published in 1926, one year before the final collection of Sherlock Holmes stories. The influence is immediately obvious: Taverner possesses many Holmes-like attributes both in his mien and his working method. He is even accompanied by a sidekick, Dr. Rhodes, his trusted assistant at a highly exclusive English nursing home just after the First World War. Even more true to formula, Dr. Rhodes is the narrator of the tales and acts as a proxy for the reader, marveling at Taverner's eccentricities and abilities. The opening of "Blood Lust," the first story in the collection, has little to distinguish its narrative from any dozen of Sherlock Holmes pastiches. But there is much more to Taverner's sleuthing than a faithful devotion to the Holmes formula.

Dr. Taverner is an initiate of an ancient occult order and is concerned with his own peculiar type of crime. His antagonists are neither bank robbers nor blackmailers; neither are they industrial saboteurs or political spies. Having access to a large number of mentally disturbed inmates in his nursing home, Dr. Taverner pursues the psychic demons, vampires, hell hounds, black magicians, astral entities and disincarnate spirits that haunt his patients. In "Blood Lust" he helps a war veteran rid himself of the astral energy of a man he killed in battle who had latched itself onto his etheric body. "The Death Hound" involves a psychic attack by an astral beast, quite unlike the scientifically explainable *Hound of the Baskervilles*. In short, Doctor Taverner completely accepts a realm of reality that Holmes would have considered an irrational delusion. Doctor Taverner explains to Dr. Rhodes that his suffering patients would ordinarily be buried by the medical industry and dismissed as mentally ill, not seen as victims of psychic attack who require either an exorcist or a ceremonial magician to cure their ailments.

Dion Fortune was trained as a psychoanalyst, and the teachings of Sigmund Freud about the unconscious cast a large shadow on the Taverner stories. On the cover of the new edition by Weiser/Red Wheel, Dr. Taverner is even illustrated as a Freud look-a-like, cautiously taking notes while a vampire reclines before him on the analyst's coach. While Holmes occasionally used psychology to solve crimes, the detective of Baker Street would have been uninterested in the mystical and sexual irrationalism unleashed by the technique of psychoanalysis. The early decades of the 1900s was a time of great discovery in the field of the subconscious, and many occultists, including Fortune, leveraged this knowledge, fitting theories about the inner life of the mind into their own magical world views.

Several of the stories in the collection involve the careful nursing of a mentally and spiritually broken person back to a deeper sense of wholeness. "The Soul That Would Not Be Born," "The Daughter of Pan," and "The Man Who Sought" in particular swap out the typical beginning of a mystery story (a client coming to the detective's consulting office) for a mental patient being brought to the nursing home. It is Taverner's diagnostic method to perform an etheric reading of the patient's condition, and then attempt either to guide his soul to spiritual healing or to go after the psychic vampire causing the condition.

As an occultist, Taverner has the training to tackle a variety of unusual crimes. In "The Return of the Ritual," he dives into the Ashakic Record in order to locate an occult manuscript that had been stolen from his Order during the reign of the Medici. He never reveals the name of the Order, but in true Holmes fashion, he does caution Dr. Rhodes about the evil genius behind the Black Lodges. His references to the Order of the Cowled Brethren and the Lodge of Set the Destroyer are particularly amusing and worthy of Aleister Crowley's sense of parody. Yet a strong master villain never truly emerges, leaving many of the stories a bit lacking in drama. Dr. Taverner himself possesses little of the multi-dimensional characterization of Sherlock Holmes; he is often too perfect and never disagreeable in his personal habits. Much of the fun of the Holmes stories resides in Dr. Watson's frustration dealing with his roommate's slovenly habits, his drug addiction, and his utter lack of concern for the humanity of his clients. By making Dr. Taverner such a perfect initiate and brilliant psychoanalyst, Fortune has robbed her character of much literary fascination.

Sadly, Dr. Rhodes himself is almost completely two-dimensional. He doesn't even come close to the type of narrator that Doyle had in Watson. This is too bad, considering that Rhodes and Taverner were based on two very real people: the author herself and a physician she apprenticed with after the war. In fact, she claimed that many of the fictional cases in the stories were based on actual ones that she experienced alongside her teacher whose name, oddly enough, was Dr. Moriarty. Perhaps her admiration for the man clouded her literary judgment, and she refrained from making him more of a flawed character. It feels like a great missed opportunity since there are tantalizing hints that Dr. Taverner has a dark side. Fortune has Taverner confess to Rhodes, "If you are ever offered your choice between being an occultist and a blacksmith, choose the lighter job and enter the forge rather than the Lodge." There is a story left untold and one only wishes that Fortune would have invested more literary art into Taverner and Rhodes.

Dion Fortune, born Violet Firth Evans in 1890, was, like Dr. Taverner, an initiate in an esteemed occult order, in her case a variant of the Hermetic Order of the Golden Dawn presided over by Moina Mathers. She penned several occult novels, including *The Sea Priestess*, *Moon Magic*, and *The Demon Lover*, but she is best known for *The Mystical Qabalah*, a non-fiction summary of the western tradition of Hermetic magic that has since become a classic, continuously in print since 1935. Her other non-fiction classic is *Psychic Self-Defense* (1930), reprinted by Red Wheel/Weiser in 2001.

Reading the non-fictional *Psychic Self-Defense* just after *The Secrets of Doctor Taverner* was a revelation in itself. The author constructs her manual for protection against paranormal attack in the form of personal anecdotes, many of them clearly the case studies used as inspiration for the Taverner stories. While the book exposes the occult and paranormal

causes of mental illness that traditional doctors ignore, the author delin-
eates between a physician one goes to for the curing of physical ailments
("Not so long ago," she explains, "I came across a case of alleged obsession which turned out to be neglected constipation, and which was
effectively exorcised with castor oil") and the occultist one turns to for
the curing of etheric, astral, and spiritual maladies.

In fact, much of this book is written as a training manual for occult
professionals, not so much a handbook for ordinary people to have
around the house in case they are occasionally attacked by unbalanced
elemental forces. Fortune gives lengthy instructions about how to diag-
nose patients and intuit their psychic illnesses, addressing the reader as
if he is about to rent a London flat and set up his shingle as exorcist or
psychometrist. Much of the author's advice runs parallel to that given by
Dr. Taverner to Dr. Rhodes in the short stories, which makes reading
these two books in tandem especially illuminating. One can almost hear
Dr. Moriarty lecturing to the young Dion Fortune on the the process by
which a healer should treat the damaged aura of a patient.

However, much of *Psychic Self-Defense* now seems dated. We are
instructed that when one of our patients is suffering from psychic
assault, look to see if he lives around any Roman or Druidic ruins (no
doubt sound advice for one living in England just after World War I)
and that a good way to avoid the effects of a fiendish psychic vampire
is to be at the cinema roaring with laughter at Charlie Chaplin. At the
very end of the book, Fortune gets positively absurd and flat-out racist, declaring that Jews know nothing about the mystical Qabalah and
that the occult lodges are shunned by Bolsheviks because occultists are
hardly political.

Fortune has been accused by many to be writing with too much
of a Judeo-Christian bias, emphasizing the Christ-center nature of
Tiphareth and centering much of her prayers upon her Osirian-Aeon
religious mythology. However, in her defense, her magical training was
with some of the original members of the Golden Dawn, an order that
clearly based much of its teachings upon Judeo-Christian mythology.
And where is it written that the Old and New Testaments, two books
of great spiritual power, can't be part of your magic? I believe her bias
against witchcraft and a disdain for anything remotely related to Aleister
Crowley may have provoked much criticism of her Christian-style magic.

Despite all this, *Psychic Self-Defense* includes some eloquent and
beautiful writings on the spiritual and occult maladies that plague us as

we navigate through a world populated with elemental and discordant entities that often wear the fleshy bodies of those around us. Many of Fortune's anecdotes, methods of diagnosis, and suggestions for psychic healing are firmly rooted in her years of experience with spiritual as well as mental illnesses and give strong lessons in how we can identify them within ourselves as well in others. If you ever doubt that there are such things as psychic vampires or astral hell hounds, just look around you at the people you share your life with to see where those entities are manifesting.

And if the entity is more disincarnate and the assault so damaging to your etheric body that an exorcist is needed, perhaps a visit to Dr. Taverner's nursing home will do the trick.

First published in *Behutet: Modern Thelemic Magick & Culture*, Issue 50, Autumn, 2011.

BETWEEN THE GATES
BY MARK STAVISH

Back in elementary school, I read the *John Carter of Mars* series by Edgar Rice Burroughs and marveled when the gallant Virginian Civil War hero was transported to the planet Mars just by slipping out of his physical body and drifting across the vastness of space to the Martian soil. It was super cool that after toiling as a slave of the green-skinned warrior bad guys called Tharks, he gained his freedom and led an army of red-skinned good guys to victory. He even became an emperor and married the most beautiful female in the city state of Helium (can anyone say White Supremacy?), but to me his biggest accomplishment was to travel across the void of space without a spaceship, leaving his physical body behind on Earth.

In the short-lived DC Comic *Weird Worlds*, I even got a beautifully colored cartoon version of Carter's transportation across space to the martial sphere. From that moment on, whenever I thought of astral travel, I thought of that comic book drawing. Carter was a man of war, a soldier who had seen brutal combat and led men into battle, who was now rising up through the spheres of consciousness to his supreme God, the planet Mars. In Kabalistic terms, he was elevating himself to Geburah, the Sephiroth at the top of the pillar of Severity of the Tree of Life.

Likewise, Burroughs' other fictional heroes had their own respective Sephiroths to conquer. Carson Napier, otherwise known as Carson of Venus, arrived, albeit by spacecraft instead of his astral body of light, on the green planet, otherwise known as Netzach. Admiral Julian invaded the Moon a.k.a. Yesod. Tarzan of the Apes lorded over the earthy and primitive world of Malkuth. From a very early age, a science fiction writer was teaching me fundamental Kabalism.

So when I later discovered the teachings of the Mystical Kabala, initially through the works of Israel Regardie and Dion Fortune, it was not a great leap for me to visualize the Sephiroths of the Tree of Life as science fiction landscapes: Malkuth is a harsh, great jungle full of prehistoric beats; Yesod is a lunar landscape of rock and dust; Netzach is a lush and brilliant forest full of cyclopean trees; Hod is a city of alchemical laboratories and planetariums inhabited by bearded wizards; Tiphareth is a golden landscape of sun temples; Geburah is a bloody battle field patrolled by barbaric hordes on horseback; Chesed is a sky-line of cathedrals and palaces where mighty kings take counsel; Binah is a city of pyramids where a powerful witch crone rules with tyrannical excess; and Chokmah is a vast and largely empty temple leading to an altar of brilliant white light.

Between the Gates: Lucid Dreaming, Astral Projection and the Body of Light in Western Esotericism is a new book by Mark Stavish, published by Weiser Books. It sells itself as a book on Hermetic magic in theory and practice, with an emphasis on how to create a body of light and transport your consciousness into other realms. The young kid in me that was still reading about the exploits of John Carter got very excited half-way through the first chapter. This was not going to be a dry manual on how to visualize yourself floating through a wall to spy on your neighbor -- this was going to be a challenging journey through different worlds and levels of consciousness. I flipped ahead and saw alchemical drawings by Robert Fludd, drawings of the chakras and the Tree of Life, listings of Hebrew letters and their correspondences. It seemed very promising.

Stavish is the founder of the Institute for Hermetic Studies and the author of several books on the Hermetic tradition, alchemy, and Kabalah, including a book on Freemasonry with Lon Milo DuQuette. His credentials are impressive, his writing style very reader friendly and clear. And he does indeed give us some fundamental exercise on how to develop the body of light, how to rise through the spheres of consciousness and seek a deeper integration between our spiritual selves and our physical manifestations. However, the book, lightly sprinkled with visualization exercises and instructions on how to vibrate Hebrew letters and god-names, is not so much a textbook on Hermetic magic, as a collection of previously published essays and articles, many of them still available on-line, well-written and informative, valuable to the student of the magical arts, but far from a practical beginner's guide or even a resource for advanced students.

Stavish is a good writer, and his explanations of the synthesis between Hermeticism, Kabala, and alchemy are quite readable and inspiring. He talks about the various spiritual disciplines and magical systems as different languages all trying to signify the same reality. He guides us through fundamental Kabala, the mysterious drawings of the alchemists, the philosophical foundations of alchemy, the use of the magical voice and the holiness of the Hebrew letters, the creation of the body of light and the assumption of God forms. He ties everything together by the essential image of the Tree of Life, explaining how Kabala's biggest contribution to humanity was a model of consciousness that explains the relationship between the divine realm and the material.

In Stavish's own words, "The working assumption behind contemporary and modern Hermetico-Kabalistic practices is that we as conscious beings originate in the Ain Soph Aur, or Limitless Mind of God. We incarnate through various stages of increasing density and matter into the present world in order to gain the experiences that will allow us to go from potential beings to self-actualized or self-created beings. In our journey of development, we take on characteristics and 'bodies' of various vibrations, and on our 'return' we shed these bodies in exchange for increasingly subtle bodies and worlds of Light."

Topics are briefly introduced and then abandoned, like the four-and-half page section on Enochian. Concepts like the Sephiroths and their meaning are used to make valuable points, but technical terms are utilized long before they are actually defined and explained, leaving a beginner a bit confused by words like "Tipareth" and "Ain Soph." To a seasoned reader of mysticism who by definition may not even need this book, these technical words barely pose a challenge, but this book does presume to appeal to aspirants of all levels. Also, crucial visuals like the actual Hebrew letters themselves are not even included as illustrations. This is more of a set-back as one may think, for a beginner would not be motivated to put the book down and go find another one that actually includes the letters.

The biggest strength of the book is the beautiful way that Stavish explicates various Kabalistic, alchemical and Hermetic principles. Having just ploughed through a few books on quantum physics right before starting *Between The Gates*, I was in the right mindset to think about how all reality is a continuum between the pure white light of the Ain Soph and the material universe of Malkuth. While there has been, for almost three decades, a cultural impulse to compare the findings of quantum mechanics to the ancient Eastern philosophies, I would be curious to see the multi-dimensional universe of superstring theory and the rest of modern physics compared to Kabala and alchemy.

Although Stavish doesn't mention anything about the mystical trends in modern physics, he is a good magical philosopher and despite my many years of reading about these subjects, I felt a fresh voice putting hard concepts into well-crafted phrases that I could understand with a new perspective.

As for the exercises included in this book, I am in the middle of trying them out. They are mostly visualizations to help develop a body of light and explore the astral worlds. Hopefully, if they are truly effective, I will soon find myself either drifting through my neighbor's wall to spy on him, or arriving on the soil of Mars to become enslaved by the green-skinned Tharks and marry the Princess of Helium. I'll let you know which happens first.

HISTORICAL WOMEN AND TRUE CRIME

THE REVEREND AND
THE MILL GIRL
An Unsolved Fall River Mystery

The study of unsolved murders from the past can often teach us about the people and culture of another time and place. Reading about Jack the Ripper opens up a window into the murky underworld of Victorian London; Lizzie Borden reveals much about the genteel culture and private living conditions of industrial New England society; even the assassination of JFK, now so distant in time, resurrects the political paranoia of the Cold War era and offers a glimpse of what America had been like on the other side of the 1960s.

It is now one hundred and seventy-five years since Sarah Cornell, a thirty-year old weaver in a Massachusetts cotton mill, was found strangled to death on the edge of a farm near Fall River in December of 1832. The physical evidence at the crime scene, plus incriminating but unsigned letters found among Sarah's possessions, led to the arrest of the Reverend Ephraim Kingsbury Avery, a Bristol, Rhode Island, Episcopal Methodist minister. The resulting trial, besides being a great newspaper sensation, was, up until that point, the longest, and most complex in American history. Like that other great Fall River mystery, the Borden Murders of 1892, the case remains unsolved and a matter of great controversy.

However, the seasoned Lizzie Borden student would be quite surprised to find in the Sarah Cornell story a very different Fall River than the one depicted in the newspaper accounts, police reports, and trial transcripts of the Borden Affair of 1892. Here, we are transported to a more primitive society, one more rural and driven by religious factions, a world being reshaped by the industrial revolution, but not quite close to the great industrial nations that would build the Titanic and the Panama Canal. The Bristol/Tiverton/Fall River axis upon which the story pivots is indeed a scene filled with familiar elements: present are the Borden and the Durfee families, the worshippers at the First Congregational Church and the shoppers going about their afternoon business on South Main Street. But this is not Lizzie's Fall River; it is the town of Andrew Borden's childhood, the Fall River of David Anthony and Oliver Chace (two of the great early mill owners), where no street cars clatter along the cobblestones, no telephones are to be had at the corner stables to summon the police, and you can converse with many a man who still remembers the Revolutionary War. The world of Sarah Cornell and the Reverend Ephraim Avery was as different from Lizzie's as our world today is different from the days before the Cold War.

Sarah Cornell died just a few short years after Fall River had given birth to its textile industry, an enterprise that would make the city one of the country's most important manufacturing centers and establish a vast economy built upon the labor of young women like Sarah. The bulk of that industry and wealth was still in the future at the time of her death, but a study of the complex social web in which she had become enmeshed, the religious community in which she struggled for approval and found nothing but condemnation, the society that scorned her for her amoral lifestyle and choices, the factory system that swallowed her up as a mere cog in the wheel of labor, has a lot to teach us about New England's deep roots and our own collective cultural history.

Sarah Cornell was born on May 3, 1802, into an established Connecticut family. Her grandfather had been a successful paper manufacturer and Sarah would have grown up in a genteel affluent environment if her mother had not tragically run off with a worker from her father's mill. Fallen out of favor with the family, and ultimately abandoned by her husband, Sarah's mother inherited only enough money on which to survive and spent many years in a furtive rambling existence with her daughter. Young Sarah was first trained as a tailor, but soon became a weaver working in various factories. The girl had been condemned to the life of a skilled laborer in the mills of New England, a consequence of her mother's exile from their family's wealth.

To make the situation worse, Sarah seems to have grown fond of misconduct and often was the subject of much scandalous rumor about her sexual proclivities. There is no doubt in Sarah's own letters and confessions that she saw herself as a bad woman. Musing upon the death of a gentle black servant, she wrote, "Sometimes I think why I am spared, perhaps it is to commit more sin" (Kasserman 31). No doubt, in today's day and age, she would be viewed as a girl whose poor choices led to complications and confusions; but in Sarah's age, ruled by rigid laws and religious judgment, such misconduct was enough to make her an outcast from society.

While staying in Providence and working as a weaver, Sarah got into trouble over some clothing that she took on credit from a tailor and then never paid for, a controversy that seemed to have cemented her reputation as a thief and fallen woman. Although accounts of her activities are often contradictory and their truth suspect, Sarah was clearly a reckless youth who sank deeper into trouble no matter how far she fled. She moved from town to town, sometimes changing her name and inventing a past for herself to start life anew, but bad luck followed her. Sometimes it was the simple fact that she was seen walking with a strange man after work that strengthened her reputation for promiscuity.

Soon she was looking to make amends and return to the fold of her family. "God in his mercy has shown me the depravity of my own wicked heart" (Kasserman 35), Sarah wrote to her mother and sister in an attempt to reconcile with them and to throw herself under the protective umbrella of religion. She became a member of the Congregational Church, but her later shift to the Episcopal Methodist Church may have been prompted by the appealing Methodist belief that all can be saved, not just the elite, and that salvation had more to do with deeds and faith than the randomness of being born into a well-positioned family.

Sarah was by now a poor laborer with a sinful reputation, so the Methodist Church may have seemed a logical haven for her. Their tent meeting culture, modeled after the tribes of Israel wandering in the wilderness, must have struck a chord in the mill workers whose survival depended upon a migration from one town to another, drifting about as factories burned to the ground, and labor disputes forced unemployment.

Sarah's own assessment of the four-day-long tent meetings where ministers gave their impassioned impromptu sermons was that all the Methodists should be "as strangers and pilgrims having no continuing city or abiding place, but seek one to come" (Kasserman 40). Clearly, her spiritual yearnings were authentic, and, in the Methodist Church, she found the closest she would ever come to a central home and a self-identity. But sadly, this safe haven proved to have no lasting value for her.

After more accusations of being in the company of strange men—on one occasion taking up lodgings in a hotel together—Sarah took flight to Lowell, Massachusetts—at that time a great industrial center—looking to reinvent her life yet again. When she arrived there in May, 1828, she was armed this time with a certificate of membership in the Methodist Church, a piece of paper that, because of her poor moral reputation, meant the difference between work and starvation.

Daily life in the Lowell mills started for Sarah, and many other young women like her, at five in the morning and often lasted until six at night. They were paid by the piece, not by the hour, and the girls had to live in boarding houses owned by the factory. Condemned to such a life and hounded by rumors and whispered stories of her sinful past, Sarah decided to jump once more to another profession, one that would put her squarely into the arena of her Church and perhaps redemption in the eyes of her fellow Methodists: she applied for a job as a domestic in the home of the Reverend Ephraim Avery.

Ephraim Kingsbury Avery was a young man from Connecticut, thirty-four years old at the time that Sarah Cornell first knocked on his door in 1830. A decidedly handsome man with a sensuous mouth (a trait that was much played up by his detractors during and after the trial as proof of his libertine nature), he was originally slated to be a man of medicine but followed a calling into the Methodist Church. He carried about with him his own baggage of scandal, mostly a zealous and rash preoccupation in reporting the ill conduct of members of his flock. On a few occasions, he had spoken out against fellow Methodists and what he perceived to be their bad behavior and morals. At the time, the hierarchy of the Methodist Church was ordered into societies, assemblies, and conferences—creating a culture in which the ranking ministers could ensure a person a stable life by awarding them a certificate of good standing within the church. A denial of such a certificate would result in banishment and often the inability to find employment.

Avery's rise in the community and the New England Methodist Conference contains several interesting revelations about the changing dynamics of New England society at the time. It was a period of vast cultural and economic expansion, and it was inevitable that the old Protestant religious order that had pioneered life in New England and had served as a fabric of society for so long, was starting to respond to the rising phenomenon of modern capitalism and the impositions it made upon the lives of ordinary people who were destined to work the factories. The Reverend Avery's subsequent unrelenting, almost paranoid, judgment of Sarah Cornell is representative of the avidity of the old order reacting to the changing conditions of modern life, where wage labor and ownership of property were forging a new culture and a new way of responding to the world.

Interestingly enough, the Methodists had laid down their presence in Fall River by 1827 with the organizing of their first church there. The Methodists were a relative newcomer on the scene and planted them-selves down in the midst of the factory-owning Congregationalists. The Methodists came across as anti-intellectual and non-elitist. The value of the minister seemed more in his ability to spontaneously sway a crowd through impromptu sermons and crank up the level of energy in a tent meeting, rather than in his learned study and integration into the local business community. Clearly, in the meeting of the mill girl and the Reverend, the two conflicting halves of New England's emerging new order were headed for a confrontation. This may explain the severity of the passions that the Methodists and the Industrialists exhibited towards one another in the long ordeal of Avery's capture and trial. In this way, Sarah's death was to ignite an eruption of hidden social, political, and religious forces that were in stressful conflict within the community.

Sarah only worked for Avery for a short time (it was rumored that the Reverend's wife detected an attraction between the two and dismissed the poor girl unfairly), then went back to the mills, but she persisted in attempting to get good references from him. The Reverend's stub-born need to discredit the character of those he considered to be amoral created a tension between them, and a struggle of wills became more entangled as time went on.

When Sarah asked Avery to supply her with a certificate, he insisted on an open statement of her sinful behavior. She readily admitted to illicit sexual activity with several men, but she could have been lying to impress Avery with her willingness to repent. He eventually gave her a certificate of good faith, but then proceeded to initiate a church trial against her. Shortly after, Sarah showed up at a doctor's office diag-nosed with a venereal disease and then left town, taking Avery's prized certificate with her.

As Sarah traveled about the state trying to secure employment, she kept presenting the document that would be her only hope to reintegrate herself into her Methodist community, but Avery never hesitated to inform any inquiring minister of Sarah's ill character and evil past. When Sarah wrote him letters of confession, Avery renewed her certificate, only to denounce her the next day because he had uncovered a falsehood.

Having been excluded from Methodist circles by Avery's persistent outcries against her, Sarah eventually took refuge at her sister's home in Woodstock, Connecticut, where her brother-in-law took her on in his shop as a seamstress and office manager. She had been welcomed into her new church but was hounded by the thought of the Reverend Avery having her letters of confession, documents that he could use to destroy her reputation at any moment. In fact, Sarah posted several letters to Bristol, Rhode Island, where Avery now lived as a minister. While it cannot be proven that she was writing to him, it does seem likely, since she knew no one else in Bristol, was negotiating with him for the letters, and was possibly arranging for a face-to-face encounter at an August tent meeting of the Methodists in Thompson, Connecticut.

At the meeting, Avery seemed determined to get Sarah ejected from the grounds, but according to Sarah herself, he arranged to meet her in the forest near the camp grounds where he traded sexual intercourse with her in exchange for the letters of confession. Although great pains were taken at Avery's murder trial to show that he could not possibly have slipped off during that evening to meet with Sarah, there is no doubt that several months later she was known to be pregnant.

At the suggestion of a lawyer, Sarah moved to Fall River ostensibly to be close to Avery's home in Bristol so she could negotiate support from him. She obtained employment in the Fall River Manufactory run by David Anthony, and, despite her pregnancy and bouts of sickness, held onto the job. Sarah bravely approached Avery and begged him not to destroy her in Fall River as he had done in Lowell and elsewhere. Avery's response was typical of his consistently heartless attitude towards the poor girl, that he had done nothing to destroy her—she had destroyed herself.

The next evening, October 20, 1832, Avery disappeared after a Methodist meeting for an hour, later claiming that he had been at some stables, but Sarah later confessed that Avery had met with her to give her references to Thomas Wilbur, a South Main Street doctor. Dr.

Wilbur, who examined the girl, was horrified to learn that Avery (or at least as Sarah told the story) had instructed her to take 30 drops of oil of tansy to induce the abortion, a dose that certainly would have proven deadly. In short, if Sarah is to be believed, Avery was trying to get Sarah to take a fatal overdose.

Throughout November and December, Sarah allegedly negotiated with Avery via secret letters. The ones that were found in Sarah's possession after her death, unsigned and in a hand never determined to belong to the Minster, clearly were about arranging for a meeting in Fall River on December 20, 1832. Indeed, on that day, Sarah left her job at the Mill early, ate a quiet supper in the rooming house where she was staying, and then wrote a penciled note before taking off into the night: "If I should be missing enquire of the Rev Mr Avery of Bristol he will know where I am Dec 20th S M Cornell" (Kasserman 73).

The next morning, Sarah was found dead, hanging in a haystack just outside of Fall River.

Sarah Cornell's body was discovered on the morning of Friday, December 21, 1832, at nine o'clock in the morning on the Richard Durfee farm in Tiverton, not far from the Fall River border. She was suspended from a pole attached to the roof of a haystack, her cloak fastened about her with her hands inside, a significant fact that was later to be pointed out by Avery's prosecutors. Elihu Hicks, the Tiverton coroner, gathered a jury of six men to observe the body, and after she was identified as a girl from the weaving room of the Fall River Manufactory, Dr. Wilbur was called upon. The Fall River doctor promptly came to the circumstantial conclusion that Sarah had killed herself because of the betrayal of the Reverend Avery, the man who had fathered her unborn child. The coroner's jury gained access to Sarah's personal possessions at her boarding house, including letters found in a bandbox that clearly showed she had been negotiating a meeting with an unnamed person (known only in the letters as B.H., which were the initials of Avery's niece, Betsey Hill), and promptly came to the conclusion that she had committed suicide over her pregnancy and betrayal by Avery.

From the start, tensions between different political and religious factions charged the case with high drama. The Methodists refused to bury Sarah since she had not been on good report with the church, and, further, a letter of resignation from the church in her handwriting had been found in her bandbox. The Reverend Ira Bidwell, a Fall

River Methodist minister who had been called to the scene of the crime, immediately ran off to Bristol to tip off Avery that he was about to get into serious trouble. Reverend Orin Fowler of Fall River's First Congregational Church took on the duty of burying Sarah, possibly at the request of her last employer, David Anthony, a Congregationalist. The people of Fall River were now experiencing a sense of empathetic identification with the poor young girl who had died over the machinations of a Rhode Island Minister who had done her wrong, and was, almost as serious, a Methodist.

The coroner's verdict and Sarah's funeral on Saturday, December 22, were a bit premature, since it was after the services that the penciled note she had written the night of her death implicating Avery was found. It was further rumored that her body showed bruises and other signs of abuse, and that the clove hitch knot that had been tied around her neck could not possibly have resulted in a self-inflicted hanging. The cry of "Murder" was immediately raised.

Stirred with the conviction of foul play, the coroner's jury was dismissed—two of the men were not landowners, a technicality that invalidated the verdict—and the body was exhumed for re-examination. While Dr. Wilbur worked hard to obtain a legal judgment of murder against Avery, the Reverend Bidwell was in Bristol warning Reverend Avery that trouble was brewing. After a bizarre cat-and-mouse game in which two Fall River men traveled to Rhode Island to obtain an arrest warrant for Avery at a time when the murder did not yet legally exist, the Reverend was finally arrested on the evening of Sunday, December 23.

Fall River came together as a community during the days immediately following the discovery of Sarah's body. The crime had been committed outside their jurisdiction, in Tiverton, and Avery was to appear before a court in Bristol where he had been arrested, so Fall River, determined to see that justice be done, had formed a committee of vigilance and a committee of investigation that was to aid the Rhode Island officials in whatever way they could. While the case against Avery seemed open and shut, largely due to Sarah's own confessions to the Reverend Bidwell and Doctor Wilbur, as well as the content of the letters found in her possession, the gap between the Fall River Congregationalists and the Rhode Island Methodists was widening. There was also a decidedly anti-Masonic atmosphere to the whole business since certain members of the Fall River committee were staunch anti-Masons and associated the Methodists with that fraternal community. Clearly, the death of Sarah Cornell and the Reverend Avery's association with it, as unproven as it was at the time, caused the internal stresses between Fall River's industrial and religious factions to bubble to the surface.

On Christmas Day, the Fall River committee boarded the *King Philip* to be ferried to Bristol to demand the release into their custody of the Reverend Avery, whom they were determined to have examined in Tiverton. The engineer of the ferry was John Orswell, a man who had delivered to Sarah one of the letters, in an unknown hand, which had proposed a meeting in Fall River. Orswell claimed that the letter had been given to him by the Reverend Avery to deliver into the hands of Sarah Cornell. If such a connection could be proved, it would seem a simple case that only needed its day in court to see Avery hanging from the gallows.

The Fall River men soon found that truth and justice often can take a back seat to political and religious factions. When Justice Howe of Bristol insisted on keeping the case in his jurisdiction, the committee marched to Avery's home where he had been allowed by the court to reside, towing Orswell behind them, and confronted the Reverend during a tense scene that almost turned into mob violence. Avery, after being identified by Orswell as the stranger who gave him the letter, put on his spectacles and asked Orswell again if he looked familiar.

"Sir," said the Ferryman, "your glasses do not alter the features of your face" (Kasserman 26).

The Fall River Committee eventually retired to their hometown, empty-handed. Avery was to stand before a court in Bristol.

Reverend Avery's examination began before Rhode Island Justices John Howe and Levy Haile, with the Reverend himself reading from a carefully prepared statement. From the very beginning, it was clear that his defense was based upon two tactics, the first being the denunciation of Sarah Cornell as a woman of evil disposition, no better than a whore, and someone who had used him as an innocent scapegoat in her boundless machinations. The court was being asked to interpret all the testimony and evidence against the defendant in the light of Sarah's sinful existence which, contrasted with Avery's impeccable reputation and serious concern for the moral correctness of the Methodist society under his protection, seemed to be conclusive proof of his innocence. In short, it was Sarah Cornell, the victim, who was now on trial.

Secondly, the defense was determined to prove that all the evidence against Avery—the letters found in Sarah's possession, the confessions she made to confidants about her carnal relations with Avery, his role in her pregnancy, and any testimony dealing with the Reverend's whereabouts on December 20—was circumstantial and based on the clever lies of a very desperate woman and her Congregational supporters. All in all, Avery hoped to prove that he was a righteous servant of his flock, and Sarah was a fallen woman who could not be believed, even in death.

Avery's opening statement also provided his own explanation for his whereabouts on December 20 during the crucial hours in question. Claiming to have been curious about a coal mine on the island between Bristol and Fall River where he could obtain cheap heating for his church, the Reverend decided to ramble over some of the island's countryside, a hobby that many of his friends testified he was very fond of, and to negotiate a coal purchase. Having crossed over to the island on the Bristol ferry, he headed towards the mines, only to discover that there was no coal to be had, so he took off towards the house of a friend—which he could not find in the descending darkness of winter. He claimed to have returned to the ferry, a location some nine miles or so from the site of Sarah's death, at nine o'clock in the evening, approximately around the time the coroner fixed Sarah's death, which was a strong argument for his innocence. He absolutely denied having crossed the stone bridge into Fall River at any time.

The Reverend, however, had no definitive witnesses that placed him on the island besides the ferryman at Bristol. The hearing and the second trial later that year included a parade of witnesses who claimed to have seen the Reverend, or someone who looked like a Methodist minister, at various points of the island, at the stone bridge, and even at a tavern in Fall River, closer to the time of the murder. Avery's stroll across the island is just as elusive and frustrating to fathom as Lizzie Borden's own sworn whereabouts at the time of her father's murder.

During the course of the hearing, the defense attempted, through objections, to prevent the jury from hearing any testimony that implicated Avery in Sarah's pregnancy, including second-hand accounts of her own confessions. Persuading the court that Sarah's words were hearsay and not sworn testimony or deathbed confessions, the defense unexpectedly barred the prosecution from posing any direct quotes. As a result, Dr. Wilbur testified as to Sarah's physical condition of pregnancy, but he was prevented from quoting her word that Avery had been the father. Likewise, Sarah's brother-in-law was prevented from telling the jury how she had told him in confidence all about Avery's seductions and carnal blackmail. Even when various Methodists were called to remember confessionals from Sarah's own letters, they were not allowed to quote from memory because it was judged that nothing could be proved without producing the letters themselves, which no longer existed. This was potentially a killing blow to the prosecution, although they tried their best to get the court to allow the testimony.

The hearing ended after fourteen days of testimony with a verdict in favor of Avery. Justice Howe delivered his decision to the shock of the angry people of Fall River and those who had sympathy with the dead mill girl. He did not believe the signs of abuse on her body were anything more than an attempt at a self-induced abortion, and even questioned whether a clove hitch knot had actually been used on the cord that strangled her—a clove hitch would have ruled out suicide. In regard to the unsigned letters, the Thompson meeting, and other occasions where Avery could have sneaked off to meet with Sarah, the Justice put significant weight on the number of Methodist ministers who were paraded before the court to account for Avery's whereabouts on crucial dates. Howe found the timetables, as defined by the Methodists, unimpeachable.

Not only did Howe find Avery innocent of the charges, but he also summarily decried Sarah Cornell as a girl addicted to every imaginable vice, and no better than a prostitute. Most shockingly of all was his declaration that even if Avery had met Sarah in Tiverton that evening, he most likely would have just given her a cautionary speech, which the Justice conjured from his own dramatic imagination for the sake of the court. In short, the Justice could believe that Avery lied about meeting her, but it was beyond all doubt that such a man could not have murdered her. When Justice Haile concurred, Reverend Avery was set free.

A storm erupted. Newspapers cried out for justice, and in Fall River, David Anthony, called a meeting of seven hundred people in the vestry of the Congregational Church to determine how best to get a new warrant issued for Avery's arrest and re-trial before the Supreme Court of Rhode Island. The Fall River Committee of Investigation, in turn, claimed to have come up with new evidence—a letter that Sarah Cornell had written describing her relationship with Avery and her attempts to meet with him. With the prospect of such damning evidence being introduced to a court without objection from the defense, Harvey Harnden, the deputy sheriff of Bristol County and a committee member, set off on a dramatic chase across three states to track down Reverend Avery, who had secretly slipped away to a hiding place in New Hampshire.

Tracking his prey through Rhode Island and Boston, Harnden, who was very familiar with the pursuit of criminals, canvassed the taverns where Avery's carriage had halted, and visited the homes of the Methodist ministers, whom he bullied with threats of legal action if they did not give him information as to Avery's whereabouts. Harnden eventually cornered Avery in his New Hampshire hideout and stormed the building, finding the Reverend cowered in an upstairs bedroom. Avery was brought back to Rhode Island where Harnden was dismayed to find that, although the Governor had posted a reward of three hundred dollars for the capture of the accused man, the offer had been posted after the capture. The deputy sheriff walked off with a mere reimbursement of his travel expenses. One new report announced that Harnden had "commenced the pursuit for the acquisition of the glory it might produce; he enacted the part of a hero, and let the trophies of the hero be his reward" (Kasserman 127). This did nothing but further the resentment against Avery and hardened the shell of support and protection forming around him from his fellow Methodists.

Avery was now back in custody in the hostile territory of Tiverton and swarmed about by a hostile Fall River crowd. He anxiously awaited a hearing before the Rhode Island Supreme Court. A defense dream team headed by Jeremiah Mason, a lawyer friend of Daniel Webster's, and the collective resources of the New England Methodist Conference, was quickly assembled. The tempers and fevered antagonisms among all the different religious and social strata of New England society had reached a high pitch. The trial promised to be more dramatic, passionate, and desperate than the Bristol hearing.

In a bizarre but significant footnote to the preparation for the new trial, Sarah Cornell's body was once more exhumed, more than a month after her death, and found to show signs of an attempted abortion and/or sexual abuse.

Reverend Avery's second trial began on Monday, May 6, 1833, at the 18th century Colony House, in Newport. This time, big guns were pulled out of the state's pockets to fill the prosecution, including Rhode Island Attorney General Albert C. Greene and former attorney general Dutee J. Pearce, who actually gave up his seat in Congress to prosecute the case. Over a hundred candidates were screened over three days to create a jury of twelve—such was the mounting dramatic pitch of the trial. By the end of the trial, which, according to Fall River historian Henry Fenner, lasted 21 court days, 238 witnesses were called to testify.

Avery listened to the indictment brought against him, which included that he had been "moved and seduced by the instigation of the devil" (Kasserman 136)—a grim reminder to a modern reader that we are dealing with a very specific New England culture, one still rooted in the blurred boundary between church and state.

The prosecution's case had a bumpy start as the jury was denied the right to retain paper and pencil for note taking. This was a denial that worked in favor of the defense, since the trial, which lasted a month, was so long and complex—the 1830s were a time when trials were spectacular if they lasted a week—that the conflicting facts, dates, times, and places that were paraded before the empanelled jurors became, as the weeks went on, a confused jumble.

The main strategy of the prosecution was to place the Reverend Avery in the right places at the right times with the right motives. They needed to prove that Avery had maintained a relationship with Sarah Cornell, had been at the Thompson tent meeting where she allegedly had become impregnated, was in Fall River when the letters to her had been mailed, and had lied about his trek over the Island, making it plausible that he had traveled into Fall River on the evening of December 20. The second thrust of this attack was to finally place before the jury Sarah Cornell's own confessions to her doctor and family that Avery was the father of her child. These two combined would toll the Reverend's doom.

Much rested upon the condition of the body during the initial examination and upon subsequent exhumations. The fact that the neck had shown only one set of marks, due to the strangulation from the cord and not from any assault by Avery, suggested suicide, while the bruises and discolorations on her abdomen and the fecal matter upon her undergarments suggested that at one point in her ordeal she had been lying upon the ground suffering some form of abuse. However, sexual modesty prevailed when the four women who had been charged by the Reverend Orin Fowler to prepare Sarah for burial were called to testify to Sarah's physical condition and found that they could not speak plainly about the dead woman's body. One witness kept insisting that Sarah had been "dreadfully abused" (Kasserman 144) and would not shake her chosen description even when pressed by the court to be more accurate. In the end, their testimony was considered lacking in the expertise that would have been present in the report of a more expert medical man or coroner.

Further, some testimony as to the condition of the body was based on the examination 38 days after her death, when her decomposed body had been exhumed for the second time. These less than optimal forensic conditions practically disqualified all talk of bruises, which could have been caused by blood settling after death, rather than any physical evidence of rape or attempted abortion.

As in the initial hearing in Bristol, witnesses were produced to prove that Avery had mailed Sarah the letters arranging a rendezvous at the Fall Meeting, that Avery had crossed the stone bridge to Fall River on the afternoon of December 20, and that Sarah Cornell was not in a suicidal mood in the last days of her life. Even the justices from the Bristol hearing were called as witnesses to prove the inadequacies of their own legal proceedings. Much of the trial seemed a rehash of the previous one, but with a dramatic increase of the emotional ante.

As predicted, when Dr. Wilbur was asked about Sarah's confession to him that Avery was the father of her child, the defense objected that Sarah's words were hearsay, and not sworn testimony or a deathbed confession, and therefore inadmissible. After several fumbled attempts to get Sarah's words to the doctor before the jury, the prosecution struck upon a clever plan. They noted that the doctor had been given a statement that had been published in a newspaper called the *Microcosm* about Sarah's accusations. Claiming that the statement, as published in the newspaper, differed from the statement he had made in court, the prosecution requested that the newspaper copy be entered into the trial as evidence, thereby getting it in front of the jury. The plan failed when it was determined by the court that the two statements did not significantly differ.

The defense team attempted to prove that Sarah was a manipulative and troubled woman, often unstable and suicidal. Doctor William Graves of Lowell testified as to Sarah's mental condition: "I was almost inclined to think she was insane" (Kasserman 163). However, the defense quickly pointed out that Dr. Graves had been the Reverend

Avery's personal physician. Sarah's promiscuity and alleged history of venereal disease were put on display, and an unproven tale was related by a tavern keeper that once Sarah had extorted money from a man by pretending that a blanket wrapped under her clothing was his unborn child, proving a tendency towards desperation and deception.

The defense went on to claim the forensic evidence was insufficient to prove murder, that all of the testimony of a stranger who looked like a minister on the island during the murder could be discounted, and that Avery's whereabouts could not be proven. A medical expert testified that the fetus found in Sarah's body could have been too old for it to have been conceived during the Thompson Methodist meeting.

Another moment of sexual modesty occurred when a woman who had seen Sarah bathing at the Thompson meeting could not bring herself to describe the state of her breasts, whether or not they were in a swollen state from pregnancy. "Her countenance looked as though she was in a state of pregnancy," claimed the Methodist woman (Kasserman 172). The lawyer examining her broke all decorum and insisted upon a description of the state of her "bosom." All the woman could insist was, "I noticed nothing but her countenance." After much harassing from the lawyers, she finally broke down and said, "Her bosoms appeared rather full." A few moments later, when asked to clarify her description, the woman, shocked and impatient, withdrew her statement, claiming she did not know if Sarah's bosoms were fuller than usual. From the prosecution's point of view, this was a far cry from a valid medical opinion on pregnancy.

More Methodist witnesses from the Thompson meeting were produced to account for almost every second of Reverend Avery's time there. The tension between the Methodists and the Congregationalists was increasing as more of Avery's kind flocked to his defense. The Methodists, in turn, seemed rather paranoid that the Fall River Committee was no better than a crazy mob giving in to hysteria, much like the Salem Witch Trials of 1692.

At the defense's summation, Mason emphasized that not only was all the evidence circumstantial, but that it could not even be proven that a murder had taken place, which led to another moment shocking to the modern reader: Mason declared that suicide "may almost be called the natural death of the prostitute" (Kasserman 202), and that "if you were to seek for some of the vilest monsters in wickedness and depravity, you would find them in the female form" (Kasserman 201-202). As an illustration, he painstakingly laid out all the vices in Sarah's short life—her venereal disease, promiscuity, and unwedded pregnancy—as proof that the "termination of [her] career" (Kasserman 202) would naturally be suicide. The Reverend Avery, on the other hand, had no history of depravity or murderous tendency. How could such a righteous man take such a huge leap from his pious self to deranged killer? It was more likely that Sarah Cornell framed him.

Mason took Fall River to task, painting a portrait of that town as run by a mob of vigilantes who would rather fanatically pursue a man to the gallows than carry out a reasoned and disimpassioned search for the truth. He pointed to the large number of pamphlets and newspaper accounts that shouted Avery's guilt and made the claim that an unbiased trial was, by this stage, almost impossible to achieve.

This last charge was addressed in the summation by Attorney General Greene, who defended the actions of the Fall River citizens, emphasizing that they were not driven by any anti-Methodist passions or a blind belief in Avery's guilt. Respectable citizens and an experienced lawyer, who had performed their civic duties in the face of the tragedy, guided them. Greene concluded that none of the flimsy medical testimony could sustain a conclusion of suicide, that it was nearly impossible for witnesses to have remembered Avery's movements on certain days down to the last minute, and that the final note found in Sarah's bandbox explaining that the Reverend Avery would know of her whereabouts in case of her disappearance were all proof that she had met with him in Fall River at the hour of her death.

Finally, after 21 days in court, a short deliberation of the jury came back with a Not Guilty judgment and the Reverend Ephraim Avery walked out of the Newport courtroom a free man.

A third trial followed shortly thereafter—the church trial by the New England Methodist Conference. Essentially a formality, the proceedings did nothing more than provide seven Methodist ministers the chance to review the trial transcript that had been liberally published in various editions in newspapers around the country. Predictably, they dismissed the witnesses for the prosecution as unreliable, chalked up the work of the Fall River Committee as the hysteria of a lynch mob, and criticized a climate in which "shadows become embodied into substantial forms, dreams are changed into realities, and vague impressions become known and vivid conceptions" (Kasserman 215). The biggest ammunition on their side was not their own investigations or judgments, but the verdicts of the two previous trials. The Reverend was quickly cleared of all charges within his own Church.

However, his expectations that he could return to a quiet life as a Methodist minister were shattered when a visit to a Boston shop resulted in his being surrounded by close to five hundred angry citizens. Newspaper campaigns were waged against him, especially by the *Rhode Island Republican,* where an anonymous journalist named Proteus accused the defense team of conspiracy and jury tampering. Other newspapers followed suit with attacks and cries for justice. Proteus continued to attack the minister as the year 1833 progressed, even pursuing his own form of investigative journalism, at times claiming to have dug up fresh incriminating evidence.

Like the more infamous Fall River accused murderess Lizzie Borden, the Reverend Avery was subject to the wicked barbs of child rhymes such as "He killed the mother—then the child;/What a wicked man was he!/ The Devil helped him all the while:/How wicked he must be" (Kasserman 220). As if such an association with the Devil wasn't enough, the songs went as far as to cry out for belated justice: "Hang him, hang him on a tree/Tie around him Avery's knot/Forever let him hanged be/And never be forgot" (Kasserman 220).

Some in the city of Fall River even hung effigies of Avery in public, one of which was torn down and dragged through the streets, followed by a screaming mob that reportedly numbered in the hundreds. At particular sermons, Avery was booed, and more than a few times threatened physically by a hostile crowd. Even Lizzie Borden, who suffered a bitter cold relationship with the people of Fall River in the wake of her acquittal, did not receive such violent ill treatment.

It wasn't long before the saga of Sarah Cornell's death reached the public through artistic outlets. In September, a play opened in Newport, Rhode Island, called *The Factory Girl, Or, The Fall River Murder.* A play with a similar title opened in Richmond Hill, New York, and soon the story of Sarah's murder had been published as a book, *Fall River, An Authentic Narrative* by Catherine Williams (1833). These works were indicative of the growing anger and resentment against the Methodist religion that was replacing specific personal anger toward Avery. Strong public criticism was growing towards this Church that had an unelected governing body ruling over people with laws that were antithetical to the Constitutional freedom of American citizens. Newspapers shouted that the Methodists were not content with merely subverting American justice but were ambitious enough to wield political influence for the promulgation of their own ideology. Uncomfortably enough, this situation mirrors the modern climate—with the Christian Right Wing and their powerful influence in Washington being counter-balanced by secular critics who profess that such religious extremism is incompatible with a free society.

The storm finally broke with Avery's publication of his own defense, *Vindication of the Result of the Trial of Reverend Ephraim K. Avery, etc.* (1834), a collaboration with the Methodist Church to clear both the Reverend and the Church Conference of all guilt or charges of conspiracy. However, Avery's position in the church was permanently compromised, and the Reverend ended his days in Ohio working as a farmer.

The story of the death of Sarah Cornell and the trial of Reverend Ephraim Avery is a fascinating and richly detailed one, and for those who are addicted to studying such matters, an unsolved mystery of great complexity. In fact, it is not even clear if a murder took place, and in a review of the newspaper accounts, trial transcripts, and subsequent books written about the affair, a bizarre puzzle appears that is as compelling and interesting as the Borden Murders of 1892. In both cases, there were sensational murder trials that ultimately crashed upon the shoals of circumstantial evidence and bungled forensics. Both cases ended in an acquittal of a defendant that many people thought to be obviously guilty, and both of the accused were denied a settled and guilt-free life in the aftermath.

However, the most startling picture to emerge from a careful study of the Cornell/Avery case is how removed in time those events now seem, and how different the world of 1832 is compared to even the nearly-modern industrial world in which Lizzie Borden lived. It is very likely that Lizzie would have heard about Sarah's death, although it was six decades before her own ordeal. For obvious reasons, Lizzie may have identified more strongly with the Reverend Avery's struggle to prove his own innocence, but for all those years that Lizzie lived in Maplecroft on the Hill, she could have strolled over to Oak Grove to visit Sarah in her final resting place. Perhaps Lizzie, on a summer's afternoon, after a short visit to her family plot, would have wandered amidst the winding paths between the rolling hills, manicured lawns, and carpets of stones to see Sarah, even out of plain curiosity. It's possible Lizzie knew little or nothing about the events of 1832-34, but in the wake of her own tragedy, she may have been curious about Fall River's most famous other unsolved murder.

Sarah Cornell is on Whitethorn Path, just a short walk from Lizzie's own plot. The grave marker is severely weathered and almost unreadable, but she is there forever in Fall River, amongst the graves of those Congregationalists who were the only respectable men and women who gave her unconditional community support. Tragically, she did not live to enjoy it.

WORKS CITED:

Champlin, Kenneth M. *History of the First Congregational Church & Fall River, Massachusetts: The Early Years 1699-1838*. Fall River: First Congregational Church of Fall River, Inc, 2003.

Fenner, Henry M. *History of Fall River*. NY: Smiley Publishing Company, 1906.

Kasserman, David Richard. *Fall River Outrage: Life, Murder, and Justice in Early Industrial New England*. University of Pennsylvania Press, 1986.

Peck, Frederick M., and Earl, Henry H. *Fall River and Its Industries*. NY: Atlantic Publishing and Engraving Company, 1877.

First published in *The Hatchet: Journal of Lizzie Borden Studies*, Vol. 5, Issue 2, April/May, 2008.

A Murder in Gotham:
Helen Jewett

"And turning to the body he said, "Dorcas, arise." And she opened her eyes and, seeing Peter, she sat up. Then Peter gave her his hand and raised her up and calling the saints and the widows, he gave her back to them alive."

—*Acts 9:40-41*

One: The Death of a Prostitute

Late in the evening of April 9, 1836, Rosina Townsend, the madam of an upscale New York City brothel at 41 Thomas Street, not too far from the future site of the World Trade Center and just west of Broadway, was presented with an unusual request from one of her more popular prostitutes, Helen Jewett: to deny admission to Helen's regular Saturday night client. Instead, Rosina was told to expect a man by the name of Frank Rivers, who had been seeing Helen since the previous summer and with whom she seemed to be having much difficulty. Indeed, sometime between 9 and 9:30 p.m., Frank Rivers appeared at the brothel, his face covered by a cloak, and, with hardly a word of greeting, briskly disappeared into Helen's second floor bedroom. Rosina saw Frank again after 11 p.m., when she delivered champagne to the room; after which, she joined her own guest for the night, and at a quarter past twelve, went to bed.

Awakened at three in the morning, Rosina noticed that a globe lamp was on a table in the parlor at the back of the house that should have been in Helen's room, and that the door to the rear yard was ajar, a clear violation of the house's protocol. Pushing through the oddly unlatched

OF MOONS AND MONOLITHS: COLLECTED ESSAYS

OF MOONS AND MONOLITHS: COLLECTED ESSAYS

door of Helen's room, Rosina was shocked to find billows of smoke, and Helen lying on the bed, "her nightclothes reduced to ashes and one side of her body charred a crusty brown," by the flames that were consuming the mattress [Cohen 7].

Pandemonium erupted in the brothel on Thomas Street: watchmen were called from the street (New York did not yet have an organized police force); male clients of the other prostitutes hastily pulled on their trousers and fled into the night; and the surviving women labored to extinguish the flames that threatened to engulf the building. After all was over, they were left with the burnt body of what had previously been a twenty-two-year-old prostitute.

Jewett had been hit three times on the forehead with a hatchet, two light blows followed by a heavy one that cracked into her skull, killing her instantly. Blood in her thoracic cavity told the coroner that she had been dealt a heavy blow to the chest, perhaps the result of being held down brutally while the killer attacked her face with the hatchet. There was little doubt that the extensive burns to her body happened after her death. The killer may have intended to burn down the brothel, thereby erasing evidence of his crime.

A horrified Rosina Townsend told all who would listen about Frank Rivers and his late-night visit to Jewett. He was last seen lounging in Jewett's bed, just three short hours before the discovery of the body. Townsend had observed him from behind but had noticed a bald spot on the top of his head, a detail that helped identify him. Others who worked at the brothel named, as being amongst that night's visitors, a nineteen-year-old clerk, Richard P. Robinson, who lived in a boarding house at 42 Dey Street.

Two constables arrived at the boarding house, pulling Robinson out of bed and placing him into custody. Appearing blank and dispassionate, Robinson claimed that he had arrived home the night before after 11 o'clock. His roommate, another young clerk who was a frequent visitor to the Thomas Street brothel, backed up his alibi, claiming that he had awoken at 1 a.m. to find Robinson in bed. Both were brought back to Thomas Street and unceremoniously paraded before the remains of Helen Jewett. Robinson remained stoic and unflinching, consistently denying the allegations against him. By early morning, he was in Bridewell jail in Lower Manhattan, stridently protesting the injustice that was being done to him.

As the case unraveled and the press became more involved, it was clear that this act of homicide was not, as violent as New York was at the time, typical of the city's criminal activity. Helen Jewett was a well-known prostitute who worked at a wealthy brothel; she was frequently seen parading down Broadway in her characteristic green antebellum attire, a style of which she owned many splendid examples. Jewett also counted amongst her clients some respectable New Yorkers, and not merely the young clerks typified by Robinson. Here was no mere street-walker: Rosina Townsend's establishment was situated in the same neighborhood as Park Row, Columbia College, New York Hospital, the Astor House (owned by John Jacob Astor), and the College of Physicians and Surgeons. The close proximity of Columbia students and wealthy doctors guaranteed the prostitutes of the area respectable clients with reliable cash flow, unlike the more degenerate women who haunted the back alleys of Five Points and Corlears Hook (from which locale the name "hooker" came to be applied to women of that profession).

So, very rapidly, Helen Jewett and Richard P. Robinson seized the public's imagination. The press coverage was both lurid and sensational, and the attention of America (barely sixty years old) began to turn to the bizarre tale of the store clerk and the prostitute.

Two: Sex and the City

Richard P. Robinson was from a moderately successful Connecticut family, and had come to New York City to apprentice himself in a trade and to seek his fortune. He was a typical example of the sporting male sub-culture that had arisen in the 1830s, of the young men who lived in boarding houses where their private world would remain unmonitored by adults that are more responsible. These sporting boys cultivated an aggressive male dominance over women, preferred bachelorhood to marriage, and a long-standing financial arrangement with a prostitute over any sort of committed relationship. As time progressed, this sub-culture even generated its own newspapers: the *Whip*, the *Flash*, and the *Libertine*; this community of rakes even printed its own guides to the city brothels, publications that were little better than consumer reports about the women who were their purchased merchandise. Richard P. Robinson, thrust into the public spotlight by his dramatic arrest, the sensationalism of the murder charges, the revelations of his letters to Helen, and by his puckish and non-repentant attitude during his incarceration and trial, nevertheless would become a pronounced symbol of this sporting culture. Indeed, Robinson came to embody a defense of the group's principles, and an affirmation of the antebellum youth culture of libertinage.

Sometime around 1820, New York City had emerged as a major center of commercialized sex. Prostitution had evolved from a marginalized phenomenon of the working class to an economic trade that was an integral part of city life. One of the major contributing factors to this evolution was the privatization of much previously held municipal real estate, which placed, to a degree theretofore never experienced, economic and cultural development issues into the hands of landlords. These investors were struggling with the effects of a tidal influx of immigrants, an unprecedented migration of poor people into New York, a phenomenon that gave rise to the tenement culture. It made sound economic sense for landlords to place more faith in the ability of a well-managed brothel to pay the high rents they demanded, than to rely on the questionable resources of the working-class poor. As New York City rents increased (scandalously so: livable apartments were renting for several times the annual salary of a typical laborer), both the exploitation of large masses in the tenements, and the unusual license and privilege extended by landlords to brothel madams, became acceptable infringements of the social order that were readily overlooked by the law. In fact, New York barely had any anti-prostitution laws on the books in the 1820s. Accordingly, the proliferation of the profession throughout the city, even in well-heeled neighborhoods like Park Row and Water Street, was greatly stimulated by a legal tolerance that protected the investments of the landlords who owned the buildings in which the brothels enacted their business.

John R. Livingston, for example, was the landlord who owned the Thomas Street property in which Helen Jewett was murdered. Livingston had rather substantial real estate holdings. He came from a wealthy family that included Robert Livingston, a founding father, Chancellor of New York, and one-time minister to the court of Napoleon. Garnering a reputation as a war profiteer during the American Revolution, John R. Livingston had secretly sold out to the British, at one time working in cahoots with Benedict Arnold—later distancing himself from his business partner when Arnold's traitorous plans were revealed in 1780. Livingston, who once said, "Poverty is a curse I can't bear," then became a New York real estate investor, coming to own much of the property that constituted the Five Points, one of the most crime-ridden and dangerous slums in the city. Over the first half of the 1800s, he had been the owner of thirty brothels in total, including many of the most fashionable and lucrative. The Madams had an unholy alliance with him, and while circulating their business through many Livingston properties, the number of protesting neighbors increased. Other wealthy families, including the Lorilards, followed Livingston's profitable example, since owning brothels tuned out to be quite a sound real estate investment. Indeed, the brothels' economic viability was a principal reason why so few anti-prostitution laws were passed by the city [Gilfoyle 43].

Despite community protests and the increasing crime rate that formed on the periphery of the prostitution world, the industry flourished as a collaboration in a symbiotic relationship: the wealthy landlords who rented the houses; the municipal government who turned a blind eye to the thriving sex trade; the affluent clients who wanted sex; and the young women themselves who needed the profession as a way to survive in a harsh capitalist world. The combined efforts of law enforcement, religious leadership, and community action all failed to curb the rapid growth of the sex trade.

The theater houses in New York, such as the Park Row and the Bowery, were notoriously saturated with ladies of the night since they often used the convenient darkness of the theater stalls to arrange amorous and sexual liaisons. The "third tier" was an infamous denotation for the upper balcony of these theaters, a territory where such women patrolled freely, undisturbed by law enforcement and isolated from the more dangerous life of street-walking. Here, amidst the cacophony of actors on stage, musicians in the orchestra pit, and the roar of the audience (who often treated the theater more like a social picnic than a place to passively watch a work of art), the young sporting men cruised for their sexual liaisons. Richard P. Robinson's letters to Jewett, found under her bed after her death, made constant reference to their encounters at the theater. They had clearly found this to be a place they could meet privately to make sexual plans for the evening.

As more successful madams like Rosina Townsend gained prominence, many brothels were going private, with arrangements being made by appointment only, and with the cost of services increasing to the point that a courtesan like Helen Jewett became wealthier than many of her contemporaries—the mainstream women who had resigned themselves to more respectable, but less remunerative, professions. Some of the lower-class gangs of youths took exception to this and the violent, disturbing practice of brothel raids began. These unprovoked attacks were *Clockwork Orange*-style assaults on private houses, where drunken, angry men with bats and knives would force the prostitutes to serve drinks, then they would terribly abuse them and vandalize the property. The brothel raids were increasing in frequency around the time of Helen's murder, which was the main reason for Townsend's having employed such a tight security protocol on the evening of 9 April.

At first, the case against Robinson seemed open and shut. Witnesses saw him with Jewett right before her murder and he was the last known person to see her alive. The security at the brothel necessitated that a lady of the house let out midnight visitors through the locked exits, but no lady had reported letting Robinson out at any time. The only way he could have escaped was through the back door, which had clearly been opened by someone from the inside after a globe lamp from Helen's room had mysteriously found its way downstairs. In the courtyard beyond, a cloak was discovered similar to the one Rosina that had seen Rivers wearing, and a hatchet was found discarded near the rear wall. This was determined to have been the weapon that ended Jewett's life and was similar to one that had gone missing from the grocery store in which Robinson worked. Few were in doubt that Richard P. Robinson, a.k.a. Frank Rivers, had done the deed, and a coroner's jury thrown together at the crime scene confirmed this belief.

Under ordinary circumstances, such a crime would have passed notice in the obscure filing cabinet of crime statistics, hardly worth a second thought, but this one struck a particular note, touching the raw nerve of several social and cultural conditions that were unique to the age. Robinson, as a representative of a privileged middle-class youth population, soon had a large number of supporters who believed in his innocence. That these supporters were themselves mostly young men who frequented prostitutes was no cause for surprise. Helen, further, was hardly like the ordinary profile of a prostitute. She was an educated woman who had a passion for literature, poetry, and the performing arts. Her room was stocked with novels and books of poetry, and the wall over her bed boasted a portrait of Lord Byron, itself an expression of her erudite romanticism.

The sensational details of the relationship between Robinson and Jewett, which had been going on for almost a year, before she had ever started working at the upscale brothel, were revealed in the letters found at the crime scene. The psychological scope of this correspondence was worthy of a tragic novel: the complexities of their feelings for each other, Robinson's outrageous bouts of jealousy and anger, coupled with Helen's coy and manipulative game-playing, shocked many readers who had presumed that young men only saw prostitutes for hastily-performed sex acts and nothing more. This rare peephole into the world of antebellum "yuppies" and their sensual lifestyle were cannon fodder for the news journals and penny sheets, which exploited the situation with unprecedented news coverage sparking a nation-wide media sensation.

James Gordon Bennett of the *New York Herald* was one of the few newspaper editors who made an appearance at the Thomas Street brothel, personally interviewing Rosina Townsend and the other prostitutes. He also viewed the body, vividly portraying to his readers his impressions of Helen's corpse:

> Not a vein was to be seen. The body looked as white—
> as full—as polished as the pure Parian marble. The
> perfect figure—the exquisite limbs—the fine face—
> the full arms—the beautiful bust—all—all surpassing
> in every respect the Venus de Medicis. . . . For a few
> moments I was lost in admiration at this extraordinary
> sight—a beautiful female corpse—that surpassed the
> finest statue of antiquity [Cohen 16].

However, below all this idealization of Helen's prostate form, Bennett neglected to describe her mutilated face, or to mention the horrible burns on her body. Nor did he disclose the fact that, shortly before he viewed her, she had been autopsied, with her breasts parted thus by a hideous gash from the coroner's blade. Such were the distortions of the sensational press that had begun full force to exploit the tragedy.

Bennett did have one advantage, however, relative to other reporters: his physical presence on the scene and his contact with the prostitutes who had known Helen (not to mention the possibility that he was also a client at the establishment), gave him the scoop on her real identity.

Three: Dorcas Doyen

Bennett thus identified Helen Jewett as Dorcas Doyen from Augusta, Maine, a poor "virtual" orphaned girl who had been taken at age thirteen into the home of State Supreme Court Justice Nathan Weston (her father and stepmother lived nearby but could not take care of her). So placed, Dorcas was raised in a cultured, upscale environment. Dorcas had also been graced with the advantages of a quality education, due to the generous nature of Judge Nathan and the fact that his father-in-law had founded the Cony Academy, one of the country's first boarding schools for young girls. Despite her humble origins, she had spent much of her younger years in middle-class surroundings, albeit as a servant.

The judge himself found out about Helen's murder from an Augusta newspaper and was shocked to discover that the fallen woman found murdered in a New York brothel had been the little girl that he had sheltered until the age of eighteen. It was only a matter of time before Helen's journey from Maine to Thomas Street was made public, and a portrait emerged of a woman that was as unlike any ever associated with the profession of prostitution.

Dorcas' family could be traced back to the French Huguenots who had fled France to the New World. Her ancestors' early trials in the wilds of New Hampshire, before the American Revolution, remain largely uncharted since they did not distinguish themselves in the historical records. Jacob Doyen, her grandfather, fought hard in the war, having been wounded in the battle of Saratoga; he wintered at Valley Forge with George Washington, and finally engaged in grueling and savage combat with the Iroquois Indians in the Finger Lakes region of New York. In the 1780s, he settled near Augusta, Maine, where his registered profession was that of hog reeve (a man who gathered wandering hogs), a not-too-distinguished office for a man in a frontier society bristling with opportunities for the industrious.

John Doyen, Jacob's son, who was recorded in history as a shoemaker, brought Dorcas into the world on 18 October 1813. She was named after a saintly woman in the Bible who performed charitable work for the poor, and, indeed, at that period in history, many women's charity groups were called Dorcas Societies. Ominously enough, Dorcas was also the woman in the Bible whom Saint Peter had resurrected from the dead in the Book of Acts.

Sometime between the age of seven and ten, Dorcas' mother died and her father chose to put her into service, placing her with a prominent Augusta family who boasted the largest private library in the state. This situated the working-class Dorcas within the influence of cultured

living and education. When she was thirteen, her services were transferred to the family of Judge Nathan Weston who made a deal with
Dorcas' father that he would house and support her as his girl servant
until she reached the age of eighteen, a favorable prospect to her father
as this would ensure that Dorcas would come of age associated with
middle-class respectability.

By that time, Augusta itself had grown in but a few short decades
from a frontier fort community to a thriving and civilized society, now
home to two learning academies, banks and bookstores, newspaper
offices and law firms. Powerful families like the Bridges, the Williams,
and the Westons had forged a gentile antebellum society on the landscape that had once been a wild frontier. Dorcas may have been scrubbing
dishes in the kitchen and running laundry most of her day, but she did
so in a privileged atmosphere. She attended the First Congregational
Church and went to school with a sponsorship from Judge Weston.
Further, she got to observe the daily affairs of a distinguished family,
whose sons themselves would later become, respectively, a Senator and a
Supreme Court Justice. Dorcas was also rapidly developing a devouring
passion for books.

One of John Adams' main visions of America was a nation of literate people, whose education would make them worthy of exercising a
true voice in a democracy. In 1823, when Dorcas came to Augusta, these
ideals of Mr. Adams, who was still very much alive, were freshly minted
upon the American imagination. In such fashion, Augusta, which was
petitioning to be made the capital of Maine, boasted not one, but two
bookshops. One of these, just a few short blocks from Judge Weston's
house, was run by Harlow Spaulding, a young man who helped to raise
the intellectual level of the town through his literary and bookselling
efforts. His bookstore boasted newly printed books, including novels,
which were still a controversial art form in the 1820s. It was then particularly believed that romanticism and novelistic fantasy had a corrupting
influence on the young, since it was perceived as encouraging impres-
sionable minds into flights of fancy. Lord Byron, whose works were
sold at Spaulding's store, drew particular criticism, and Dorcas' love for
the romantic writer's stormy works was evident at her death scene more
than a decade later—her scorched and mutilated body lay under a portrait of the poet. Spaulding's initials were the same as the ones used in
a article run by the *New York Herald* in 1836, which claimed that Helen
Jewett had been corrupted by an "H---- S------g," a seduction that

was portrayed as having led to Dorcas' fall from grace and her descent
into prostitution.

While it cannot be proven that Harlow was Dorcas' lover and such
a corrupting influence, there is no doubt that they knew each other,
for, in any event, Dorcas' love for books would have inevitably drawn
her to Spaulding's store. There Dorcas had access to writers like Walter
Scott and Washington Irving, not to mention the works of Lord Byron.
Anne Royall's *Black Book* trilogy, a non-fiction account of the travel
author's experiences in Augusta, a book series that was also to be found
in Spaulding's store, actually boasted an encounter with little Dorcas in
the household of Judge Weston. This was to mark Dorcas' first appearance in print, though sadly, it was hardly her last.

In 1828, Spaulding's bookstore proudly presented the first novel by
Nathaniel Hawthorne, a work that actually premiered on consignment
at Harlow's. In fact, Hawthorne's literary agent was also cited by the
New York press as having been Dorcas' alleged corrupting lover. Years
later, Hawthorne was to visit a wax exhibit in Boston depicting Helen's
murder and wrote about it in his *American Notebooks*. History does not
record if Hawthorne then had recognized her as Dorcas Doyen, the
servant girl from Augusta, Maine.

Although there were a few other candidates besides Harlow
Spaulding who may have qualified as the man who had seduced Dorcas
(and in the eyes of antebellum society, once a woman was seduced by
a man, she was seen as a fallen woman—not so for the seducer, apparently), it is clear that there was someone who was intimate with her,
emotionally as well as physically. In a letter to Robinson many years
later, she wrote, "I have met very few persons who could share in all
my feelings so largely as—, who was my earliest companion. When I
walked, read, or conversed with him, I whispered to my heart, if I could
find one like him how much I should love him" [Cohen 193].

Although Dorcas was prone to weaving fantasies, fabricating false
identities, and exaggerating the truth, it was clear that she had been
seduced by someone and that this fact was brought to the attention of
Judge Weston. When the Judge forced her to leave his home, she fled
initially to Portland, and later to Boston, surviving, despite her young
age, by learning the trade of prostitution. For three years after leaving
Augusta, she wrote back and inquired often about Harlow Spaulding,
the young bookseller who, subsequently, in 1836, would vehemently
deny having had any association with the dead prostitute in New York,

but who may very well have been the one true physical and intellectual love of her life.

FOUR: THE SPORTING BOY

From the moment that Helen Jewett was murdered and Richard P. Robinson was taken into custody, Helen and the sensational details of her life and death particularly fascinated the newspapers and the public; hardly any attention was paid to the accused. However, there was much to find that was sensational in Robinson's life.

Regardless of his guilt or innocence, Robinson was an example of a new breed of young American men. He exemplified those from respectable backgrounds who had come to a big city to apprentice themselves for a white-collar career, but, who, unlike their eighteenth-century predecessors, were living on their own in boarding houses. These sporting boys led lives that were unmonitored by families or employers, freely indulging themselves in libertine lifestyles that involved affairs with prostitutes (sometimes several at once), sporting events, gambling, and other such vices that rapidly-growing mercantile cities like New York had to offer. The image of Robinson spending his energies on a woman like Jewett, forming emotional and physical bonds with a woman who was continually manipulating him, who was flaunting her other lovers in his face and playing coy games with his emotions, is one straight out of a dark and stormy Gothic novel.

The press virtually ignored him at first. Perhaps it was the fact that Robinson's employer, Mr. Joseph Hoxie, a small business man and a local politician of the Seventh Ward, vouched for his young clerk as an upstanding gentleman and insisted that the boy's alibi was sound; or perhaps it was the existence of Robinson's middle-class family in Durham, Connecticut, that led the New York press to hold back on its reporting about the boy's character and life-style. However, it was only a matter of time before the letters that Robinson had written to Helen, over a period of ten months, were revealed. Moreover, as events unfolded, Robinson began to appear as a disturbed man whose emotional condition worsened the more he struggled to turn his tryst with a prostitute into something resembling a real love affair.

Robinson's roommates and fellow clerks also had affairs with the women of the Thomas Street Brothel. In fact, George Marston, who went by the name of Bill Easy, had been Helen's regular Saturday night visitor, whom she had turned down on 9 April in order to receive Frank Rivers into her bedroom. Marston was an unstable youth from Massachusetts who had been accused of arson and denounced by his family as a mindless dolt destined for self-destruction. Both Marston and Robinson were examples of what the moral reformers at the time were decrying as youths who were bringing themselves to ruin through their rakish lifestyles and voluptuous indulgences. They were the 1830s equivalent of the Wall Street yuppies of the 1980s, who also frequented prostitutes and had a dangerously unmonitored amount of money. Oddly enough, those yuppies, who were to ravage New York City in a similar vein more than one-hundred-and-fifty years later, worked and sometimes lived in the same neighborhood as Helen Jewett and Richard P. Robinson.

The story of their curious relationship, which began in June of 1835, is told through a series of some fifteen letters written by Robinson and some forty-three penned by Jewett. Oddly enough, only one of the letters out of the sixty-eight that were extant was admissible as evidence at Robinson's trial, but all of them were published years later in the *National Police Gazette*. James Gordon Bennett of the *Herald* reported that actors at the Bowery Theater, the same venue so often frequented by Robinson and Jewett and which served as their secret meeting place for so many months, were performing passages from the letters on stage as if they were "a scene from Shakespeare" [Cohen 249].

The letters, as reproduced in the press, are curious and strange: certainly not meant to be read by any third set of eyes; definitely not revealing any back story (events are commented upon but not explained); and are replete with a large amount of emotional and psychological game-playing, especially from Jewett towards Robinson. After all, Jewett's job required that she put on a mask and not dare reveal her true motivations or feelings. It is a testament to her professionalism that she devoted so much time to letter writing, particularly inasmuch as this activity was the administrative work of her relationships with her clients.

An early letter written on 20 June 1835, reveals how masterful Jewett was at hooking her new customer:

> There is so much sweetness in that voice, so much intelligence in that eye, and so much luxuriance in that form, I cannot fail to love you. The pleasure I feel in your presence and your smile, speak of hour and nights

> of joy; I long to see you, to hear your conversation
> animate your features once again, but I must defer that
> pleasure until your next visit [Cohen 252].

It is clear from this passage that intense flattery is a mere prelude to a subtle suggestion that Robinson come back to visit her, presumably at $5 per night. Her affection for him, apparently, isn't enough for her to demand his presence right away, but only during regular business hours at the brothel.

In subsequent letters, Helen is downright passionate about her alleged love for him, and even compares him to an unnamed lover from Augusta, the one with whom she shared her deepest feelings and with whom she had a deep intellectual relationship (this, perhaps, being Harlow Spaulding). Robinson's response to these proclamations is over-the-top and perhaps even self-delusional: "At best we but live one little hour," he writes in June of 1835, "strut at our own conceit and die. How unhappy must those persons be who cannot enjoy life as it is, seize pleasure as it comes floating on like a noble ship, bound for yonder distant port with all sails set. Come will ye embark?—then on we go, gayly, hand in hand, scorning all petty and trivial troubles, eagerly gazing on our risingsun, till the warmth of its beams (i.e. love) causes our sparkling blood to o'erflow and mingle in holy delight . . ." [Cohen 256].

In this heavily romantic and embarrassingly over-metaphorized passage, Robinson's highly theatrical reaction and his bad imitation of Shakespeare demonstrates that he has taken much away from his visits to the Bowery Theater. The same letter, despite its descent into romantic fantasy, ends with a tinge of jealousy for another man: "Did Cashier come to see you after I left?" he asks [Cohen 257].

Jewett's strategy at this point was to begin feigning her own unworthiness for Robinson's love, as if she were preparing him for an inevitable break, or at least keeping him at a distance. She also began to dangle before him the reality of her other clients. In a letter in which she beams over how exhausted she was from a night's love-making with Robinson, she ended with the anecdote of how she joined another client called The Duke and a few other prostitutes in breaking out some champagne bottles and having a party immediately upon Robinson's departure. She ended another romantic letter with the ominous and jealousy-provoking statement that "the parlor is full of persons, and I am called off from writing . . ." [Cohen 260]. In other words, Jewett had other men downstairs in the brothel's parlor who wanted to have sex with her.

Soon, Robinson's pathology started manifesting. Perhaps it was more than a mere theatrical flourish when he wrote to Helen in June: "I am not without my bitter moments of dismal misery, when I loathed all, myself and everything on earth" [Cohen, 257]. And soon he would be writing to her of events whose true nature history must bar from our sight:

> Helen, I must now again, beg your pardon, for my most ungenerous and ungentlemanlike conduct last night. You have always treated me well, *too* well, and why I should thus requite you, I myself know not. . . . When you told me you were unhappy and wished me not to act so foolishly, I felt for you, and pitied you, yet *I* could not have spoken a pleasant word, if *I* would [Cohen 261-262].

He ended the letter by reminding Helen that it was Bill Easy who had slept with her the night before, which implies that he had erupted into an irrational rage over her relationship with his fellow clerk.

Soon the tables would be turned when Jewett finds out that Robinson has been seeing another prostitute, and she writes him a restrained, but highly manipulative, letter:

> There are very few men who *understand* the feelings of poor women. We are often obliged to smile and hide with a cold exterior, the feelings which sometimes nearly cause our hearts to break. Women only can understand woman's hearts. We cannot, dare not complain, for sympathy is denied us if we do [Cohen 263].

She begged Robinson to come see her and explain his infidelity, but it is difficult, reading through the letters, to sense how much of her described emotions are genuine and how much reflects a prostitute trying to hold onto a client who is threatening to take his business elsewhere.

At Robinson's trial, several of the prostitutes other than Helen, with whom he had had relationships, painted an ugly picture of a libertine youth making the rounds of the local brothels, including having an affair with a seventeen-year-old girl. One of the prostitutes who knew him testified that, "F. Rivers told her if any women exposed him he would blow out her brains" [Cohen 267]. Such testimony is particularly stunning considering Jewett's fate, and it serves to highlight the nature of the letters Robinson wrote throughout the fall of 1835. Here

Robinson refers to his awful treatment of Jewett, his own ill-temper, and sense of unbalance. He recognizes that he is being bad to her, but cannot control himself.

Through the winter of 1835-36, the two lovers were locked in a disturbed battle of intense emotions and psychological manipulation. Jewett went farther than she had ever gone with respect to her other clients, and clearly her relationship with Robinson was spiraling upward in intensity. They wrote intricate and fiery letters to each other, engaging in spasms of jealousy and genuine hurt. To read the letters in chronological order is to witness a deteriorating condition that Helen Jewett, a very skilled and successful prostitute, seems no longer to be able to control.

FIVE: THE MURDER AND TRIAL

During the cold opening months of 1836, Jewett and Robinson continued documenting their jealous rages and their desperate longing to fix a relationship that was perhaps beyond repair. There were times where they seemed to be separated, and Robinson frequently patronized other prostitutes; and there were times when the two of them were involved in some sort of intrigue that involved personages with names like Gilbert and Cashier, who shift below the surface of history forever out of our sight.

It was only a few weeks before her murder that Jewett went to work at Rosina Townsend's brothel at 41 Thomas Street. In the final days, it is clear that the two were breaking up for good, and Jewett requested that her letters to him be returned (which he seemed to honor). However, a miniature portrait of him that he had given her to wear about her neck, which had been seen in her possession before his visit, had vanished from the crime scene. This portrait was found later at Robinson's boarding house. Further, although Rosina Townsend saw Robinson's bald spot and recognized him, by the time of the trial Robinson had shaved his head and was wearing a wig.

However, the rest of the circumstantial evidence against Robinson was overwhelming. His presence at the brothel, identified by several women, combined with the difficulty of anyone else having gained access to Jewett's room due to the security measures of the house, made it unlikely that anyone but Robinson had been with her before her murder. Further, the black cloak discovered at the scene was identified by

OF MOONS AND MONOLITHS: COLLECTED ESSAYS

one of Robinson's roommates as having belonged to him. The hatchet that had been found in the backyard, its blood washed off by the late-night rain, had been stolen from Hoxie's store where Robinson worked. In addition, a white string tassel tied to the hatchet had been found to be broken off the fringe of the cloak. As for motive, Robinson's diary, which had been taken from his boarding house and subsequently published, along with the sordid portrait of his character that emerged from it, presented such difficulties that any legal defense team would find it troublesome evidence.

In the weeks leading up to his trial, a large New York City contingent of sporting boys and dandies publicly came to Robinson's defense. These supporters engaged in vocal protests in the streets and printed pamphlets emphasizing the circumstantial nature of the evidence against Robinson. They even adopted his foppish manner of dress, including the floppy silk hat he wore, which quickly became popularized as "Frank River caps" [Gilfoyle 98]. When a crowd of fifteen hundred people responded to a meeting of the Men's Moral Reformers at Chatham Street Chapel, many of them were Rivers-supporting hooligans who disrupted the somber proceedings by pelting the stage with garbage and breaking the stage lamps, thereby inciting a riot.

Lithographs of both the accused and the victim were widely distributed. The likeness of Robinson, cherubic and wide-eyed, beaming a boyish innocence, stood in stark contrast to the ugly picture that had emerged from his diary and letters. Jewett's lithographs portrayed her in her famous green silk dress, heavily flounced and ribboned, carrying a parasol, handkerchief and letter; she was presumably on her way to a post office to mail a letter to one of her clients, perhaps Robinson himself. These lithographs sold like hot cakes, turning the two into overnight celebrities.

The trial opened on Thursday, 2 June 1836, on the second floor of City Hall, with Judge Ogden Edwards, a descendant of Puritan Jonathan Edwards, presiding. An estimated six thousand people surged around the building trying to gain entry to the spectacle, including, as was expected, a large contingent of Rivers-style sporting boys. Their presence in the court caused much disruption and added a strange atmosphere when the testimonies of several prostitutes provoked murmurs and giggles from those who recognized the women from the various brothels that they had frequented.

The case for the prosecution emphasized the circumstantial evidence, including Robinson's access to Hoxie's hatchet and his ownership of the tasseled cloak. The defense attempted to build a case for a conspiracy designed to frame Robinson, focusing particularly upon the fact that the hatchet was found outdoors in the morning, hours after the murder, and easily could have been planted by one of the prostitutes. A roar of applause ripped through the courtroom as Rosina Townsend admitted that more than one client used the name Frank Rivers, and more than a few of the witnesses for the prosecution were pushed by the defense attorneys to admit their own sympathetic ties to the world of prostitution. Much was made out of the casual manner in which unknown men, also at the brothel that night, had quickly vanished from the scene without being questioned or even having their names recorded. One of the biggest blows to the prosecution was its failure to get Robinson's letters admitted into evidence, due to the inability to positively identify his handwriting (Joseph Hoxie, Robinson's boss, who certainly would have known the boy's script, failed to give a positive identification of it, thus adding weight to the defense's position that the letters should not be admitted).

One of the biggest surprises of the proceedings was the examination of Frederick W. Gourgons, a clerk in a Broadway apothecary shop, who testified that Richard P. Robinson had been in his shop sometime in early April, before the murder. Robinson was inquiring if he could buy arsenic, a request that Gourgons refused. This implied that Robinson, before settling on a hatchet as the means to dispatch Jewett, had tried to poison her first. Gourgons' testimony, frustratingly enough, was inadmissible into evidence because arsenic was not the specific murder weapon mentioned in the indictment, and the day and hour of the visit to the apothecary did not match the specifics of the actual murder. One can only speculate how the case would have turned out if Gourgons' testimony had been ruled admissible by the judge.

The defense also launched a surprise witness, the owner of a downtown grocery, who claimed that during part of the evening Richard P. Robinson was in his store, sitting on a barrel and smoking one of twenty-five cigars that he had purchased that evening. It did not help the prosecution that the owner was a friend of more than one juror in the jury box. In fact, as the case for the defense unfolded, there was a distinct feeling that Robinson's greatest advantage was the camaraderie in the sporting life that he shared with many in the male-dominated proceedings.

Robinson was well-heeled and connected, from a prominent Connecticut family (the brother of the presiding judge was Governor of Connecticut at the time), and that was worth more to the jury than the testimony of prostitutes, madams, and common watchmen. Time after time, the reliability of prosecution witnesses was called in question. It was suggested that Rosina Townsend ignited the bed herself in order to collect on insurance, and that Robinson had brought Hoxie's hatchet to the brothel (much in the same way women today would carry a can of mace) and left it there only to be used by Jewett's murderer after Robinson's departure. The barrage of doubt, and suspicion of all the circumstantial evidence, led to a verdict of Not Guilty on the fifth day of trial.

SIX: AFTERMATH

No sooner had the trial ended, and Richard P. Robinson released back into private life, then an outcry emerged from the press and public that a great miscarriage of justice had been effected. There was even a demand for Judge Hoffman's resignation. The appellation of "poor boy," in which Robinson had cloaked himself during the trial, quickly evaporated when a twenty-year-old by the name of William Gray was arrested for theft and had walked into a courtroom with more than a dozen letters written to him by Robinson. Indeed, Gray had been a boarding house roommate of Robinson's, and had lent him the cloak that had been found at the scene of Jewett's murder. Gray's handing over the letters to the court may have constituted a plea bargain of sorts (an unsuccessful one, however: Gray was sentenced to Sing Sing).

Yet the letters produced by Gray clearly showed another face of Robinson, a sporting boy unashamedly talking to one of his own, engaging in a shared misogynistic and narcissistic vocabulary. Robinson reveals to Gray, who was engaged to be married, that he had indeed had sex with his fiancé, and would gladly do it again once they were married if it would help Gray secure a divorce on grounds of adultery. "She will not be the first married woman, who has felt my persuasive powers," Robinson proclaims, after announcing that he has performed this service for other men before [Cohen 376]. He also boasts of his sexual conquests in New York and threatens a servant girl with abuse if she testifies against him. The swagger, hostility, and the perception of a monstrous ego that emerged from Robinson's letters to Gray, added fuel to the fire of controversy that dogged Robinson until the end of his life.

In July, an anonymous clerk friend of Robinson's published a pamphlet called "Robinson Down Stream: Containing Conversations with the GREAT UNHUNG" in which Robinson, ever the sporting boy, sneered once more at the world and all its vanities: "I have nothing more to hope from the patronage of this hypocritical world," Robinson announced. "I have no desire to flatter it. Mankind! I love ye not . . . I know your disguise; I have worn it—I know your arts; I have practiced them—I know the trickery of the stage; I have myself been behind the curtains—examined the scenes, scrutinized the tinseled wardrobes—sneered at the elements of a thunderstorm, and convivialized in the green room. I can unmask one half of New York and uncloak the other." Besides revealing all the dramatic flourishes that he learned from the theater, he also shows his outrageous narcissism: "Half the women in New York were in love with me," he announced when asked if Helen Jewett really had feelings for him. "I can go back to Gotham and marry an heiress" [Cohen 382, 383].

Yet, instead of returning to New York to marry an heiress, Robinson took flight on a steamboat and headed down to Texas to enlist in service in the war against Mexico. Not suitable as army material (he was mysteriously discharged from the First Regiment of the Texas Army), Robinson withdrew to Nacogdoches, a frontier town in East Texas. He adopted the name of R. Parmelee (his mother's maiden name) and became the owner of a billiard hall and saloon. Exploiting the hard-earned skills that he had gained in New York, Robinson-Parmelee also became the clerk of the County Court, got married, and invested in real estate. In time, he even owned twenty slaves, and was one of the ten wealthiest men in Nacogdoches. He had prospered into a hard Texas aristocrat in a place that was wild enough for his misogynist and egomaniacal temperament.

There is evidence that some of his fellow Texans knew of his true identity, but for the most part he evaded any real scandal. While dime novels and pamphlets about the murder of Helen Jewett continued to be published during the 1840s, Robinson enjoyed his wealth and property. In 1855, while traveling on the Ohio River via steamboat, he contracted yellow fever and had to be brought ashore in Louisville. An elderly black woman who attended him at the end claimed that in his last moments Robinson ranted feverishly about Helen Jewett, calling her his wife.

While this dramatic flourish is quite compelling, it cannot be proven, and Richard P. Robinson passed into eternity, enigmatic and unhung.

As for Helen Jewett, born Dorcas Doyen, she was buried in the churchyard of St. John's Episcopal Church in what is now the neighborhood known as the West Village. Sadly enough, medical students from the College of Physicians and Surgeons dug up her grave just four short nights after her burial, dissected her and boiled her down to her skeleton. Her physical body, once a habitation of life, a source of income, and an object of desire for lustful New York City youths, mutilated and scorched and brutally murdered, may have found its final resting place in the collection of Dr. Valentine Mott, "the foremost snatcher of his day," labeled as Item 714, a "lacerated cerebellum." In the 1860s, a fire destroyed Dr. Mott's gruesome collection, and, if this was she, Dorcas' remains passed into eternity. The closest we can now come to a final resting place for Dorcas is the James J. Walker Park in New York City's West Village, not too far from the brothel where she died. Under its asphalt and park benches is the soil where she lay for four days before her exhumation [Cohen 463].

As Helen Jewett, she continued to make frequent appearances in decades to come in pamphlets, in best-selling lithographs, and in the pages of dime store novels. Even a depiction of her murder was displayed in a Boston wax museum, along with the black-cloaked, hatchet-wielding Robinson; she was placed just a few exhibits away from a recreation of the murder of Sarah Cornell, a Fall River, Massachusetts, mill girl who was murdered in 1832. Cornell's alleged killer, the Reverend Ephraim Avery, also escaped the gallows and similarly lived out the rest of his life under an assumed name, haunted by his past.

There is a sadness to the story of Richard P. Robinson and Dorcas Doyen. If not for one brief evening of homicidal rage, their sexual involvement and emotional tragedy may have disappeared into the secret flow of history as a passing fancy, enacted by a hot-blooded young man and a professional prostitute that he had hired for his pleasure, nothing more and nothing less. Eventually, Robinson would have moved on to his professional career, leaving behind his youthful foray into the world of whores. Dorcas, however, would have been trapped in that fallen world, incapable of any advancement, beyond the hope of marriage, and destined to either become a madam or to seek support from an on-going parade of lonely men who chose to rent out some little intimacy in the closed bedroom of a brothel.

WORKS CITED:

Cohen, Patricia Cline. *The Murder of Helen Jewett*. New York: Vintage Book, 1998.

Gilfoyle, Timothy J. *City of Eros: New York City, Prostitution, and the Commercialization of Sex, 1790-1920*. New York: W.W. Norton and Company, 1992.

First published in *The Hatchet: Journal of Lizzie Borden Studies*, Vol. 5, Issue 4, November/December, 2008.

THE STRANGE CASE
OF TYPHOID MARY

"The price of liberty is good behavior."

—*Preventative Medicine and Hygiene*, 1935.

While there has always been debate as to whether Lizzie Borden murdered her parents, there was no doubt in anyone's mind that Mary Mallon, popularly known as Typhoid Mary, between 1900 and 1915, transmitted the deadly disease known as Typhoid to forty-seven distinct individuals, causing the death of three.

Borden and Mallon came from radically different socioeconomic backgrounds—Lizzie was the pampered daughter of a prominent businessman while Mary was an Irish immigrant who labored as a cook—but both were accused of killing people and both spent the rest of their lives languishing in solitary prisons. True, Lizzie's prison was a large Victorian home in Fall River's wealthier neighborhood surrounded by a cordon of servants, and Mary Mallon's was a one room shack on a medical quarantine island with only a nurse who sampled her stool for contagion to keep her company, but both outcasts suffered from social stigmas that kept them isolated and painfully alone.

One can only suspect that if the two could have met and traded notes, they would have understood each other as no one else of their time could. Lizzie the Hatchet Killer and Mary the Human Pandemic, forced by the cruel stereotyping of history into their perceived roles as killers, remained unrepentant to their dying days.

Off the north shore of Queens, New York, just beyond Bowery Bay, sits the landmass of Riker's Island where the Department of Corrections maintains a notorious prison facility for those who have committed crimes against society. But off the northwestern tip of this island is a smaller landmass facing the Bronx known as North Brother Island where the abandoned ruins of a large hospital and other health facilities tell the story of a very different kind of prison. Between the years 1907 and 1938, a solitary woman was there incarcerated for almost one half of her life-span. She committed no crime and had been condemned by no court of law, but here Mary Mallon a.k.a. Typhoid Mary was kept in medical quarantine against her will for almost three decades.

The name Typhoid Mary has become a part of our culture. To say that someone is a Typhoid Mary is to describe them as spreading disease, causing those about them to die as they themselves move about unharmed. For this reason it shocks many people to hear that Mary Mallon was only responsible for three deaths and those were certainly unintentional. Mary had the misfortune to be the first healthy carrier of the disease verified by the New York City Department of Health. Her sequestration one hundred years ago, with her subsequent vilification by the press, is a controversial case study of how far we would go to protect ourselves from disease, even at the price of civil liberties.

Mary Mallon was born in 1869 in County Tyrone, Ireland and immigrated to America as a young woman, alone and determined to survive, like so many other Irish girls of her day, as a domestic cook. By all accounts, her cooking career was a success: she worked for many wealthy families on Long Island and in Manhattan. Between the summer of 1900 and March 1907, she worked in Mamaroneck, Sands Point, Tuxedo Park, Oyster Bay, and on Park Avenue. However, at all these locations, members of the family and/or the domestic staff came down with typhoid, twenty two cases altogether. One person died of the contagion.

It is easy to believe that Mary had no awareness that she was spreading the disease. In 19th Century America, typhoid was a tragically common occurrence and it is hard for a modern reader to appreciate just how widespread the disease was. Statistically, there was little reason to think that her presence in so many infected households was unusual. Of the several thousand people who contracted typhoid in New York State in 1906, there were more than 600 fatalities and only one of them happened in a household where Mary worked. To her, she could not possibly be the carrier because she herself exhibited no symptoms of the disease. She had even stuck around to nurse the sick and quit soon after in fear she would catch typhoid.

At the beginning of the last century, it had become a primary directive of many health departments in the United States to fight the disease, largely through the improvement of living conditions, cleaner water supplies, better sanitation and the reduction of physical filth. Moreover, the emerging science of bacteriology focused on attacking the bacilli themselves, but of course, to attack them, these invisible enemies first had to be found. The thought that they could be lurking in a healthy individual who worked in impeccably clean conditions was pushing the boundaries of what we knew about disease propagation at the time. In 1907, science had not yet proven that such a thing as a healthy carrier actually existed and there were no laws on the books to determine how to handle such an individual should they be discovered.

George Soper, who had made his reputation as a sanitary engineer specializing in epidemics, was hired by Mr. and Mrs. George Thompson to investigate the outbreak of the disease at their Oyster Bay mansion where their summer tenants, the Warren family, resided. Soper was determined to make a name for himself by capturing America's first scientifically recognized healthy carrier. After learning that Mary Mallon had worked as a cook in Warren's household in the summer of 1906 and left shortly after the outbreak, Soper traced her employment history and found the large number of typhoid cases in her wake. This led him to pay a visit to Mary as she worked in the kitchen of the Bowen family on Park Avenue.

Soper approached Mallon with a passionate argument that she may be causing the infections in her clients through her cooking and her failure to clean her hands properly after bowel movements. He requested that she supply stool and urine samples to determine if she was indeed a carrier. Mary responded by pulling out a roasting fork and chasing him from the premises. Determined to put his name into the annals of bacteriological history, Soper buddied up to Mary's working class boyfriend, confronting her for a second time in her own apartment on Third Avenue and Thirty Third Street. She responded with an equally violent reaction and Soper beat a hasty retreat.

Feeling that this was indeed a job that required a woman's touch, the Department of Health sent in S. Josephine Baker, a city medical inspector, with an ambulance and five police officers. When they confronted Mary at her place of employment, she fled and hid in a staircase closet for over three hours as Baker and the policemen searched several houses. When discovered, she put up such a fight that in the wagon, while she howled obscenities and hostile imprecations at her captors,

Baker had to physically sit on her to keep her from escaping. Mallon was removed to an isolation cabin on North Brother Island where she was to remain, with the exception of a few brief years of freedom (1910 to 1915), for the rest of her life.

Almost from the moment of Mary Mallon's capture, serious legal and ethical issues had been raised about her arrest and captivity. While Soper and Baker gained some notoriety for identifying and isolating the typhoid carrier, Mallon herself was deprived of her freedom. The charter for the New York City health department did mandate that it should protect the public health of the city by removing "or cause to be removed to [a] proper place to be by [the Board] designated, any person sick with any contagious, pestilential or infectious disease..." [New York City Department of Health Charter Section 1170]. The problem with this directive is that it was written before the discovery of healthy carriers. It is one thing to deprive someone of his or her liberty because they are burning up with a 105-degree fever from an infectious disease. It is quite another matter to incarcerate a perfectly healthy individual.

However, there was no lack of evidence. The health department did take several stool samples a week from Mary in the beginning. Of the 163 samples taken during the period from 1907 to 1909, 120 tested positive for the typhoid bacteria, and 43 tested negative. When her case did get reviewed by a court of law in 1909, Mary produced test results that she had done with an independent lab, all of which tested negative. However, it was believed that the longer amount of time between the excretion of the samples and the delivery of them to the lab gave the typhoid time to degrade. Another possibility is that Mary went through periods where the bacilli were not active, as can be seen in the 43 negative tests done by the health department.

There was no doubt in anyone's mind, excepting perhaps Mary's own and her lawyer's, that she was a perfectly healthy woman who carried the typhoid bacilli about in her gall bladder and had spread the disease to others through a combination of food preparation and poor sanitary habits. Although a judge ruled against her release in 1909 in a hearing where bacteriology itself seemed to be on trial, the Hearst newspapers unexpectedly drummed up public sympathy.

In a lengthy article in the June 20, 1909 edition of the *New York American*, Hearst seized upon the name "Typhoid Mary," which had been used in a medical journal to mask Mallon's identity (in a modern scientific paper she would be called Mary M.), and published a drawing of a domestic cook tossing small human skulls into a frying pan as if they were eggs of death. It declared her "most harmless and yet the most dangerous woman in America" and did drum up public outrage against her incarceration on North Brother Island. Other newspapers such as the *New York Herald* and *The Times* followed suit in casting her in a sympathetic light, although they all milked the strongly evocative term "Typhoid Mary."

What happened to turn the tide of popular opinion against her was what she did when she was finally released from the island in 1910 due to the sympathies of a new health commissioner. She unashamedly violated the conditions of her release, which were to remain in touch with the Board of Health and to refrain from making her living as a cook. In 1915, after being off the radar for several years, she reemerged at New York's Sloane Maternity Hospital where twenty-five individuals came down with typhoid fever, two of them eventually dying from their illness. Sure enough, Mary was found working under an assumed name and she was unceremoniously dragged by the Board of Health back to North Brother Island, this time for good.

Because of her deliberate disregard for public health precautions and her continual refusal to admit the danger she posed to those around her, public sympathy for her almost completely vanished. This time she had clearly spread the disease with full awareness of what she was doing, although she still claimed that she was perfectly healthy.

While Mary grew accustomed to life on North Brother Island and over the years became less enraged over her predicament, she continued to deny that she was a threat to anyone. She obtained a position working in the island's hospital and there is evidence that she even took day trips into Long Island and Manhattan. The public soon forgot her, she grew old and sick, and then in 1938, after several years bed ridden from a debilitating stroke, she passed away. The last known photograph of her on the island shows a big beefy woman with a partially paralyzed face. She never gained back her full liberty and she never accepted the scientific evidence of her being a healthy carrier of typhoid.

The questions remain about how Mary Mallon, who was not the only healthy typhoid bacilli carrier in New York in 1907, became so notorious and well known, and why her incarceration and treatment at the hands of the Department of Health was more severe than any of the other known healthy carriers, and why she became an American icon for pathogenic hysteria? Some of the other carriers identified by the

New York City Department of Health were responsible for more infections and more deaths than Mary Mallon; however, the other carriers played nice, agreeing to the restrictions of the officials, reporting to their case handlers on a regular basis, giving stool samples to track their condition over time, and agreeing to refrain from certain professions like food preparation. Mary disregarded all these directives, attacked officials with a weapon, and violently denied she was the cause of the suffering about her. By setting a stern example with Mary Mallon, the Department of Health had their Typhoid poster girl to serve as a warning to other healthy carriers who may consider rebelling against them.

At the time, the growing concern over public health had reached a frenzied peak and was fueled by scientific discoveries over the bacteriological origin of diseases. For many decades, the understanding was that filthy living conditions bred disease, but the new thinking, sparked by the isolation of microorganisms in the bodies of the sick, actually stirred a debate over whether the approach to eliminating diseases was to enforce better sanitation and living conditions or to simply go after the microorganisms. While we now understand that disease is a collaboration between the two—filth helps to propagate the bacteria—in the early 1900s, many medical men and social reformers fanatically favored one approach to disease eradication over the other.

In 1907, science seemed to be winning the bacteriological battle on both fronts. With health organizations well funded in every state, sanitation programs and municipal strategies for cleanliness of water and living conditions were taming the deadly epidemics that were plaguing the country. The possibility of healthy carriers, people who were in fine bodily health but who carried the bacteria in their bodies and could spread it to those about them if they were not being mindful of their sanitary habits, helped to sustain a paranoid fear much akin to the AIDS scare of the 1980s. Clearly for science to complete its victory, it would have to come up with a way of handling this fearsome source of contagion. Mary Mallon was one of the first widely publicized cases of a healthy carrier that scientific investigation had isolated. She stood as a symbol of science's ability to seek and destroy disease wherever it was hiding, whether in spoiled food supplies, unhealthy drinking water, or Mary Mallon's gall bladder. By isolating her, apprehending her, and forcing her into quarantine for the rest of her life, public health science was asserting its authority and its ability to defeat a deadly epidemic.

The severity by which her liberty and rights as a human being were denied was part of this triumph. Mary's defiant stance against the Department of Health made her even better press and put her in alignment with the disease itself. Other healthy carriers played by the rules, taking care of themselves and adhering to strict guidelines in order to protect others from their own disease. They would use exclusive toilets and limit their employment opportunities that often put them under financial hardship. Mary refused to do any of this, and caused many infections as a result. She had to be restrained, against her own will, for the public good. No other healthy carrier made such a stink, and by refusing to cooperate with the Board of Health, she was deemed, in the view of many, to be no better ethically than the disease. To isolate and contain Typhoid Mary became synonymous with isolating and containing typhoid itself.

Like Lizzie Borden, there have been many novels, plays, and even an interpretative dance that were either based on or inspired by Mary Mallon's tragic life. While in her day she was viewed through the lens of society's desire to eliminate pandemics through the power of modern science, the creative arts generated from her story in the last few decades has largely focused on feminist issues, comparisons to the Reagan administration's policies towards victims of AIDS, and larger existential issues. Barry Drogin and Peg Hill's 1988 dance production Typhoid Mary has the Irish cook preparing a meal on stage that is subsequently fed to the audience, forcing them to confront their fear of being infected by the outsider.

Few people today know or remember the actual facts of Mary Mallon's case, but everyone knows her nickname, even if they are surprised to hear that Typhoid Mary was a real person. She is buried in the Bronx, far from her Irish homeland but only a short distance from North Brother Island where she lived in isolation for three decades.

Satellite photography on the Internet gives a sad testament to the legacy of Typhoid Mary. At Wikimapia, you can examine the landmass of North Brother Island as it stands today, abandoned and overgrown with forest. At a higher magnification, you can see the roof of Riverside Hospital. The location of Mary's isolation shack is completely covered with trees. Nothing remains but the name Typhoid Mary, one that she personally despised but which has been embraced by our collective cultural imagination.

WORKS CITED:

Bourdain, Anthony. *Typhoid Mary: An Urban Historical.* NY: Bloomsbury Press, 2001.
Leavitt, Judith Walzer. *Typhoid Mary: Captive To The Public's Health.* Boston: Beacon Press, 1996.

First published in *The Hatchet: Journal of Lizzie Borden Studies*, Vol. 4, Issue 3, August/September, 2007.

HETTY GREEN:
WALL STREET WOMAN

During the first decade of the 20th century, the streets of lower Manhattan played host to an almost daily event that unnerved and bewildered many a pedestrian: Hetty Green was walking to work.

The eccentric millionaire and resident of Hoboken, New Jersey, infamous for her stinginess and unwillingness to spend a dollar on her own creature comforts, came across the Hudson River each morning on a New Jersey ferry, draped in a black dress that was literally falling apart from being worn continually without being washed, topped by a dark flowery hat that made her look like a ghost from another era. Now in her 70s, an advanced age that enhanced her wraith-like appearance, she was soon dubbed by New Yorkers the Witch of Wall Street.

Her destination was her offices in the financial district where she would spend her days surrounded by her stocks and bonds, reportedly eating oatmeal that she heated up on the radiator because she would not pay for proper food, controlling her wealth with a spectacular talent for success that awed even the most prosperous of her fellow financiers. Having taken an initial inheritance of $5.7 million and turned it into an astonishing $100 million by the time of her death, she made history as a woman who ran the bull on the market harder and longer than most investors of her day and being a female in a male dominated world of power and wealth, just compounded the scope of her astonishing achievement.

Henrietta Howland Robinson was born in 1834 in New Bedford, Massachusetts, one of the most important cities in the history of American whaling. She came into the world less than five decades after New Bedford's incorporation as a town in 1787 and thirteen years before it officially became a city. Its close proximity to Nantucket and its natural seaports made it an ideal capital for the American whaling industry. Many of the down-to-earth humble Quakers who inhabited the area became extremely wealthy due to the immense profits that were to be had from the butchering of the Leviathan. Indeed, Hetty's family fortune came from investments in the whale industry.

Whale oil was, in its day, a crucial source of energy and light, making the industry that surrounded its production the 18th century equivalent of Consolidated Edison. But so great was the demand for the oil that the hunting fleets out of Nantucket and New Bedford dramatically altered the world's whale population in just a few short decades. The hunters all but exhausted the fisheries in the North Atlantic, so great was the slaying, and they would often sail on voyages that lasted years, traveling as far as the Pacific Ocean. So compellingly exotic was the life of an American whaler that Herman Melville (who sailed out of New Bedford as a whale man) was to score a commercial bestseller with *Moby Dick*, a 700+ page description of every grueling aspect of whaling imaginable and which painted a vivid portrait of New Bedford in its opening scenes before the story heads out to the open ocean with Captain Ahab and his crew.

Hetty Green, whose father, Edward Mott Robinson, owned a whaling fleet, grew up amongst opulence and was no doubt sheltered from the harsh realities of the seafaring life and the slaughter of the great mammals. Besides being pampered and privately schooled, her Quaker heritage enforced a humble austerity that may help explain some of her later life-style contradictions. Never possessed with any desire for ostentation or opulence, she was trained to value every penny of a dollar. From an early age she was reading financial reports out loud to her family and learning all she could about money management and investment. At the time of her father's death in 1864 Hetty inherited $5.7 million dollars. One of the first signs of her eccentricities towards money was a lawsuit she initiated against her own aunt's estate to prevent $2 million dollars of her fortune to be donated to charity. She was suspected of forging a crucial document. She lost the case because the judge threw out the foundation of the civil suit. Hetty appealed, but then the parties compromised.

But at the time that Hetty inherited her money, the discovery of petroleum as an alternative source of energy had cast the whaling industry into its twilight years and Hetty felt compelled to reinvest all of her money in depreciated Civil War Bonds. During the war, the U.S.

government had issued paper money or "greenbacks" which didn't always have full-value, and they were considered, at the time, unstable as a long-term investment. But Hetty kept a cool and level head, navigating through the financial turmoil of the post-Civil War period as a highly successful investor.

As uncharacteristic as it may seem, Hetty had a husband and children. She married Edward Henry Green, a wealthy man himself, shortly after obtaining her inheritance, and attempted to separate the management of his fortune from her own. It had been rumored that Edward even signed a prenuptial agreement renouncing all claim to her money, but their marriage suffered eventually from financial stress. Hetty found out in 1885 that her financial house, John J. Cisco and Son, had secretly made deals with her husband, and when the house failed, she withdrew all her securities and deposited them in Chemical Bank. Further, she dropped her husband like he had been a bad investment, reconciling with him only near the end of his life when she nursed him during his last illness.

Hetty invested mostly in real estate and railroads. She was always quick to loan at reasonable rates, but never to borrow. In 1907, during a financial crisis, she gave New York City $1.1 million in exchange for revenue bonds. She used offices at the Seaboard National Bank in lower Manhattan but refused to pay rent, opting to take over random desks, surrounding them with her suitcases and financial papers, making her resemble a bizarre cross between J.P. Morgan and a bag lady.

Over the years the wild stories of her shabby existence ran rampant, so much so that biographers have difficulty weeding out what is fact from what is fantasy or mere exaggeration. It is true that she took the Hoboken Ferry to work each day, and rode on public streetcars, during an age when she could have owned her own private railroad. It is also a fact that she tried to save money on hospital bills, dressing shabbily when visiting doctors with her young son after he injured his leg. Over time, she tried treating his injury with home remedies, but it never fully healed. At the age of twenty, her son's leg was amputated. In later life she resorted to a wheelchair because she didn't want to pay the $150 to fix her hernia. Finally, she spent much of her last years drifting between small apartments in various cities, afraid of tax collectors and growing increasingly paranoid that people were after her money.

But while history always paints a portrait of Hetty with an emphasis on her reclusive eccentricities and extreme parsimony, it is worth a moment to examine a few aspects of her financial strategies that in and of themselves earn her an esteemed place in the Wall Street Hall of Fame. According to the Museum of American Financial History, these strategies were very simple indeed: Hetty never borrowed but always lent, she never consumed her investment principal, and she shunned the short-term risk in favor of long-term stability. It is a mathematical fact that Hetty increased her wealth from under $10 million to $100 million over fifty some odd years, and according to the Financial Museum, "This feat can be accomplished with an annual compound rate of interest of less than 9.5%." Clearly there was no magic involved in the growth of her colossal fortune other than a life-long stubbornness, an unusual ability to navigate through stock panics and a refusal to speculate. Paradoxically, part of her success was her inability to give in to greed.

What is most fascinating about Hetty Green, beyond the stories of her rotting clothing and radiator-cooked meals, is that she spanned a wide plank over two very different eras of American history. Her life started in a New England whaling community just about half a century after the American Revolution but ended in a very modern looking Manhattan which, by the time of her death, was filling rapidly with the technological marvels of the 20th century—electricity, telephones, movie palaces and automobiles. While she always lived in the presence of wealth and only wanted for material comforts by her own choosing, she remained at heart a colonial working woman who brought to her Wall Street obsession a frontier mentality of fortitude and deep survival instincts. Her eccentricities may have been merely an extension of the ever-diligent sacrifice paid by her ancestors as they worked the land and spent years at a stretch hunting the whale, while the newly born America grew up about them.

Indeed, Hetty Green was witness to American industry's financial growth spurt that started with the colonial whaling fleets of the pre-industrial age, and moved to the giant banking houses and corporations of the modern world. In her youth, she learned well from the Captain Ahabs of New England with their austere Quaker ways, profound earthiness and steadfast vigilance on the seas as they waited for the spouting signs of their mighty sea beasts. As a grown women, she played hard with the tycoons of the Wall Street towers, besting them at their own game with her stern obsessive patience and fierce slow burning aggressiveness.

It can be argued that her controversial life style was a defense against the male dominated financial community that would have preferred their playing field be kept free of the female sex. Perhaps she chose not to partake of material self-indulgence in order to define herself as a down-to-earth pioneer who knew that every dollar earned through patience, labor and sacrifice was a gem dug harshly from the earth at a very dear price.

Perhaps if she had been more ordinary, less reclusive, or more connected to the fads of her generation, she wouldn't have fared as well. It seemed to have been her deep alienation from the world and her stubborn refusal to nurture anything else in her life other than her fortune, that made her so unique a woman in American history.

Author's Note: A brilliant fictional parody of Hetty Green can be found in Kurt Vonnegut's 1979 novel *Jailbird* (Delacorte Press) in the character of Mary Kathleen O'Looney, a New York City bag lady who is in reality the CEO of the fictional RAMJAC Corporation.

WORKS CITED:

Actual Virtual Vermont Internet Magazine. "Hetty Green." 21 January 2007. 27 January 2007 <virtualvermont.com/history/hgreen.html>.

Grinder, Dr. Brian and Dr. Dan Cooper. "Hetty Green: Legendary Wall Street Investor." *Museum of American Financial History.* 2005. 27 January 2007 <financialhistory.org/fh/1996/55-1.htm>.

Lewis, Arthur H. *The Day They Shook the Plum Tree.* NY Harcourt, Brace & World, 1963.

Philbrick, Nathaniel. *In the Heart of the Sea: The Tragedy of the Whaleship Essex.* NY: Viking Penguin, 2001.

Sparkes, Boyden and Samuel T. Moore. *The Witch of Wall Street.* Doubleday, Doran & Company, 1935.

First published in *The Hatchet: Journal of Lizzie Borden Studies*, Vol. 4, Issue 1, February/March, 2007.

CARRIE NATION:
ANOTHER AMERICAN
HATCHET WOMAN

Carrie Amelia Moore Nation was a flamboyant, theatrical and completely outrageous woman, who was a self-described "bulldog running along at the feet of Jesus, barking at what he doesn't like." At nearly 6 feet tall, she cut an imposing figure. Her intimidating presence was not eased any by the hatchets that she often wielded, when, in the name of Christian temperance, she entered bars and saloons to chop up furniture and bottles in an attempt to destroy the drunkard's watering hole at its source. She often described her victims as "rum-soaked, whiskey-swilled, Saturn-faced rummies" and led her attacks with the rallying cry of "Smash, ladies, Smash!"

Although not the only famous teetotaler of her generation (Susan B. Anthony and George Bernard Shaw were known for their temperance work as well) she was certainly the brassiest and the most feared. Arrested over 30 times between 1900 and 1910, she also went on whirlwind lecture tours, published her own newspaper (*The Smasher's Mail*) and provided mail order autographed postcards of herself that still pop up on eBay from time to time. From all over the country her supporters would send her hatchets to show their approval of her Elliot Ness-like tactics in fighting the evils of alcohol. She even had her name, Carry A. Nation, officially trademarked to exploit its fearful symbolism.

Carrie Nation was born in 1846 in Kentucky and later moved to Missouri where she married a hopeless drunk who died after two years of marriage. Remarried to David Nation, a lawyer and minister, and moving to Medicine Lodge, Kansas, Carrie got increasingly involved with the state temperance movement, at first advocating peaceful protest to close down saloons and drive out the drunks.

Kansas has been one of the first American states to prohibit alcohol by constitutional amendment in 1880, but it took a while for the saloons to close, and Carrie Nation and the Kansas State Temperance Union certainly did their part to hurry along the process. But political corruption, a sagging US economy, and a less than enthusiastic law enforcement community allowed the dens of iniquity to continue to ply their trade.

Sometime in the spring of 1900, Carrie seemed to have re-evaluated the efficacy of non-violence. Apparently, standing outside a saloon singing hymns and reciting Biblical temperance poetry wasn't cutting her mustard. So, fed up with the hypocrisy and the on-going spread of alcoholism, Carrie, at 54 years of age, tucked a stash of bricks and bats into her buggy and drove out of Medicine Lodge to go on an infamous tour of violence through several towns and cities.

Urged on by the voice in her head telling her that He would stand beside her in any action she felt compelled to take against vice, she burned through Kiowa, Wichita and Topeka, landing several stints in jail of several weeks each. She was beaten by saloon keepers' wives, heckled by irate citizens, and criticized widely, even by the Kansas State Temperance Union, which disapproved of her extreme tactics in advancing their own cause.

Eventually, however, her charisma and ability to draw a large approving crowd, not to mention stirring new membership for the KSTU, won over the public, and before the end of 1901, Carrie had organized groups of Home Defenders, all armed with their pokers and bats and hatchets. At their approach, no keg, cask or stein was safe. Chairs, stools and billiard tables were chopped into splinters. Expensive glass windows were shattered. Slot machines were broken. Befuddled drunks were tossed to the gutter. According to contemporary accounts, few put up any significant resistance and Carrie's popularity grew exponentially.

The Home Defender's attacks on the rum halls of Topeka led to a confrontation with the state senate after Carrie targeted Topeka's Senate Saloon, an establishment frequented by legislators. "You refused me the vote," Carrie told them, "and I had to use a rock!" The senate eventually passed significant legislation that did not completely wipe out alcohol from the state of Kansas but established a stronger prohibition than the weakly enforced one that had driven Carrie Nation to violence.

After her triumph in Kansas, Carrie went on to give lecture tours and to publish a newsletter. She ran a lucrative mail order business that sold autographed postcards and miniature hatchets. Her writings were often filled with religious justification for her deeds, but the fad that she had created was non-sectarian and appealed to a wide variety of reformers and women's rights activists. Eventually Carrie hired a talent agent and went on a theatrical tour, smashing barrels on stage and singing her temperance songs to enthusiastic audiences who howled for more.

Her acts of violence against saloons became known as "hatchetations." Prizefighter John L. Sullivan, "the Boston Strong Boy," reportedly broke down out of fear when Carrie Nation entered his New York saloon and he converted to a staunch prohibitionist. Such stuff was the material of legends.

Carrie Nation, despite her over-commercialized theatrics, did contribute much to the wider movement in which she is situated in history. The Woman's Christian Temperance Union, of which Lizzie Borden was once a member, started in Fredonia, New York, in the early 1870s. It not only addressed issues surrounding alcoholism in society, but also prostitution, recreational drugs, domestic violence, prison reform, public health and eventually women's voting rights. As early as 1875, the WCTU tried to raise public awareness of the dangers of tobacco, quite a large leap for the time. Their particular Christian bent, unfortunately, forbade Jewish or African American women from joining their ranks, but despite that gross lapse in political correctness, they indirectly helped all women in this country empower themselves and addressed serious substance abuse and health concerns that plagued a society just emerging from a frontier mentality and a male-driven industrial expansion.

The movement spread quickly all over the world, and although Carrie Nation represented an extreme measure within its larger tactics, she certainly was acting in accord with its principles. Carrie was very much a woman of her time and place. Medicine Lodge, Kansas, was a very different type of society than Fredonia, New York, and the genteel women of the gilded age who marched in the streets of New York were not dealing with the wild frontier drunkard of the western states. Moreover, as we have seen, Kansas was a state struggling with its own prohibition legislation, and awareness of the corruption and legal indifference to the state's own laws provoked people like Carrie into extreme measures. After all, Carrie was merely demanding that the Kansas State Government enforce their own neglected laws. From her perspective, she was not only doing the work of the Lord but adhering to her own Constitution.

As she advanced in years, her overly ostentatious behavior became more relevant on the national stage as women's passions for their own suffrage heated to a violent boil and the modern woman's movement swept through the sweatshops and inner cities of the country. Even before she died in 1911, women were taking more daring political and social action, like Jewish Anarchist Emma Goldman declaring to a group of workers in Union Square, "Ask for work; If they do not give you work ask for bread; If they do not give you work or bread then take bread" and getting arrested for her incendiary words.

Carrie Nation was indeed a fiery spark in American history. Her bizarre presence was also a curious prelude to the modern age of celebrity where people are famous for being famous. She rose to notoriety almost overnight, and very shortly after she smashed up her first saloon in Kiowa, her image was marketed widely throughout the States. One could easily imagine her appearing on the David Letterman show or staging a stunt in the middle of Times Square *a la* David Blaine. In her time, in fact, popular songs were written about her with lyrics such as:

> When time shall build the marble guild,
> That marks man's reformation,
> Its arch of fame shall bear the name
> Of dauntless Carrie Nation.
> Her righteous scorn of rum and wrong—
> May all creation catch it,
> And join the "Woman's World Crusade,"
> Armed with "our nation's" hatchet.

> (Minna Irving in *Leslie's Weekly*)

Although never a profound intellectual (she had more in common with Calamity Jane and Annie Oakley than Susan B. Anthony or Emma Goldman), Carrie Nation definitely stirred the American collective imagination, giving it a new icon to emblazon in its hallowed history. And while this sassy frontier woman from Kentucky who wielded a hatchet in the name of her Lord never quite knew the genteel upper middle-class quietude of Lizzie Borden's life, something tells me the two of them would have found much to talk about.

And by the way, as far as we know, Carrie Nation never involved herself with animal rescue, ironing handkerchiefs or teaching Chinese school children, but it would have been wonderfully coincidental if she had.

WORKS CITED:

"Carrie Amelia Nation." *Kansas State Historical Society.* 2 November 2006 <kshs.org/people/nation_carry.htm>.
"Crusades." *Woman's Christian Temperance Union.* 2 November 2006 <wctu.org/crusades.html>.
"Early History." *Woman's Christian Temperance Union.* 2 November 2006 <wctu.org/earlyhistory.html>.
Nation, Carrie. *The Use and Need of the Life of Carry A. Nation.* 10 October 1998. Project Gutenberg. 2 November 2006 <gutenberg.org/etext/1485>.

First published in *The Hatchet: Journal of Lizzie Borden Studies*, Vol. 3, Issue 4, November/December, 2006.

HELEN DUNCAN: THE BLITZ WITCH

Britain's Last Great Witchcraft Trial

The city of Portsmouth has always been of strategic importance in England's long history of trade, warfare and empire building. Located across the Channel from the shores of Normandy, it has been, for centuries, a major base of the British Navy, boasting the world's oldest working dry docks. For these reasons, Adolph Hitler chose Portsmouth as the primary target in the first Luftwaffe air strike of the Battle of Britain.

On August 14, 1940, Hitler launched Eagle Day (Adler Tag), the first of many air raids that would collectively become known to history as the Blitz. England's declaration of war on Germany after the September 1939 invasion of Poland was followed by what had been dismissively called the Phony War, a reference to the failure of either side to launch an offensive; but the waiting was now over, and the Germans struck over and over on England's shores and cities, killing tens of thousands and devastating cities with a ferocity that many feared was a prelude to a decisive invasion.

While the general morale of the people was bolstered by the inspirational and defiant broadcasts of Winston Churchill, many English, fearing death and having suffered the loss of loved ones, turned to the Spiritualist movement as a means of giving them hope and comfort. The Spiritualist movement had grown exponentially in Britain since the First World War, evolving into thousands of circles loosely federated by the Spiritualist's National Union. The SNU helped protect the rights of mediums and Spiritualist groups, distribute literature, and defend the civil rights of practitioners.

One of the laws used by the government to combat the movement was the Witchcraft Act of 1735, passed by Parliament to acknowledge that the state no longer believed in the actual existence of magic and witchcraft. Those who were caught practicing magic were prosecuted for believing in its existence, not the actual practice. Nonetheless, it was a weak law. The law held a maximum sentence of only one year in prison. While by today's standards, this is a violation of fundamental rights, in 1735 it was considered quite enlightened, recognizing that the killing of magicians was barbaric since magic, in their minds, didn't even exist. The last woman burned for witchcraft was Janet Horne from Scotland, seven years before the Witchcraft Act, which makes the Act a marker for the end of that great period of persecution that Wiccans still call the Burning Time.

By 1940, the Witchcraft Act was a strange remnant of a by-gone age, and one that seemed most irrelevant as Hitler's bombers were devastating London; but oddly enough it was invoked several times before its repeal in 1951, the most dramatic of which was the 1944 trial of Helen Duncan, a Scottish Spiritualist medium whose fame and, quite possibly, her all-too-real powers, led to her arrest and trial as a witch in wartime England.

Helen Duncan was born Victoria Helen MacFarlane in 1897. Growing up in Callander, Scotland, she had a strange childhood in which she regularly communed with the dead spirits who inhabited the magical landscape of the Highlands. Because of her abilities, which included having the spirits write the answers to her school exams on her slate, the locals gave her the nickname Hellish Nell, one that was later exploited by the press at the time of her trial. She grew into a large woman with a thick heavy Scottish brogue. Not surprisingly, she became first a clairvoyant and then a successful seance medium. Her husband, Henry Duncan, was a war veteran who believed in her abilities and acted as a manager of sorts for her profitable performances on the Spiritualist seance circuit.

Helen's act would begin with a thorough examination of the stage set by members of the audience to ensure that there was no hidden panels or trapdoors. The set consisted of what was called a medium's cabinet, an armchair surrounded by curtains which would all be examined in turn. The audience was always invited to search her seance clothing, a black robe and slippers. Women from the audience were then ushered to a dressing room where a quite nude Helen Duncan would subject herself to a full body search before robing up and taking the stage.

Her spirit guide was an entity called Albert, allegedly an Australian soldier who had died in the First World War. Slipping into a trance, Helen would start channeling Albert, who spoke through her, his educated London accent proving a sharp contrast to her own Highlands speech. Albert would take over the proceedings, entertaining the audience with witty banter and the manifestation of spirits through the portal of the Cabinet, enabling the audience to communicate with their dearly departed.

Albert had a personality that contrasted sharply with Helen's. While she was shy and reserved, Albert was uninhibited, cracking insulting jokes much like a ventriloquist's dummy or a king's jester. He even went so far as to insult Henry, Helen's husband, who manned the phonograph in the back of the parlor (the act was accompanied by recorded music, mostly pop songs). In a bath of eerie red light, Albert would run the show and make sure that the audience got an entertaining pop for the pound.

Whether Albert was real or not, Helen did fake one crucial part of her act. She rigged up a mixture of cheesecloth, capped with doll heads and faces cut out of magazines, to simulate ectoplasm, that mysterious substance mediums appeared to exude from their body orifices. While witnesses claim to have seen this ectoplasm emerging from Helen's mouth and nostrils, Harry Price, the Director of the National Laboratory of Psychical Research, thought otherwise. He performed tests on the substance confiscated from one of Helen's seances and proclaimed it to be a fake.

Harry Price wrote about how he proved the trickery in the early 1930s:

> At the conclusion of the fourth seance we led the medium to a settee and called for the apparatus. At the sight of it, the lady promptly went into a trance. She recovered, but refused to be X-rayed. Her husband went up to her and told her it was painless. She jumped up and gave him a smashing blow on the face which sent him reeling. Then she went for Dr. William Brown who was present. He dodged the blow. Mrs. Duncan,

without the slightest warning, dashed out into the street, had an attack of hysteria and began to tear her seance garment to pieces. She clutched the railings and screamed and screamed. Her husband tried to pacify her. It was useless. I leave the reader to visualize the scene. A seventeen-stone woman, clad in black sateen tights, locked to the railings, screaming at the top of her voice.

A crowd collected and the police arrived. The medical men with us explained the position and prevented them from fetching the ambulance. We got her back into the Laboratory and at once she demanded to be X-rayed. In reply, Dr. William Brown turned to Mr. Duncan and asked him to turn out his pockets. He refused and would not allow us to search him. There is no question that his wife had passed him the cheesecloth in the street. However, they gave us another seance and the 'contro' said we could cut off a piece of 'teleplasm' when it appeared. The sight of half-a-dozen men, each with a pair of scissors waiting for the word, was amusing. It came and we all jumped. One of the doctors got hold of the stuff and secured a piece. The medium screamed and the rest of the 'teleplasm' went down her throat. This time it wasn't cheesecloth. It proved to be paper, soaked in white of egg, and folded into a flattened tube. Could anything be more infantile than a group of grown-up men wasting time, money, and energy on the antics of a fat female crook.

As comical as this may sound, Helen Duncan did cause a huge stir in the highest levels of power in the British government during the height of World War II, a stir that would result in her being one of the last women tried and convicted under the Witchcraft Act and, for a brief period, considered a serious security risk to the British Empire.

Helen Duncan had long been under investigation from seance-busters like Harry Price, but she continued to have a lucrative career as a medium and support her eight children in Edinburgh. Skeptics in Blitz-besieged England were few and far between. Many of the higher-ups in the Royal Navy were staunch spiritualists. Air Chief Marshal Lord

Hugh Dowding, the hero of the Battle of Britain, had gone completely over to the faith when he felt that dead airmen who had lost their lives under his command were trying to communicate with him. He issued a call to the country's mediums to help the tormented spirits to communicate with their loved ones, giving millions of scared people hope that the war would not prevail over their immortality. In short he was equating seance with spirit manifestation as a legitimate part of the war effort. The popularity of seances soared and mediums, especially Helen Duncan, were in hot demand.

This all changed on November 25, 1941, when three British battleships hunting for a German convoy in the Mediterranean were attacked by a U-boat. The *HMS Barham* sank with almost nine hundred lost when its magazines exploded. The U-boat submerged and retreated so soon after the attack but before the fatal explosion that the German High Command had no knowledge of the true damage sustained by the Royal Navy. Security was so air tight around this intelligence that not even the families of the dead crewmen were informed of the tragedy.

That is until Helen Duncan gave a seance in Portsmouth where an ectoplasmic entity wearing an *HMS Barham* cap announced to a stunned audience that his ship had been sunk. The wife of a sailor from the Barham was in the audience, and she immediately contacted the Admiralty. The affair was hastily hushed up, the widow was talked into believing that her husband might still be alive, and the Germans continued to remain in the dark over the fate of the battleship.

Helen's security breech did not go unnoticed by the Portsmouth constabulary led by Chief Constable Arthur West. Because of the strategic significance of Portsmouth, West had the advantage of receiving intelligence from the War Office, Scotland Yard, Military Intelligence and the Home Office. His latitude in detaining, arresting and imprisoning people was quite wide and in light of the savage German onslaught and the imminent invasion, it would seem that the fraudulent antics of a working-class medium with her cheesecloth puppets would be far below his radar. But the name Helen Duncan rang a bell and suddenly her seances did not seem so innocent. Several months earlier he had received a report that a medium named Helen Duncan had announced during a trance that a ship had been sunk in Norwegian waters. The seance was performed on the very day that *HMS Hood* was sunk by the German battleship Bismarck. Now, Helen had once more channeled sensitive military intelligence. Coupled with the fact that she was playing in

West's backyard, the Chief Constable thought to keep a close eye on Duncan. Arresting her outright was unwise since that would certainly draw German attention to the sinking of the *Barham*. Besides, the belief in Spiritualism was so rampant in the British navy that West, a hardcore skeptic, would have a tough time suppressing Lord Dowding's treasured weapon of morale. It would have to take either proof that Helen Duncan was a spy for the Germans or a complete exposure of her stage act as a fake to get her out of the way. In the winter of 1941, Chief Constable West had neither.

But he did have patience. He waited until January, 1944, when a report came in that once more involved Helen Duncan. By that winter, everything had changed. The invasion of the British islands now seemed highly unlikely, the Germans had been beaten back on the Eastern Front and were now losing Italy, and the Allied Forces had a grand invasion of France planned for the summer. Most of the intelligence that came across West's desk involved not only the planning of that invasion, but the counter-intelligence that would deceive the Germans into believing that the invasion would strike in other areas besides Normandy. In the midst of all this critical work that would decide the fate of Western Civilization, the Chief Constable of Portsmouth had not forgotten the Scottish Highlander with her ectoplasmic cheesecloth and uncanny knowledge of military secrets.

So, when a complaint was filed against Helen after she had performed in Portsmouth, West sprang into action and ordered her arrest. It seemed to be a perfect way out of his dilemma. If she were to be detained in prison until after the invasion, she would not have a chance to interfere. Arresting her for fraud would require no explanation on behalf of the Constabulary. The risk of her compromising the war effort would be eliminated, and Britain would be rid of one more confidence trickster trying to make money off another person's grief.

Helen Duncan was arrested in the midst of a seance at the Master Temple in Portsmouth, along with the High Priest and Priestess. The arresting officers scrambled to find her cloth and puppets without compromising the dignity of the women present but came up with nothing. Without this evidence, she could not be charged with fraud but was hastily removed to Holloway Prison, a dank and medieval hold in the middle of London. The news of her incarceration spread like wildfire throughout Spiritualist circles, many of whose members began raising their voices that she was being unfairly held. Her "crime" was merely to tell fake fortunes, a misdemeanor at best, and her punishment should have been a fine of a few pounds. Instead she was locked up in a prison without bail.

High ranking Spiritualists got together and organized a defense fund, which included the appointment of a defense lawyer, Charles Loseby, an imposing and cold barrister who intimidated the police into releasing Helen on one hundred pounds bail. To continue to hold her would be to give the impression that the British government, backed by the Anglican Church, was attempting to weaken the Spiritualist movement. This would amount to nothing less than religious persecution.

West had lost the first round of the battle. The medium was now at liberty to talk to the press and the public and there was still no evidence that she was a fake, the only charge that would justify her arrest. West set into motion a plan to put Duncan back in prison for a duration of at least nine months, long enough for the Allies to invade France. He scrutinized her past for any legal violations or any evidence of fakery. Did anyone nab a cheesecloth? Have any paranormal investigators complained about her? The goal was to focus on the fraud charges and draw all attention away from the political and military reasons behind the persecution.

The witch trial began as a hearing on February 29, 1944, at the Portsmouth Magistrate's Court, which was presided over by the Lord Mayor of Portsmouth. Helen's co-defendants were Mr. and Mrs. Ernest Homer (the High Priest and Priestess of the High Temple, the venue at which Helen had been busted) and Mrs. Francis Brown, her seance assistant. Also present for the hearing was a large gathering of Spiritualists. The charge brought against the defendants was conspiracy to defraud with phony spirit materializations and communications with the dead. A shock wave ran through the audience when the prosecution added heresy to the charges. After Helen's arrest, the inner circle had been comparing her arrest to that of Jesus Christ, a highly controversial comment that did not go unnoticed by the Court.

The hearing resulted in a ruling that the trial would commence at the Old Bailey's Central Criminal Court. By doing so, the case was now an official sensation. The Spiritualist cause would have its day in court and, if all went well, would conclude with a landmark decision that would validate the Spiritualists and help to protect the civil liberties of practitioners. None of them suspected that the real motivations behind the move against Helen Duncan was the war itself and the most incredible military secret of all, the armed invasion by the Allied Forces of Hitler's Europe. If the Portsmouth Constabulary couldn't get their conviction, then no military secret was safe in the hands of the Blitz Witch and her cheesecloth spirit guide.

The King's Counsel appointed for the trial was a military intelligence veteran named John Cyril Maude. He immediately agreed with Chief Constable West that the goal of the trial would be to lock Helen Duncan away for as long as it took for the Allied Forces to invade Europe. But this agenda could not be publicly admitted for matters of national security. The problem was to decide on what exact charges should be brought against her. She had already been tried on conspiracy to defraud the public; however, there was a thorny problem with this: Helen Duncan never made the claim to be able to manifest spirits. She remained silent during her seances; an assistant collected the monies. In regard to the fakery involved with Albert and other spirits cut from cheesecloth, the prosecution did not have a single shred (literally) of evidence. No cloth had ever been confiscated, and there was currently no proof that the ectoplasm had been fake.

The magistrates finally settled on a strategy, one that would shock the nation and push the war off the newspaper headlines in favor of Helen Duncan. The Scottish medium was to be tried under the Witchcraft Act of 1734: "If any persons shall pretend to exercise or use any kind of witchcraft, sorcery, enchantment, or conjuration, or undertake to tell fortunes, every person so offending shall suffer imprisonment by the space of one whole year without bail."

This strategy cut the Gordian knot. If it could be clearly be proven in court that Helen Duncan had performed these acts, she could be put away for an entire year (just long enough for the Allies to invade Europe), and the true meaning of her persecution need never be disclosed. No charges involving the taking of monies need be invoked. However, despite any fraud involved in Helen Duncan's performance, the invocation of the Witchcraft Act as a means to protect a military secret was a risky gamble. This assumed that Helen actually had access to military secrets through paranormal means, something that Constable West and King's Counsel Maude clearly didn't believe in.

In his opening remarks on the first day of the trial, Maude played a clever hand. He admitted the impossibility of the conjuring of spirits, but he considered Duncan's seances, in light of the number of families that had lost their loved ones in the war and the bombings, to be deplorable and her conduct in exploiting their loss to be "a false and hollow lie." He further appealed to the Spiritualist community who packed the courtroom, concerned about any medium who was *faking* the conjuration of spirits. His reasoning was that any true-hearted Spiritualist should be just as appalled by fakery as a non-believer. Despite this plea, however, the trial in the Old Bailey continued to be seen as religious persecution.

When Attorney Charles Loseby opened the case for the defense, he announced he would prove that Helen Duncan was not guilty of witchcraft charges because she merely acted as a conduit through which the spiritual forces of the universe were working. There was no conspiracy; it was all being done by the spirits. To this end, he paraded one witness after another who testified to the supernatural deeds done during Helen's seances and even suggested to the court that Helen Duncan materialize her spirits directly in the courtroom, a request that the King's Bench denied.

Loseby's strategy was to give credibility to the Spiritualist movement. Invoking Lord Dowding, a staunch defender of the faith, he pummeled the jury with Spiritualist propaganda and testimony. The witnesses explained in great detail how they saw their departed loved ones take shape out of Helen Duncan's ectoplasm. Spiritualism was a religion based on the existence of life after death, and since Christianity preached life after death, there was kinship between the two religions. The presiding judge unnerved the prosecution when he summarized that the goal of Spiritualism is to try to "prove the central feature of the Christian belief."

A witness also testified:

> [T]hose who profess the Christian religion have left out the part that pertains to Spiritualism, that pertains to spirit. They follow the letter of the law, instead of the spirit. The orthodox church teaches us that by faith alone we are saved, while we, as Spiritualistic people, believe that the Word of God is still living. God has not stopped talking. He reveals himself to his people daily; and therefore we cannot be bound by creed.

Such testimony made Helen Duncan seem less of a paranormal quack and more of a religious leader at the vanguard of the true

Christian faith. As Loseby stated in his closing argument, "This is the essence of my case: Through Mrs. Duncan, God shows himself in an unexpected way, in humble surroundings."

Despite the espousal of the Spiritualist faith, the testimonials towards the medium's uncanny ability to channel spirits, the attempts to prove that the alleged victims of fraud had truly experienced what they had paid their money for, despite all this Helen Duncan, without having testified in her own defense, was found guilty under the Witchcraft Act of 1734.

At no point during the trial was it even hinted at that the real motivation behind the persecution of Helen Duncan was political and military; however, during the sentencing phase, Portsmouth Chief Constable West, who had initiated the entire affair, informed the judge and the courtroom that Helen had transgressed security laws back in 1941. To a judge who had a tolerance for alternative religions and a record of protecting civil liberties, this revelation may have made all the difference. His sentencing was as follows:

> Helen Duncan, Ernest Homer, Elizabeth Jones and Francis Brown, you have been convicted of pretending to recall spirits of deceased persons in a visible and tangible form. There are many people, especially in wartime, searching for loved ones. There is a great danger of their susceptibilities being exploited, out of a yearning for comfort and assurance. There are those, unfortunately, who are ready to profit. Many of these persons who seek solace are trusting by nature, and in poor circumstances. The law endeavors to protect such persons against themselves. I have considered very anxiously the course I should take and have come to the conclusion that Mrs. Duncan has made the most of this. The sentence of the Court upon her is that she be imprisoned for nine months.

Upon hearing this sentence, Helen Duncan fainted to the floor in the courtroom. The hopes of getting off with a ten pound fine for playing hocus-pocus with a cheesecloth had been dashed. She was now being treated like a traitor to her own country during wartime. And the stigma of being prosecuted under the Witchcraft Act was equally devastating. Despite the fact that the Witchcraft Act did not actu-ally recognize magic as real (it merely forbade people to pretend that they could perform magic), it was a sad and lamentable blow to the Spiritualist movement to see Helen Duncan so incarcerated. All the more tragic since its motivations remained a state military secret. If not for the war, no action would have been taken against the medium resulting in anything more than a petty fine.

Instead Helen Duncan was sent to jail. At her appeal hearing, Loseby reminded the court that Helen Duncan had been imprisoned under the Witchcraft Act, one that had originally ended the wide scale persecution and slaughter of women accused of conjuring spirits. However, the jurist pointed out, the Act was never intended "to punish those gifted with psychic powers." The basis of the court's prejudice against Helen Duncan rested on their legal definitions of "conjuration" and "witchcraft," both of which involve active dealings with the Devil.

Claiming that all the great advances in human knowledge were all initially greeted with skepticism, Loseby insisted that the court had dismissed any of the claims that Spiritualists made to the afterlife and the spirits they have conjured, and instead reduced a valid religious faith that was not incompatible with Christianity to a mere superstition practiced by ignorant and grieving people. While forty-five witnesses had testified to Helen's powers, not a single shred of material evidence had been presented by the prosecution, and the offer to have Helen demonstrate her abilities by giving a seance in the courtroom had been denied. Hence, the court had shown severe prejudice.

Despite this somewhat valid argument, Helen Duncan, having been branded a witch, lost her appeal and was destined to serve her sentence.

As D-Day approached, civilian travel on the English coast was restricted. The wounded streets of Portsmouth became an armed camp and the centuries old dry-docks were congested with thousands of ships that would take part in the invasion fleet. Helen Duncan, behind bars, had no access to the public ear to propagate whatever mystical knowledge she had about the invasion. If only she had used her powers to give the Allies information about the Germans, circumstances may have turned out very differently for her.

Not every high-ranking member of the British government felt justified in locking her away. Winston Churchill, who had more reason to care about national security than anyone else in Britain, became very upset when he read about the trial in the Old Bailey. On April 3, 1944, he wrote to the Home Secretary: "Let me have a report on why the Witchcraft Act of 1735 was used in a modern Court of Justice. What was the cost of the trial to the state, observing that witnesses were brought from Portsmouth and maintained here in this crowded London for a fortnight, and the Recorder kept busy with all this obsolete tomfoolery?"

As the world waited for the appeals court to come to a verdict, a new assault began as if the Devil was pronouncing its own sentence on the English Empire. Hitler's V-2 rockets, a last attempt to terrorize and damage the London populace, began to fall upon the city. With terrifying ferocity, the rockets—which in themselves were technological advancements over the bombs that had hitherto been dropped—spread terror and renewed the sense of siege that had characterized the Blitz in its heyday. Old Bailey itself had been hit and suffered great damage, forcing the courts to convene in bomb shelters underground. Perhaps the severity of the bombardment, the terror that was spread in the wake of these weapons, and the renewed feeling that despite the Allied invasion, Britain was quite vulnerable to the German war machine, kept Helen Duncan in prison despite her appeal. Once the conviction had been obtained, no one cared that it had been bought with "obsolete tomfoolery."

Helen Duncan was released from Holloway Prison on September 22, 1945. By this time, the Allied Forces had overrun France, liberated Paris, and driven the Hun back over their border. The victorious armies were halted at the gates of German by their very success: the Allied armies pushing forward towards the Rhine had run out of gas for their tanks. Instead of thrusting forward into the heart of Germany and ending the war by Christmas, they were destined to suffer another winter in the liberation of Belgium and the Low Countries. But His Majesty's government did not see fit to keep Helen Duncan restrained from that point onwards.

She returned to her home in Scotland after nine months in prison, and kept relatively quiet. She did continue with her medium services, eventually going back out on the circuit, and was busted a few more times before her death in 1956. However, the Witchcraft Act was revoked in 1951 and replaced with the Fraudulent Mediums Act, a more dignified title and not one that suggested obsolete tomfoolery.

For believers in the manifestation of spirits, Helen Duncan was a martyr, a victim of religious persecution and ignorance. At best, she was a pawn in the war between the Church of England and the alternative new age religions that gave empowerment to pagans and women alike. Yet to skeptics, she was a pest and to the government she was possibly a German spy.

It is doubtful that had she been a spy, she would have chosen the venue of spirit seances to convey military secrets. More likely she would have passed secret messages to the German High Command. To have her spirits tell us battleships sunk in foreign seas to the paying audience only drew attention to herself.

There is little doubt that she was at least partially a fake. The ectoplasm was cheesecloth and the spirit faces were pictures cut from magazines. But even some of her most ardent defenders admit that she had to resort to theatrics in order to give an audience their money's worth. Yet it has never been determined how Helen obtained the information about the sunken ships or how some of her spirit manifestations had been accomplished. If anything, she can be given Brownie points for putting on a really convincing show.

The conviction of Helen Duncan under the Witchcraft Act seemed almost arbitrary. While she did her time in Holloway prison, other occultists like Aleister Crowley and Gerald Gardner formed and maintained secret societies; and new religions, organizations like the Golden Dawn and the Rosicrucians, continued their operations despite the political warfare waging around them, and practitioners of High Magick were quite active in their own circles. The suggestion that a fat woman tossing cheesecloth and puppets about was a serious threat to the British Isles and their military security is now laughable at best.

The Chief Constable of Portsmouth had pursued a complaint in his own backyard. He was in the sensitive position of maintaining security in an area that was crucial to the successful launch of D-Day and the Allied invasion of Europe. For a man in such a position, he had a stronger case against a woman who was faking spirit manifestations than he would against a secret society with fifty years of history behind it, one that boasted aristocrats in its ranks like the Golden Dawn.

Perhaps the intense focus on mediums came from the atmosphere of death that had accompanied the war. The bombing of England had struck a chord never before felt, and death became a constant companion on the home front. Grief, loss and the wounds of war always bring out the deeply buried need to believe in an afterlife, and Spiritualist mediums, more than High Magicians with their tables of correspondences and ceremonial invocations of various planetary spirits for the benefit of inner spiritual growth, were the ones to which the masses were drawn. The Great Work just wasn't as comforting as a quick fix for the fear of death.

For Helen Duncan to be incarcerated for nine months in order to satisfy a hidden military agenda raises many issues. Constable West deliberately withheld his true intentions from the public. In today's climate where political transparency is dismissed in the name of national security, her case has particular resonances. What would we think of our own government if they imprisoned a religious practitioner purely on the belief that he posed a threat to the war effort. Hmmm. Sound familiar?

Let us remember Helen Duncan for what she was: a seance medium of the Spiritualist faith who tossed as much fakery at her audience as she did true spiritual energy, but who, I am certain, had no more access to military secrets than the average English citizen in 1944. To prove that she was a one-hundred percent fake wouldn't diminish the lessons learned from her ordeal. Calling her a martyr may be too dramatic, but to call her a tragic victim of government paranoia would be quite appropriate and very relevant to our own struggle for liberty, both spiritual and political.

First published in *Behutet: Modern Thelemic Magick & Culture*, Issue 57, Winter 2013.

About the Author

{~~}

Richard grew up in Queens, New York, and although he left the city as a young man, he remained a New Yorker at heart for all of his short life. Richard attended Stuyvesant High School where Greenwich Village was his campus. The school had a major impact on his life, shaping him into a deep thinker and a writer. Here, both on and off campus, he was first exposed to the Beat writers, avant-garde foreign films, experimental music, the teachings of Tibetan Buddhists and Chinese philosophy, and surrealist art. He also discovered mysticism, which deeply resonated with him. He studied various mystics and used many of their principals as the guiding force of his creativity and of his daily life.

While living in New Jersey, Richard met and married his wife Anna, and soon afterward they moved to New England. It was in this, the happiest period of his life, that Richard was able to focus on his writing, film-making and podcasting. Richard and Anna co-founded Nine Muses Books so they could personally publish his writings, including his *Lizzie Borden, Girl Detective* series of mysteries, for which he is best known. Richard wrote easily in many genres, in both fiction and non-fiction. His fiction short stories and non-fiction essays have been published in a variety of journals. He was also a lecturer on historic Victorian women and on silent film comedy. Richard also was a budding actor and appeared in several local plays. His GardenBayFilms

Channel on YouTube contains a variety of short films Richard made, mostly centered on Lizzie Borden. Richard's *Lizzie Borden Podcast*, available on iTunes, examines the Lizzie Borden case with various historians, as well as contains a radio play of *The Agitated Elocutionist*, one of his *Girl Detective* short stories.

Richard had plans to continue to create films, write stories, deliver more lecture series, and to interview more historians for his podcast, but his ill health caused him to put his plans on hold. When he learned that he did not have much time left, he said, "But I am not finished yet!" After it became tragically clear that Richard would not recover, he indicated to his wife that he wished his writing to be published posthumously.

Anna, with the help of Richard's sister Susan, gathered Richard's writings and sorted the finished pieces into three different books: Richard's personal writings, which would be part of his *Garden Bay Stories*; his non-fiction essays, which would be part of the *Of Moons and Monoliths* essay collection; and his *Lizzie Borden, Girl Detective* stories collected into one complete volume, *The Audible Amnesiac and other Lizzie Borden, Girl Detective Mysteries*.

Richard is sorely missed, but he leaves us a legacy of fine work in a variety of media and genres.

www.ingramcontent.com/pod-product-compliance
Lightning Source LLC
LaVergne TN
LVHW051447080426
835509LV00017B/1692